All Our Yesterdays

ALL OUR YESTERDAYS

*an informal history of
science fiction fandom
in the forties*

by Harry Warner, Jr.

Introduction by Wilson Tucker

Advent:Publishers, Inc.

Chicago: 1969

TABLE OF CONTENTS

Illustrations

Many of the photographs in this book are from the collections of Bob Tucker and Ed Wood, whose assistance is gratefully acknowledged. The photographers include: Martin Alger, page 62; Lynn Bridges, page 241; Paul Freehafer, pages 21, 99, 101, and 248; Dean Grennell, pages 18 and 82; Jerome, page 85; Roullard & Butler, page 212; Bob Tucker, pages 20, 34, 234, and 270; and Julius Unger, page 48. The author and publishers wish to thank each photographer, known and unknown, whose work has been used.

INTRODUCTION

Harry Warner and the late Cecil B. DeMille have certain fine points in common, although each of them would be rather astonished to hear me say it. In the language of the movie posters, their greatest works were years in the making, employ a cast of thousands, and are so incredibly long in the unfolding that the viewer cannot hope to get from here to there in one sitting. Although I haven't yet read the whole text of this volume (175,000 words!) I am reasonably certain Warner is a better craftsman than DeMille— a more meticulous craftsman. If, in these pages, the waters part and a suffering people are chased across the sea-bed by Egyptian chariots, it's a safe bet Warner will *not* have permitted their scurrying feet to raise clouds of dust.

Harry Warner first found an interest in science fiction in 1933, perhaps in a stack of yellowed pulps stashed away in that ubiquitous closet or second-hand shop; many an unsuspecting youth was subverted and led down the primrose path in the same manner, with neither politician nor reformer present to recognize the danger and pass laws to protect him from himself. Harry was hooked, as this book reveals.

I discovered him, or he discovered me, sometime after he encountered fandom in 1936. My memory isn't that keen, and unlike him I do not keep carbons of my correspondence from the Year One; I know only that we discovered each other by mail in a year when a first-class postage stamp could be bought for three cents, and a first-class letter traveled from Hagerstown, Maryland, to Bloomington, Illinois, overnight by rail. The trains were still operating when Franklin D. Roosevelt was re-elected to his third term in the White House, and mail fandom was the only means of contact we could afford. It has been a richly rewarding correspondence.

I met Harry—the first time—in 1939. I saw nothing in him that would give me to suspect he was capable of writing and publishing this history thirty years later—or even that he had an interest in such a task; and he saw nothing in me that could give him the suspicion I would be doing *this* later on. Who peers thirty years into the future of fandom? We were only a couple of gawkish faaans (three vowels please, typesetter) staring at one another and privately wondering what-the-hell? He was a grinning, gangling teenager suffering through a visit by a passel of traveling fans and wondering how he could possibly explain them to his parents. I was a grinning, gangling graybeard

Harry Warner, Jr.

in my mid-twenties, wondering why he preferred to be "The Hermit of Hagerstown." (Harry did not attend his first convention until nearly a quarter of a century after discovering fandom. Remarkable abstinence.)

He was and is a creature latterly known as "a publishing jiant" although that fact does not seem obvious at first glance: in these many years he has not produced the scores of titles or numerous one-shots or engaged in any other frenzied mimeograph cranking that might earn him such a label. But he *has* succeeded in publishing one fanzine continuously for three decades, and I would be pleased to know any other practitioner who approaches such a record. The first issue of *Horizons*, containing twelve pages, was dated October, 1939. The one-hundred-and-fourteenth issue of that same journal, now containing the usual twenty-four pages, was dated Spring, 1968. I suppose the following issue is on the press as this is written. Other fanzines boast a higher numerical count, but other fanzines cannot boast the same publisher and title—the same deep continuing interest—for thirty years.

He also published *Spaceways*, a general-interest magazine which attracted wide popularity, from November, 1938, through September, 1942. The thirty issues of that fanzine are much in demand today and, if one may speak of filthy lucre for a moment, prices asked for copies have ranged as high as a dollar each. I am one collector who will readily grant the worth: *Spaceways* always published meaty stuff by names large and small, for Harry was an astute editor worthy of the name. He edited. He selected his material with care, rejected what he thought inferior, and let the chips fall as they might. When it was my turn to fall, I remembered the lesson.

The Hermit of Hagerstown has also been responsible for three other publishing ventures, but I can describe only two of them. He published *Harrisons* while he was a member of IPSO, an amateur journalism society; and in 1942 the pair of us collaborated on a brief fling known as *Fanzine Service for Fans in Service*. Collectors need not bother hunting for that; I believe the two-paged flyer endured for only one issue, although the service may have later been incorporated into some other publication. The Hermit's only remaining fan title is a mystery to me. I am reasonably certain it existed somewhere, somewhen, because he once dropped a clue to that effect—but the mystery was never explained to me.

Harry Warner, Jr., was born six days before Christmas in 1922. When I saw him last year, he was still the tall, gangling, quiet man of earlier years, but now given to longer, almost taciturn silences; he did not utter aloud enough words to fill one page of *Horizons* although he fills each twenty-four pages with the written word quite handily. He is a newspaper reporter, and I suspect he sometimes doubles as night editor as well. During one of those infrequent visits to his cave, I was amused to see cub reporters and beautiful lady editors jump and run when he snapped his fingers. I asked him what would happen if one of us darted into the press room crying "Stop the presses! Scoop! Scoop!" He was quite certain the shockwave would send the press-gang fleeing into the night, and the paper would not get published for days. I think the same thing would happen if I ran into his office, shouting.

He has held several offices in the Fantasy Amateur Press Association—probably every office except that of Editor, which is passing strange—and has served as Director of the National Fantasy Fan Federation. Among his other credits are membership at various times in the Futurian Federation of the World, The Order of Dagon, the Dixie Fantasy Federation, the Goon Defective Agency, and the Cosmic Circle. In short, he is as guilty as the rest of us.

Harry is a packrat.

His storied attic—and all the other rooms of his large house on Summit Avenue—are crammed with several thousand records (a marked weakness for opera), several thousand more books and magazines, and several million fanzines. Stashed here and there among the stacks are an unknown number of radios, tape recorders, record players, and television sets. How he also manages to be an avid baseball fan isn't known to me. He has one inflexible rule: none of this accumulated treasure is ever piled atop his bed. He also likes to sleep. The mammoth fanzine collection served as his prime source for this history, and it was mined carefully—exhaustively. Consider this comment published in *A Sense of FAPA* in 1962:

"I have just completed a preposterous project: the task of leafing through every page in every publication distributed through FAPA since the middle of 1939. This represents more than nine-tenths of the club's bundles since its organization, and even more of its total output by bulk. Omission of the first eight mailings from this review was a necessity, not a chickening out on my part. I didn't join until FAPA was beginning its third year (1939). It took spare moments over a couple of months to do the leafing and to type out notes on many matters that turned up during the scrutiny. It was done as part of my homework for the fan history that I hope to be ready to write before FAPA's 200th mailing." (But the research was already underway in 1961—perhaps earlier.)

Harry broke into the professional prints several times. His earliest appearance was in *Astounding* in November, 1942, with an entry in that magazine's "Probability Zero" department; additionally, he placed about a dozen short stories in various magazines during the middle 1950's.

His fanzine appearances are something else again.

It isn't too much of an exaggeration to claim that Harry has appeared at least once—and at least in the letter columns—of every fan magazine published from 1936 to date. He is an indefatigable writer of letters of comment, and the young fan editor who publishes two or three issues without receiving such a letter is apt to fold his presses and steal away in shame. Harry's output of fannish writings is simply incredible, and a complete collection of his work would fill a book as thick as this one; his newspaper training has made him over into a prolific, speedy creator-composer-typist. It may be quite true that he can type with one hand while he is changing records with the other, and at the same time be reading the latest issue of *Other Worlds*— or one of the many fanzines which arrived in his mailbox that day.

All this may tell you more than you really want to know about Harry Warner. I hold what I believe to be good reason for going into much detail: in all the 175,000 words of this history, you may—if you peer closely— find a scant few hundred words about *him*. The Hermit still values taciturnity. There is a brief bit in Chapter Two confessing his part in a clever hoax—the really brilliant *Odd Tales* hoax of 1942—which may add up to a hundred and fifty words. In the same chapter is a low-key statement concerning the longevity of *Horizons*, and another concerning the circulation boost of *Spaceways*. Again, in Chapter Eight, one will find perhaps seventy-five words about the author; and another piece in Chapter Twelve will add another two hundred words if you are charitable. Other than that, and other than listing himself as an officer of some organization in a most perfunctory manner, Harry has edited himself out of the book.

An old fan, and tired, who has helped make fan history since 1936 does not deserve such a muted fate.

Wilson Tucker
Heyworth, Illinois
July, 1968

FOREWORD

This is the first volume of a history of science-fiction fandom. Two explanations of that statement are in order: one for the initiated, the other for the bewildered.

The initiated are those who are already fans or have renounced that status. These readers will, however, encounter certain puzzles in what follows, if they have sampled the main portion of the book before starting the introduction.

This does not pretend to be a complete history of fandom, either in the factual or in the chronological sense. This volume deals basically with some of the important events of the forties. A second volume will cover the fifties. There is no particular reason why there should not be a third book about the sixties, other than the probability that twenty years of fandom are enough to wear out any historian. I have dealt in this volume with such matters occurring before *ca.* 1940 as are necessary for understanding of events in this decade and with some aspects of fandom that were omitted from other reference works. I have penetrated into the fifties only when it was expedient to finish off a topic once and for all. If you're shaky about fandom's history before 1940, try to find copies of the *Fancyclopedia* (first edition by Jack Speer and second edition by Richard Eney) and *The Immortal Storm* by Sam Moskowitz.

This history is intended to entertain, inform, and infuriate its readers, but not to exhaust them. To this end, I have renounced the entire scholarly apparatus. Completely absent are footnotes, reference listings at the end of the book, bibliographies, and the other paraphernalia that delight the intellectual few and distract most of us. A few dates and other facts may have slipped into the text past my close guard, but a rapid reader will hardly notice them. There are several reasons why I did not insert one footnote for each sentence. To list the source of information and to advise where other facts about the matter appeared would make a plump volume impossibly big. Moreover, the mere sight of such documentation might make the concept of a history of fandom seem laughable and not worth the effort of reading. Finally, such references in normal historical works tell the reader where he can find additional facts. Such instructions would be useless in a history of fandom. With trifling exceptions, all the information contained in this history comes from sources that are unobtainable, for all intents and purposes. Why should I refer a reader to a fanzine that might require three years of searching to find, to correspondence files in my attic that are out of bounds to everyone except close friends, or to conversations that exist only in my memories?

However, my notes for this work are fully annotated. Anyone who simply must know more about the source of any particular matter can find out by the simple process of writing me a letter.

Nobody will fail to notice the fact that I've expressed opinions in this work. I felt it was more honest to do it openly. Every historian must exercise some prejudices and predilections, to permit him to decide what to omit and the amounts of space he will give to included material. I was involved in many of the events described herein and was an excited spectator of almost all the others. At the time, I felt that the New York Futurians pretended to mature intellectualism that they lacked and that good fans were becoming bad professional writers; I prefer to make these biases and many others quite obvious, rather than suffer the accusation of hidden slanting. Anyone who wants to spend the next six or eight years working on a history of fandom is invited to produce one that is free from such human failings.

The contents of this book are as accurate as I can make them, otherwise, with one reservation. I've occasionally pieced together quotations without the use of points of elision and brackets to show where words were omitted or words were added. I am certain that I haven't changed the sense of any remarks. Most of the quotations are from the pages of hastily stenciled fanzines. It would be as impious to quote literally in a volume as permanent as this one from such ephemeral publications as it would be unkind for the press to publish word-for-word the remarks made at a press conference by a president or batting champion.

A listing of credits and thanks will go into the second volume. This volume does contain an index. A brief glossary is also included here, for the use of those who are shaky about special meanings of common words in fandom and the words that fans have invented. Many of the terms that are briefly defined in the glossary will be found explained at greater length somewhere or other in the text.

Before you scream that I've omitted some vital events of the forties from this volume, please wait and see if they are in the second volume. Some of the history of the fifties can be most conveniently written by starting with happenings in the forties that are skipped here to avoid future duplication.

This history does not pretend to any more thoroughness than the patience of the writer and the economics of publishing for a limited audience will permit. Given unlimited time on my part and a potential readership as large as that enjoyed by Sir Winston Churchill, each chapter in this book could be expanded to the length of a normal book, by the inclusion of all the curious details, interesting remarks, and fascinating fans involved.

It is unlikely that many persons unacquainted with fandom will open this book. But accidents happen, and so a brief explanation follows. This history deals with a hobby enjoyed by some readers of science fiction, weird fiction, and fantasy fiction. The hobby is called simply "fandom" throughout this book. For no reason in particular, some readers of these types of fiction yield to the impulse to do something more than simply read their favorite type of literature. No other specialized type of fiction has produced a fandom of these proportions. Even more curiously, many persons continue active in fandom long after they have lost an interest in reading these types of fiction.

The mainstream of fandom arose when professional magazines specializing in these types of fiction began a consecutive existence in the twenties. They made it possible for the first time for fans to find one another with fair ease. Fans met when they saw one another reading the magazines on buses or buying copies at the newsstand, or when they wrote to the people whose names appeared in the correspondence sections of these prozines. Fans began to visit one another and to correspond. Soon they formed clubs in some cities, published amateur magazines that they called fan magazines, and tried to organize in a national sense. Informal corresponding must have begun to thrive as soon as the letter sections were introduced. The first surviving fanzines of mainstream fandom appeared around the start of the 1930's. Large-scale meetings appeared in the last half of the same decade, soon after formation of local clubs.

Just as newspapers devote only a minority of their columns to news, and just as musicians perform or listen to music less than half of their waking hours, so do most normal fans spend only a small amount of their hobby time reading, discussing, and writing about their favorite type of fiction. This situation scandalizes a few fundamentalist fans who think it somehow blasphemous that two fans should talk about the current war threat or murder mystery novels. The reality of the situation cannot be denied. That is why so much of the content of this book has no direct relation to stories about the future, vampires, and leprechauns.

Fans are mostly young men, middle class in their social status, slightly above average in their intelligence, noticeably more conservative in their thinking than might be expected from their literary tastes, and their numbers are in the hundreds at any given time. Only a few of them are unfortunate or hardy enough to spend decades as active fans. Many fans enter the field and vanish soon without doing anything memorable. Perhaps the average stay as an active fan might run between two and four years.

There must be some reason why I have spent so much time and effort to write a history of a completely insignificant hobby group. As far as I can sort out my motives, they are:

Fandom could wither and die in the near future, if the habit of reading fiction in this nation continues to sicken. I'd hate to see fandom forgotten without leaving some slight trace behind, because it is a harmless hobby that has given innocent pleasure to many good persons. A hard-cover history book might survive in a few libraries if all the fanzines crumble into dust and every convention memory is extinguished by death. I feel no particular mission as a destined and fated historian of fandom; but I do recognize that very few of us who lived through these past events still have the interest and the patience to write about them at great length. If I hadn't done the job, perhaps it would never have been accomplished. Someone who came into the field recently and gained his knowledge of the old fannish days without personal participation might accidentally unbalance his chronicle more severely than occurs in the present volume through prejudice. There is a remote chance that one or more fans mentioned in this work will survive in the future halls of fame as important literary men, scientists, politicians, or other celebrities. If this should happen, a history of fandom might be the only source of filling in some of the background activities and influences involving these men.

Finally, I cling to a hope that today's active and gafiated fans will find pleasure in reviewing the events in which they took part, and that the fans who came into the hobby recently will find in the book reason to take more philosophically their fannish troubles, through the discovery that we went through the same mishaps so many years ago.

Harry Warner, Jr.
Hagerstown, Maryland
October, 1968

GLOSSARY

Annish—Anniversary issue; the issue of a fanzine celebrating its birthday, usually but not necessarily containing extra pages and/or features.

Apa—Amateur press association; a group whose members bulk-mail a specified number of copies of their fanzines to an official who distributes them in bundles to the entire membership at stated intervals, usually every third month.

Ayjay—Amateur journalism; usually with reference to amateur press association activities, occasionally covers any fanzines, sometimes intended to distinguish mundane apa members and activities from fans.

Big name fan (bnf)—Semi-cynical designation of the best known fans.

Blitzkrieg—Drastic action to accomplish something difficult, originally expeditions to dislodge apa publications from a lazy official's home.

Boskone—Boston conference; pun involving New England fan gatherings and E. E. Smith's fiction.

Carbonzine—Fanzine that is reproduced by carbon paper.

Chainzine—Something like a carbonzine, but sometimes it doesn't even use carbon paper; each recipient in a designated list adds to it and mails it to the next person.

Chicon—Worldcon in Chicago.

Cinvention—Worldcon in Cincinnati.

Clubzine—Fanzine published by a fan club.

Con—Convention or conference; a meeting of fans, who normally use "convention" to refer to the largest annual national event and "conference" for statewide or regional gatherings.

Degafiate—To resume fanac after gafiation.

Denvention—Worldcon in Denver.

ESFA—Eastern Science Fiction Association; fan group in New York area.

Faan—Usually a fan who has lost most of his interest in science fiction and is now mainly interested in other fans and faans; occasionally a particularly enthusiastic fan.

Fanac—Fan activity; something that a science fiction fan does while pursuing his hobby.

Fanzine—Fan magazine; amateur publication, sometimes free and sometimes sold for a price, published and written by fans without expectation of profit.

FAPA—Fantasy Amateur Press Association.

Fiawol—Fandom is a way of life; the philosophy that fandom is important enough to dominate life, antonym to **fijagh**: fandom is just a goddamned hobby.

Filthy pro—Semi-affectionate term for someone who makes money from science fiction.

Fringefan—Someone who is just barely a fan, or sometimes an individual who is not a fan at all but enjoys the company of fans.

Fugghead—Originally, bowdlerized written version of a vivid slang word, later an independent insult of only medium severity.

Futurians—A group of New York fans active in the thirties and early forties.

Gafia—Getting away from it all; growing inactive in fandom, and as a verb, to gafiate; originally it meant the opposite, getting away from the mundane world by engaging in fanac.

Hugo—Award, named after Hugo Gernsback, given at worldcons for outstanding pro and fan accomplishments.

ISA—International Scientific Association.

JEAJA—Nobody knows what it stood for, because no historian was handy.

LASFS (LASFL)—Los Angeles Science Fantasy Society (Science Fiction League).

Letterhack—Anyone who gets published with some frequency in the letter columns of prozines or fanzines.

Mailing comments—Reactions, reviews, and comments inspired by the contents of an apa mailing, a sort of postal conversation.

Mundane—Everything and everyone except fanac, fans, and their literature.

NAPA—National Amateur Press Association, mundane ayjay group.

Neofan—Newcomer to fandom.

Newszine—News magazine; usually, fanzine emphasizing news.

Noncon—Meeting of fans unable to attend a bigger fan meeting, usually being staged at the same time; sometimes, a diplomatic term for a meeting set up in direct competition to a con.

Nycon—Worldcon in New York City.

Pacificon—Worldcon on the west coast of the United States.

Philcon—Worldcon in Philadelphia.

Phillycon—Annual autumn conference in Philadelphia; frequently called Philcon despite strenuous efforts to reserve that term for worldcons.

Postmailing—Magazine that the publisher sends out to everyone on an apa mailing list after the official bundle has been distributed.

Pro, prohood, prodom—Professional, the state of being a professional, professionals as a subdivision of humanity; the pro is normally someone who earns money from science fiction as an author, artist, editor, publisher, or agent.

Prozine—Professional magazine; normally, one that publishes science fiction, weird fiction, or fantasy fiction.

SAPS—Spectator Amateur Press Society.

Science fiction—Stories in which future science plays a part, frequently stories about the future in which science has little or no role, occasionally fiction about the prehistoric past; in this history, it frequently implies weird fiction and fantasy fiction as well, since science fiction fans frequently like the other types of non-mundane literature.

Sercon—Serious, constructive; sometimes compliment, sometimes insult, depending on the intent.

Shaggy—Familiar name for Los Angeles clubzines, *Shangri-La* and *Shangri-L'Affaires*.

Shaverites—Those who believe in or are fond of Richard Shaver's stories, which appeared in Palmer-edited prozines.

Subzine—Subscription fanzine; contrasted to those given away, or to apazines distributed only to apa members.

TAFF—Trans-Atlantic Fan Fund.

Torcon—Worldcon in Toronto.

Trufaan—Particularly active and loyal faan.

VAPA—Vanguard Amateur Press Association.

WAPA—Nineteenth century ayjay group whose full name is lost.

Worldcon—Biggest fan convention, staged annually, generally in the United States, but occasionally transferred to foreign soil.

Zine—Magazine.

1. "IT IS A PROUD AND LONELY THING TO BE A FAN"

1. Prerecorded Fandom

It is customary to assume that Columbus discovered America in 1492, although there is little doubt that many explorers purposely or inadvertently reached this continent before him. We speak of *Amazing Stories* as the first science fiction prozine, in spite of the irrefutable evidence of the existence of science fiction dime novels that came decades sooner. Such misnomers are the result of the custom of considering as the original whichever late-comer begins a persistent pattern or trend. Columbus didn't really discover, but he did a good publicity job on what he did accomplish, and began to populate the Americas with people who were not red in hue. Gernsback's magazine resulted in numerous imitators while the dime novel prozines did not enjoy uninterrupted lives. Something of this sort must be understood when we speak of fandom's origins. We say that fandom began in an un-organized sense with the letter sections in the prozines and at the start of the thirties with the first fanzines and first fan clubs. But fandom really dates much further back into the past. The earlier forms of fanac do not get the credit, because they resulted in no continuing publications and because their major forms of activity differed somewhat from those that were pop-ular in the thirties. They either died or simmered until general fandom of the thirties evolved. Like the real discoverers of America, the predecessors to general fandom are difficult to track down in full detail and it is impossible to be sure that we have detected them all. We are doubtlessly ignorant today of numerous small groups of readers and collectors who formed short-lived clubs. It is unreasonable to assume that there were not occasional carbon-copied or hectographed publications from science fiction fans before the appearance of the first fanzines that are known to us. It is impossible to be sure that groups of readers didn't elect officers and meet regularly in large cities, leaving behind no traces for lack of a prozine publicizing medium. There are enough references to something closely resembling primitive fanac in biographies of great writers to make it probable that much more of the same thing happened involving obscure folks.

The first stirrings of fandom, even though isolated and nonconsecutive in nature, go back to the middle of the nineteenth century. Like prehistoric monsters known only through an occasional fossilized thigh or pelvic bone, these primitive fans must have been infinitely more interesting and colorful than the occasional relics by which we know them today. Usually they survive only in fragmentary bits of evidence. For instance, it wasn't until 1962 that an unknown, ardent collector was discovered to have been active a century earlier. He had published, in 1878, in *The University Magazine*, a British publication, an article on space operas. It listed classics that are still well known, and added one that is completely obscure: *Les Voyages de Milord Seton*. The author's name was not given. The name of this protagonist is curiously like the surname chosen by Dr. E. E. Smith for another pioneer space traveler.

2. Lewis Carroll

Better documented is the stirring of fannish instinct in one of the most celebrated of all filthy pros, Lewis Carroll. He followed an old Victorian custom of compiling collections of his writings in manuscript form, arranged as if they were a printed magazine, and neatly bound. The first Carroll production of this type bore the ominous title of *Useful and Instructive Poetry*. It covered a half-year during 1845, when he was thirteen. In 1848 he got material from outside for *The Rectory Magazine*. After that, his titles sound like an array of fanzines: *The Comet* lasted six issues in 1848; *The Rosebud* came next with two issues; *The Star*, less ambitious, and a half-dozen numbers surviving; *Will-o'-the-Wisp*, whose triangular format no fanzine has yet imitated; *The Rectory Umbrella*, hardbound and made up at a time when Carroll was already selling professionally, actually reprinted in 1932; and *Mischmasch*, begun in 1855 and intended to set higher standards for what Carroll called domestic magazines. *Mischmasch* has received credit for helping to develop Carroll's Alice style. One biographer, Derek Hudson, sounds like certain pros recalling their fanzine days: "Gradually—and with no very ambitious motive—he began to give literary shape to some of those whimsical intimations and impressions that had haunted him since childhood, fantasies that belonged to the wonderland country and to the other side of the Looking Glass."

3. Howard Scott

Another fascinating near-miss in this instinct toward the fanzine was experienced by one Howard Scott, an amateur journalist in the 1870's. He issued a publication called *The Rambler* and collected ayjay publications of others that laid much stress on speculative science. A surviving bound volume of such apazines contains such items as an article about possible inhabitants of other worlds, information on the more abstruse habits of birds, mesmerism facts, and a discussion on the possibilities of phonetic spelling. There must have been trufaanish instincts among Scott's circle. Some of these magazines lamented the personal abuse and anger that had grown prominent in ayjay arguments, and this group was getting together for conventions. They met in 1878 at the Palmer House in Chicago and the following year convened at Hotel Hunt in St. Louis. They had organizations, known now mainly by initials like WAPA and JEAJA, official organs, and feuds. Any possibility that Scott might achieve a real breakthrough into genuine fannishness was effectively ruined when he was 35 years old. He was murdered by someone whose identity is unknown but not, hopefully, another fan.

A British girl, Grace Burns, summed up the difficulties besetting potential fans before 1930. "When I was in my youth, we too had our science fiction and very keen we were on it, I assure you. Of course, organized fandom was nonexistent. As for rubbing shoulders with authors, that was impossible, separated from us as they were by the impenetrable barrier of the editorial office. I think that the main difference was that our enthusiasm had a political bias, whereas modern enthusiasm seems to be non-political. I was a keen socialist in my youth and naturally a secret supporter of the suffrage movement."

One may only conjecture what primitive fanac is betrayed by such a slender clue as a flyleaf that Donald A. Wollheim discovered in a copy of *The Island of Dr. Moreau*. Dated April 4, 1909, the inscription reads: "To my dear James A. McCreedy in memory of the gabfests that have gone with the days when we talked of strange tales and queer things. William King Fisher."

Only a newspaper clipping enables us to know about Anna Marie Miller. She was a Brooklyn housewife who admired the works of M. P. Shiel too early in the century to have the opportunity to join in the feuding that was available to the area's residents in the fandom of the thirties. But she wrote a letter to Shiel in 1931 about *The Lord of the Sea*. A correspondence resulted, in the course of which Shiel proposed to her. She objected on the grounds that she already possessed one husband. The writer died in February, 1947, willing a house complete with garden in Sussex, England, to her thirteen-year-old son, Patrick.

4. Jules Verne

Shiel was not unique in finding admirers ardent enough to qualify as active fans. The most famous science fiction writers had lives that occasionally brushed early stirrings of fannishness. Jules Verne was born February 8, 1828, at Nantes, France. As a youth he belonged to a club with the discouraging name of Eleven Without Girls. When he broke into print professionally with "A Balloon Journey" in *Musee des Familles* in 1851, he belonged to "a club of science writers." These are all the facts we know about his own amateur interests. But there is no doubt that he was the first fantasy writer to gain a specialized fandom of his own, like Edgar Rice Burroughs and J. R. R. Tolkien.

Like the Burroughs fans a century later, most of the Verne admirers were young. Starting with *Five Weeks in a Balloon*, Verne wrote a series of novels aimed at young people that "immediately gripped not only the boys of fifteen but their parents as well," one of his biographies says. "Children, those spontaneous judges, had instantly accepted him." While *From the Earth to the Moon* was running serially, many of his fans clamored to be written into the story with a place in the imaginary projectile. Verne also had a letter-hack problem that later pros have not faced. His feminine admirers used to send him samples of their hair. He kept a pair of tweezers handy to extract it from the envelopes. "Young inmates of reformatory schools used to devour his novels," we are told. "Schoolboys, workmen, clerks, shop assistants, invalids, all those with shut-in lives were the constant companions of all his adventures.

One fan went somewhat further than any modern fan in demonstration of his intensity of feeling about science fiction. He shot Verne. The wound in the author's foot gave him trouble for the remainder of his life. This event, in March, 1886, was explained by a theory that the youngster "from excessive work had been overcome by an attack of brain fever." The Boys Imperial League of London did its best to make up for the inconvenience by purchasing a fine walking stick for Verne. He got much posthumous recognition from his fans. Roze, a famed sculptor, designed a monument after Verne's death in 1905 that depicted the author on a pedestal, three young fans at his feet. A hurricane that hit Amiens in 1925 beheaded three of the figures, but there was still enough enthusiasm over the writer to inspire its repair within a year. The more celebrated monument that *Amazing Stories* once used as a front cover is a different one, standing at the Verne grave at the Cimetière de la Madeleine at Amiens.

The only specific Verne element in general fandom until the 1960's was a kind of early groping toward Hugo awards. This was the Jules Verne Prize Club that had a frail and temporary life around 1933. Raymond A. Palmer was its chairman. It cost two bits to join. The purpose was to sponsor voting for the best science fiction stories of the year, and provide cups for the authors. It seems never to have accomplished its purpose even once. Unconnected with fandom and known only by rumor is a retiring, obscure Verne organization that was reported attempting to produce a prozine in 1940 that would publish previously untranslated Verne fiction.

It should be noted that Verne was proof that Hugo Gernsback could be right, under certain circumstances, in his claim that interest in science fiction is good for science. Simon Lake read *Twenty Thousand Leagues Under the Sea* as a ten-year-old sunning himself at the beach, told himself that he wanted to be Captain Nemo, and eventually invented the submarine in practical form. A celebrated balloonist, Charles Richet, credited his interest in air travel to *Five Weeks in a Balloon*. Admiral Byrd said after a flight to the South Pole: "It was Jules Verne who launched me on this trip." A French scientist, Georges Claude, said: "It was through his extraordinary prophetic insight that I first conceived the ambition of placing at the service of humanity some of the countless resources nature offers us. I am sure that my enthusiastic reading of his works made just as great an impression on my subconscious as on my conscious mind." It must be emphasized that Gernsback's theory had opposition even then. An early insurgent was Pope Leo XIII who said: "I am not unaware of the scientific value of your works. But what I esteem in them most of all is their purity, their moral and spiritual value."

5. H. G. Wells

Biographies of H. G. Wells give the impression that here was an individual who was constantly attempting to become a fan but was always foiled by a success in this or that venture. He was born an impressively long while ago, on September 21, 1866, in a London suburb. He grew up with a fondness for toy soldiers that lasted through adulthood and once inspired him to publish a leaflet of rules for playing with them. As a twenty-year-old student at London University's Normal School of Science, Wells started an amateur publication, *Science Schools Journal*, intended to serve interests of both literature and socialism. Previously, he'd practiced with a handwritten newspaper, *The Up Park Alarmist*. A teacher forced him to give up the editing of the *Science Schools Journal*, blaming it as the cause of poor marks. But he published in it the first three installments of an amateur science fiction story that he wrote during convalescence from a football accident. He called it "The Chronic Argonauts." After these installments, April through June, 1888, Wells decided that the story wasn't written quite right. Later in life,

Wells bought up all the copies he could find of issues that contained his fiction, articles, and mailing comments, and destroyed them, in the hope of preventing researchers from tracking down his immaturities, but he failed to make a clean sweep. He later revised "The Chronic Argonauts" and it began to appear professionally in *The National Observer*, which collapsed before the story ended. Under a new title, *The Time Machine*, it eventually was published serially in *The New Review* and in book form.

Wells' science fiction stories developed lots of personal fans. Artists, writers, and sensation hunters took their wives along when they visited their hero. This procedure was more devoted than it may seem on the surface, for those were prudish times and Wells was living with a woman to whom he was not married. On a visit to the United States, Wells discovered that Teddy Roosevelt had read and thought a great deal about *The Time Machine*. Alas for Gernsback, the President was mainly interested in its sociological implications. Wells lived long enough for real fans to hear him speak but he had no real association with general fandom. He was an old man when he died in London on August 13, 1946, pathetically confident that because so many of his predicted inventions were coming true, the world union and universal peace he had also prophesied were equally imminent.

Fans had begun to show interest in the variant versions of *The Time Machine* as early as 1934, when R. H. Barlow wrote about them in *The Fantasy Fan*. But, curiously, there seems to have been no attempt to compile a bibliography of Wells in fanzines until Forrest J Ackerman produced a memorial fanzine soon after his death. Paul Spencer probably wrote the most typical fannish obituary: "Wells' fantasies are the most completely satisfying ever written. Wells' prose at its best was remarkably vivid, flowing and poetic, his characterization delightful, his plots engrossing. Despite his often incredibly poor evaluations of current events, Wells had on a general level a vigorous insight into both the evils and the potentialities of human society which deserves acclaim." Independently of fandom, an H. G. Wells Society was formed in England around 1960. It intended to stimulate interest in his writings and ideas. It published a complete bibliography in the first issue of its fanzine, *The Wellsian*.

6. The Dime Novel

The first genuine prozines in the English language did not develop a fandom while they were at their height. They were dime novels. They meet all the tests to qualify as prozines and they contained original fiction instead of the reprints with which Gernsback filled up the first few years of *Amazing Stories*. The best-known dime novels are the Frank Reade, Jr., series. This began with an issue dated September 24, 1892, containing "Frank Reade, Jr., and His New Steam Man, or The Young Inventor's Trip to the Far West." Boys who wondered about the name of the hero might have learned from their parents that this was the son of Frank Reade, whose adventures began to appear serially in *Boys of New York* in 1876, then were reprinted complete in Wide Awake Library publications beginning in 1882. That first Frank Reade, Jr., novel must have been patterned after the January 24, 1883, issue that contained "Frank Reade and His Steam Man of the Plains."

The Reade magazines followed the dictum that Wells later laid down as the way to write science fiction: introduce one unfamiliar factor in a normal environment, and describe what results from the combination. Thoughts of airplanes, submarines, and automobiles were running through boys' minds at the end of the 19th century, so these dime novels put heavy stress on the use of known forms of power to create such futuristic transportation machines as the electric air canoe, electric submarine, steam horse, deep sea diver, and the slightly anticlimactic electric tricycle. There were other dime novel series that also laid stress on science fiction. The Boys Star Library of the late 1880's and 1890's had an extensive series of science fiction novels starring Jack Wright, who also liked to use electricity for travel purposes. One novel by Richard R. Montgomery, "Two Boys' Trip to an Unknown Planet," was such a popular example of early space opera that it appeared in the Boys of New York series in installments in 1889, and turned up in 1901 in *Pluck and Luck*.

Quite prominent men were avid fans of the dime novels. Irvin S. Cobb never forgot them. In 1926, he told an acquaintance that he would like to present to a hypothetical son equally imaginary leather-bound collections of the old dime novels with this speech, on the nonexistent youth's fourteenth birthday: "Here, my son, is something for you; a rare and precious gift. Never mind the crude style in which most of them are written. It can't be any worse than the stilted and artificial style of your school reader. Read them for the thrills that are in them. If fortune is ever kinder to you than it was to your father, you may be inspired to sit down and write a dime novel of your own."

A most unlikely enthusiast was Frederick Delius. He encountered parental opposition to the British version of dime novels, penny dreadfuls. Delius as a boy devised a scheme more practical than the type of music he wrote as a man would indicate. He ran a cord from the gaslight in his bedroom over a system of pulleys to the head of his bed, read the tales from between the sheets until he heard footsteps, yanked the cord and doused the light, and pretended sleep. His mother finally discovered the subterfuge, but the tale has a happy ending. She glanced at one of the novels herself, began reading it, and became a penny dreadful fan as a result. Sweeney Todd, the demon barber, was Delius' favorite hero.

Dime novels survived in the United States until March 6, 1929, when *Pluck and Luck* published its final issue. Even before then, dime novel fans were reprinting the older ones and were publishing fanzines. Many of these reprint and fan publications had science fiction as their content. Frank Fries, of Orrville, Ohio, seems to have been the first enthusiast who began an elaborate reprint program. He concentrated on the Reade and Reade, Jr., series. Beginning in 1928, Fries produced 82 issues of a small fanzine that republished some Reade tales in serial form and supplemented them with articles, letters to the editor, and such fillers as a request for information on the real first name of Pomp. Fries continued this fanac at least through 1935. Another famed dime novel fanzine was *Happy Hours Magazine*, published by Ralph P. Smith, of Lawrence, Massachusetts. It flourished during the twenties. Walter A. Coslet was apparently the only member of mainstream fandom with much interest in this specialized field. His collection contained some 400 issues of dime novel fanzines, including many of interest to science fiction readers.

George Sahr began to reprint the *Frank Reade Weekly Magazine* in 1931 in facsimile form. The Dime Novel Club also issued numerous facsimiles of the Reade, Wright, and other series. Prices at which they were offered were generally higher than the cover prices of the originals, which had often sold for only a nickel despite their generic name, but still much lower than the going price paid by collectors for originals. Fries, for instance, sold a facsimile of *Frank Reade's Steam Man* for 50¢ in 1927. Nobody has issued a checklist of dime novels with science fiction and fantasy themes. Collectors who sought them all, fantastic and mundane, had big jobs. Sahr spent fifteen years attempting to complete his run of *Frank Reade Weekly Magazine*, despite the benefit of a huge headstart when he bought up all but ten issues from the original publisher.

One way to be certain that there was an early fandom lies in the survival into contemporary times of various individuals who were ardent collecting fans long before the first issues of *Amazing Stories*. Laurence Manning was known to fandom only as the writer of prozine stories in the thirties. But he had been a fantasy book collector long before that. A Canadian by birth, a Staten Islander by residence, and a nurseryman by profession, he specialized in utopias, assembling more than 500 volumes on this theme. The mysterious fan W. S. Houston quite possibly antedates fandom as a collector. This enigmatic figure is old enough—reputedly in his eighties—and subscribed to most fanzines from their start. Lynn Hickman, one of the few fans who has visited him, described his collection as one of the finest of all. C. A. Brandt, known today as the first managing editor of *Amazing Stories*, had a tremendous collection of fantasy books in English and other languages in the early days. This German-born chemist was reputed to be the world's greatest authority on science fiction when a second-hand book dealer put him in touch with Gernsback to be wet nurse for *Amazing Stories*. A letter in *All-Story Weekly* in 1917 in which he asked help with a bibliography of George Allan England is proof that he did more than read the books he collected. Brandt, who was credited with introducing calculating machines to the United States, suffered the loss of his collection when it was sold out from under him while he was overseas in World War II. Nothing daunted, in his sixties, he began to rebuild this collection. He willed the second collection, upon his death in 1946, to Ackerman. He had attended his first fan meeting, a postwar convention in Newark in March, just before his death. Wilbur C. Whitehead, an auction bridge expert who also helped with the early editing of *Amazing*, was described as another fan. Gernsback himself might have qualified as a semi-fan. He'd gone into wild enthusiasm at the age of nine when he encountered a German translation of Percival Lowell's *Mars as the Abode of Life*, almost memorized the novels of Verne and Wells, and wrote his own science fiction stories as a boy.

7. H. P. Lovecraft and His Circle

The most prominent fandom before the One True Fandom was the cult of Howard Phillips Lovecraft. This differed only slightly from general fandom and came many years earlier. For convenience's sake, we call it Lovecraft fandom, although it acquired that title only after the death of HPL. The name is misleading, in the sense that it was not originally as piously devoted to the writer as later fans might assume.

Lovecraft might have been described as a fan looking for a fandom for many years. He was born in Providence, Rhode Island, on August 20, 1890. He was a child semi-genius, learning to read when four years old and creating at the age of five the imaginary character of Abdul Alhazred, later disguised as the mad Arabian author of the *Necronomicon*. Lovecraft was a Roman fan when six, building altars and organizing sacrifices for pagan gods. He wrote fiction thrillers, including ghost stories, when nine. His first publishing venture came at the age of eight. He used a pencil and carbon paper to produce a weekly *Scientific Gazette* devoted to chemistry. He persisted with this for four years, then used a hectograph to publish in his teens the *Rhode Island Journal of Astronomy*. He circulated this in a 25-copy edition, and didn't lose interest for another four years. When little more than a boy, he acquired the interest in mundane amateur journalism that caused him to write for these publications at least as early as 1908, when he published "The Alchemist," a weird tale that he later disowned, in *The United Amateur*.

When eighteen, Lovecraft destroyed most of his fiction, inadvertently simplifying the later labors of August Derleth.

For some reason, Lovecraft did not join an apa until 1914, when he became a United Amateur Press Association member. Curiously, in view of his kind and friendly nature, he plunged almost at once into ayjay politics and became a key figure in a literary clique. He was president of UAPA in 1917-18, and remained a force in its politics until the middle twenties. As early as 1918, the UAPA contained such members of Lovecraft fandom as W. Paul Cook, Edward H. Cole, Samuel Loveman, Arthur Goodenough, Clark Ashton Smith, and Frank Belknap Long, Jr., all interested to varying degrees in fantastic fiction. One authority on mundane amateur journalism, Helen Wesson, is convinced that "Lovecraft generated a tidal wave of literary achievement in amateur journalism and the ripples lapped on the shores of contemporary American literature."

There is nothing to disqualify these people from the title of fans. They were not primarily interested in science fiction, but neither were many other prominent figures in general fandom. They corresponded, wrote amateur fiction, articles, and poetry, visited one another, feuded, letter-hacked, collected, and although they did not have conventions for fantasy fiction fans, they did enjoy the conventions of the apas to which they belonged. They published amateur magazines that frequently featured weird and fantasy fiction and articles about its authors.

Lovecraft's first night spent away from home occurred when he was thirty years old and attended a get-together in Boston, a primitive sort of noncon for those who couldn't make it to the 1920 National Amateur Press Association convention in Cleveland. Moreover, Lovecraft came close to prophesying literally the fiawol philosophy in his talk to the Baltimore Conference of Amateur Journalists in 1921: "What amateur journalism has given me is life itself." UAPA was his first love. He was its president three times, won three laureates, and attempted to kidnap members of the ultra-NAPA Hub Club as recruits for his faction. But he finally joined the NAPA in 1917, waiting until then because of a fuss with one of its prominent members, Graeme Davis. Lovecraft caused an ayjay sensation when he became the NAPA president in 1922 and managed to calm down its squabbles during his year in office. As late as 1935, he still served on the NAPA bureau of critics.

Lovecraft contributed frequently to apa publications. George Wetzel traced 57 contributions (under Lovecraft's own name and known pseudonyms in the years from 1918 to 1926) among the collection of amateur journals that Lovecraft bequeathed to the Fossil Library of Amateur Journalism in Benjamin Franklin Memorial Library, Philadelphia. These were mainly poems, augmented by essays and fiction. Lovecraft's own publication was entitled *The Conservative*. It appeared first in 1915 and lasted for thirteen issues through 1923. Literary discussions predominated in it. Lovecraft later dismissed his amateur journalism writing as "a mass of mediocre and miserable junk," and we may never know exactly how much written material he turned out during nearly three decades of activity.

For a person with reclusive tendencies, Lovecraft showed impressive stamina and gregariousness at ayjay meetings. His death undoubtedly deprived the first fannish worldcons of a professional focal point. He was particularly skillful at the art of going without sleep from start to finish of a con. But it was his corresponding that made him best known to fans. His letter-writing was extensive beyond belief. R. H. Barlow estimated that Lovecraft wrote 100,000 letters, averaging eight per day, some of them up to sixty pages long, always in handwriting. Lovecraft carried out fully a philosophy of dislike for machines, like typewriters, similar to that which Ray Bradbury later espoused. The Lovecraft correspondents varied from fifteen youngsters with whom he became penpals in the last year of his life to the antediluvian C. W. "Tryout" Smith of Haverhill, Massachusetts, who began amateur publishing in 1872, had produced 369 zines by the time he marked his 91st birthday in 1943, and handset into type some of Lovecraft's fiction. Lovecraft normally kept from fifty to one hundred correspondences in motion at all times. One individual received a letter a week from Lovecraft for twelve years, ranging in size up to thirty pages.

Lovecraft's status as a writer never equalled that of Henry James and Lord Dunsany, though some of his fans claimed that distinction for him. But his goodness as a human and as a fan remained unchallenged. He never published a fanzine in general fandom, although he had planned one in collaboration with Duane Rimel in the last years of his life. He participated in many other fannish activities. As a letterhack for the prozines, he was quite persistent. His letters frequently appeared in *Argosy*, where he once complained because a story ended with a love scene, an event that Lovecraft rarely observed in the wake of a real-life drama. He loved hoaxes. It was not until after his death that the nonexistence of Abdul Alhazred became generally known. Claire Beck then published letters that Lovecraft had written to Jim Blish and William Miller, Jr., admitting his invention. Lovecraft did suffer some mild remorse when people wasted time at public libraries hunting for that Arab's book. The *Necronomicon*, supposed to exist only in a Greek translation published in 1567 in Italy, was listed in at least one catalog of rare books, as a sentimental gesture by a dealer who knew the truth. Another Lovecraft devotee somehow smuggled reference cards into the catalog of the Yale University Library, causing repeated false alarms about the book in that institution. In a sense, the book really exists. John Boardman found in a Brooklyn home a slender black volume that contained all passages from the

Necronomicon that are quoted in fiction by Lovecraft and his followers. It appeared to have been printed privately.

Lovecraft was probably responsible for a mysterious pioneer piece of faan fiction mailed anonymously from Washington, D.C., in the summer of 1934. This single-sheet "The Battle That Ended the Century" was a tale of a fight on the eve of the year 2001 in which H. C. Koenig, Julius Schwartz, Franklin Lee Baldwin, W. Paul Cook, and Forrest J Ackerman appeared under thinly disguised names. Even after he became a professional, Lovecraft liked to introduce fannish references into fiction. Robert Blake in "The Haunter of Darkness" is Bloch, with an altered name but an accurate home address. Others in the circle reciprocated. Lovecraft died in ways invoking various degrees of nausea in four professionally published stories: Bloch's "Shambler from the Stars" and "The Dark Demon," Long's "The Space Eaters," and Kuttner's "Hydra." A brutal editor kept the Kuttner story's reference from getting into print.

Lovecraft's personal characteristics have been recited and exaggerated to absurd excess. It is true that he was eccentric, but this condition is common to perhaps half of the nation's adults. He was allergic to cold air, in a degree slightly more severe than that exhibited by half of the women on this continent. He could live on 30¢ a day, and this has been publicized as a wildly freakish thing, while writers who can go into debt at the rate of $3.00 a day pass unnoticed. Lovecraft put many of his fears and emotions into his fiction, a procedure that almost all good fiction utilizes. The only harm from this trick of the trade has been the ruin it brought to stories by imitators who tried to convey horror over matters that didn't affect them personally. In any event, the outward milestones in Lovecraft's life are quickly told. He spent most of his life in his beloved Providence, where various elderly female relatives watched over him. At the 1921 NAPA convention, he met Sonia H. Greene, whom he married in 1924. They separated in less than two years, and were divorced in 1929. When Lovecraft moved to New York City for a couple of years during the twenties, he joined the Kalem Club that contained such fantasy fiction figures as Long, Samuel Loveman, H. C. Koenig, and Donald Wandrei. Lovecraft first sold fiction in 1922. Many of the stories that brought in cash had seen original publication in amateur form. Death came on March 15, 1937, at Jane Brown Memorial Hospital in Providence, of cancer of the intestines and Bright's disease. The legend that he starved to death is incorrect. He ate adequately but irregularly, and thought that a lot of food prevented a clear mind.

W. Paul Cook was a pioneer in the circle of HPL admirers. Fruits of his labors to publish Lovecraft became treasured, expensive collector's items within a decade. At least two Cook preprints are even rarer for they never saw publication: *The Shunned House,* which Cook withheld, and the uncompleted second issue of *The Recluse*, which he destroyed. Something similar happened to Barlow's edition of *Fungi from Yuggoth*, a batch of Lovecraft poetry, whose pages were printed but never collated. Other primitive fans also helped to put Lovecraft into print. "The Quest of Iranon" first appeared in an amateur magazine, *The Galleon*, issued by Lloyd Arthur Eshbach. "Tryout" Smith was publisher for at least three stories.

Like many greater writers, Lovecraft experienced a great growth in his fame and quantity of admirers after death. August Derleth has generously devoted a substantial portion of his adult life to handling the posthumous literary matters of Lovecraft. With the help of Wandrei, Annie Gamwell, and Barlow, Derleth did much of the work on what was originally thought of as a one-shot memorial volume, *The Outsider and Others*. In 1939, when Derleth was putting between hard covers some of Lovecraft's best fiction, it was possible to publish 1,200 copies of this fairly large volume for a printing bill of $2,500. Derleth borrowed some of this money, and made up more of the expense by purchasing personally 100 copies of the book. Wandrei made a similar 100-copy purchase. The 554-page volume was offered for $3.50 before publication and $5.00 thereafter. Wandrei and Derleth warned that they would not give a go-ahead signal to the printer without sufficient advance orders. But they risked the venture despite failure to sell more than 150 copies in advance. When it took four years for the edition to sell out, the sponsors must have understood why both Simon & Schuster and Scribner's had rejected the typescript.

The Kalem Club staged a get-together to celebrate publication. Then the book went into the hands of purchasers with tedious slowness, despite all sorts of fanzine publicity. Finally, when it went out of print, something unexpected occurred. It immediately became the most fascinating object in the history of fantasy, one that every reader must own immediately, preferably in duplicate or triplicate. The second-hand price soared to at least ten times the original cost. There were reports that $100 had changed hands for a single copy, and advertisements offered the book at that figure. Nobody has ever produced proof that the figure was ever reached. Wandrei and Derleth, after risking their money and donating huge amounts of valuable time, found themselves accused unjustly of profiteering. Grimly and patiently, Derleth explained what had happened: he and Wandrei had released their own copies after the remainder of the edition sold out. Derleth sold his hundred for the list price, and an extra 30¢ had been added to the list price for the Wandrei copies, because of added transportation requirements. It was a nasty treatment for a man who had put into the publication expense some money that the bank had lent him for improvements on his house. Derleth also denied the tales that he was selling books in quantities to individuals for speculative purposes. Even after the inflation occurred on

the price of that first Arkham House volume, there were only three individuals on his mailing list who bought two or three copies of each new title.
This bull market for the Lovecraft collection did not return profits to
anyone except second-hand dealers. But Derleth continued his publishing
under the name of Arkham House. Cautiously, he published another batch
of Lovecraft stories in 1943, *Beyond the Wall of Sleep*, in a 1,217-copy
edition. The next year *Marginalia*, odds and ends of HPL, appeared. The
less happy series of literary scavengings from Lovecraft leavings began after
that and the great age of Lovecraft fandom subsided simultaneously. Francis
T. Laney, long one of his foremost prophets, expressed the fandom-wide re-
vulsion: "Why should any fanzine ever again publish anything by Lovecraft
or even about him? If fanzines more or less drop HPL from consideration
and one or two other pros stop beating the drums for Lovecraft for even
as little as one year, HPL will drop back to his proper status in American
literature—almost completely unknown and forgotten."

Although Derleth controls the Lovecraft writings themselves, other enthu-
siasts have done a great deal of publishing of Lovecraftiana of other types.
An early effort was *Rhode Island on Lovecraft*, issued in 1946 by Thomas
P. Hadley and Donald M. Grant. This contained useful reminiscences by
Providence residents who had known Lovecraft personally, including Win-
field Townley Scott, Mrs. Clifford Eddy, Dorothy C. Walter, Marian F.
Barner, and Mary V. Dana. Printed professionally, it sold for only 50¢.
Laney meanwhile had issued *The Acolyte*, one of the time's finest fanzines,
specializing in material by and about the Lovecraft circle.

The tedium of indexing and glossing Lovecraft's writings was taken up
enthusiastically by some scholarly-minded fans. George T. Wetzel, who
alienated general fandom by his manner of arguing, has been one of the
hardest workers in Lovecraft lore. He began research around 1946, and
started publishing his findings in 1951, in the fourth and fifth issues of
Destiny. Leon Stone, an Australian, started in 1948 to publish a Lovecraft
bibliography. It ran for five issues or so in his annual publication, *Koolinda*.
Edward Cole issued a superbly printed number of *The Olympian*, devoted entirely to material about Lovecraft. Barlow served as literary executor, pre-
serving hundreds of books and magazines, vast numbers of amateur publications, and countless manuscripts found in the study at 66 College Street.
Ray Zorn began in 1949 to publish *The Lovecraft Collector*, a printed leaflet
produced "in the interests of amateur journalism and to further the collecting of the works of Howard Phillips Lovecraft." Another aspect of Lovecraft fandom must have been more exciting if it indeed existed. Laney
claimed that Cthulhu worshippers were active in Boston and some other
cities during the forties. They were alleged to believe that Lovecraft wrote
truth under the guise of fiction.

8. August W. Derleth

Some notables in Lovecraft fandom can be introduced through the manner in which they were influenced by HPL. August W. Derleth, for instance, had been known to Lovecraft at least as early as 1929, when Lovecraft wrote a letter of favorable comment to *The Dragnet* about the Solar Pons detective stories that Derleth was selling then. Derleth was born in Sauk City, Wisconsin, on February 24, 1909. He began to write as he was entering his teens, was graduated from the University of Wisconsin, and scored professional success more regularly and quickly than Lovecraft managed to do. Derleth read *Weird Tales* from its first issue, getting acquainted with science fiction there. He was an *Amazing Stories* reader from its start, too. Around the middle twenties, Derleth began to correspond with many fantasy notables, entering penpal relations with Lovecraft, C. A. Smith, Henry S. Whitehead, Wandrei, Robert E. Howard, Bloch, Kuttner, and Fritz Leiber. But he was not as obsessed with fantasy fiction as many of those gentlemen. He wrote much mystery fiction as a devotee of Sherlock Holmes, held editorial posts on such diverse publications as the *Capital Times* of Madison, Wisconsin, and *Mystic* magazine, and earned a Guggenheim fellowship in 1938.

Derleth never published a fanzine or showed any great interest in fandom. His first big adventure in the field was not too pleasant in nature. He threatened in 1937 to sue Corwin F. Stickney over the latter's publication of a 25-copy printed edition of ten Lovecraft poems. Derleth did not resort to the law, in the end, possibly in consideration of the facts that the booklet was to be given away, that Lovecraft had granted permission to Stickney to publish some of the poems, and that part of the contents was already in the public domain because of previous fanzine publication.

9. W. Paul Cook

Less known today, but much more important during Lovecraft's lifetime, was W. Paul Cook. The details of Cook's devotion to his hobby sound like a hoax created specifically for this history. Cook printed Lovecraft's second published story and much of his other work, long before the prozines became interested. Cook published the first surviving fanzine. Fans marvel in recent years at fanzines that contain 100 mimeographed pages, but Cook published an amateur magazine that contained 312 superbly printed pages. I have been unable to track down the early details of his life, but he was elderly at the time of his death on January 22, 1948, and had been active in amateur journalism for a half-century. Even before Lovecraft fandom coalesced, Cook published *The Monadnock Monthly* for thirteen years early in the century. From 1923 to 1927, he issued *The Vagrant*, whose final edition was the 312-pager. In that same year of 1927, *The Recluse* came from the Cook press, the one-shot that represented the first undisputedly amateur magazine devoted entirely to fantasy. It contained the first appearance of Lovecraft's essay "Supernatural Horror in Literature," fiction by Wandrei and H. Warner Munn, poems by Wandrei and Frank Belknap Long, Jr., a checklist of the writings of George Sterling, and other material by Samuel Loveman. Only 100 copies were printed. Cook described it as "The realization of a dream, long cherished, of the publication of a magazine to please the producer only. Nothing will be paid for contributions and the magazine will, as have former efforts, be issued as an amateur and money cannot buy it." He had been the individual who persuaded Lovecraft to write the essay, a pioneering survey of the field of weird fiction. Cook's final major publishing effort was *The Ghost*. Five issues appeared from 1943 to 1947, each containing fifty pages that emphasized Lovecraft and collectors. It contained almost every type of verse, fiction, biography, and literary reminiscing, turning it into one of the rarest, most sought-after bits of Lovecraftiana. "Cook's finest gesture was dragging from a darkened den that super-craftsman, Howard Phillips Lovecraft, pushing him with cajolery and encouragement into the lighthearted circle of United Amateur journalists where most members play with little journalettes, not knowing the difference between a manuscript and a mausoleum," Earle Cornwall said.

10. Henry Kuttner

Henry Kuttner was only a fringefan when he began to sell stories in 1937. But his association with Lovecraft had one special result, unique in the Lovecraft circle. HPL helped Kuttner to meet his future wife. The two men began corresponding in 1935, at a time when Catherine L. Moore already had a stall in the stable of Lovecraft's numerous correspondents. Lovecraft sent Kuttner a batch of his unpublished stories with a request to read them, then to forward them to the girl. She and Kuttner fell into correspondence over the matter. They met in Los Angeles and in Indianapolis, romance ensued, and they were married on June 7, 1940. Working as a bank clerk, C. L. Moore had already been selling fiction for a decade when she became Kuttner's bride. Until Kuttner began to hit the prozines, he had done few things in fandom in addition to a lot of correspondence. Older than most of the Los Angeles fans—he was born in 1914—he had contributed to some West Coast fanzines while residing in Beverly Hills. At the time, he claimed he was too lazy to use his ability to write for the slicks. He was not gregarious, but he was among the best-liked of all the highly admired men in

Lovecraft fandom. "I never heard a bad thing about Henry Kuttner. I never saw evil of any kind in him. I never knew I could miss so very much someone I had seen so seldom. He shouldn't have died," Ted Sturgeon said in obituary remarks in 1958. The Eastern Science Fiction Association staged a half-day con in honor of his memory.

11. R. H. Barlow and Farnsworth Wright

Little has been written about R. H. Barlow. He had little or nothing to do with general fandom, aside from his activity in Lovecraft fandom. He published two issues of *Leaves* in the thirties, modeling them after Cook's *Recluse*. Even his death is an uncertain matter. Dr. C. L. Barrett found him still alive in Florida a few years ago and took advantage of the discovery to purchase most of his collection.

Another famous fantasy figure had an amateur publication that could conceivably have taken on fanzine characteristics if an act of God hadn't intervened. Many mishaps have befallen fanzines, but none has ever been swallowed up by an earthquake. Farnsworth Wright was a Californian, born there in 1888 and a resident of the state until the San Francisco earthquake. He'd published *The Laurel* for the National and United APAs until the earthquake ate it. Wright had written, edited, set and printed it himself on a hand press. Many years later, he became the villain of Lovecraft fandom, for his rejection of much HPL fiction while he was editor of *Weird Tales*.

12. Robert Bloch

Robert Bloch is the only member of the Lovecraft circle who both made the transition to general fandom and survived as a fan. Born April 5, 1917, in Chicago, but a resident of Milwaukee most of his early life, he was precocious enough to be a fourth-grader when eight years old. At that age, he discovered the ecstasy of scaring oneself to death, by viewing the Lon Chaney *Phantom of the Opera*. "It scared the living hell out of me," he remembers fondly. Two years later, an aunt offered to buy the boy any magazine in the display at a railroad depot. He chose his first issue of *Weird Tales*. Out of fondness for Lovecraft's fiction, Bloch began to correspond with HPL in 1932. With typical kindness, Lovecraft immediately offered to lend him books, encouraged him to write fiction, and introduced him by mail to such notables as Derleth, C. A. Smith, and E. Hoffman Price.

Uniquely, Bloch broke into general fandom and into prodom at almost the same moment. He made his first sale to *Weird Tales* in 1934, two months

Bob Bloch (l.) and Bob Tucker

after being graduated from high school. Almost simultaneously, he began to show up in fan publications, starting with *Marvel Tales*, then *The Fantasy Fan*. Until 1937, Bloch had met more pros than fans. Jack Darrow paid a call on him one Sunday. That was his only encounter with the fannish breed at a time when he'd already walked and talked with such legendary personages as Stanley Weinbaum, Ray Palmer, Ralph Milne Farley, Farnsworth Wright, Eando Binder, Otis Adelbert Kline, August Derleth, Donald Wandrei, Julius Schwartz, and Mort Weisinger.

In 1937 the shock of Lovecraft's death caused Bloch to try to divert himself by traveling to California for a visit to Kuttner. Immediately he met the Los Angeles Science Fiction League members. He made a trip to New York in 1939 but skipped that year's Nycon, then couldn't afford to attend the first Chicon in 1940. But after the war, Bloch and conventions became both synonymous and symbiotic. Acting and floor show experience in his teens may have helped to prepare Bloch for the starring role that he played in many later conventions.

In and out of the fantasy field, Bloch built up a major reputation as a fiction craftsman that won him entry to more profitable fields than the pulps where he began. "Yours Truly, Jack the Ripper" probably put him before the public more prominently than any other work until the movie *Psycho*. Arkham House published *The Opener of the Way*, a collection of Bloch fiction, in 1945. A French edition appeared through Editions Fournier. Both the *Kate Smith Show* and *Mollé Mystery Theater* put the Ripper on radio, then Bloch adapted 39 of his stories for *Stay Tuned for Terror*, a syndicated transcribed radio program. In Milwaukee he held a weekly spot on a local television panel program, *It's a Draw*, in 1954-59. Writing long remained a sideline with Bloch, who had a job with an advertising agency until 1953. He then spent the following six years as a free lance writer, living in Weyauwega, Wisconsin. On weekends he commuted to Milwaukee for his television appearances.

In 1959 Bloch's novel, *Psycho*, was sold for filming. Then he went to Hollywood to cash in on the reputation he'd built up through his first ten books. He apologized to fandom for taking the time to make real money for a change.

More than almost any other professional, Bloch donated his time and efforts to write for the fanzines. He didn't toss them the leavings in the form of stories that hadn't sold. Instead he wrote non-fiction for them, polished and wise articles that bear the evidence of ample thinking-out and the most careful composition. The best of them were assembled by Earl Kemp in *The Eighth Stage of Fandom* and edited just enough to remove the more mysterious fannish language and references. Advent:Publishers issued it in both hardcover and paperback editions in 1962. Bloch put fandom into the prozines repeatedly in fictional form, most elaborately in "A Way of Life," which used fandom as the basis for a science fiction story in *Fantastic Universe* in 1956.

Typical of his willingness to pay attention to his own spawning pool was Bloch's kindness to a completely unknown fan who bobbed up in 1951, William E. Neumann. While many fans snubbed Neumann as a neo, Bloch talked with him for hours about psychopaths and schizophrenia, topics familiar to the new fan, who worked as an attendant at a mental institution. "I appreciate more than anything else the friendships and contacts that fandom has brought me through the years," Bloch wrote in 1949, and he hasn't forgotten the gratitude. More recently, he described himself as a middlebrow, "The forgotten man in an era when everyone is being called upon to stand up and be counted. Either you take your stand with the exultant lowbrow majority and glory in the fact that the very biggest names are all catering to your taste or you bare your breast with the young intellectuals and dig moderne the most. Nobody is a middlebrow any more. You're either a company man or a rebel without a cause." His own position, oscillating between prodom and fandom, offers an interesting parallel to his philosophy.

13. H. C. Koenig

H. C. Koenig was a New Yorker whose age was never officially revealed but must have been considerable. He had read *All-Story* and *Argosy* before they combined in 1920, to give you some idea. He was an avid subscriber to fanzines, unlike most members of the Lovecraft circle, and published for FAPA *The Reader and Collector*, a unique fanzine. Its specialness consisted in the fact that Koenig's secretary did the work. Koenig worked as an electrical engineer for Electrical Testing Laboratories, in New York, where he could enjoy the luxury of writing his scathing comments on inane professional writing and stupid fannish opinions, turn the manuscript over to the girl, and let her do all the rest. He even used part of his office to house some of his fantasy collection. Koenig was celebrated for his diligent cam-

paign against prozine stories in which characters "hissed" statements that
contained no sibilants. As a collector, Koenig was fond of first editions,
a phase of the hobby out of the financial reach of most fans. He also liked
to restore neglected authors to favor. William Hope Hodgson was his biggest
reclamation project. Somehow Koenig was enthralled by a short story by
Hodgson in a 1931 weird fiction anthology. Koenig persuaded Lovecraft to
include consideration of Hodgson in "Super-
natural Horror in Literature," then published
essays in *The Fantasy Fan* and *The Phanta-*
graph on this writer, devoted an entire issue of
The Reader and Collector to Hodgson in 1944,
persuaded *Famous Fantastic Mysteries* to print
three Hodgson stories between 1943 and 1945,
and helped influence Arkham House to publish
four Hodgson novels in 1946 and his weird detective stories the following year. When out-of-
town fans visited New York in the earlier days,
Koenig and John Campbell used to toss a coin.
The loser played host to the fans.

H. C. Koenig

14. Duane Weldon Rimel

Duane Weldon Rimel was distinctive principally for the fact that he almost
published a fanzine in collaboration with Lovecraft, then did publish one in
cooperation with Laney. Rimel grew up in Asotin, Washington. Inflamma-
tory rheumatism in his early teens left him a semi-invalid. Franklin Lee
Baldwin, another Asotin resident, and Rimel got acquainted in the early
thirties and entered Lovecraft fandom together. Both contributed to fanzines and Rimel sold his first story to *Weird Tales* in the nick of time.
It appeared in the last issue of that magazine that Lovecraft lived to see.
Rimel made many linoleum cuts for *The Fantasy Fan* and *Fantasy Magazine*.
An interest in jazz got him acquainted with Laney. The fanzine collaboration
with Lovecraft aborted because they couldn't make arrangements for a press.
The Acolyte emerged from the Laney association. Its full story is told else-
where in this narrative.

15. Clark Ashton Smith

The hermit impulses and eccentricities attributed to Lovecraft might with
more justice be ascribed to Clark Ashton Smith. It takes a considerable

imagination to find fannish things
to tell about him, despite his long
presence in the Lovecraft circle.
Born in 1893, he hid away from
the world in a cabin at Auburn,
California, for a long time until he
got married, then resided in Pacific
Grove in only slightly less secluded
conditions. He knew Lovecraft
from 1923, when Smith sent Lovecraft a copy of his privately-printed
writings, *Ebony and Crystal*. Lovecraft also provided him with a nickname, Klarkash-Ton. Only a few
fans made the pilgrimage to visit
him through the years: Kuttner,
Price, Wandrei, Henry Hasse, Emil

Clark Ashton Smith

Petaja, Paul Freehafer, Derleth, Barlow, and a scattering of Los Angeles area
people. His last years were difficult ones, with financial demands forcing
him to sell off most of his land and treasured items from his collection.

There must be many lost members of Lovecraft fandom. Nobody today
knows anything about Howard Davidson, for instance. This Columbus, Ohio,
man died leaving behind an old trunk that eventually reposed in a second-
hand store. There it was found to contain a Lovecraft manuscript, numerous
letters from the same writer, amateur stories by Davidson, and ayjay magazines. Internal evidence showed that he'd been active in UAPA and NAPA
before World War I.

16. Near-Miss Fans

There is no doubt that quite celebrated people have had fannish instincts
that were overshadowed by their success in other fields. Thomas Wolfe, if
we may trust his description of Eugene Gant, "liked all weird fable and wild
invention, in prose or verse, from the *Golden Ass* to Samuel Taylor Cole-
ridge, the chief prince of the moon and magic." Helen Traubel says in her
autobiography: "I have a dozen long shelves packed with fairy tales from
all over the world. For years, I have collected the doings of never-never land
with the same devotion that a miser might count his gold. I enjoy reading
them over and over, smiling at their pleasure, and feeling my eyes moisten
at their disasters. The adventures of the children, dwarfs, kings and princes,
swans and geese, heroes and cowherds, giants and elves—these, I find, are

not unreal at all. They seem to me to be more genuine than many of the happenings in real life. In the best sense, my own life has been a fairy tale."

Robert Butman, in his essay "Modern Mythological Fiction," even proposed the theory that a sort of fandom can be traced through the majority of the important English novelists and poets of the past three-quarters of a century, originating in the theosophical writings of Madame Blavatsky, and evidenced in such men as Lawrence, Yeats, and Huxley. Then there was the first known Spanish fan, Manuel de Falla. He also formed a precedent for Coventry, a later Los Angeles mythology: As a boy, around 1890, he invented an entire imaginary city, Colón, complete with a newspaper, *El Mes Colombino*, and satirical weeklies, *El Burlon* and *El Cascabel*. This had genuine science fictional elements, because de Falla arranged for letters and messages to go from Colón to Seville by "a rapid vehicle of his own invention," an old friend recalled. There is no telling how far de Falla would have gone with this dream city-cum-publications, if he hadn't been so engrossed in it that he failed to watch the carnival revelry in the street below the balcony of his home at the start of one Lent. His parents investigated this sudden disinterest, found him busy collecting taxes, discovered all the receipts and papers involved in the city, and called a doctor. The physician ordered all the records taken away from the youth, lest it end in madness. The disappointed de Falla had to settle for the life of a composer.

The lack of a rallying point like a full-fledged prozine must have prevented a consecutive fandom from originating many decades before the thirties. Too many persons with intense interest in science fiction simply did not realize the existence of others with similar devotions. Thus, around 1918, when a great deal of collecting and bibliography was already in progress, we find one Edward Shanks writing in *The New Statesman* an article about novels set in the future. He claims that no amateurs have begun collecting the books. Shanks, writer of a fantasy book of his own, *The People of the Ruins*, published in 1920, anticipated in his essay much of modern fanzine fandom when he recommended fantasy as a theme for anyone seeking essay material that could combine literature, sociology, and the psychology of the slightly insane.

But it must also be remembered that amateur journalism could not flourish until economic conditions and technology set the stage. The first known amateur publications date back to 1750, but they were issues of a university magazine financed by well-heeled students of Oxford and Cambridge in England, not susceptible of imitation elsewhere. It was not until just after the Civil War that low-priced printing presses became available in the United States and literary-minded youngsters could find a way to express themselves without a professional medium. It is significant that the National Amateur Press Association was formed in 1876. The British ayjay organizations did not arrive until 1890. Mimeographs did not become generally available until the twentieth century. The only copying system available in the nineteenth century was a device that permitted making only a single copy of a document. The inventor of the hectograph for obvious reasons has concealed so well all trace of his identity and details of its discovery that I have been unable to determine the date on which he unlocked this secret of nature. But the devilish things must have been available before the turn of the century. Frank Swinnerton's autobiography tells how, as a teen-aged office boy, he published a small monthly journal with the help of a hectograph. Swinnerton, incidentally, gives credit to the Boer War, of all imaginable things, for helping to create a great deal more amateur journalism. He thought that it supplied a rallying point for young minds with liberal tendencies and thoughts.

But fan historians have overlooked the most telling piece of evidence proving the existence of a numerous body of enthusiastic fans before 1926. Gernsback, who reprinted in *Amazing Stories* several items from *The Lane Tech Prep*, a student publication of a Chicago boys' high school, put the evidence into black and white in *Amazing Stories* at a date when he cannot be accused of falling victim to an unreliable memory. In the June, 1926, *Amazing* he wrote: "From the suggestions for reprints that are coming in, these 'fans' seem to have a hobby all their own of hunting up scientifiction stories, not only in English, but in many other languages. There is not a day, now, that passes but we get from a dozen to fifty suggestions as to stories of which, frankly, we have no record, although we have a list of some 600 or 700 scientifiction stories. Some of these fans are constantly visiting the book stores with the express purpose of buying new or old scientifiction tales, and they even go to the trouble of advertising for some volumes that have long ago gone out of print." This passage is also notable as the first public use of "fan" as the name for the person who likes science fiction too much to be content with merely reading it occasionally. The reference to "fans" quite possibly settled the general name for the hobbyists, and prevented us from acquiring as distinctive a term as the hams of amateur radio or the buffs of Civil War lore.

2. FANDOM: Manners and Mores

1. Numbers and Types of Fans

What was fandom like during the forties?

Efforts to determine how many fans existed in the decade bog down immediately into sticky semantic swampland. There were few of the convention fans who sprang up during the fifties, those hundreds of fans who appear at world cons and regional conferences, more rarely for local club functions, and remain hidden the rest of the time. No worldcon during the forties attracted more than perhaps a hundred persons who were not prominent fans or professionals. But there must have been large numbers of a type of fan equally hard to track down most of the time, during the forties: the collecting fans, who pursue their hobby in an idyllic seclusion rarely shattered by eruptions of fanzine-publishing and feud-promoting. There were enough of these collecting fans to make possible the temporary success of semi-pro publishing houses that broke even or nearly did so by selling just a couple of thousand copies of each title of a science fiction or fantasy book to mainly a little coterie of collectors, rather than through the normal bookstore outlets. Enough of these collectors were known to provide fan dealers with mailing lists containing more than a thousand names.

The number of fans in the fanzine sense showed a gradual gain as the decade progressed. One poll in the late thirties asked for estimates on how many fans existed. The answers averaged 216. At various times during the forties, the number of fans in this category might have varied between 300 and 500, at a rough guess. Then there were the prozine letterhacks, not very numerous, but sufficiently prominent and often enough migrating to general fan status to be worth consideration. If a fan is defined in the most liberal sense, perhaps as the person who does something more about his interest in science fiction than the simple process of reading stories of this type, there must have been at least a couple of thousand individuals deserving the fannish label at any given time during the forties. If the term is restricted to the sense of the active fan, the fan who is aware of his environment and occasionally makes himself felt in it in some way more strenuous than sending checks to dealers, perhaps 500 would be the average figure for the decade.

In any event, most polls of fandom in that decade took more interest in determining the fan's literary and artistic preferences than in delving into his personal characteristics. An occasional pollster meddled with the facts of fandom, however. In the middle forties, Art Sehnert got replies from 65 fans to a questionnaire that revealed two-fifths of the group to possess German ancestry, and most of the remainder to claim English descent. One-third of these fans claimed that their jobs were highly technical, more than one-fourth of the group described their work as skilled, and only one-eighth admitted to manual labor for a livelihood. Around the same time, Art Widner took a poll of 40 fans that produced such mysterious bits of information as the fact that the average fannish hat size was 7¼, larger than the national norm, that little type A blood ran through the veins of fans, and that the average age of the grandparents of fans was ten years over the national expectations. Bob Tucker dredged up some information on the familial habits of fans in 1944, when 74 replied to a quiz. He found that only 20 of the group were married, that there were nine divorces or separations in the experience of the fans replying to his questionnaire, that there were only 36 children deriving from these fans, that 23 of the group had not reached their 20th birthday, and that 55 of them were under the age of 30. Somewhat dubious in its application to active fans is the survey that John W. Campbell made at the end of the decade about the readership of *Astounding*. If we assume that the reader who replied was more likely to have fannish tendencies than the reader who remained silent, we might like to know that the average income of the 3,000 who answered was almost $450 monthly, quite high for 1949, that two-fifths of them were technicians, engineers, or professional men, and that the college students most frequently followed engineering courses.

The average age of fans probably advanced with the progress of the decade, because many fans remained active right through it, to counterbalance the rejuvenation created by the gafiation of older fans and the appearance of neofans. Jack Speer had found an average age of only 20, when he took a poll in the late thirties, and a median of 18.

2. Feminine Fans

Women were gradually emerging as genuine fans as the forties went along. Around 1940, it was possible to claim that there was no such thing as an independent, honest-to-goodness girl-type fan, because virtually all the females in fandom had a fannish boy friend, brother, husband, or some other masculine link. But by 1948, a Tucker survey showed that eleven per cent of all fandom now was feminine. There is some reason to assign to Barbara Bovard the pioneering role as an independent female fan. After she began to contribute to fanzines, Ackerman dragged her into Los Angeles fandom by brute strength, and she was quite active in most fannish phases until she got wartime work in Washington, D.C., and subsided. She flourished around 1941, a couple of years after Virginia Kidd had become a slightly less prominent lone girl-fan, mainly by letterhacking and corresponding from her home near Baltimore. She bobbed up years later as Mrs. Jack B. Emden in VAPA, and later married James Blish.

In age, fans ranged from nine-year-old Mary Helen Washington, who was more active than some more-celebrated feminine fans, through her contribution of "The Monster of the Cave" to her brother Raym's fanzine in 1942, up to the legendary W. S. Houston, already in his late sixties and early seventies during that decade. Fandom had become large enough and old enough to stratify to some extent. Jimmy Kepner thought he could trace in it an analogy to the nation's social structure. He described an upper upper class composed of the old aristocracy of fans who had been prominent for years, a class impenetrable without a long record of achievement; a lower upper class, containing most of the outstanding fans, an area that could be entered with fair ease and one whose members would not admit subordination to the upper uppers; upper middle class fans, who never finished in the top ten in popularity polls but were familiar to everyone and frequently wrote or did something notable; the lower middle class, comprising neofans, prozine letterhacks, and older fans who had never fulfilled early promise; the upper lower class, consisting of today's fringefans category, a sprinkling of juveniles, and the few thoroughly disliked fans; and the lower lower class, containing those fans with personality problems or possessed of subnormal mentality.

Except for the few women, fandom was composed almost entirely of English-speaking, white males. With the exceptions to be noted later, fans with other native tongues had made themselves evident only rarely. A Negro had been one of the earliest fans in the New York area, another had occasionally attended the LASFS meetings, and there had been some bitter controversy when a few U.S. fans demonstrated anti-Negro prejudices despite the apparent lack of fans to hate for the color of their skin. However, it is quite possible that one fan proved to himself through fandom that he could receive equal treatment even from the prejudiced, as long as he wasn't visible to them. A Portland, Maine, fan named Russell Harold Woodman published four issues of a good fanzine named *Triton*, contributed well-liked manuscripts to other fanzines, and along with Ed Cox threatened to revive Maine fandom at the end of the forties. Then he gafiated suddenly and completely and wrote to me on May 24, 1949: "Perhaps a storm wave would sweep certain frontiers of the fan world if I had stayed in publishing long enough to reveal that I am a Negro. That fact would have surprised a lot of people, I think."

3. Sources of Fans

Where did all the new fans come from? Mainly, from sources that have dried up during later years. First and foremost, from letter columns in the prozines. These provided an inexhaustible stream of addresses of potential new fans for fanzine publishers who wanted to send out sample copies, for the lonely fan who feared that nobody else in his city read science fiction and welcomed an opportunity to visit a fellow admirer who wrote to "Brass Tacks" or "Discussions." The letter columns provided to many potential fans the first giddy exhilaration from seeing one's words in print, a delight that often was repeated in the modified form of fanzine contributions or publishing. Tremaine made an early attempt to turn a letter column into more dignified science chatter, when he substituted "Science Discussions" for "Brass Tacks" in the February, 1937, *Astounding*. But after less than a year, he recanted, and soon other prozines were turning their letter columns into less formal departments than the Gernsback and Sloane magazines had ever permitted. Standard Magazines went a bit far even for fans, when "Sergeant Saturn" began to treat letterhacks realistically, like a batch of kindergarten students. But in general, the letter columns were a unique breeding ground for the fanzine type of fans. Only at the very end of the decade were the first ominous signs evident of what was to follow in the fifties: *The Magazine of Fantasy and Science Fiction* was started in 1949 without a letter section, probably in imitation of *Ellery Queen's Mystery Magazine* after which it was patterned. *Galaxy Science Fiction* was launched in the same letterless manner in the next year, and evil days soon followed for the letterhacks.

Another source of fresh blood was represented by clubs sponsored by prozines. *Wonder Stories'* Science Fiction League had begun in 1934; no later prozine club approached its elaborate structure, but even the sketchiest imitation group sponsored by a prozine had the ability to encourage formation of local clubs. Even though most of these clubs met instantaneous death, one or two members frequently survived in a less local sense in fandom. The Science Fictioneers, sponsored by Fred Pohl's *Super Science*, probably represented the most ambitious of the later prozine groups, appearing so likely to represent a major force that some existing local groups wrestled mightily with the question of whether to give allegiance to it or to the SFL. Wollheim's *Cosmic Stories* sponsored the Cosmian League with fewer pretensions: its activities seem to have been pretty well limited to sending a Dollens-designed membership card to anyone who asked for it, and Wollheim himself admitted there was no need for another group of the Science Fictioneers' high purposes. *Captain Future* sponsored a club with only two rules, but they were tough ones: read the magazine and persuade others to read it. Ed Hamilton, who wrote the novels in this publication, was once threatened with excommunication from this club for failure to get his manuscripts in to the editor promptly enough. Great hopes for such things as black masses and continental table-tipping were held when *Weird Tales* Club was announced in 1940, but it did nothing in particular for its members except to publish lists of their names. In any event, partly through the existence of the prozine encouragement, fandom could count anywhere from 30 to 50 local groups in existence at the end of the forties, depending on how you defined the point at which a club had collapsed completely.

4. Rocket Societies and Other Subfandoms

Almost wholly lost by the forties was the old breeding ground of new fans, science enthusiasts who read science fiction as an offshoot of their interest in experiments. We hear little about fannish efforts to build rockets during the new decade. On the other hand, the forties had not begun to produce the large regional conferences that became in the fifties the source of large quantities of sociable fans. Most regional events in the earlier decade were small, and received publicity only in fanzines. A surprisingly large number of good fans had reached the field during the forties by the accident of attending the same high school as an already active fan. And finally, the prozines became more generous than ever before during the forties with departments catering to fans, aside from the letter sections, making casual readers aware that the hobbyists existed. Hornig, for instance, published fanzine-type articles in *Future Fiction*. *Startling Stories* was the first to publish fanzine reviews regularly, as contrasted with the occasional brief plugs that other prozines had permitted in letter sections. *Amazing Stories* attempted to distract fans from the quality of its fiction through its "Club House" department, consecrated to all phases of fandom. Sometimes

Amazing produced a spectacular, like the contest that Rog Phillips conducted in 1948 to locate the best fan writing of the year, with a top prize of $25 that went to Marion Bradley.

By the end of the forties, then, there was no reason why any reader of magazine science fiction should be unaware of the existence and nature of fandom. So it was finally obvious to everyone that the old dream of fandom expanding to include all readers of science fiction had some built-in inability to become reality. Even today, nobody is sure why a fraction of one per cent of all science fiction readers become fans. But it seems proven, after all these years, that fandom will never grow into a hobby containing tens of thousands, and that the peculiar few will become fans whatever difficulties may be posed by lack of prozine publicity.

Meager attendance at worldcons during the forties should not be taken as proof that fandom wasn't growing, incidentally. It is true that no worldcon topped by very much the estimated 200 who went to the first Nycon, until the monster events began in the fifties. But there were special circumstances affecting most of the cons. The depression was hardly broken up in time for the Chicon and Denvention. The Pacificon suffered from lack of publicity outside of fanzines. The Torcon was far out of the way, New York's numerous fandom was partially angry at the Philcon, and the Cinvention was also quite a distance from large congregations of fans.

Fandom has never been one homogeneous organization. Even at its start, there were those who preferred to collect and those who preferred to publish: the fans who wanted to talk a lot about science and those who preferred the literary outlook on the hobby. But the tendency to create subdivisions partly within, partly outside fandom became noticeable as the forties proceeded. The science element in fandom was no longer a major factor, although there was a certain amount of continuing interest in amateur rocketry. The only reported casualty among the science fans in this decade was Bill Dubrucq, a Memphis lad who lost his eyesight temporarily in an effort to concoct a stable rocket fuel in a chemical laboratory used by the Lunarites, the local science fiction club. History is silent on the question of whether the lab recovered as fully as the eyes. The rocket group that made the biggest splash in America's fandom during this decade was the non-fannish United States Rocket Society. It worked out a deal with me at the start of 1942 that provided it with a page in my fanzine *Spaceways* for publication of its news. In return, I got an imposing number of new customers: everyone on its membership roster. R. L. Farnsworth, Chicago, was the president. By 1946 it had its own lithographed 16-page publication called *Rockets*, but the science had become adulterated with mysticism and Forteanism. Toward the end of the decade, the American Rocketry Association had headquarters in Washington with a science fiction fan division. It numbered among its members such pros as Murray Leinster, George O. Smith, A. E. van Vogt, and Richard Shaver. The British Interplanetary Society belongs in the narrative of British fans.

Also described elsewhere are such subfandoms as those devoted to dime novels, Shaverism and Lovecraft. Collecting fandom also has its own chapter. Burroughs fandom was a phenomenon that became a nuisance in the sixties, but its roots can be traced back to the end of the forties. Vernell Coriell and Darrell C. Richardson were the Burroughs fans who were most vocal in general fandom in those years. Coriell was already publishing the *Burroughs Bulletin*. He lugged around much of his collection in the trailer in which his father, three siblings and he traveled around from circus to circus where they would be performing. Vernell walked up a 30-degree sloping wire, and he also juggled. Richardson was hot on the trail of collectors' items like yoyos with Tarzan pictures on the side, and the 50 picture cards, distributed in 1933 with candy, that contained the story of "Tarzan and the Crystal Vaults of Isis." One of the 20-cent Whitman Big-Big books with a Burroughs adventure published in the late thirties had already sold for $10 before the forties ended, and a first McClurg edition of *Tarzan of the Apes* brought $70.

The works of Charles Fort formed the bible of a small, dogged subfandom. The Fortean Society had been founded in 1931 by moderately well-known non-fannish literary people. Eric Frank Russell was the first science fiction personality who got involved in the fandom based on the skeptic's books. He became its British representative in the thirties. The Fortean Society publication, *Doubt*, reached some fannish homes. Fans who were identified to some extent with the movement in the forties included some reasonably mature souls like Everett F. Bleiler, Erle Korshak, Fred Shroyer, and Vol Molesworth.

5. The Intelligence of Fans

When fanzine essayists struggled with the implications of fannishness, intelligence was a factor frequently claimed as distinguishing fans. Testing to prove the theory was not done systematically. The results could easily be affected by the inclination of the tester to try his luck with fans whom he believed to be particularly bright. The first big splash over the matter of extra mental capacity for fans came when Speer administered to a dozen or more the mental alertness test used at George Washington University. It was this test that produced a remarkable score of 194 for Al Ashley, later mistakenly claimed by Ashley or his enemies as his IQ. Three who took this test made scores in the tenth decile, five were in the ninth decile, and only one was as low as the sixth decile. Speer concluded that almost all fans belong in the upper fourth of the population with respect to brains, that the average fan is in the top tenth of the national population, but there is no basis for claiming that most fans are geniuses. A real IQ test was given by Bob Pavlat to Washington fandom as the decade closed. This Otis self-administering test of mental ability produced scores ranging from 127 to 140 for the seven who took it. A gigantic Tucker survey that did not demand notarized proof showed that seventy per cent of those responding believed themselves smarter than the average man. An occasional fan claimed an extreme IQ; J. Chapman Miske said that his was near 150, Lester del Rey admitted to an IQ of 200.

But there is little doubt that many fans were precocious. Some of them began selling to the prozines at a tender age. Bob Bloch amazed some fans by beginning to hit *Weird Tales* when he was 17. But earlier, Kenneth Sterling had sold a humorous story to *Wonder Stories* when he was 13 years old—the quality of the story proves this fact—and Charles Cloukey had made his first sale to *Amazing* when only 15. The Edison Scholarship Contest had shown Cloukey to be the seventh highest participant from the entire nation's high schools.

A. G. W. Cameron, an obscure subscriber to fanzines during the forties, never became an active fan, but as the next best thing he became second in command at the Institute for Space Studies two decades later.

Various other efforts were made to link fannishness with physical or psychical genius. Philadelphia fans at one time devoted most of their meetings to showing off their muscles. Hyman Tiger could bend double a silver dollar, using only one hand. Elmer Perdue could crumple a tomato juice can one-handed. Some theorists began to speculate about a relationship between fandom and muscle development, then stopped when they saw various other fans. The virtue most frequently ascribed to supermen in fiction, telepathy, was also sought in fans with varying results. If Al Lopez wrote truthfully in an issue of *Necromancer*, he was the most skilled telepath in fandom, for he claimed that a fellow experimenter could produce exact sketches of objects which he pictured mentally.

Even then, scholastic ability was not rated a true test of fannish brains, because of the probability that fans truly interested in such matters as literature and science would work hard in college and might produce better results than more intelligent non-fan students who were there only for prestige purposes. But in the middle forties, when the majority of high school graduates did not go on to college, a remarkably large proportion of fans were quite well educated. In 1946, R. D. Swisher, Langley Searles, and Thomas Gardner possessed their doctorates, advanced degrees were imminent for Bill Evans and Milt Rothman, while many other fans like Russell Chauvenet, Art Widner, and Chandler Davis were doing specialized advanced work in scientific fields.

In the end, common sense generally triumphed over the temptation to find superiorities in fans. Francis T. Laney summed it up: "If we fans had the necessary ability to be New Order leaders, we would be demonstrating that superiority in actual research and inventions, rather than spending our time reading escape fiction, publishing fanzines, and writing whacky letters. There are mighty few fans with the real ability to be any more than mere ciphers in our civilization. If fandom could take over and lead the way to the New Age, just what sort of an asinine, screwball world would it give us?"

One curious aspect of fandom in this period that added to the suggestion of unreality always hovering around the field was the apparent immortality of its population. That fans could die violently was proven by suicides and by World War II casualties. But death from natural causes appeared only at the rarest intervals in this group of individuals who were mainly young and sensible enough to take proper care of their bodies. Two important fans who died in fandom's dawn did so at their own hands, inspiring the first batch of the innumerable jeremiads that have shouted down through the years how much harm fandom can do to an individual. Fortunately, fan suicides became quite rare as the field expanded and matured. David R. Daniels took his life on April 17, 1936, at his Ignacio, Colorado home, soon after *Astounding Stories* had called his short story "The Far Way" one of the three best it had published in 1935. Two years later, J. Francis Hatch followed suit. He had been first-prize winner in the *Fantasy Magazine* cover contest for September, 1934, and had also sold professionally. Even the war seemed to spare fans to some extent. One count shows only five American fans died in the conflict: the number varies in respect to the definition of fan, but it is lower than the number of young fans in the service would normally produce.

6. Paul Robinson Freehafer

However, one of the best-balanced, best-liked fans did die during this decade. He was Paul Robinson Freehafer, who was aware that a rheumatic heart doomed him, but did not let this knowledge affect his ability to publish *Polaris*, one of the most literate fanzines of the era, or his determination to stay on good terms with all factions in Los Angeles. John Cunningham wished, on learning of the death, that he could have seen Paul one last time, to thank him "for being such a liberal, intelligent man." Paul's home was in Payette, Idaho, but he moved to California to attend the California Institute of Technology, and

Paul R. Freehafer

spent most of his time there until he went home to die just after the mid-March, 1944, housewarming of Fran Shack. He was only 27. Much less celebrated in fandom but equally liked by the few who knew him was Steve Weber, who died on February 21, 1949. He co-edited *Astra's Tower* for a time when Marion Zimmer was a neofan, and he had provided to *Famous Fantastic Mysteries* copies of several scarce books needed for reprinting purposes.

7. Slan Shack

Even those who held no brief for the case for fan as superman occasionally speculated about the possibilities of a separate fannish civilization. "Slan Shack," where a batch of active Battle Creek, Michigan, fans lived for nearly two years, was the most famous example of a fannish island in the sea of mundania during the forties. It is true that Futurians in New York City had lived in clumps in an interminable series of apartments with fancy fantastic names. But those New York ventures were motivated principally by the fact that the Futurians were trying to earn their livelihoods in free lancing and found that starvation advanced a little slower when they shared expenses. Slan Shack was inspired by more philosophic considerations about fandom as a way of lives. Theoretically, Slan Shack was not a goal in itself but a modest beginning on a more imposing project. The fact that fans took this major project seriously enough to speculate on it in print is the best proof of the decade's atmosphere of fans and fandom as something apart. Slan Center was conceived by Battle Creek fans early in 1943, when civilians suddenly were earning salaries of previously unimagined proportions, the advertisements told how wonderful everything would be after the war, and all fans in Battle Creek liked each other. Slan Center was to consist of an entire city block on the outskirts of Battle Creek, available for something less than $5,000. A corporation of fans would purchase it, would obtain jobs in Battle Creek, then would purchase on the cooperative plan homes that would be built in this block. Slan Center was to contain a cooperative grocery store, a general store, a common heating plant, and as final proof of the disdain for mundane facilities, its own electrical generating plant. Al Ashley calculated that ten to twenty fans with $300 to $500 each could get the thing started. He urged interested fans to save during the war years, then to invest in the project as soon as building materials became available with the return of peace. Francis T. Laney, who had energetically derided much less imposing fan projects, was so enthusiastic that he calculated the probable living expenses to the last penny, and announced that a couple could enjoy such a semi-cooperative housing project for $152.75 monthly.

Slan Shack scene—sitting, left to right: Thelma Morgan, E. E. Evans, Else Janda, Ken Krueger, Frank Robinson; standing, l. to r.: Al Ashley, Abby Lu Ashley, Delvin Coger, Jack Wiedenbeck, Mari Beth Wheeler.

Meanwhile, Slan Shack came into reality at the end of October, 1943, when the Ashleys bought the eight-room house at 25 Poplar Street. The fannish occupants promptly named the rooms. E. E. Evans' ground-floor room was the Temple of the Old Foo. The Ashleys' bedroom was Playground. Upstairs was Walt Liebscher's room, Chanticleering, distinctive because it was necessary to move one wall to enter. Jack Wiedenbeck's Artesian Well even included two named closets: Stuff and Abattoir. Communal rooms were Gorge Room, the dining area; Nitrosyncretic Lab, the kitchen; Control Room, the bathroom; and Shottle Bop, the giant attic that was used as a studio and collection room. The front door bore a simple inscription: Civilization.

Slan Shack instantly became a mecca for every fan who could surmount wartime travel problems to make a pilgrimage. Upward of twenty ate there at some meals. It was the scene of Michicons, NFFF crises, publishing sessions for some of the finest fanzines of the era, interminable poker sessions, and political shenanigans. FAPA mailings emerged from Slan Shack. So did the Wiedenbeck airbrushing whose color technique has never been surpassed in fandom. Ashley and Evans had known each other as long ago as 1926, when both belonged to the Battle Creek Scribblers Club, a literary group. Now they began to clash. If the dissensions didn't originate from fannish matters, they became manifest in many fannish ways: Ashley disliked Evans' tactics in the NFFF, Evans thought that he wasn't getting enough egoboo from angeling Ashley's *Nova*, and Evans became the first to leave Slan Shack, in mid-1945. The great experiment ended on September 7, 1945, when the rest of the occupants piled into a 1942 Plymouth with exceptionally delicate tires and spent two weeks driving to Los Angeles. They met a sobering collection of fates: Evans became a filthy pro, Abby Lu Ashley turned into a chiropractor, Wiedenbeck hid deliberately and completely, Liebscher took a job with a railroad, and Al Ashley became a straight man for Burbee and Laney.

8. Fandom Qua Fandom

Slan Shack exemplified the tendency for fans to find one another's company pleasant at times when science fiction and fantasy were not the topic of conversation. Much milder manifestations of this tendency provoked numerous diatribes from persons who felt that some fundamental principle was being outraged if a fanzine published an article that dealt with a mundane topic. American Legion post homes are not exclusively devoted to conversations about the latest wars of the nation. A high school newspaper rarely mentions the studies for whose sake the school exists. Churches have been known to sponsor activities that have no direct connection with a higher power. But primordial instinct has caused occasional people in and out of fandom to feel a duty to stamp out heresy, when a fan acts as if science fiction is not the only thing in the world worthy of thought and comment. The criticism during the forties took either of two starting points: a club meeting did not restrict its programs to speeches about the importance of Raymond Z. Gallun in the world of letters, and a fanzine did not censor someone's mention of jazz; or much more critical, a fan admitted that he was getting sick and tired of reading science fiction stories. This conflict between fundamentalists and liberals seems to afflict almost any type of word-oriented activity. The first example that I have been able to trace is a great controversy that sprang up in the early stages of the nineteenth century, when Sir Walter Scott complained that Francis Jeffrey was editing the *Edinburgh Review* in such manner that Whig partisanship had become evident in its reviews of books. One expert on periodicals of the period tells us that by the 1850's, the *Review* had undergone the same change that some persons would deny to fanzines a century later: "Literature came more and more to take second place to politics and affairs."

Curiously, those who have complained about the dilution of science fiction in fanzines always get alarmed because they believe that this phenomenon has just begun. Those who lament for the good old days when fanzines were devoted to science fiction could find in the January, 1934, *Fantasy Magazine* that already the battle was launched. Julius Schwartz and Milton Kaletsky were answering critics who wanted to know what the articles about hoaxes that they were publishing had to do with science fiction. The editors justified them "in view of the fact that all these hoaxes were fakes, frauds, fic-

Fantasy Magazine, September 1934

tions, and based on scientific or pseudo-scientific principles. These hoaxes do not conflict with the spirit and purpose of *Fantasy Magazine*." Then as now, the science fiction magazines escaped this sort of criticism, even though the prozines frequently transgressed the fundamentalist ideals. When Schwartz and Kaletsky were thinking up excuses for their series, *Amazing Stories* was preparing to serialize Verne's completely mundane "Measuring a Meridian." By the start of the forties, sensible fans were no longer inventing reasons but were making straightforward challenges to critics. Bob Tucker in 1941 summed up the new attitude: "The time is coming when fans and fanzines will no longer revolve about the professional magazines. We shall revolve strictly about ourselves; an unorganized society that has cast aside the core it began on, and moulded a much better substitute. We are outgrowing professional magazines." At the same time, on the other side of the Atlantic, Doug Webster demolished the opposition in a more systematic way: "Science fiction is important because it draws fans together. It's not science fiction which starts fans pondering on any abstruse problem they come on. It is science fiction which makes possible and stimulates discussion on these problems. And once science fiction has done this, its task in very many cases is done. Fans can be quite independent of science fiction, once they're in touch with each other. I hold that many a fan magazine is worth more from a literary point of view than are most of the pros."

There were temporary efforts to hold the line. Francis T. Laney expressed disillusionment in 1944 when he accompanied Frank Robinson on an exhausting expedition to collect old books and magazines, only to learn that Robinson disdained reading any of his finds. "Upon making inquiry among local collectors," Laney revealed, "I was amazed to find that few of them read the stuff. I should think that it would necessitate quite an elaborate bit of mental gymnastics to term a mere accumulator a fan."

But already quite celebrated fanzines were deliberately almost free of contamination from science fiction and fantasy material. *VOM*, the Ackerman-Morojo successor to *Imagination!*, was perhaps the best of the generally circulated fanzines of this type. Jack Speer had produced for limited circulation in FAPA *Sustaining Program*, an important proof of how far fanzine material could range without collapse of the heavens on the editor's mimeograph and stapler. Time after time, we find mute evidence of the trend in the determination of new publications to hold the fundamentalist line. *The Fanscient*, for instance, once insisted: "The contents will deal principally with stories, authors and publications, rather than with fandom."

9. Science Fiction Becomes Respectable

The conflict may seem more significant if we recall the fact that science fiction was becoming respectable enough in the forties to be fought for in such ways. The use of rocket-powered weapons in World War II and the culminating atomic bombing of Japanese cities were the first major evidence in decades to show the general public that those crazy Buck Rogers stories might come true after all. Science had made ample progress during the twenties and thirties, but its manifestations had not become so suddenly apparent as in the previous years when the airplane, automobile, general use of electricity, X-rays, and a dozen other wonders had impinged on every life. The prozines grew up in a land where there was a temptation to feel that the age of new marvels had ended.

Just as important, from the standpoint of prestige for science fiction, was the fact that it finally became accepted by hardcover publishers during this decade. The prozines, for all the fine things they possessed inside, were indistinguishable in outward appearance from the hackiest sport and western story magazines that swarmed over the newsstands. Anthologies in the United States customarily ignored science fiction before Phil Stong rather grudgingly edited *The Other Worlds* in 1941. Wollheim, obviously fonder of science fiction, soon produced the first paperback anthology, *The Pocket Book of Science Fiction*. But the decisive event was the first Groff Conklin anthology in 1946. Almost at once, the appearance of new science fiction novels in book form became more frequent, anthologies popped up from even major publishing houses, and an almost forgotten development of great importance occurred: science fiction of recent vintage found its way for the first time to school libraries. Kids who didn't have a quarter for a magazine, or lacked a place to hide the cover of a magazine if they acquired it, could now indulge in science fiction more modern in theme than Verne and Wells. Yet another important, frequently forgotten factor was the four-year life of *Unknown*. This was the first time in history that a periodical had specialized in pure fantasy and in weird fiction that did not use fear and fright as the principal gimmick. This sane, lighthearted attitude to fantasy must have helped to make some readers more tolerant of the gothic type of weird fiction, now that they could change off from it each month, and it must have brought into fandom some individuals who would never have taken great interest in the murky *Weird Tales* type of fiction.

During this decade, fandom first became known in the nation at large through publicity in non-specialized periodicals. *Time* had given fandom its first bad taste of publicity in 1939, when it called fans "jitterbugs of the pulp magazines" in an item on the first Nycon. But in the forties, this sort of publicity became somewhat more dignified. A *Writer's Digest* article alleged in 1947 that fans are "intelligent, literate, and have broad mental horizons." In the same year, *This Week*, the Sunday newspaper supplement, described fans as the "most scientifically hep reading public in magazine history." The *New Yorker*, in an item by Angelica Gibbs in 1943, termed science fiction readers in general "one of the most contented minorities in the country today." Central Press provided a widely syndicated article on the Cinvention in 1949. *Time* even acted to rectify in 1949 the damage it had imposed on fannish dignity a decade earlier, with a reference to fans as "a special cult which specializes in collecting the classics and faithfully supports the worthy publishing ventures." *Harper's Magazine* also gave fandom a good plug in 1946.

10. Science Catches Up With Science Fiction

Meanwhile, fandom was also reacting to the sudden proof of the advance of science. Fans had been charged by the Futurians with refusal to do anything about the world that lay ahead of them. When the United States began to atomize the Japanese people, fans showed little evidence that they had thought out what this science fiction theme would do when it became reality, or how to react to it. Judith Merril, then Judy Zissman, talked to some New York City fans on the night after Hiroshima. "They said they were ready to run to the hills. They talked about world extermination and atomic explosion, monster mutations, tyranny, ruin and destruction." Rick Sneary wrote down a list of things that he felt he might need for the first time: a hunting knife, army sewing kit, compass, and *Boy Scout Handbook*. He chose central Arizona as the preferable hideaway from the atomic holocaust that seemed to be the next prospect. Norm Stanley recalled that when his mother broke the news to him, "I confess my first reaction was one of elation, which even the obvious misgivings couldn't quench. 'Geez, we might blow up the whole planet,' I thought, 'but it's still wonderful.' " Forrest J Ackerman used his army editorship to write in his post publication: "Atomic power could be humanity's great boon. Or great boom." E. Everett Evans found fandom "in a blue funk. They are actually afraid to let themselves think seriously and deeply about the very thing of which they have been reading and talking for 20 years." Milt Rothman read the news in *Stars and Stripes*, while he was serving in Europe. "To a person who had been raised on stories such as 'The Final War,' this was both a terror and a hope. Man could use this to destroy everything. He could also be scared so badly at its possibilities that impending wars could be staved off long enough for a world organization to get going properly." Don A. Wollheim himself wrote: "Science fiction fans we may have been, but we ourselves for all our visionings were caught short. We knew it was coming—but the manner of its entry, the sudden change in world thought—that was shocking, almost sinister. What is there left to science fiction? Have not the basic ideas now all ceased to belong to the realm of imagination?" Elsewhere, he said: "Humanity has a way of surviving its doomsayers, its errors and its deadly turns, and showing up bigger and bigger. We have not the slightest doubt that atomic energy and rocketry will do more to better humanity in the long run than they can do to hurt mankind, which seems to be the immediate prospect."

True to the failing that Wollheim had scolded them for, most fans did nothing about the atomic threat. Not even Sneary headed for the wilderness. A few more fans took to science as a vocation after this, but they may have acted with increased financial rewards as their real incentive. Two exceptions lived in the no-man's-land between fandom and prodom. Chandler Davis was sufficiently frightened by a particularly idiotic proposed bill to become a one-man lobby against it in Washington. Jim Blish participated in a nationwide draft card-burning demonstration conducted by the Break With Conscription Committee, despite a severe handicap: he had lost his draft card before he decided to put it to the flames.

11. Fannish Culture and Slang

Jack Speer, a fannish pioneer in so many ways, was the first to emphasize the manifestations that demonstrated fandom's gradual acquisition of cultural traits during the late thirties and forties. One proof of the existence of a subculture is its consistent use of its own dialect or a plentiful supply of slang. Fandom's slang is used consistently enough to cause bafflement and resentment in many individuals who encounter a fanzine or attend a club meeting for the first time. Moreover, fandom's own special words are in some instances different from the colorful words that are distinctive to many other interest groups, in that they are neither exact synonyms for an existing, suitable word ("pad" for an individual's room, or "padre" for chaplain), nor terms created to describe an object or process peculiar to the field ("imperforate" for stamp collectors, "isorhythmic" for musicologists). Instead they are words devised by fans to cope with situations that are not unique to fandom but have failed to produce a really adequate word in mundania. Thus, "gafia" is a resounding fannish word that satisfies the soul when spoken with sufficient feeling and it has a meaning that is not quite defined by *dolce far niente* or escapism or resignation. Gafia is formed from the initials of "getting away from it all," is credited to Dick Wilson's inventiveness, and was in use at least as early as 1940 when there was a Loyal and Benevolent Order of Gafia. But the term has a curious history. It originally referred to the condition of a person who was doing fannish things in order to forget or avoid the unpleasant things in the warring world around him. Much later it was generally accepted as possessing the opposite connotation: the dropping of fannish activities and obligations. The mechanism by which the change occurred has not been systematically investigated, but it seems to have occurred around 1949. Art Rapp has been suspected as the triggerman, for having used it incorrectly in fannish circles where few remembered the original meaning. Fafia, forced away from it all, was a later variant on the second meaning of the root word.

Egoboo, a convenient term to express the concept of boosting one's ego through praise or even impartial mention in fannish circles, seems to have become popular around 1945. The next year, a Burbee invention swept fandom: crifanac, or critical fan activity, the process of fanning strenuously, praised by Ackerman as a term that "explains all, excuses all, enthuses all." Laney failed in an attempt to honor the top ten fans by calling their doings crucial and varying the term to crufanac.

Yet another useful term that ran wild through fandom around the same time was an accident. It was not intended to be a word, was never meant to be pronounced as written, but was merely a means of reproducing another word while respecting the amenities of print. But when Laney began to write "fugghead," some fans started to speak the word in situations where the parent word seemed a trifle too strong. Less sophisticated fans occasionally got into trouble when they used the word without realizing its origin, in the presence of mundanes who did not understand the subtlety of pronunciation. Technically, Laney tried to restrict the use of fugghead to refer to those whose fuggheadedness overshadowed their more useful and reasonable characteristics.

Less dangerous and even more sweet to the soul was "fout" as a fannish expletive. A younger brother of Phil Bronson apparently discovered the term in an inspired instant of utmost dissatisfaction, fortunately with attentive members of the Minneapolis Fantasy Society within earshot. Fout spread over fandom so rapidly and was so instantly comprehended that it has been suspected as a survivor of some former universal tongue that still lurks in the subconscious. Walt Willis, however, suspected that it came, through some unknown mechanism, from the vivid French verb whose infinitive is *fouter*. If so, it goes all the way back to the Latin *fosso*, which possesses exciting connotations regarding fertility rites. Originally, fout meant all-out disgust, and gradually subsided to exclamatory evidence of mild impatience or a sense of being provoked.

New words of fandom that are pretty much limited to the field itself are numerous. "Fanzine" and "prozine" were discovered after years of striving to find euphonious, fast terms for fan magazine and professional magazine. Ironically, the stone deaf Louis Russell Chauvenet devised those perfect words, around 1941, after many other fans had tried uselessly to popularize ugly words like "fanmag" or Freudian terms like "fmz." Tucker is responsible for the use of "space opera," which he proposed in the January, 1941, *Le Zombie* as a name for the "hacky, grinding, stinking, outworn spaceship yarn." Space opera eventually became a generic name for all stories about space and even many stories occurring on other planets, regardless of quality.

Various celebrities helped to invent and popularize more specific subdivisions for the generic term "fan." A sercon fan originally meant insultingly someone who took his hobby too seriously or engaged in it too ploddingly. It has since come to refer more usually to anyone who gives serious thought to the articles he writes or the opinions he expresses. It is made up from "serious" and "constructive." "Trufan" has slowly turned into a noun with much the same meaning as faan: the individual whose interest lies more in fans than in professional science fiction or its authors. Originally, it defined the fan who devoted every available minute and his total supply of energy to his hobby. "Faanish" originally was pronounced with a bleat indicated by the double vowel, because Tucker invented it to symbolize the sheeplike follow-the-leader habits of lots of fans. Now it usually sounds just like fan and means simply one whose hobby is fandom, not science fiction. Jack Wiedenbeck was the first "fakefan": one with no basic interest in fandom but with a pleasure in the company of fans. In recent years, it has been diluted often to refer to a person with a mild interest in fandom. "Bem" got into the dictionaries after Martin Alger coined it in the early forties to refer to the bug-eyed monsters on the covers of *Thrilling Wonder Stories* and similar publications. Almost forgotten is the fact that Alger ruled at the outset that a bem need not have bug-type eyes.

Other manifestations of fanspeak are less confined to newly created words. As if by instinct, fans have inserted from time immemorial the letter h as the second letter in many words that begin with a consonant. Donald A. Wollheim attributed it to the all-powerful influence of Ghughuism. It is equally possible that there is a rational explanation: Mencken's fondness for "bhoys," perhaps, or the frequency in fantasy fiction of words like ghost and ghoul. The use of the slash or hyphen as a strikeover to partially obscure words for

humorous effect (e.g., "I l̸o̸a̸t̸h̸e̸ love Joe Fann") is something that seems
pretty much confined to fandom. It is the fanzine equivalent of the humorous aside of stage convention, something that the writer pretends to have
decided that he shouldn't have said, but doesn't try to conceal thoroughly.
Les Perri used it as early as 1941, when she took the time to write a postal
card declining Art Widner's mock offer of marriage.

"Rosebud!" is an almost forgotten former rallying cry of fandom. There
is some reason to believe that it spread from fandom to become in some
parts of the nation a fairly well known euphemism for a more vivid verb.
It formed a clue to the character of the main subject in Orson Welles' movie
Citizen Kane, although it was only the name of a sled in that movie. Next,
a character muttered it just before violent death in a Lowndes fanzine story,
"Trigger Talk at Green Guna." It first became audible in real life at the
climax of a picnic in Bloomington, Illinois. In addition to its own word for
this particular physical accomplishment, fandom has its own special disease,
unknown to medical dictionaries. Twonk's disease is believed to be spread
by germs that live on mimeograph stencils. It is much worse than all other
diseases, in that it has no symptoms whatsoever, making it impossible to
know when an individual is suffering from it. Fortunately, it is never fatal.

Joe Fann as a fictional symbol was created by Tucker in *Le Zombie* in
1940. He personified the young goshwow enthusiast of fandom. Willis
turned him into Jophan in *The Enchanted Duplicator*, but this was in a time
beyond our immediate concern. The prozines occasionally found a justifi-
cation for their existence by providing a useful fannish term. Van Vogt's
Slan appeared at a time when fans were trying to decide if they are superior
to the average person. It proved irresistible because it sounds so much like
"fan" and denoted beings of superior intelligence and powers. "Fans are
slans!" became the rallying cry of the Cosmic Circle; later it turned into a
derisive taunt for anyone who wanted to disparage the quality of fannish
labors. Forgotten or ignored was the fact that Ray Cummings had written
about Slaans. They were Venusian slaves in "Tarrano, the Conqueror."
Yngvi, an unimportant character in de Camp's and Pratt's "The Roaring
Trumpet," touched off a years-long argument in fanzines over the accuracy
of the statement that "Yngvi is a louse." Another van Vogt story, "The
Weapon Makers," set fandom to talking a great deal about sevagrams, using
it pretty much as a nonsense word. Most fans liked its sound even if they
didn't realize that it came from the end of van Vogt's story about a race
that would "rule the sevagram," or that it was derived from an Indian word
for village that Gandhi had frequently used.

Dirty old pro, a term that denotes more affection than insult, seems to
have begun with a report at the Torcon that the professionals in the Hydra
Club sought the next convention for New York City because they needed a

market place to hawk their wares, followed by the Hydra importation of a professional model at the Cinvention, a promotion that angered even the placid Bloch for its crude publicity motivation. Ray Nelson cartoons in which pros always carried money bags helped to strengthen the fondness for the term. Cartoons also helped to solidify the beanie as a symbol of fandom, always possessed of a propellor at its apex. Ray Nelson purchased the first helicopter beanie in a dime store at Cadillac, Michigan, and George Young became the first to wear one at a convention when he attended the Torcon. *Spacewarp* and other Michigan fanzines immediately put helicopter beanies atop all the fans in cartoons, and Cincinnati merchants suffered mightily during the Cinvention next year, as delegates sought for fresh variants and extra-luxuriant models of the headwear for prestige purposes.

The fannish proclivity for inventing words got official recognition from the *Saturday Review of Literature*. Its April 7, 1945, issue told how fandom had coined such terms as Nycon, fen (as a plural for fan), gentlefen, faps, and dyktawo (probably false credit, for this initialese for "don't you know there's a war on" probably had mundane origin). But the tendency to create a special language, accepted as necessary in most fields, has caused some people to look with alarm on fandom. As early as 1942, someone wrote to H. C. Koenig complaining: "My impression is that the fantasy boys, by and large, are keen and clever commentators, and if I knew what they are talking about, I might even grant them a distinct shade over the average NAPA publications. It seems to me that they have one curious trait in common: an addiction to obscure lingo for its own sake." From within fandom itself, there was an occasional dire warning like this one from Donn Brazier a couple of years later: "One of the channels that leads men to shock an unsuspecting audience is some action or expressed thought which is abnormal or highly exaggerated. Oddly enough, after this initial shock the audience soon becomes distressed with the calculated eccentricity, now grown tiresome from constant repetition."

"Fan" as a word was frequently under attack as insufficiently distinctive or lacking in dignity. "Stefnist" was proposed as a substitute on several occasions, either as a new term for fan or to represent a former fan with little surviving interest in professional science fiction. James Kepner found little support when he tried to make all fans call themselves futurians. The word was too long, too closely associated with ill-tempered New York City fans, and capable of religious misinterpretation if abbreviated too far. "Fantast," another proposed new name for fans, was also too long and susceptible to reversion to the original word if abbreviated. "Tem," as a radical new synonym for fan, was suggested by Ashley. It derived from the temporal aspects of the time-binding ability that science fiction readers allegedly possessed. Widner liked "imaginist" and when it didn't find favor, Jay Chidsey tried to shorten and inflect it: "im" for a male fan and "ime" for a female fan. Despite subtle hints from dictionaries that fan probably derives from fanatic rather than fancier, fans remained fans.

Almost from their emergence, fans have taken occasional delight in organizing burlesque religions, possibly as an ancestral memory of the way scientific discoveries had been discrediting fundamentalist tenets of Christianity in recent decades. Sometimes genuine emotion occurred when theological controversy over these synthetic beliefs grew complicated. GhuGhu and FooFoo were the earliest of the fannish deities. It is difficult to separate fact from heresy about them, because of the merciless nature of the literary campaigns waged. But GhuGhu was either an incarnation of Wollheim or a beetlebodied monster on Vulcan. Michel was high priest of GhuGhu and the other Futurians held the other principal subordinate posts. The purple theme of the creed lost most of its significance when the hectograph lost favor in fandom and the ineradicable stain of purple as a basic tenet puzzled rather than awed the younger fans. The opposing sect, FooFooism, acknowledged a mundane creator in the person of the comic strip creator, Bill Holman. He used to put the word foo onto all improbable places in his panels for "Smokey Stover." Mary Corinne Gray, better known in fandom as Pogo, was credited with establishing this order at almost the same instant as a similar impulse overcame Speer. Speer, who thereupon became Pogo's left-hand man, claimed that FooFooism was a burlesque on GhuGhuism and on militarism, rather than on religion in general. But both beliefs fell into such sad neglect that they offered no opposition when newer powers sprang up toward the end of the forties. Ignatz was revealed and publicized by Nancy Share, first in SAPS, after she was overwhelmed by the discovery of the old Krazy Kat cartoons in which he was the long-suffering hero. The credo of Ignatzism said, basically, that he began as a squeak that resulted from the effort of thought, and from the thought images, fans were born. Krazy Kat herself was considered a latecoming pawn and tool of Ignatz, created solely as an example to fans of conformity and weakness. Believers learned that they who throw bricks at established things now and jump feet first into all fusses may be rewarded with the golden brick of Ignatz. Roscoism was less dependent on mundane revelations and was more specifically fannish in nature. Roscoe was Art Rapp's revelation, a gay young beaver who is invisible, protects fans wherever they may be, can be seen flying his spaceship across the sky on Independence Day, and must be toasted on his birthday, Labor Day, at the worldcons, which really exist only for this purpose. Roscoe is the supernatural cause of the occasional willingness of mimeograph styluses to remain on the table instead of rolling off. He has been known to cause an occasional dealer to sell an old prozine for only half the asking price.

Fandom failed to come up with a philosophy, genuine or fake, all its own, to accompany the religions. Time-binding was in the fannish eye for many months after Heinlein's Denvention speech, and was perhaps the closest approach to filling the lack. Time-binding was supposed to mean that science fiction enthusiasts have more than the usual ability and willingness to relate the past and future to the present in their thought and to consider the triple temporal chain in their actions. E. Everett Evans was the most eloquent and wordy of the admirers of the concept. But the idea seems to have had its own built-in deadend that caused it soon to wither and pine away into oblivion. Perhaps the trouble was that nobody ever proved that the assumption was true or showed what benefits would result if it were acted upon. General semantics attracted some attention, after van Vogt began writing it into stories, but it had no more lasting effects than the technocracy and Esperanto spasms that shook the field briefly in the thirties. *Unknown* was tremendously popular in fandom, but few fans gave much indication that they had begun to take seriously the Fortean philosophy that some of its stories echoed.

Ethics did not trouble fans too greatly during the forties, partly because they got together rarely enough to make it unnecessary to create unwritten agreements on how fannish behavior should differ from that of mundane people. Almost from the start of fanzines, however, there had been signs that different mores were inevitable. Nobody is known to have done more than complain bitterly when a fanzine publisher failed to refund the unfulfilled portion of a subscription when his publication folded without warning. The reluctance to take fannish disputes to law became evident as fandom grew, despite certain obvious exceptions: the lawsuit that smashed to fragments the former Futurian crowd in New York City, and the astonishing retraction made by Francis T. Laney, when A. Langley Searles threatened a lawsuit. A gradually evolving tradition of open house and all-out hospitality when a rare fan ventured out into the great world and visited other fans required hasty revision with the coming of Claude Degler. The high degree of courtesy and reticence that had prevailed in the earliest fanzines was lowered considerably when Laney began the realistic school of writing about other fans.

With respect to the arts, fans did not often create their own music for specific fannish purposes, but they were fond of fitting new lyrics with special connotations, usually unfavorable, to existing melodies. But there were isolated instances of a musical counterpart to the literary manifestations of fannish culture. Tigrina, a once-famous California fan, published around 1941 a "Hymn to Satan" that had been widely heralded but proved to sound like a beginner in the study of harmony attempting for the first time to imitate a Bach chorale, in a key that nobody could possibly sing. The first respectable publication of music in fandom was Jim Blish's setting of Korn-bluth's poem, "Cry in the Night," distributed in the May, 1945, VAPA mailing. It may not be great music, but it was a capable imitation of a fairly modern school of composition. Fandom's big chance to get its music before the mundane public took the form of Vanguard Records, a project that the present Vanguard recording firm has probably never heard about. Just after World War II, Blish and Robert W. Lowndes got outside funds for their attempt to found a firm producing 78-rpm discs. One fan composition, Chandler Davis' "Song of Worlds Unseen," performed by pianist Bertha Mel-nik, was among the works on Vanguard discs that actually got distributed. There were ambitious plans for a fat album of music by various fan com-posers. The company was in search of recording rights to works by non-fans like Stravinsky and Bartók when it collapsed after it lost an angel.

Many fans had some ability as artists. But they were so obsessed by the habit of imitating prozine art that individual styles were hard to find, fan-centered art was hardly thought of, and not even the artists thought enough of their abilities to organize fan art shows. Harry Jenkins, Jr., managed to produce two issues of a fanzine devoted to pictures and articles about them in 1941. The then unknown Virgil Partch did wonderful caricatures of Los Angeles area fans in various publications in that city during World War II. But few fan artists took these hints that fan art could be something in and of itself. Mostly they drew for the fanzines pictures in the style of those that they saw in the prozines, or tried to commercialize their artistic ability in some way. The semi-pro fannish art projects were usually tied to prodom in some way. Thus, Ronald Clyne discovered an almost forgotten artist with fantasy inclinations, Wallace Smith, and promoted the reprinting in 1944 of a $1.00 portfolio of drawings. The NFFF was behind the reprinting of a couple of Finlay portfolios. In 1949, ten fan artists drew a series of pictures, Dr. David H. Keller wrote a story to fit them, "The Final War," and the whole thing got published by Portland, Oregon, fans as a series of fantasy postcards.

One curious manifestation of fandom as a subculture was the attempt to popularize a fannish substitute for money, a new form of currency designed to fit the peculiar needs of fans more neatly than the stuff produced by the national mints. This was fan wampum, invented in 1948 by Stan Woolston when he designed a sheet of paper containing his name at the top and space for other signatures lower down. This was intended to pay fannish debts of a nature that standard money was not suitable for or not available for. Each piece of this fan wampum was intended to circulate almost indefinitely. Orville W. Mosher III revived it by charging three cents for each piece of fan wampum. The scheme may have been derived from the system of "obs" made famous by Eric Frank Russell in "And Then There Were None."

The only fannish game with survival value was Interplanetary. Art Widner created it and introduced it at the end of 1942 to the Stranger Club. He borrowed elements of Monopoly and Auto Race, well mixed with new gimmicks like planets that maintained suitable motion. Interplanetary's principal distinction was the enormous amount of time consumed in completing one game—at least eight to twelve hours. Much later Bill Evans, Bob Pavlat, and Ted White revised the original Widner rules, cutting out some preliminary procedures and making it possible to play a game in a normal evening. One former fan got a game into the commercial markets, but this was a mundane game: Mort Weisinger introduced Movie Millions in late 1938. Los Angeles fans experimented occasionally with fantasy elements grafted onto the standard rules of chess. These included such things as a piece that could move through time and another that exploded at some point in the game.

It will be more suitable to consider fannish foods and drinks in a later place, since the nuclear fizz was the only famous product of the forties. But this decade did produce the first fannish calendars. *Poor Pong's Almanac*, featuring events of humorous and fantasy import, was a popular feature of *Le Zombie*. The same publication seems to have also distributed the first genuine calendar for fans in 1942, when three wildly dancing Roy Hunt natives were lithographed above a set of prosaic calendar sheets.

Another fannish tradition that became firmly established during the forties was the hoax. Some of the most dramatic events of the decade never occurred, in accordance with a precedent that had been set repeatedly in the past. Perhaps the first fannish hoax took the form of a letter in the May, 1931, *Astounding* that offered for sale collectors' items. Those who bit learned eventually that the stories did not exist. Two years later, Hugo Gernsback unbent sufficiently to run in *Radio-Craft* a fake advertisement for a radio so small that it would fit into the palm of the hand. He called this a WestingMouse. Hundreds of credulous readers sent orders to Westinghouse, and the corporation got very angry with Hugo.

But these imaginative lies did not contain the suspense and mystery of the Earl Singleton case. He almost succeeded in hoaxing fans with a suicide that eventually became known as the pseuicide. In February, 1941, several fans received letters from one Oliver King Smith, who identified himself as a roommate of Singleton at Massachusetts Institute of Technology, and wrote: "He shot himself in the temple with a small calibre pistol. He evidently died instantly." Singleton was a popular, talented fan who had been giving away fat issues of a fanzine devoted to poetry, *Nepenthe*, holding a powerful role in New England fandom, and contributing literate articles and verse to fanzines in quantities. Fans promptly found forebodings of this February 9th suicide in the tone or content of various letters and fanzine items written in the weeks immediately preceding. However, Singleton absent-mindedly mailed on February 10th a letter to Jack Chapman Miske. Moreover, the chronology of what happened after the shooting seemed dubious: far distant parents seemed to have reached the scene and obtained release of the body from authorities with entirely too much speed. Louis Russell Chauvenet grew suspicious enough to egg Art Widner into contacting MIT authorities. This caused immediate and real trouble for Singleton, who was now in Washington, D.C. Widner and Chauvenet kept quiet for a while about the truth that they had discovered. Trudy Kuslan put on a tremendous emotional outburst over the handsome lad at a Boskone at a time when she probably knew the truth, confusing other suspicious fans. But by instinct or by rumor, Donald Wollheim and Forrest J Ackerman broke into the fannish prints almost simultaneously with their own doubts about the matter. Those in the know made everything public.

The real reason for Singleton's curious hoax was never agreed upon in fandom in general. It was variously attributed to a need to disappear because of secret wartime work, overwork, a desire to get rid of fannish ties with the least possible ceremony, a desire to make the manner of his going more spectacular than any previous gafiation, or an uncompleted plot that would have brought him back into fandom almost immediately under a penname. Perhaps the most believable explanation came five years later from Smith, who said that Singleton had found himself hopelessly swamped with the combination of all-out fanning and college studies, and decided to quit both completely. In any event, Singleton eventually completed his studies and now operates Amalco, an important electronics firm in Los Angeles. A curious sequel to the whole thing was the unanimity with which fandom

Odd Tales

assumed that Singleton had faked not only the immolation but also the roommate. Oliver King Smith turned into a legend, his mythical character was kept alive by occasional fanzine references, and when the real person turned up later in Los Angeles, the sensation was almost as great as the original hoax had been. Smith did not become a real fan but he occasionally took part in fan gatherings in the years that followed.

The atmosphere of the decade was favorable to hoaxes. Hardly a convention was complete without some kind of a fake telegram or synthetic message from extra-terrestrials. There were a couple of widely disseminated, fully false reports of the deaths of prominent fans. But these fake obituaries were hardly elaborate enough or carefully enough planned to qualify for the dignity of hoaxes. They were just plain lies. The Lovecraft fans convinced occasional trusting souls that various props in the HPL mythos really existed. Perhaps the nastiest hoax of the decade, for the false hopes that it raised, was *Odd Tales*. Julius Unger and I were the main culprits, early in 1942, when we attempted to make Singleton a piker with publication of a nonexistent prozine. We got permission from various celebrities in prodom to use their names as contributors of fiction for the first issue. An original painting by Hannes Bok served as the basis for an improvised cover that looked authentic enough when photographed and circulated in the form of small prints. *Odd Tales* was guaranteed to contain no hack stories, no clumsy illustrations, no fiction that anybody had ever read before. Despite generous clues to the true nature of *Odd Tales*—initials on the cover and on story titles spelled "fake," "lie," "hoax" and "false"—money began to arrive for subscriptions, authors not contacted offered their best manuscripts, and it seemed desirable to tell the truth immediately.

12. Fan Newsmagazines

These were years in which communications became increasingly significant for fandom. Correspondence and fanzines had once served as the overwhelmingly major means of keeping in touch. But by the end of the forties, personal contacts were becoming easier for most fans. Travel was growing easier, as increasing numbers of fans found themselves financially able to own automobiles. The old habit of dubbing as a conference any get-together of at least three fans ended, because of the commonness of such events. But even with this increased mobility, fandom was growing so rapidly in size and diversity of interests that conversations and occasional news columns in general fanzines were not enough to keep everyone informed on the important happenings in fandom. Fanzines devoted to news, frequently called newszines, flourished as never before. It is true that they were not new to this decade. They had begun in the late thirties. Some were tiny, like *Postal Preview* that Ted Carnell published on a postal card from London, once or twice monthly, starting in October, 1939. He produced some forty issues until the war killed it. Others were bigger and lasted much longer. James Taurasi began in the summer of 1938 to publish *Fantasy News*, partly because he wanted to provide something in return for money on hand for subscriptions to his defunct *Cosmic Tales*, partly because he didn't like the Futurian tendencies of *Science Fiction News Letter*, a Dick Wilson newszine that eventually gave up after 78 highly literate issues.

From the start, Taurasi emphasized news about prozines in his publication,

finding such success with this procedure that he got an affidavit from dealer
Unger two years later, to the effect that advertisements in *Fantasy News*
had the greatest response of any magazine in the field, fan or professional.
Fantasy News, which first appeared in June, 1938, was taken over by Will
Sykora when military induction threatened Taurasi. Sykora took the task
with the condition that he needn't accept subscriptions from Futurians. The
publication disappeared for about a
year during the darkest part of the
war, then resumed publication with
the 160th issue in May, 1943, after
Sykora had moved to the Baltimore
area. Meanwhile, Taurasi had begun
Science Fiction Times in September,
1941. He claims on somewhat dubious
grounds that it is the oldest surviving
fanzine, although its changes in editorship and title, suspended animation,
and the existence of my own *Horizons*
are somewhat strong evidence against
the distinction. The publication began
life as *Fantasy Times*, disclaiming any
intention to rely exclusively on news
for its content. It became the first
photo-offset fanzine. When Taurasi
went into the service, Moskowitz became the editor. He changed the title

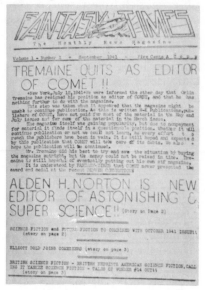

First issue of Fantasy Times

once to *Fantasy Reporter*, then dropped it altogether. Taurasi revived it
after the war, changed the title back to *Fantasy Times* and then to *Science
Fiction Times*, and in later years devoted it almost entirely to professional
aspects of science fiction. If the continuity of the publication is accepted, it
has the distinction of producing the greatest number of issues of any fanzine
in history, approaching its 400th issue as the sixties opened.

Fantasy Fiction Field was another of the long-lived newszines of this
decade. Julie Unger began it as a weekly four-pager, costing a nickel, on
October 26, 1940. It also was heavily slanted toward prozines, and regularly
published photographic reproductions of forthcoming covers. Unger had
the special attraction of Langley Searles' bibliographic projects, distributed
a couple of pages at a time with the newszine: listings of the contents of old
fantasy publications, book reviews in a standard format intended for eventual
collection into reference volumes, and a fantasy book index. After putting
out more than 200 issues by the end of World War II, Unger gafiated so
completely that he gave away his personal file of the publication, only to

revive it at the start of 1963 with the help of another reactivated fan, Harvey Inman. Unger died just after the first issue in the new series went out, but Inman struggled single-handedly with the project for a few more months before abandoning it. Sykora bobbed up again at this late date with an equally brief revival of *Fantasy News*.

Bob Tucker began a postal card publication, *Fanewscard*, on July 3, 1943, to dispense gossip and news. He put it out weekly for a couple of months and grew tired of it, Frank Robinson and Ed Connor tried to keep it going, and eventually Walt Dunkelberger assumed charge with the first anniversary issue. He wavered between full-page format and postal card size for an interminable period, experimented with daily issues for a week, then began to expand. It gave the most thorough coverage of fandom and prodom of any newszine in history, and claimed 339 issues when it suspended publication in January, 1948. This numbering is controversial, however, since Dunkelberger was in the habit of sending out simultaneously a thick sheaf of pages identified as a specific number of issues in apparently arbitrary manner.

There were many other attempts to chronicle the news. Jack Speer published *Stefnews* for a year, starting July 1, 1945. Its career was brief but it nearly destroyed the worldcon when it published prematurely information about Pacificon plans. After Richard Wilson dropped *Science Fiction News Letter*, Robert W. Lowndes tried to hold the Futurian cause before the public by issuing *Science Fiction Weekly* in 1940. Later in the forties, various projects lasted less than a year apiece: Joe Kennedy's *QX the Cardzine*, Walt Daugherty's *Shottle Bop*, Walt Liebscher's *Wee Tome Tipper*, a *Slanewscard* from Detroit fans, and *Nebula*, produced at various times by Rusty Barron, Larry Shaw, and Bob Madle. Numerous local club publications were mainly intended to spread through fandom the news about that particular city's fandom or the doings in a small region.

13. Fan Fiction

Fandom has created its own literature. Fiction about fans, as distinct from fiction written by fans in imitation of prozine stories (both were called fan fiction, indiscriminately) goes back at least to 1934. In that year, *Fantasy Magazine* published "The Ship From the Past," a story about a feud in a local fan club and a spaceship that proves in the end to be a hoax. But most fiction about fans in the earlier fanzines was tongue-in-cheek, either providing famous fans with adventures in fantastic situations, or telling about future events in fandom with the use of real fans or thinly disguised fictional counterparts of them. Thus, "Six Against the Past," a serial with several authors, in *Cosmic Tales*, told how Wollheim, Sykora, Wilson, Speer, Dan

McPhail, and Taurasi were thrown back into pre-Columbian North America, and how they managed to split up the rule of the continent among them; Arthur Clarke's "A Short History of Fantocracy," serialized in *Fantast* in 1942, put Ackerman, Clarke, Sam Youd, and other fans into a near future in which they begin to take over the whole world with the help of an itching ray. But here and there, fanzine writers realized that fans and fandom could be the topic of serious fiction. A pioneer effort was Sam Moskowitz' "The Road Back" in 1938, the story of how a fan attempted to return to fandom after gafiating. It doesn't sound like an original theme today, but at that time, a gafiated fan was generally agreed to be a goner. Redd Boggs' "The Craters of the Moon" in the July, 1948, *Dream Quest* was the most famous example of a serious science fiction story involving fans in a fanzine. It told of a fan's disillusionment with his hobby, upon completion of man's first successful flight to the moon.

The prozines occasionally published fiction about fans. *Wonder Stories* in 1934 had published "The Return of Tyme," a tiny story with characters named Jack D. Arrow and Forrest Jackerman. Westwood, New Jersey, fans were written into an otherwise orthodox science fiction story. This was Manly Wade Wellman's "Space Chore" in *Thrilling Wonder Stories* in 1940. The fans had given him the plot idea and he named characters after them. Then in 1943 fandom became a crucial element in a successful mystery novel: *Rocket to the Morgue*, published under William A. P. White's pseudonym of H. H. Holmes. As literature, it was no great shucks but it sold well. The story was a lengthy example of the type of fiction that Walt Liebscher called gay deceivers: apparent fantasy or science fiction in which everything gets a mundane explanation in the last pages. But the plot concerned professional science fiction writers and fandom. There were references to real fannish and professional events. Most of the characters had a greater or smaller degree of relationship to real individuals. Thus, Tubby Yerke served as the model for the corpse, William Runcible. The major suspect, Austin Carter, contained a great deal of Heinlein and a small seasoning of Kuttner. An original illustration by the character called Arthur Warrington was based on a real painting by fan Tom Wright. D. Vance Wimpole was a thinly disguised L. Ron Hubbard, Campbell was present under his own penname of Don Stuart, and Joe Henderson has been tentatively identified as Ed Hamilton. The book's version of a fan club, the Mañana Literary Society, actually came into existence later. It was the name of an informal group of professional writers in the California area who included White himself. White became better known in science fiction circles under another penname, Anthony Boucher.

Among professional writers, Bob Tucker was the most consistent borrower of fans for fictional use. Sometimes he brought them into his books as supers or gave them the briefest possible roles. On other occasions, he used their names in real or slightly distorted forms for the major characters. Sometimes but not always he borrowed real character traits as well as the names for the fiction. Tucker's first major success, a mystery called *The Chinese Doll*, contained such individuals as Joquel Kennedy, Donny Thompson, Doc Burbee, and August Ashley. Rothman and Liebscher became detectives in Peoria, and there was a woman-hating Sgt. Wiedenbeck. Published in 1946, the plot revolved around science fiction and fanzines, permitting the public at large to read about such creatures as faps and such publications as *Le Zombie* and *Rosebud*.

14. Previous Histories of Fandom

Fandom first became aware of its history when Speer wrote "Up to Now" at the end of the thirties, chronicling some of the events of the decade that was ending. This history set an unfortunate precedent of overemphasis on the fans who engaged in the most quarrels and the organizations that had the least effect on fans. Emphasis on politics and fannish flies conquering the flypaper caused Joe Gilbert to say that it was "as if someone had gathered up all of the hates, prejudices, and petty jealousies that have clogged the pipes of the stream of life since the world was first begun." Speer in a sense wrote a much better and longer history but disguised it as the *Fancyclopedia* of 1944. Divided under alphabetized headings like an encyclopedia, it nevertheless provided a much better-balanced compilation of fandom's past, and its bulk proved the extensiveness of fandom's culture and traditions, even at that early date.

The most celebrated history of fandom, Sam Moskowitz' *The Immortal Storm*, covers a year or two more time than "Up to Now" at ten times the length. The title has a curious origin: it began life

as the name for fiction about an imaginative future war between New Fandom and the Futurians that Moskowitz used to read in installments to the Newark Science Fiction League in 1940. The picayune squabbles between these two camps of teenagers continued to dominate, after Moskowitz shifted the title's field from the future to the past and from the imaginary to the actual as Moskowitz saw it. The history began to appear serially in *Fantasy Commentator* in 1945, and saw book form in the fifties after struggles over publication that lasted from 1951 to 1954. The work was generally praised for the obvious labor that went into it and the extreme documentation provided—we are even told the type of box in which some New York City fans carried fanzines to sell at a Philadelphia meeting. De Camp called it "an extraordinary and outstanding (if quite unintentional) study in small-group dynamics." Peter Maurer defined it as "a sad commentary on human nature" that "might have been funny had the style been less deathly serious." Someone or other referred to the style as "badly translated from the Slobbovian" despite Searles' touching-up of some of the most distinctive portions of Moskowitz' syntax and grammar. If read immediately after a history of World War II, it does not seem like an anticlimax.

The historians are partly responsible for the concept of numbered fandoms. Disputes over the exact identity and chronological location of First Fandom or Third Fandom or other fandoms reached the intensity of the denominational bickering of Christianity at times. Olaf Stapledon is probably to blame, for his division of the future of humanity into Second Men, Third Men, and so on. But it is not as easy to see the need for the divisions in fandom as in *Last and First Men*. Even the faithful adherents of numbered fandom divisions admit that it is almost impossible to recognize that a fandom is beginning or ending as the events occur. They claim that such dividing points become evident in later years, when a broader overview becomes possible, and that certain distinctive traits also become apparent in the various fandoms. In rebuttal, it might be claimed that the existences of different fandoms become evident only when the events are sufficiently forgotten to cause the memory to seize upon a few isolated happenings and imagine that these were typical of the entire fandom.

Speer is generally credited with listing the numbered fandoms, first in the *Fancyclopedia*. But five years earlier, Moskowitz had divided fandom into eras, somewhat differently from the Speer separation. Moskowitz thought that the first fannish era covered everything up to 1933, the second and third came rapidly in the next couple of years when the first large fan clubs declined and underwent an afterglow, the fourth era was assigned to 1936 and 1937 when fanzines spurted with *Fantasy Magazine* at their head, a fifth era involved the collapse of *Fantasy Magazine* and resulting effects, and the sixth era began with the emergence of many new fans around 1938. Speer didn't find quite as many eras. He set first fandom from 1933 to 1936, when fanzines grew and culminated in *Fantasy Magazine*; second fandom from October, 1937, to October, 1938, when politics and feuds were thriving; and third fandom from 1940 to near the end of 1944 when older fans began to gafiate in quantities. Between these fandoms, he identified transitions, and later he was forced to assign the name of "eofandom" to those active from 1930 to 1933, a time he'd overlooked in drawing up the original scheme. Later, Bob Silverberg detected as fourth fandom the immediate postwar years when hucksters and commercialism seemed to dominate. He thought that there was a brief fifth fandom in the last of the forties, specializing in insurgency to protest the excesses of fourth fandom. Sixth fandom in the Silverberg scheme of things belongs to the fifties. This sort of trend-detecting may have been useless but it was not harmful until somewhat later, when some new fans decided that they were the destined prophets and leaders of the uncreated seventh fandom. The results were apocalyptic in the extreme.

15. Bibliographic Work

Besides fiction and history, fandom produced a fair bulk of non-fiction that could have come from nowhere else during the forties. There were bibliographic items that will be described in detail when we come to Collecting Fandom. The *Fancyclopedia* (see Chapter Twelve) was not only the biggest of the fannish reference books, but also the first proof that a few fans who were determined could produce publications of a size previously thought impossibly expensive and difficult. An almost forgotten habit that prevailed during much of the decade consisted of the publication of yearbooks, highly useful for memory-stirring, nostalgia-wakening, or more scholarly research. Tucker had published an index to the year's prozine stories in the form of the *1938 Science, Weird and Fantasy Fiction Yearbook*. Its success justified a second edition, and Tucker turned out a new one the following year. Frank Brady and Ross Kuntz of Los Angeles took over the task of the 1940 yearbook. The 1941 volume was produced by Julius Unger, under the editorship of Larry Shaw, Bill Evans, and Fred Hurter. More elaborate and comprehensive yearbooks arose later in the decade. Kennedy put out a splendid one in 1945 that omitted the prozine story index but provided a chronology, lengthy summaries of professional and fan activities, and poll results. The *Fantasy Annual* of 1948 was edited by Boggs, published by Ackerman, ran to 120 pages, and was so superlative in every way that nobody has had the ambition to try to do the same thing on such a vast scale again, to this very day.

3. BIBLIOMANIA: The Insatiable Urge to Collect

1. Early Collectors

Collecting as the major activity of many fans is fundamental but sometimes forgotten by the fans who prefer fanzines or conventions. Some of the most important fans, evaluated on the basis of the time they put into their hobby, the money that they are willing to squander on it, and the lasting results they leave in general fandom, are individuals whose names are little celebrated. It is quite probable that a lot of important collecting fans are completely unknown in mainstream fandom. Occasionally, by accident or intent, one of these previously hidden fans comes suddenly to knowledge, possessed of an enormous collection of all sorts of science fiction and fantasy items, and equipped with an all-encompassing knowledge of the field. One abiding mystery of these retiring collecting fans is where they get the fanzines that they almost invariably own in endless quantities; they are never on subscription lists of fanzines and do not advertise in an effort to buy up the things in bulk.

Before worldcons produced expensive auctions, before fanzines appeared devoted largely to collectors' advertisements, before the prozines offered lots of free plugs to fans, we know that there were advanced collecting fans. In the thirties, for instance, Fred Fischer got more than fifty replies to a tiny item that he managed to slip into the correspondence corner of *Amazing Stories*, offering old magazines for sale. Occasionally we hear of one of these early collectors surviving to this very day, still engulfed in fannish oblivion. A good example is W. S. Houston, who had been subscribing to fanzines from their start, never writes a letter to anyone, and when finally visited by Lynn Hickman, was revealed to possess one of the finest collections in existence.

He was in his eighties as the 1960's began. Active fans were baffled when the unknown Crosley Conners of Burbank, California, offered for sale in 1947 the fruits of twenty years of secretive collecting, including lots of fanzines and many items predating the start of his collecting activities. There is the celebrated Dr. M. Doreal of Denver, head of something called the White Brotherhood, who was alleged to have 25,000 items in his library of fantasy and science fiction as long ago as 1947. Even more famous in a reverse way is M. J. Miller, Cleveland, whose book collection is so legendary that nobody knows anything about it, but who once paid $25 to Walt Coslet simply for the privilege of reading a copy of *Thrill Book*.

It was easier in the early days to be a collecting fan. There were second-hand book and magazine stores everywhere yet unravaged by other collectors and wartime pulp paper drives. Moreover, the sheer quantity of items to collect had not reached outrageous proportions. Until World War II, most years produced fewer than fifty issues of the prozines, new books of fantasy import might appear in the United States a half-dozen times per year, and paperbacks were not yet popular. Even collectors of borderline items found them surprisingly easy to obtain in many cities. Just before Pearl Harbor, a Chicago collector got 400 copies of *Argosy*, nearly all of the issues during the thirties, for $5.00. Somewhere in Rochester, New York, a tiny shop with a tremendous supply of almost every old magazine was known to Larry Farsace and Elmer Weinman. In it they found complete sets of almost everything a collector might want as far back as 1880, thousands of issues in duplicated form. (Their determination to keep this useful shrine a secret from other collectors had lamentable consequences. Before they could purchase nearly all of its fantasy treasures, the store sold out its stock to a paper mill for $4.00 per ton.) When Leonard Marlowe began collecting in 1941, he virtually completed sets of all the prozines simply by visiting back-issue shops, finding the earliest *Amazings*, *Wonders*, and *Astoundings* bringing their cover prices and more recent publications going for around $1.00 per year.

2. Collecting Habits

Collecting fans differ in their habits. Some of them just accumulate the stuff without reading it. Others not only accumulate the items without reading them, but take such pains to insure their safe preservation that they are afraid even to remove them from their wrappings, cellophane encasings, or lightproof boxes. But there are collectors who put the books and magazines to their literary purposes, and a few benevolent collectors put their hobby at the service of other fans by producing criticism, indexes, historical information, and related matter about their possessions. The tradition of publishing bibliographic matter in fandom goes back at least to 1935, when the *Science Fiction Bibliography* was issued by William Crawford and D. R. Welch. It was a 12-page booklet with a rather helter-skelter set of contents: the names of some semi-pro and pro pamphlets containing science fiction, listings of some early fanzines, estimates of fair prices for various treasures, and advertisements. Even then, fans were seeking exceptional rarities or creating rarities of their own. Walter Sullivan, for instance, was proud of his unique acquisition, the first two years of *Astounding* in bound volumes, the file copies of Clayton, the publisher. Louis C. Smith had dozens of custom-bound volumes that he entitled "Fantastic Fiction." The contents were cannibalized fantasy stories untimely ripped from the wombs of otherwise mundane magazines. Albert Sidney Johnson, a Texas fan having a holiday in New York, set all fandom into a tizzy with a find that was a ten-day wonder: a copy of the January, 1931, *Amazing* that was printed on slick paper.

Many collecting fans were so reticent or so loudmouthed about the extent of their possessions that it is hard to be sure who had the biggest collections. Fred Shroyer claimed 1,300 books containing science fiction, around 1944, before the big boom in fantasy books began. Both Wollheim and Langley Searles admitted around that same time that they had not added the 1,000th book to their collections yet. But a prozine writer, Laurence Manning, claimed to possess more than 500 books on just one theme, utopias; it's not certain if this included nonfictional studies of the philosophical concept. Farsace may have been top man as a magazine collector during the forties, because he amassed an enormous assemblage of his own and later bought up the collections of two other oldtime Rochester fans, Francis J. Litz and Bernard A. Seufert. An older collector, Erle Barr Hanson, was claimed to possess the largest collection in the South. Late starters like Dr. C. L. Barrett were coming to the fore as the decade ended. And then there was Ackerman, of course, who already owned so much of everything that it was impossible to be certain just how far ahead of the others he really was.

Books and magazines were the earliest collectors' items. But fanzines soon became fashionable in the field. At the end of the 1930's, Moskowitz counted more than eight hundred issues in his collection, approximately a year's fanzine output a little later when the field had grown. Bill Miller and Russ Hodgkins were high in the earliest stages of the race. A little later, Laney claimed that he had 95 per cent of all major fannish items issued through 1946, and most of his collection eventually helped to increase the fanzine holdings of Coslet. Wollheim had so many fanzines that he tried, upon becoming a pro, to persuade fans to continue to send him their publications regularly, for continuation of a collection that up to then could hardly be duplicated.

3. The Value of Collections and Selected Items

It is tremendously difficult to determine just how valuable these collections of the 1940's were. The advertised prices for specific items were not always the figures that dealers really hoped to receive for the merchandise, and when an entire collection changed hands in lot form, it usually did so under special circumstances that lowered the price: total disillusionment with fandom by the seller, or the death of the collector whose survivors were ignorant of the worth of the stuff. However, we may be sure of two things. Prices in collecting fandom never went as high as non-fans were paying for the rarest fantasy items, while certain items rose to prices higher than the purse of the average fan might make probable. Thus, a first edition of *The Wizard of Oz* sold for prices in three and four figures outside fandom, while I know of no instance in which a fan has ever tried to save up to buy one, despite the great popularity of the Baum books in collecting fandom. Dime novels in the 1930's were bringing prices up to $475 per copy, but they were virtually ignored in collecting fandom, despite the science fictional content of many series.

On the other hand, G. Gordon Dewey once estimated the value of his A. Merritt collection at $2,000, although it is doubtful that Ackerman paid that much when he eventually purchased it. Coslet in more recent times has tried unsuccessfully to obtain $20,000 for his enormous assemblage of professional and amateur materials. Still, prices varied wildly in fandom. We find someone in 1945 offering for $15 the 39-issue set of *Unknown*, a few months before a group of fans tried to arrive at fair prices for old prozines and set the value of its first issue alone at $2.50. As early as 1934, someone offered to pay one dollar per copy for any issue of *Weird Tales* from its first year of publication. A year later, the *Science Fiction Bibliography* estimated the worth of a complete set of *Scoops*, the twenty-issue British magazine, at $10, only a year after their issuance. The same publication put $11 as the worth of the first 24 issues of *Science Fiction Digest*. There were complaints at an early date about high prices of collectors' items. H. C. Koenig gave a blast at Gernsback for advertising at $2.00 and $2.50 books that were selling on remainder counters for 75 cents or less. One dealer suffered a unique attack of conscience that impelled him to offer books at half his previous prices. And yet the receipts at the first worldcon auction in 1939 totaled only $75; included in this figure were the winning bids for such things as the original manuscripts of a Weinbaum novel, a Howard story, and "Cosmos," the pro chain story; unpublished Wesso and Paul cover art; early issues of *Time Traveller* and *Science Fiction Digest*; and an inundation of less heady material.

The law of supply and demand has undergone any number of amendments in collecting fandom. Julie Unger once theorized longingly that any good fanzine should sell for $50 per copy, a couple of years after publication, because so few copies of any given issue survive and because it is so rarely that a fan will part with this type of possession. The theory does not hold good, perhaps because the individuals who are most apt to be in search of fanzines are the new young fans who are less likely to be well heeled. Nevertheless, the better fanzines had asking prices ranging as high as $1.50 to $3.00 per issue when sold individually, after World War II. Almost anything might happen when a fan unloaded his entire fanzine collection. Dr. Barrett obtained the Chauvenet accumulation for only 40 cents per pound.

Mary Finn, an old-time Los Angeles fan, once insisted that a dealer had tried to provide her with a copy of *The Moon Pool* in book form for $600. But this must have been either a case of a missing decimal point or a nightmare. Collectors did pay $50 and more for copies of the first Arkham House book, *The Outsider and Others*, only a year or two after the $5 volume went out of print. There is no doubt that prices on almost everything were inflated during the forties. Partly, the increase must be blamed on fans who went into dealing on a mail order, part-time basis, purchasing their stock at retail prices and multiplying two or three times to arrive at a selling price. Tucker found advertisements in 1944 that asked up to a dollar apiece for paperbacks that were still selling on most newsstands or could be ordered from the publisher for the original 25¢ figure. Remaindered novels turned up in advertisements in fan publications at prices two or three times the fee at the majority of dime stores. Fans and pros in New York organized a Collectors Club in 1945 to attempt to combat the trend: it sought to buy in quantity to obtain reduced per-copy rates, provided a means for trading duplicates easily, and organized expeditions on which bookshops within a 200-mile radius were ransacked mercilessly through the weight of manpower. Mel Korshak, when he returned to dealing after three years in the armed forces, thought that the general increase in the cost of living and the drying up of sources of supply also played a big part in the increased prices. One dealer refused to give him the old trade discount, on the grounds that it was no longer possible to restock.

One effort to reach agreement on fair average prices for back issues set the value of the first *Amazing* at $8, other issues of the 1920's from $6 to $2 apiece, and knocked down the last eight years' editions (as of 1946) at 25¢ apiece. *Famous Fantastic Mysteries* in its first couple of years, 1939 and 1940, was assessed at values of $2 to $1. In general, issues with stories by E. E. Smith, Weinbaum, Campbell and Heinlein were considered justified in bringing more money.

Added to the higher prices that collectors were forced to pay for old items was the increased burden of simply keeping up with the new items. For instance, the fan who had bought every prozine from the newsstand as it was published would have spent $90 up to 1940, unless he had heard about the dime novels. In 1949, Coslet calculated that such on-the-spot purchases would have cost the veteran fan $412.67 by then, including the dime novels that everyone now knew about.

4. Fantasy Advertiser

Many fanzines paid particular attention to the collector, for either studious or commercial reasons. But *Fantasy Advertiser* was the best evidence of how many collectors existed and how many dealers were making money from them. Gus Willmorth began to issue it in 1946 as a 16-page mimeographed publication. He said that he hoped to make the fanzine "an effective instrument in spreading the gospel of fandomania through the medium of giving suitable publicity to our wares." It contained lots of advertisements and enough non-commercial material to entice the fans to read all the pages. By its fourth issue, at the end of that year, the mailing list contained 1,000 names and addresses. Two years later, *Fantasy Advertiser* had become a semi-professional publication that possessed some 40 planographed pages each issue, paid five dollars for each article accepted as of interest to collecting fans, and provided 10,000 words of such text in addition to enormous quantities of all sorts of advertisements. After a drive to boost circulation to 1,500 copies, Willmorth turned the publication over to Roy Squires at the end of 1949.

5. Major Collectors

The prominent collecting fans came from a wide variety of sources and possessed sharply contrasting habits and characters. Let's look at a few of them in some detail, to prove this.

Walter A. Coslet was one of the most ardent collecting fans to appear in the decade. Born on a Montana farm in 1922, he began to save Buck Rogers strips from newspapers when he was progressing through his tenth year. He discovered the prozines a year later, but felt only a modest interest in science fiction for a full decade. Then in 1943 Coslet moved to Helena, Montana, and got a job with the United States Employment Service. New surroundings and a steady income turned him into a collector of the most extreme type. He began to order back issues of the prozines in 1944, joined the NFFF, unearthed fans from various parts of the Montana soil, and during a

Walter A. Coslet

visit to Los Angeles underwent the twin decisive experiences of encountering lots of live fans and purchasing 550 old magazines. The next ten years were devoted to mass accumulating of huge quantities of science fictioniana and painstaking searches for exceptional rarities. By 1953, when Coslet was tiring of this hobby, he estimated that he owned 10,000 magazines, more than 2,000 books, and fanzines by the hundredweight. But another long-standing hobby finally began to win precedence in the Coslet affections: the collection of various English translations of the Bible. He was gafiating by the end of the fifties. Coslet was active for years in fanzine fandom, particularly as a publisher and writer in FAPA and SAPS. But he never managed to carry out the many bibliographic projects that he started or promised.

Dr. Charles L. Barrett, born in 1909, may have inherited his collecting instinct. His father had preserved many issues of *Black Cat Magazine* in the 1890's. Barrett began to buy *Weird Tales* from its first year, was already amassing a collection while fandom was coming into the world, and remained almost unknown until fans began to discover the delights of his company and his Midwestcons in the late forties and fifties, respectively. In appearance, he reminded some fans of Wendell Willkie. By the end of the forties, books were scattered through four houses, one rolltop desk was so tightly stuffed with fanzines that it resisted opening, and one room above his clinic had fantasy books stacked on shelves 15 feet high and 20 feet wide. Barrett didn't even realize his collection was big until Fred Shroyer told him the truth. The collection involves events as fantastic as the subject matter: he once paid a girl to tackle the job of cataloging it, he bought all the comic books from the newsstands until the number of titles reached 60 and he admitted defeat, and he credited maternity case waits with giving him time to read fanzines. The demands of his profession get the blame for his failure to do much fan writing or publishing.

Born even earlier, in 1903, was Erle Barr Hanson, long a collector but active in general fandom only for a couple of years in World War II when the Dixie Fantasy Federation lured him into the open. He was head of music for Miami radio station WIOD, head of the musicians' union, and a purchaser of *Amazing* from the first issue onward. In the forties, his collection cf prozines and fanzines was reputed to be the largest in the South. It was particularly strong in *Argosy*, bound sets of which dated well back into the 19th century. Hanson began collecting books in 1916; he later became a dime novel collector and an active member of dime novel fandom.

A. Langley Searles, first a student and then an instructor at New York University, was a collector to only a moderate degree. But his bibliographic and publishing activities made him one of the leaders in collecting fandom. He began to publish *Fantasy Commentator* in FAPA in December, 1943, moved it into general circulation after five issues, and didn't conclude its career until a 26th issue in 1952. He defined his policy in the first issue, quite pithily: "Mainly books." He put into words one of the big reasons for the magazine's success: "It is quite possible to obey the simple rules of grammar and yet to maintain a conversational style of writing. Stuffiness of content is not necessarily a corollary to obedience to forms of established correctness." Best remembered now as the original source of *The Immortal Storm*, the fanzine published an imposing series of bibliographies of fantasy fiction in many mundane magazines, scholarly and literate articles about the writers of fantasy, and original material by almost all of the most famous pros of the era—Merritt, Kuttner, Keller, Lovecraft, and Hodgson, for instance. Searles did much of the work on the first big fantasy booklist, dribbling out its pages as a supplement to a newszine, *Fantasy Fiction Field*, and almost suing Laney in a dispute over the project.

William H. Evans was a collector and a fanzine publisher, but is most celebrated in collecting fandom as a researcher. Many of his tabulations found a home in *Fantasy Commentator*. Evans was born in Salem, Oregon, in 1921, graduated from Willamette University in 1942, and began to collect under the most favorable of circumstances: a job in a second-hand bookstore. He first came to fandom's attention as collaborator on Damon Knight's fanzine *Snide*. Then came his lengthy series of solo and cooperative ventures into finding fantasy in non-fantasy publications, and other types of investigation into undocumented treasures of the past. Much later, Evans began an important reprint series from old fanzines in FAPA. He moved to Washington,

Snide

D.C., after getting a civil service job, became active in that city's fandom, but didn't begin to attend cons until the sixties.

Larry Farsace was born in Rochester, N.Y., in 1921 as Litterio B. Farsaci. He gradually anglicized his name over the years. He began to attract attention as Lovecraft did, by an interest in astronomy that was strong enough to cause a newspaper writeup. Then he discovered fandom in 1935 when he bought a year's issues of *Fantasy Magazine* that had somehow wandered into a bookstore. This was typical of the fortunate finds that constantly helped to improve his collection. Over three or four years, he built up a tremendous accumulation that was particularly strong in pioneer publications like *Black Cat* and *Thrill Book*, branched out into such novel rarities as reviews of fantasy published in 19th century newspapers, and was also strong in fanzines. Besides the discovery of the Rochester back-issue shop described in this chapter, Farsace acquired the complete files of the Literature, Science and Hobbies Club of Decker, Indiana, for transportation costs, and Graham B. Stone even started to send him Australia's fantasy rarities. Unlike most collectors, Farsace spent lots of time and money publishing material based on his collection. He issued a couple of small bibliographies for early conventions, then began in 1939 to produce *Golden Atom*. Ten issues of it appeared in the next couple of years, then the war interrupted regular publication but it has continued to bob up ever since whenever everyone is convinced that it is finally dead. One of these issues, coming out in 1955, must have been the most expensive fanzine in history: 100 printed pages and lots of art in an edition of 1,200 copies at a cost of some $1,500. *Golden Atom* emphasized serious articles about prozines and their contributors, not as scholarly as those in *Fantasy Commentator*, perhaps, but glowing with more enthusiasm.

The Rev. Darrell C. Richardson got off to a later start as a collector than most fans in this period. But he made lots of speed, after he finally got started in 1943. Within five years, he had at least a thousand books, many of them first editions; 3,500 magazines; a complete set of Burroughs first editions; and a secretary who tried for two years, off and on, to index everything. The collector accomplished this despite handicaps imposed by his status as a Baptist minister. This, for instance, permitted him to read only in intervals before meals and after bedtime. His pastorate at Fort Mitchell, Kentucky, permitted the Rev. Mr. Richardson to be active in Cincinnati fandom, until his enlistment as an army chaplain in the mid-fifties, whereupon he found it necessary to rent a truck to haul five tons of books and magazines to a relative's home in Missouri for safekeeping. He went about his collecting in a systematic manner that nobody else seems to have thought of: he wrote to 1,500 chambers of commerce for the names and addresses of local bookstores that he then contacted with his want list.

6. Indexes

The collector who worked hardest and longest on indexing was R. D. Swisher. He lived in Winchester, Massachusetts, while flourishing in the late thirties and early forties. Working as a research organic chemist, he spent his spare time writing facts on index cards. By the turn of the decade, he had 6,000 cards containing information on 3,000 science fiction stories and their authors, 5,000 fans, and the contents of unimaginable numbers of fanzines. These data files were unprecedentedly complete. Even the most unimportant letter in an obscure fanzine had its entry. Top fans like Don A. Wollheim and Forrest J Ackerman piled up two hundred or more references apiece. His wife did a lot of this clerical work while Swisher spent much of his time writing away for every new fanzine that he heard about. At this time, Swisher owned virtually every fanzine and prozine in the English language, plus less generally available items like unpublished manuscripts by John W. Campbell, Jr., and the issue of *Real Spicy Horror Stories* that is published every May 15, 1937, by Yale undergraduates. Swisher may have been a mite too thorough. He was horrified to find himself in 1941 a year behind in the task of entering fanzine references onto his cards, and he wasn't able to read the prozines at all. To be fair, he caught up on the prozine reading in 1946, but was then hopelessly behind on the indexing. The major benefit of all this to fandom was the issuance of the *SF Check-List*, a fanzine title index. Another Swisher activity was the creation of an enormous manuscript on time travel stories and theories. He had some 1,000 pages of it, when last heard from. At that time, he had solved all but one of the paradoxes that make time travel impossible. He has disappeared so completely that he may have solved that final paradox.

Without that Swisher fanzine index, the first big research project to be published for fans, it might have been another decade or more before anyone proved that there is enough egoboo and satisfaction deriving from such things to make them worthwhile. Moreover, it is quite probable that nobody would have ever had the heart to tackle the fanzine indexing task, if Swisher hadn't done it a mere ten years after the start of mainstream fandom, before the things had become overpoweringly prolific. Swisher went about this index with typical overthoroughness. He listed not only all the fanzines he owned and all the fanzines he didn't own, but also the fanzines that had never appeared but had been mentioned by someone, whether abandoned before publication or jokes that were never intended for creation. Swisher completed the first checklist by the end of 1939, published a revised version during the next couple of years to cover new information and recent issues, and continued his file card activities until 1946. Although it takes us out of the period under consideration, this is a convenient place to note that Bob Pavlat began in 1952 to publish an up-to-date edition of the checklist, finally completing its issuance in 1959. Harold Palmer Piser is trying to update and correct the listing.

Other obvious and less taxing indexing projects were tackled early in fandom. Some of them were completed quite well. Frank Brady and A. Ross

INDEX to the SCIENCE FICTION MAGAZINES 1926-1950 DAY PERRI

AIR WONDER STORIES * AMAZING DETECTIVE TALES * AMAZING STORIES * AMAZING STORIES ANNU
AMAZING STORIES ANNUAL * AMAZING STORIES QUARTERL ASTONISHING STORIES * ASTOUNDING
ASTOUNDING SCIENCE FICTION * ASTOUNDING STORIES * FANTASY READER * CAPTAIN FUTUR
CAPTAIN FUTURE * COMET STORIES * COSMIC STORIES C STORIES * FAMOUS FANTASTIC
FAMOUS FANTASTIC MYSTERIES * FANTASTIC ADVENTU ASTIC NOVELS * FANTASTIC STOR
FANTASTIC STORY QUARTERLY * FANTASY (British TASY BOOK * FANTASY FICTION * FANT
FANTASY STORIES * FUTURE combined with SCI CTION * FUTURE FANTASY and SCIENCE F
FUTURE FANTASY and SCIENCE FICTION * FU TION * GALAXY SCIENCE FICTION * GALAXY
GALAXY SCIENCE FICTION NOVELS * IMAGIN MAGAZINE of FANTASY * MAGAZINE of FANTA
MAGAZINE of FANTASY and SCIENCE FICT ARVEL SCIENCE STORIES * MARVEL STORIES * M
MARVEL TALES * A. MERRITT FANTASY LE STORIES * NEW WORLDS (British) * OTHER WO
OTHER WORLDS * OUT OF THIS WORLD URES * PLANET STORIES * SCIENCE FICTION * SCIE
SCIENCE FICTION QUARTERLY * SC CTION STORIES * SCIENCE WONDER QUARTERLY * SCIE
SCIENCE WONDER STORIES * SCI DETECTIVE MONTHLY * STARTLING STORIES * STIRRING
STIRRING SCIENCE STORIES * SC E NOVELS * SUPER SCIENCE STORIES * TALES of WO
TALES of WONDER (British) ILL WON STORIES * TWO COMPLETE SCIENCE ADVENTURE
TWO COMPLETE SCIENCE A E NO TORIES * UNKNOWN * UNKNOWN WORLDS *
WONDER STORIES * WOND RIES RTE DE STORY ANNUAL * WORLDS BEYOND * AIR
AIR WONDER STORIES NG IV TA A IN RIES * AMAZING STORIES ANNU
AMAZING STORIES O LY RIES NDI CIENCE FICTION * ASTOUN
ASTOUNDING STOR VON AN EA C TURE ME TORIES * COSMIC ST
DYNAMIC STORI AMOU FAN ERIE ASTIC ADV RES * FANTASTIC NOVEL
FANTASTIC ARTERL TA B ANTASY BO FANTAS TIC FANT
FUTURE SCIEN IT ANT SCIENCE FICTION * FU RE FI
GALAXY SCIENCE FICTION * GALAXY SCIENCE FICTION NOVELS * IMAGINATION * MAGAZINE of FA

SCIENCE FICTION MAGAZINES 1926-1950

Dust jacket of the Day Index

Kuntz published in 1940 *The Imag-Index*, a 72-page volume that listed all the stories in every prozine from 1926 to 1938. They were set down in a rather primitive way, in the order in which they had appeared on contents pages. It was not until 1952 that Donald B. Day of Portland, Oregon, made things easy for those seeking specific stories or compiling statistics, by publishing his 184-page *Index to the Science Fiction Magazines 1926–1950*. This covered more than 20,000 entries on the contents of 58 magazines from 1926 to 1950, properly alphabetized by title and again by author.

7. The Checklist of Fantastic Literature

The task of compiling a listing of all known fantasy books was as enormous as the fanzine index, in some ways. The books were less ephemeral than fanzines, but they had appeared over a span of centuries throughout the world, rather than during ten years or so and largely in English-speaking nations. Louis C. Smith kept a card index in the thirties that provided facts on more than a thousand books. But the first big bibliography that was duplicated and distributed was one compiled by Searles with the help of Julie Unger. It began to go out in mid-1942, a couple of pages at a time, with issues of Unger's newszine, *Fantasy Fiction Field*. It was eventually intended to cover some 4,000 titles. The first fantasy bibliography that appeared between hard covers was *The Checklist of Fantastic Literature* that Shasta published in 1948. Everett F. Bleiler did the editing of the 5,000-title volume. The project received some criticism because it contained the titles of a lot of whimsical and outré stories that could not properly rank as fantasy, but it was still the first thing of its kind for the nation's libraries.

No such organized effort was made to gather into one place and publish the facts on all the important fantasy stories in magazines that purveyed mostly mundane fiction. During the 1940's many such magazines were

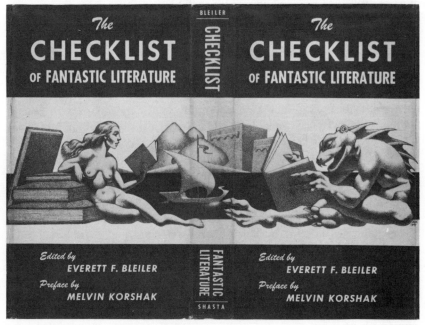

Dust jacket of the Bleiler Checklist

covered by listings of their fantasy contents, but the various fanzines that published the data are now even more difficult to locate than the old mundane magazines themselves. As evidence of the scattered way in which the listings circulated, we find an index to fantasy in *Scientific Detective Monthly* distributed through the Fall, 1942, FAPA mailing; a listing of fantasy fiction in *Harper's Magazine* in a general circulation fanzine, *The Scientifan*, for January-February, 1940; *Popular Magazine* was similarly covered in the Fall, 1948, issue of *Fantasy Commentator*; and science fiction in Gernsback publications before *Amazing Stories* was noted on a series of loose pages that *Fantasy Fiction Field* distributed in 1944, and in a pamphlet compiled by Theodore H. Engel and distributed by Hugo Gernsback at Chicon II in 1952. A few exceptionally hardy souls even dabbled in this sort of work for the contents of amateur publications. Tucker produced a complete index to *The Fantasy Fan* in 1945, and the Swisher card index files contained references to everything in hundreds of issues of fan publications. One neglected accomplishment of the era was the working out of a decimal classification system for fantasy fiction, analogous to the Dewey figures that permit librarians to put nonfiction volumes where they can find them again. Both Jack Speer and Sam Russell produced comprehensive systems that would have made it easy to indicate the general theme of stories in reference works, in 1943. But they were ignored by the compilers.

8. Pilgrims Through Space and Time

The first book-length critical study of science fiction in the English language was *Pilgrims Through Space and Time*. It was the work of J. O. Bailey, a scholar with almost imperceptibly faint connections with general fandom. He announced as early as 1935, through the letter column of *Wonder Stories*, that he was compiling a bibliography of science fiction. Then working for his Ph.D. degree, he abandoned this project, after snaring 5,000 titles, as too big a task to handle. He sent his notes to Koenig, who had helped him to gather information, and the data proved useful to Searles. Meanwhile, Bailey had sailed forth on a new tack, a Ph.D. dissertation on science fiction as a separate form of literature. The resulting work was finally published in 1947 by Ben Abramson's Argus Books. It baffled some fans, infuriated others, but still remains the best source of lots of synopses of old science fiction stories. *Pilgrims Through Space and Time* was mainly criticized as a catchall that was neither a history of science fiction nor a criticism of the field nor a set of synopses of all famous stories, but something of all three. It was defended as a work intended for the general public who wouldn't have as much interest in the prozines that fans liked as in the books that could be found in big public libraries. This was the crux of the dissatisfaction of fandom. Bailey had paid next to no attention to the science fiction written after 1914. This accounted for his neglect of the prozines.

9. The Fantasy Foundation

The project that might have given to collecting fandom the focal point that worldcons became for mainstream fandom was the Fantasy Foundation. The concept of a permanent

Dust jacket of Pilgrims Through Space and Time

home for a great collection of fantasy stories and related items, for the benefit of all fans, was in Ackerman's mind from times unguessable. It first became evident to fans in 1943 when he insured his life for a thousand dollars, assembled his parents, grandmother, aunt, and his friend Myrtle R. Douglas (better known as Morojo), and explained his intention. In case of his death, the insurance money was to establish a science fiction foundation. Morojo was to be the executrix of the plan, with Paul Freehafer backing her up. At about the same time, Ackerman willed his entire science fiction collection to fandom through this foundation. It is possible that Francis T. Laney was the catalyst that caused this vague future possibility to be altered into a definite project for immediate realization. Laney drew up an outline for a plan, showed it to Ackerman, then to other Los Angeles fans. This called for a dynamic organization that would do many things in Ackerman's lifetime. It was not to be the quiet museum that Ackerman had envisaged, and right there lay the seeds of the eventual disaster.

Fandom didn't hear about this project immediately. In May, 1946, Ackerman mailed invitations, without publicity, to a number of fans to become directors of the imminent Fantasy Foundation. He defined it as "simultaneously a showplace and a shareplace, where the work of operation is shared by volunteers and a museum of imaginative literature is eventually created which surpasses any individual collection." Pending bequests, it was to exist through dues ranging from $25 annually for clubs to various smaller amounts for individual fans, according to the category of membership that each might choose. Much of the collection was to come in the form of donations of fan and professional treasures. In this first organizational statement was listed a group of potential foundation projects that outdid the NFFF: a rented headquarters housing the physical possessions, publication of annual checklists of fantasy material, a circulating library, establishment of duplicate collections in big cities of this nation, overseas branches for England and Australia, and drives for donations. The biggest dream of all was to make the FF independent financially, eventually, through creation of annuities by better-heeled fans.

The formal announcement to fandom was held up until the Pacificon in July, 1946, perhaps in the thought that the resumption of worldcons after the war marked the best time to launch a new idea into this postwar world. At this time there was already a split in Los Angeles thinking. Ackerman felt that the FF should be basically a museum in the custody and care of fans; Laney and many followers pushed for an active organization that would not devote its money to a building but would bum space from a public library so that its resources could be reserved for collecting, distributing, and publishing. The worldcon disclosure of plans didn't go quite as intended, because Ackerman became ill at a crucial moment. But this illness could have been temporarily beneficial to the plan: fans were so concerned over Ackerman's health that they didn't risk it with arguments over the FF. The new group got general lip support and some actual money at the outset. Russ Hodgkins became treasurer, Don Bratton served as librarian, Ackerman volunteered storage space for donated articles, and also became general manager for life. The directors were Art Widner, Jack Speer, Milt Rothman, Al Ashley, Bob Tucker, and my much younger self.

Almost at once, the foundation could report donations as cheering as the $20 that Earl Leeth contributed, sufficient duplicates for its collection to start a circulating library, and the availability of three publications: a checklist of fantasy prozines, a fanzine checklist for 1945, and a catalog of the 1,300 books in the collection Ackerman had willed to the FF. In the closing weeks of its first year, the treasurer could report the donation of 256 items that included 89 prozines, 80 fanzines, 50 books, and some original manuscripts. There was $300 on hand, not enough to move into a museum building as yet, and nearly half of that sum represented *Fancyclopedia* profits. There were 57 financial supporters at this time. During 1947, the FF re-

The 1948 Fantasy Annual

mained alive and green, but fans quickly began to understand that it wasn't destined to accomplish great things immediately. The collection did indeed grow to cover a thousand items by the end of 1947, including a trunk filled with books and a crate of magazines that C. A. Brandt, onetime literary editor of *Amazing Stories*, had bequeathed. Derleth provided a mint copy of every book that Arkham House had in print and Dewey provided an imposing assortment of duplicates from his famous Merritt collection. Even microfilms were in the archives.

But Laney resigned as editor, after a dispute with Ackerman, who had failed to mention publishing plans in prozine publicity about the FF. The organization took credit for helping to publish the enormous 1948 *Fantasy Annual*, a 120-page yearbook of prodom and fandom edited by Redd Boggs and Don Wilson. There is good reason to believe that Ackerman and the LASFS would have produced it if lightning had struck the FF dead. At the end of that year, Tucker lamented that the FF had run into a chronic condition of "dignified silence," but consoled himself with the knowledge that its possessions were safe in an Ackerman garage and some of the members still had some letterheads left over. Then for a decade fandom virtually forgot the FF. Ackerman remembered it. In the absence of continued help from fans, he revised regularly a list of heirs: trusted and currently active fans who would assume charge of his fantasy possessions in the event of his death. One-third of the Ackerman estate was intended for maintenance of a museum in the house which he owned, with space enough upstairs for living quarters for the curator. In the event that Ackerman's will should be activated by reason of an airplane crash, the procedure would change considerably: the heavy insurance in effect for every air trip would provide enough additional money to erect a new museum building on the site of the existing structure.

Ackerman's deviation from the mainstream of fandom as the fifties progressed caused his collection to weaken in fanzines, but he continued to keep it fully stocked with the professional form of fantasy and science fiction. In more recent years, there have been attempts to put the collection into something resembling order, none of them particularly successful. Some fans like Bill Ellern tackled the frightening assignment as volunteers and gave up hastily. Ackerman hired a secretary in 1961 but before her cataloging was complete, she quit to get married. The remaining funds of FF went to help pay the rent on garages where the collection was stored, and Ackerman now considers the FF and his giant personal collection as synonymous, since fandom will get everything in the end, anyway. Some west coast fans like John and Bjo Trimble, Steve and Virginia Schultheis, Rick Sneary, and Al Lewis have talked in recent years about a revival of Fantasy Foundation as an active group. However, a submeeting on the topic, at the Chicon III in 1962, failed to disclose great fannish interest in the project.

4. FANS INTO PROS: The Irresistible Need to Write

1. Fans Into Editors

The vast spawning of prozines devoted to science fiction during the early forties caused fans to realize that some of their number were defecting to the professional ranks in increasing quantities. This gravitation toward prodom had existed in milder degree in fandom for a long while. Few fans were so fervent in their amateur principles that they didn't undergo at least an occasional vision of controlling a prozine from the editor's desk or quitting some dull job to engage in the excitement of writing science fiction novelettes. The opportunities to make money out of science fiction became more numerous as the number of prozines swelled. Moreover, the more experienced fans arrived at something approaching maturity, and began to acquire some writing and editing ability through their fanac years.

Unfortunately, this partial conversion of hobby into vocational school has not been an unmixed blessing for either fandom or prodom. One major trouble has been the failure of some excellent fanzine editors to be equally successful as prozine editors. Few made a mark as significant as Campbell, Gold, and Boucher, who weren't fans originally, and some fans edited prozines that either died promptly or offered awful stories during long lives. Fans did much better when they became authors for the prozines. Perhaps one difference lies in the fact that the writer works only with words while the editor must handle people as well as words. Many fans became editors when they were too young and inexperienced with people to handle them as well as they did words.

Smaller numbers of fans yielded to the clink of gold through other trades. A few became agents, fewer turned into prozine artists, and a bunch of others became dealers, large or small, in science fiction.

2. Charles D. Hornig

The first prominent fan who became a prominent pro underwent the transformation without really trying. Charles Derwin Hornig was born in Jersey City on May 25, 1916, and discovered the prozines with the September, 1930, *Amazing Stories*. A year later he was manifesting his first fannish impulses. He was typing out one-copy issues of a four-page magazine, *Science Fiction Monthly*, keeping it up biweekly through the fall of 1931 and turning the unique copy of each issue over to a friend. He got a more solid type of editing experience with his high school's magazine. Carl Swanson caused Hornig to discover *The Time Traveller* in 1932. Hornig immediately was inspired to start a fanzine of his own, *The Fantasy Fan*, in September, 1933. He sent a copy of it to each prozine editor. At this very moment, Hugo Gernsback had just fired David Lasser, the editor of *Wonder Stories*. Gernsback liked the editorial in the fanzine so much that he decided that this should be his new editor. At a dazed seventeen years of age, Hornig took the job, going to night school until he completed high school. This prozine post helped to pay the expenses involved in eighteen monthly issues of *The Fantasy Fan*, for Hornig did not give up fandom in his new exaltation. Moreover, he never blasphemed about his literary nursery, as others who made the transition later were prone to do. "As a fan, I knew what the fans wanted," he wrote in 1934. He put his fannish ideas to work in a new policy for *Wonder Stories*.

Charles D. Hornig

Hornig remained almost as active in fandom during his *Wonder Stories* tenure as before it. He was one of the first big fannish travelers, covering 60,000 miles between 1933 and 1938, largely to visit fans and pros. He paid long visits to Lovecraft and Clark Ashton Smith, looked at Bloomington, Illinois, with Tucker as early as 1934, and during a vacation in Los Angeles he produced his last fanzine. This was his guest-edited issue of *Imagination!* in July, 1938, for the LASFL. Hardly anyone else could have accomplished in it what he did: he got rid of Ackerman's simplified spelling for that one issue without breaking up the club. *Wonder Stories* collapsed under Hornig, but he bobbed up again in prodom in 1939 as editor of *Science Fiction* and *Future Fiction*. Under Hornig, *Wonder Stories* had helped to expand fandom with the Science Fiction League. The new magazines were equally helpful for their columns of fannish interest. There is no telling what further benefits fandom might have received from this individual who had made the best of two worlds, if Hornig's firm pacifism hadn't clashed with the war. He was assigned to a civilian public service forestry camp at Cascade Locks, Oregon, in March, 1942, as a conscientious objector. He consoled himself with the thought that the trees he was chopping down might someday be reincarnated as prozine pages. But the firmness of his views caused him untold difficulties during the war years.

3. Mort Weisinger

Mort Weisinger was the second to make the transition, when he became editor of *Thrilling Wonder Stories* in 1936, after it passed from Gernsback's hands and acquired its new name. However, the transition wasn't quite as abrupt for him as it had been for Hornig. Weisinger had already been gravitating toward the professional side of the field by serving as an agent for many of the big names. Moreover, Weisinger didn't participate in fannish doings after he became a full-time professional. He turned the agency over to the sole charge of his former partner, Julius Schwartz, and dropped his assistance to *Fantasy Magazine*, then the leading fanzine.

4. Ray Palmer

Much more exciting in all respects was the transition for Ray Palmer. His adventures in prodom were almost as exciting as the mishaps that seem to have dotted his earlier life, for he was apparently an accident-prone, if we may believe all the accounts of mishaps and misadventures that he supplied at various times in his own writings and in interviews with fans. Born August 1, 1910, in Milwaukee, he was hit by a truck when he was seven. The result was a broken back, a long hospital stay, and the acquisition of love of reading during convalescence. He had another two-year stay in bed, beginning when he was thirteen years old, and recovered just in time to buy the first issue of *Amazing Stories* from the newsstands. He began building a prozine collection, hiding it under floorboards in the attic because of parental disapproval. His family commandeered the money he earned with a newspaper route, but Palmer managed to continue to purchase prozines by taking on a surreptitious second route. *Amazing Stories* was only a year old when Palmer had decided that he wanted to be its editor some day. His grandmother told him one day in 1929 that he would never become a writer, a statement that goaded Palmer into revising a story three times and selling it, "The Time Ray of Jandra" (*Wonder Stories*, June 1930). There is a less dramatic version of his first fiction sales, which says that he could not find a job and wrote stories to earn money. There was another long spell of physical disability in 1930. Palmer once summed up some of these troubles laconically: "Falls off roofs, off ladders." At least one accident allegedly resulted from steeplejacking three stories up. He was supposed to have somehow broken several fingers while bowling. Baseball also cost him fractured digits. The last traceable smashup occurred in 1940 in Los Angeles, a motor vehicle mishap that caused only bruises.

As writer, editor, and organizer, Palmer worked off enough fannish energies to give him the $100 prize in a Gernsback contest on "What I Have Done to Advance Science Fiction." He blamed hard work for fandom and for science fiction with causing him an eight-month stay in a sanatorium recovering his health. An early example of his habit of blaming fans when anything went wrong was revealed when he said that a fan stole his mimeograph while he was *hors de fanac*. As a fan turned pro, he was not happy at first with the prozine editors. As 1937 started, we find Palmer writing in a fanzine like one of the average fans whom he castigated a few years later: "As for what's wrong with science fiction, nothing. The trouble is with the editors. They have found a certain type of fiction which sells their magazine. They are interested solely in profit. And they will not change. How to remedy this? You can't."

When Ziff-Davis bought *Amazing Stories* in 1938, the new owners immediately fired T. O'Conor Sloane, tottery with age, as editor. Ralph Milne Farley visited the Davis half of the ownership, saw that he didn't know much about the magazine he now owned, and suggested Palmer as the proper person for the open editorship. Davis asked Palmer to write a letter outlining his qualifications. Instead, at Farley's suggestion, Palmer applied in person at the editorial office in Chicago. An unidentified timekeeper chronicled the day's events like this: Palmer arrived at 10:22 a.m., began to go through the pile of manuscripts on hand at 10:41 a.m., received complete charge of the magazine at 5:11 p.m., and got home at 9 p.m., having gone without food and drink for 27 hours. "Here at last," Palmer said, "I had it in my power to do to my old hobby what I had always had the driving desire to do to it. I had in my hands the power to change, to destroy, to create, to remake, at my own discretion." He accepted only one of more than a hundred manuscripts left over from the Sloane regime, solicited another type of story from writers known to him, and arranged for a photographic cover because the new issue was due in two weeks and prozine artists were mostly in New York. Palmer claimed that he made the transition to editor at great personal sacrifice: living in a strange town, earning seventy per cent less than he had made writing, and finding it necessary to rewrite almost every story he accepted. Circulation figures were not officially published in those years, but Palmer claimed that *Amazing* was selling only 27,000 copies when he got hold of it, that his first issue sold 45,000 copies, that 75,000 copies were sold of the following issue, and that the figure eventually reached a peak of 185,000.

Palmer attracted more attention among fans than most prozine editors in the following years, because of his curious habit of swinging unpredictably between wheedling and alienating them. He had already shown his readiness to gripe at fans in 1936, when the Weinbaum memorial volume was published. Palmer charged then that the fan readership

Little Chicon, 1944—left to right: Ray Palmer, Frank Robinson, W. Lawrence Hamling, Howard Browne, and Chet Geier.

of *Fantasy Magazine* had failed to support the volume and that the non-fan purchasers of *Astounding* had done the job with support from *Thrilling Wonder Stories* readers. Long after, he took the same attitude toward Shaver's stories, warning fandom that it had missed the boat that was transporting the new Shaver fandom to unknown seas. But Palmer became a 'hero for the young fans who sprang up in Chicago in the late thirties. He was generous with original illustrations and manuscripts to fans, gave visiting fans a fine reception at Ziff-Davis, and made it easy for fans to contact his writers and artists. Elsewhere in the nation, the change in the literary standards of *Amazing Stories* caused the hero worship to be somewhat adulterated with other emotions. Palmer's habit of publishing in his magazines old fanzine stories must have been an early cause of the more realistic attitude that fans began to adopt toward the pros. It was hard to take seriously the assumption that prozines were better written than fanzines, when the household word for bad fanzines, Tom Ludowitz' *Space Tales*, became the source of a Hamling story, "The Man Who Spoke Too Late," that sold to Palmer.

Shaver's stories caused the breach between Palmer and fandom to become outfitted with barricades and artillery. Events of the time are chronicled elsewhere in this history. Palmer allegedly got a $250 per month raise out of the excitement that the Shaver stuff provided, while fandom in turn got a fan column in *Amazing Stories* as an indirect result of Lemuria. The course

of events that led Palmer and Ziff-Davis to sever ties is still classified information. The most specific words about it that Palmer put into print were:
"A terrible accident took your editor out of the driver's seat, and when he
got back in, the damage had been done. Science fiction no longer had human
interest and apparently was no longer of interest to humans." Subfandoms
devoted to flying saucers and Shaver became more congenial to Palmer from
this time onward. Occasionally he took the trouble to test the atmosphere
in general fandom, usually finding the fallout in it from previous detonations
too heavy for him to risk. Thus, he sent free copies of the November, 1955,
issue of *Other Worlds Science Stories* to many fans, accompanied by a
mimeographed letter couched in such terms as these: "This is Ray Palmer
talking to you, man to man. No matter who you are, or what your opinions
about science fiction in general, this letter steps over minor issues and takes
in a situation that is above the small-time politics that involve 'taking sides.' "
This meant that fans should rally around Ray Palmer while he restored
science fiction to a not too clearly defined former glory. The subscription
certificate said: "Dear Ray: I want to bring science fiction back to its former
greatness." But a little later, he got hold of an issue of *Dream Quest*, in
which I had written in most unflattering terms about the part that Palmer
had played in causing "greatness" to require an adjective. He ran it in the
October, 1957, issue of *Flying Saucers From Other Worlds*, describing it as
"one of the most interesting and informative editorials we have ever presented," but neither asking my permission nor paying me for the involuntary
contribution. He picked an individual who had at the time almost no knowledge of fanzines, Guy Terwilleger, to review the things. Palmer's publishing
ventures during the fifties became almost as frequent as his fictional projects
had been in earlier times. He seems to have veered endlessly between success
and failure in his projects. Thus, we find him in 1952 pleading for readers
to pledge $5.00 so that *Other Worlds* might appear more frequently; and the
next year he is building a splendid new home in Amherst, Wisconsin, with a
fireplace large enough to barbecue whales. One legend says that he designed
the house around some I-beams that he purchased at a bargain price. Palmer
is the type of person around whom legends cling.

5. Frederik Pohl

Three of the most prominent New York Futurians became prozine editors
during World War II. Frederik Pohl was a fan who dabbled in agenting and
professional writing with occasional success, until he became an editor on
October 25, 1939. Convinced that he could do a better job than some of
the individuals who held the reins on prozines, he had attempted to get the

editorship of *Marvel Science Stories* at a time when the magazine's fiction policy was changing for the worse. Robert Erisman of *Marvel* didn't take up his offer, but sent him to Roger Terrill at Popular Publications. This chain published no science fiction magazine at the time. But a conference with Harry Steeger, its president, put Pohl in charge of two new titles, *Super Science Stories* and *Astonishing Stories*. These received a new house name, Fictioneers, Inc., because they weren't destined to spend the princely rate of a penny per word that the main chain lavished

Frederik Pohl

on its writers. *Astonishing*'s first issue in February, 1940, represented the first prozine since the dime novels to sell for ten cents. The low word rate did not prevent it from offering stories by such notables as de Camp, Hubbard, Asimov, and Heinlein. *Super Science* began the following month. Pohl began in the latter a hasty imitation of the Science Fiction League, the Science Fictioneers. It became the parent organization for a few new and some old local clubs, but it did little otherwise to affect fandom's history.

6. Donald A. Wollheim

Donald A. Wollheim, leader and elder of the Futurians, claimed that he was reading science fiction back in the *Science and Invention* epoch when Ray Cummings' "Into the Fourth Dimension" was serialized. He first sold professionally in 1933, when Hornig bought "The Man From Ariel." Wollheim eventually instituted legal proceedings against Gernsback about not having received payment for this story when due. He found other writers who signed over to him for legal purposes their similar claims against *Wonder Stories*. Wollheim eventually got his money on the installment plan. As a result of this episode, fandom blinked several times when Wollheim accepted eagerly the chance to edit two prozines that asked for stories for which they did not offer payment. Somewhat fed up with fandom, Wollheim had been trying during early 1940 to persuade various publishers to enter the prozine field. In September, he found one who agreed to do it, Jerry Albert, editorial director of Albing Publications. The results were *Stirring Science Stories*, which first appeared in February, 1941, and *Cosmic Stories*, whose first issue was dated the next month. Wollheim claimed that he sought to fill with them a gap in fictional quality between *Astounding* and *Astonishing*. Fans made such a loud noise over the payment policy that Albert issued an explanation in late 1940: "Our two magazines are unable, for the present, to pay for stories. We authorized Donald Wollheim to furnish the best available material, both through his own creative efforts and through the efforts of his confreres as might be inclined to cooperate in furthering a sincere venture of this sort. Those who cooperate now will be given preference when stories are actually bought, which we have every expectation will be in the near future. Our methods are clearly open and above-board." *Cosmic* lasted

three issues, *Stirring* four. But Wollheim accomplished two things in their brief existence. One was his establishment as holder of a niche in the editing field. This helped him to get the task of editing the first paperback science fiction anthology, the *Pocket Book of Science Fiction* in 1943, later a similar volume for the Viking Portable Library series, and eventually jobs as editor of the all-reprint Avon *Fantasy Reader* and *Science Fiction Reader*, and more recently as science fiction editor for Ace paperbacks. His other achieve-

Donald A. Wollheim

ment was that he provided a place where Futurians could get their stories published in a newsstand magazine and build reputations of their own as fiction writers. The Futurians filled most of the issues of *Stirring* and *Cosmic* for free. Cyril Kornbluth's contributions stood out somewhat in this pile of indifferent science fiction, bringing him to the attention of more affluent publishers and editors. The other Futurians returned the compliment by printing Wollheim's stories in their magazines. He sold seventeen stories to magazines in 1942 and 1943, and managed to hit other markets only in the form of one collaboration in *Astounding* during this same period.

7. Robert W. Lowndes

Wollheim's career in fandom was marked by endless arguments and intricate politics. Pohl had been a less prominent fan but still in the Wollheim tradition, with spit and polish that Wollheim lacked. Robert Ward Lowndes, on the other hand, emanated the impression of an individual more aloof and mature than his fellow Futurians, on paper. Born in Bridgeport, Connecticut, in 1916, he had a year at Stamford Community College, then joined the Civilian Conservation Corps. He discovered the prozines gradually. An *Amazing Stories* cover in 1926 gave him a nightmare, but the first prozine that he read was an issue of *Ghost Stories* in 1927. He got his first *Amazing* in 1928 by snipping a coupon for a free issue from the public library's copy of *Open Road for Boys*. Parental objections confined him to reading science fiction in book form for a while. But he became a prozine letterhack in the early thirties. He claimed credit for suggesting first, via the letter section in the July, 1932, *Wonder Stories*, that "science fiction to be more than story telling really should do something." The notion became a warcry for the Futurians for quite a spell. Lowndes joined the Science Fiction League in 1935, founded a chapter in Stamford, Connecticut, met Wollheim in 1936, and encountered the other Futurians soon thereafter. He remembered that first meeting: "The impression I received was that we all wanted desperately to express something, to do and plan something, but most of us did not know what it was, and those who did were either afraid or reluctant to bring it out." In 1938 he began publishing fanzines that had a more mature and calm atmosphere than the typical Futurian publications. By the end of 1940, Lowndes had succeeded Hornig as editor of Blue Ribbon Publications' *Future Fiction* and *Science Fiction*. He became managing editor of Columbia Publications in the middle of 1942, soon after physical reasons disqualified him for service in the armed forces. Lowndes retained some fannish features in the magazines, calling one feature "Futurian Times" out of respect to his associates and dropping Jimmy Taurasi as writer of a fan column for the sake of old feuds.

Robert W. Lowndes

8. W. Lawrence Hamling

W. Lawrence Hamling made a more gradual climb to editorial status. Born in Chicago on June 14, 1921, he started to read science fiction in 1935. Soon he was editing the *Lane Tech Prep*, the slick-cover magazine of the enormous Lane Technical High School in Chicago. He used its 10,000-copy circulation to circulate some science fiction. At school he became acquainted with other Chicago fans who came into prominence around this time. He was graduated from high school in 1939 with the intention of getting a law degree at the University of Chicago. But he had formed both the Chicago Science Fiction League and Chicago Science Fictioneers, he had served as director in both groups, he had sold "War With Jupiter," a collaboration with Mark Reinsberg, to *Amazing* in 1938, he was thinking of putting out a fanzine, and he went to work for a railroad. While publishing this fanzine, *Stardust*, he was keeping as much as 100,000 words of fiction in editorial hands at all times. Finally, in 1947, Hamling got a job helping Palmer, his old hero, with

Amazing Stories. Fantastic Adventures was turned over to Hamling a couple
of years later. He had a longer run as boss of *Imagination*. He severed most
fannish connections as soon as he became a professional.

9. Sam Moskowitz

Two other fans who flourished during the forties got their shots at prozine
editing in the fifties. More on their fannish selves will be told elsewhere, but
this is a convenient place to clean up the fan-into-editor transition in the
United States.

Two decades after he hired Charles D. Hornig on the spur of an impulsive
moment, Gernsback tried to reconquer the prozine world. Again he chose
a fan as editor, Sam Moskowitz. Moskowitz had begun making money out
of his hobby as early as 1940, when he was doing some agenting for friends
and was selling an occasional story of his own. Fandom learned about his
duties with *Science Fiction Plus* in early 1953, through a letter mailed to a
long list of names. "I predict that this can be the turning point in the history
of science fiction in publication form," the letter said, "if only the science
fiction fans will consider this magazine as the spearhead of a crusade to
establish science fiction on the highest levels of excellence and respect it has
ever known, and work with us to attain that goal." Either the fans didn't
cooperate or Gernsback's magazine ideals were obsolete. The publication
didn't last long, but Moskowitz bounced from this fall to become editorial
director of three trade magazines in the frozen food field.

Larry T. Shaw

10. Larry Shaw

Another fan who had less brilliant prozines than he deserved was Larry T. Shaw.
Born November 9, 1924, he grew up in
Schenectady, didn't discover science fiction
until 1939, became a noted letterhack in
Planet Stories, and produced a fanzine,
Leprechaun, within the next couple of
years. He moved to New York City for a
while in 1943, falling under the Futurians'
spell, and getting a job on the *New York
Times*. He edited *Infinity* and *Science Fiction Adventures*, both of which succumbed
to the blight that descended on the prozines as the sixties opened.

11. Walter A. Gillings

Walter A. Gillings was the first Britisher to turn from fan into prozine editor. He'd grown to love science fiction as a tiny tad when he read George Goodchild's "Message From Space" serialized in the *Children's Newspaper* in 1921 and Burroughs' "At the Earth's Core" in another publication for youngsters. He saw the March, 1927, issue of *Amazing Stories* in an East End shop window in London, invested four pence to find out what Stribling's "The Green Splotches" was like, and was a prozine reader. Gillings began to write to names he found in the letter columns of *Amazing*. Moreover, he found that one of these primitive letterhacks, A. M. D. Pender of Surbiton, was a source of back issues of prozines. The first recorded personal meeting among British fans may have occurred when L. A. Kippin of Ilford called at Gillings' home in Leyton. They began in 1930 or 1931 the Ilford Science Literary Circle, a group that lasted until it attempted to expand to national proportions.

As early as 1932, Gillings planned a 12-page publication, *Science and Vision*, that was intended to keep the inhabitants of the British Isles with science fiction tastes in contact with one another. But Gernsback refused to give publicity to this idea and it was another four years before Gillings saw his first fanzine. As a child, he had produced a handwritten, illustrated publication, *Merry-Go-Round Magazine*, that lasted seven issues, acquired ten readers, and failed to complete its serial story, "2000 A.D." "I had my heart set on becoming a magazine editor, and here was a field which fascinated me and remained uncultivated in this country," Gillings remembers. His fanac was of a slightly different nature from that of most fans, since much of it was intended to stir up a demand for science fiction among Britishers. Then he "made it my

Walter A. Gillings

mission in life to persuade publishers to pay more attention to science fiction's development and to exploit its possibilities." He interested Fodham's Press in 1935 in a proposed prozine that was to be known as *Tomorrow— Magazine of the Future*, with eighty photogravure pages and much emphasis on science articles and movies about the future. The publishers decided to give priority to other ventures. Gillings tackled George Newnes, Ltd., then imitating the American pulp chain idea, with no immediate result. Simultaneously, he and John Russell Fearn were planning a British equivalent of

Fantasy Magazine. It was to be called *Future Fiction*. This emerged eventually as Gillings' *Scientifiction*, still one of the most ambitious fanzines in history. Its contents were sercon. There were interviews with Fearn, Eric Frank Russell, and Festus Pragnell, it took great interest in Campbell's future plans for his prozines, and it ran photographs of rocket experiments. Eventually this merged with an even more upper-class venture, *Tomorrow*. The dreams of professionalism finally turned into reality when Gillings became editor of *Tales of Wonder*, the first of whose sixteen issues appeared in June, 1937. It emphasized reprints, but many pros and fans made their first write-for-pay appearances in its pages. World's Work, Ltd., dropped it when paper controls grew severe during the war and the publishers wanted its paper for more popular pulps in the chain. Gillings, who retained little of his fannishness after the *Tales of Wonder* venture, and had engaged in several bitter vendettas, worked after the war as a Fleet Street news editor, launched three other publications, and kept on reading and writing science fiction.

12. Ted Carnell

The tall, dark, and handsome Ted Carnell became the second Britisher to make the transition to professional editor. Curiously, the man whom he followed in the trade was one of his biggest rivals for leadership in British fandom's early days. Born in Plumstead, London, in 1912, Carnell discovered magazine science fiction in the early twenties when the *Boys' Magazine* published serials about Venus and Mars. He had loved Verne when he was only eight years old. Carnell found his first genuine prozine in the form of the Fall, 1929, *Science Wonder Quarterly*. He haunted bookstalls for years to come, hunting more of those thruppenny ballast items. Around 1935, Carnell began to do something more than read science fiction. He became a correspondent of Brooklyn's George Gordon Clark, holder of the Number One card in the Science Fiction League, after choosing Clark's name at random from a prozine letter column. Carnell soon became a correspondent of other American fans, wrote a column for Clark's *Brooklyn Reporter*, was asked for more material by Claire Beck for *Science Fiction Critic*, and started his "London Calling" column for Dan McPhail's pioneer newszine, *Science Fiction News*, in 1935 and 1936. Through Clark's help, Carnell discovered the beginnings of British fandom, contacting first Les Johnson of Liverpool, treasurer of the British Interplanetary Society. Carnell was then working for a printing firm in London, where he soon helped to produce the BIS *Journal*, sending out an issue or two through FAPA.

Carnell's first personal contact with fans came when he met Johnson and the half-fan, half-pro Eric Frank Russell. Years later, he recalled vividly that

Liverpool Street Station was the site of the great rendezvous. The trio proceeded to Ilford, where they met Walter Gillings. From this session grew much of early British fandom. In 1937 the Leeds fans formed an SFL chapter, and Carnell, with Gillings and Arthur C. Clarke, attended the first real British con, from which the Science Fiction Association evolved. Carnell was shy enough to act tongue-tied during the con, in curious contrast to the easy confidence with which he moved through most of the later British fan gatherings. Carnell soon became editor of both the *Journal* and the *Bulletin* of the BIS. Then in 1938 he was treasurer of the

John (Ted) Carnell

SFA, and with Johnson launched as a hobby a magazine trading enterprise, Science Fiction Service, that turned into a worldwide business.

Two important things happened in 1939. Carnell began publishing his first full-size fanzine, *Novae Terrae*. He took over that magazine from Maurice K. Hanson, who helped him to publish it in an attic. On June 17, Carnell married a Plumstead girl, Irene Clock. Early in 1940 Carnell tried to start a British prozine, but found war conditions too great a barrier. The venture was attempted in collaboration with Gillings. Harry Turner did the cover lettering for the magazine, whose title was to be *New Worlds*. C. S. Youd, John Burke, and Dave McIlwain, not yet prosperous writers, were among the fans who were asked to contribute stories. On the ominous date of February 13, there was a luncheon to celebrate the new prozine, topped by the announcement that the magazine would sponsor the SFA. But later in February, the publishing firm's directorate began to squabble among themselves. The project collapsed in March. Another company showed interest but could not get enough paper under wartime restrictions.

Carnell served in the Royal Artillery during the conflict, entering the service on September 30, 1940. Friends in the United States helped to keep his prozine file up to date. Carnell played in dance bands, saw duty at various points in Europe and Africa, and published in 1943 his last fanzine, *Sands of Time*, a rider to *Futurian War Digest*. He kept his hand in professional matters, by becoming British representative for many semi-pro book publishers like Fantasy Press, Prime Press, Shasta, FPCI, and Hadley. After peace returned, Frank Edward Arnold introduced him in 1946 to the directors of Pendulum Publications. They worked out a new plan to produce a prozine called *New Worlds*. Its first issue appeared in July, 1946, at the high price of two bob for 64 pages. Ackerman was American agent. After three issues, the publisher gave up. But two years later, when the first big British convention occurred in the form of the London Whitcon, Carnell offered fans the opportunity to try yet again the *New Worlds* project. A company floated limited capital shares for science fiction enthusiasts. Conferences in the White Horse Tavern produced the third and successful start for *New Worlds*, which Carnell edited until 1964.

13. American Fans as Editors

In the United States, most of the favorite prozine editors, including Tremaine, Campbell, Gold, and Boucher, had no fannish careers before taking over the prozines. If the fans did not do as brilliantly as mundane people in the editorial chairs, those who tackled the duties nevertheless helped to speed up the process of turning more fans into writers. Friendship or admiration for writing abilities caused a number of fans-become-editors to buy vast quantities of fiction from their former buddies in fandom. Editors everywhere are prone to pay more attention to the known writers, and introductory appearances in a pal's prozine helped many a fan to sell to other editors.

Sadly, many editors who had been fans developed a nasty habit of snapping peevishly at the field that had nurtured them, sometimes immediately after their transfiguration. Hornig was fairly mild in this respect. He scolded fans only occasionally about such things as their way of obtaining prozines second-handedly: "The fans who make demands should be willing to cooperate by purchasing the magazines regularly and really trying to get others to buy them," he said. It is a curious contrast to the recent reiteration by prozine editors of the insignificant part of total circulation provided by the purchases of active fans. Lowndes was more severe, soon after he became a professional editor: "Nearly all of us editors are wondering why the letters from readers and fans, particularly, seem to be so scarce today. It's really appalling at times. In comparison to the fan mail Dr. Sloane, Tremaine, and Hornig used to receive, the letters just barely scratch our consciousness. That can't be laid to a lapse of quality in the mags, because even when the Sloane *Amazing* was at its lowest ebb, it still received mail by the sack. Two explanations have occurred to me: one, so many titles that the mail has to be spread out more; two, the real fans are too busy writing letters to fanzines and articles for same, or putting out their own fanzines, to spare criticisms for such unimportant things as the pros." That was in 1941. Eighteen years later, Lowndes was still marveling at the same phenomenon: He said that new readers turning into fans, an element "which heretofore kept the letter column and the lobby for fan departments in science fiction magazines alive, now seem to be going directly to the later stage of development, the fan writing and publishing stage, which usually doesn't leave time for letter-hacking to the dirty promags." As early as 1939, Palmer was quoted in a fanzine article as claiming that those who clipped coupons from *Amazing Stories* to vote on their preferences gave different opinions from those who were fannish enough to write letters describing their favorite stories. From this, he concluded, the fans were a minority group that made the most noise.

14. Fans Into Writers

The transition from fanzine contributor to science fiction writer has been occurring almost from the start of fandom. In the earliest days, there were such cases as David R. Daniels, who had a story published in *Fantasy Magazine*, then began selling to the prozines in the few intervening years before his suicide. J. Francis Hatch first broke into print in the same fanzine manner. Chester D. Cuthbert and Henry Hasse were among the others who became prozine authors after fanzine acceptances of their material. But it would have been hard to trace down more than a dozen such cases before 1938 or thereabouts. After that, the list grew at the rate of a dozen or more transitions each year, as the number of markets increased, fandom got larger, fans grew older and more skilled, and more fans entered a position that permitted them to favor the work of other fans. The success stories of several fans who made substantial sums from professional sales are told in other chapters. Several of the fans who became prozine editors made that transition with an intermediate fiction-selling incarnation. *Astounding*'s "Probability Zero" department was the spot where a remarkable number of fans made sales, from 1942 through 1944. By 1946, Norm Willmorth could count more than sixty fans who were earning at least part of their living out of science fiction.

In all honesty, it must be remembered that these fans did not find riches of imposing proportions deriving from their prohood. When the prozine really did pay money for stories, it might give only one-half cent per word or less, and then complain if it discovered that the story in question had once seen fanzine publication. *Astounding, Amazing,* and a few other titles that were difficult for fans to hit paid better. Most prozines paid only $5.00 for an interior illustration in 1940. The editors themselves did not get rich with dizzying rapidity. One former fan reportedly earned $15.00 per week for editing a prozine, until in a burst of inspiration he arranged for the discharge of his office boy, took over that youth's duties, and got his salary doubled as a result. A prominent fan claimed that he had been offered the post of editor of four magazines, two of which were devoted to science fiction, and refused because he was already earning more than the $65.00 per week offered him. This was during World War II. Even later in the decade, when word rates rose and there were many more markets, the beginning pro envied the sort of money paid to elevator operators. E. Everett Evans, who became a successful writer after a particularly long struggle that lasted many years, claimed that in only one year up to 1954 did his expenses for paper, carbons, ribbons, postage, and agenting fees total less than his income from sales.

Larry Shaw's remarks typify the deglamorized status that prodom eventually assumed after fans had discovered the truth about it: "Becoming a pro is not the same as achieving maturity; it is simply getting a job. It is not essentially different from becoming a shoe salesman, a government worker, or a newspaper man. Prodom often seems to be full of nothing but people who are trying to knife each other in the back. Most fans tire of fandom fairly rapidly; becoming a pro may accelerate the process, but not enough to be tremendously important. Other fans don't, and continue their romance with fandom indefinitely." And by the end of the forties, most fans who made some professional sales did not try to earn a living out of science fiction, and some of them stopped selling soon enough to produce a belief that they had merely wanted to prove their ability to make the sales. Perhaps some of them saw the statistics provided by the census of 1950: for the 16,184 persons in the nation who listed author as occupation, the average income was $3,000 per year, compared with $3,500 annually for the typical elevator operator.

One curious manner in which the professional urge expressed itself among fans consisted of occasionally successful efforts to become agents with few or none of the qualifications normally associated with the profession. The precedent had been set by Mort Weisinger and Julius Schwartz, who formed Solar Sales Service in the middle of 1934 as the first agency specializing in science fiction. Later, New York fans, living close to most prozine editorial offices, were particularly prone to announce themselves as agents just after one or two sales of their own fiction, augmented by a status of being on speaking terms with at least one prozine editor. We find Pohl beginning a literary agency in 1939 and turning it over to Lowndes a year later. As Fantastory Sales Service, it claimed credit for selling or helping to sell the first stories for Dick Wilson, C. M. Kornbluth, Oliver Saari, Sam Moskowitz, Damon Knight, and Milton Rothman. Moskowitz and James Taurasi formed a literary agency late in 1940, when Moskowitz sold his first story to *Comet* and Taurasi sold a drawing to the same publication.

15. Erle Korshak and Shasta Publishers

Other fans tried to make their hobby pay off by turning into dealers in science fiction or fantasy materials. Erle Korshak's case history would be typical if it weren't so extreme. This Chicago fan issued a casual single-sheet listing in 1938 of some prozines and fourteen books that he wanted to sell. Ten years later, we find him as a full-time dealer with a staff of ten assistants, some of whom had resounding titles, like general manager Ted Dikty, bibliographer Eric Freyor, and English representative Ted Carnell. Korshak had a mailing list of 3,250 clients by 1948, and was well known in the general bookseller's field because he had formed a trade group, the Chicago Association of Bookdealers. Korshak swore that he knew personally each of the 418 second-hand book and magazine stores in Chicago.

But few ventured into dealing on this scale and many entered the profession in a small way. The result was a great deal of inflation in the science fiction and fantasy market. Fans with small dealer operations bought at retail and added a generous profit, the cost of postage, and packing fees to obtain a selling price. A science fiction hardcover novel that failed to sell would be dumped as remainders onto dime store counters throughout the nation for 29¢ or so a copy. A month later, as certain as sin, it would appear on the lists of offerings of a dozen fan dealers at prices ranging from $1.00 to $3.00. Moskowitz led a crusade that had partial success in breaking up the artificially exalted prices. He wrote in 1945 about the "hand-rubbing pack of new and old book dealers, fully acquainted with the situation and ready to capitalize on it. *The Outsider and Others* by H. P. Lovecraft is at present selling for $50.00 a copy. Almost every dealer in the country of any knowhow has heard of it. And by a peculiar coincidence, a third of the big dealers I meet seem to have a copy or copies. But do you realize that the value isn't real? That it's artificially built up through carefully calculated propaganda? Do you realize that in the space of a year and a half the value of the book has supposedly jumped from $5.00 to $50.00?" Moskowitz pointed out that a book virtually unobtainable by dealers, the Futile Press edition of Lovecraft's *Commonplace Book*, was selling for quite modest prices, despite the fact that it had been published in only a 75-copy edition.

Still another way in which fans lost their amateur status was through the book publishing field. Sometimes these books weren't very professional-looking, but they usually charged extremely professional prices. An example of semi-pro publishing might be taken from another venture with which Korshak was associated. This was Shasta Publishers, a Chicago firm formed by Korshak, Mark Reinsberg, and Ted Dikty. It planned to produce serious works about fantasy and science fiction. Everett Bleiler of the University of Chicago headed the first project, compiling the *Checklist of Fantastic Literature*. When published in the late forties, this was found to be a first-rate accomplishment: a listing of more than 5,000 titles, well-indexed, with essays by Korshak and Bleiler on relevant subjects. Ackerman called it "the greatest single contribution ever made to the field of fantasy enjoyment." Some seventy persons helped to put it together, starting with listings of the holdings of major collections, then seeking help from other experts, the Library of Congress, and the British Museum. It had a press run of 2,000 copies and the enormous price for the day of $6.00. The firm grew fast after this beginning. By the end of the decade, it possessed headquarters in the basement of an apartment hotel that also housed Korshak's second-hand business, it had two part-time employees, and it had customers on four continents. But the original intent had been modified to permit publication of noted books like Campbell's *Who Goes There?*, de Camp's *Wheels of If*, and Hubbard's *Slaves of Sleep*. Then it ran out of steam. Most of the other semi-pro firms experienced a similar high-purposed start, temporary success, and final petering-out. This might have been prophesied because it was inevitable that all the famous works would be reprinted after a few years. The firms were operating on too small a scale to pay sufficiently to obtain first-rate new novels, and the big publishers were now interested enough in science fiction to snap up most of the successful works currently appearing in the prozines.

16. Fans Into Artists

The failure of fans to become professional artists in substantial quantities may be traced to several factors. Fanzines have always been word-oriented rather than picture-oriented, so have prozine letter columns, and fanzines have been less attractive to the individual who is handier with the sketching pencil than with the typewriter. The prozines found it more convenient to work with artists residing within convenient distance of publication offices, a situation that tended to restrict the ambitions of fan artists in far-off parts of the nation. Perhaps fandom lost some good artists early through the difficulty of decently reproducing many techniques on the mimeograph or hecto-graph.

But the first big breakthrough into prodom by a fan was a blockbuster. Joe Shuster was drawing pictures for an uninteresting fanzine published by Jerome Siegel in the earliest years of organized fandom. *Science Fiction* was the title. It saw five issues, starting in 1932. Siegel had ambitions of collaborating on a comic strip even then, but was discouraged by syndicate editors who warned that he would need an artist of professional caliber. The following year, Siegel and Shuster submitted to *Wonder Stories* a cartoon strip adaptation of a piece of fiction, and got it back with the pronouncement that it was "mechanically inadvisable." The pair got a new idea, that of a remarkably strong visitor from another planet. *Superman*, by 1940, had a circulation of 1,300,000 copies in its comic book incarnation.

A few other fans began to make part or all of their living from art in more subdued manner. Ronald Clyne became most famous as a record-jacket artist. His biggest fannish accomplishment had been to arrange for a reprint of Wallace Smith's illustrations to Ben Hecht's *Fantazius Mallare* in 1944, from which he copied ten of the drawings. Some of the New York fans, such as Taurasi and John Giunta, made occasional sales to prozines or began illustrating for the comic books. A scattering of other artists became prominent to some extent in fandom after they had become professional successes. The late Hannes Bok, for instance, was a Bradbury protégé but unknown in fandom aside from his drawings in Bradbury fanzines, until he began drawing for *Weird Tales*. Ed Emshwiller has become such a friendly fixture at conventions that it is easy to forget that he was not a fan while in the egg stage. British fan Harry Turner became a professional success in his own land, after drawing the finest illustrations that fandom produced in the late thirties. Richard Bergeron, who disappeared from fandom for a long time, reappeared after he had become successful in the commercial art field. But it seems probable that the artistic equivalent of fandom's literary invasion of prodom must wait until the nation's professional publishers turn to the mimeograph as their medium of reproduction.

Hannes Bok

5. THE SECOND AND THIRD WORLDCONS

1. Chicon I, 1940

Chicago was the second largest city in the nation, but it possessed a young and tiny fan colony when Chicon planning began. Jack Darrow's letter-hacking in the early prozine years had made the city famous. But he was never one for fanac of other sorts and subsided as a letter writer when a more complicated approach than a listing of likes and dislikes began to dominate letter columns. Mark Reinsberg and Richard Meyer, just emerging from the newly hatched fannish eggs in 1937, looked up Darrow and found him totally inactive, although Reinsberg and Erle Korshak persuaded him to accompany them to the Nycon of 1939.

The Ziff-Davis purchase of *Amazing Stories* and an accident of school district lines combined to create the Chicago fandom that existed just before the Chicon. Palmer as a new editor was friendly with fans who were nice to him, and he was generous with original illustrations and manuscripts. Many of his stable of authors and artists resided in Chicago, making it an exciting city for fans who wanted to see real live pros. Reinsberg, Meyer, Korshak, W. Lawrence Hamling, and Chester S. Geier all attended the same high school. They entered fandom at about the same time. They formed such a diligent bunch of fans that one of Palmer's pros, Robert Moore Williams, got soured on fandom and didn't turn sweet again for almost a quarter of a century.

Reinsberg's *Ad Astra* was the first major fanzine of its day in Chicago. It had a greater effect on the most famous science fiction character than it had on fandom as a whole. Reinsberg interviewed Dick Calkins, one of the creators of Buck Rogers, for an article for his fanzine. Reinsberg suggested that it was time to dispose of Killer Kane, Buck's ancient nemesis. Calkins immediately put this suggestion into reality in the comic strip.

There were a few dry runs for the Chicon. A science fiction conference, billed as the city's third, was held in April, 1940, when Reinsberg and Korshak went to nearby Bloomington, Illinois, to see Tucker and Sully Roberds. They stayed four days, planning for the Illini Fantasy Fictioneers. The facts about the first two Chicago conferences have been buried under detritus of the fannish past for so long that they may have rotted away into nothingness. Without the help of a strong local organization, Chicago's fans succeeded in feuding even before the convention, establishing a pre-con tradition that plagued a number of later events. Tucker, who got caught in the middle, described conditions in late 1939 and early 1940 as "a long, running, dirty fight that just about wrecked the old Chicon."

L. to r.: Bob Tucker, Walt Marconette, Mark Reinsberg, and Richard Meyer.

The Illini Fantasy Fictioneers was a statewide group organized to sponsor the worldcon, and accepting memberships throughout the nation. It came into being in mid-1939 in Bloomington with Tucker as director, Meyer as secretary-treasurer, Korshak as advisor, Sully Roberds as publicity director, and Reinsberg as chairman of the convention committee. This group staged several meetings and called the meetings conferences. *The Fantasy Fictioneer* was published as an official organ. Sykora and Moskowitz, trading as New Fandom, charged that the IFF spurned their offers of help. "Stop this foolishness before it harms the Chicon," the Fantasy Fictioneers told the New Yorkers, rejecting any part of that city's factionalism and hatreds.

In this stone age of fandom, worldcons were conducted on the smallest possible budgets, instead of aiming for new spending records. This first Chicon ran up an expense total of $145. This was somewhat less than the sum that the third Chicon in 1962 spent on postage stamps or on the band for the masquerade ball at which very few people danced. The Illini Fantasy Fictioneers set dues just high enough to cover publishing costs. But the convention committee haggled and finagled the hotel in a remarkable manner. They got free meeting rooms in return for staging a banquet at which they needed to guarantee only fifty dinners at one dollar each. It cost only $40 to publish the program booklet, less than the $70 bill the first Nycon ran up for this purpose. The convention dispensed with the use of a paid speaker. The result was a budget barely more than half the $270 spent the previous year by the Nycon. The Chicon kept its financial facts straight, down to the smallest item. This was one cent, paid by Tucker to Cyril Kornbluth as a bribe to prevent the acquisition of a hotfoot. It is hard to imagine the recent convention committees stooping to the sensible depths of selling soft drinks and sandwiches to hungry delegates in order to augment the income, as the Chicon officials did.

Convention officers were Reinsberg, who got the chairmanship after a bitter struggle with Hamling, who claimed that he'd been elected to the post; Roberds, who edited the official publication; Korshak, as executive advisor; and Tucker, as director of the IFF. They chose the Hotel Chicagoan for the event. Fans who entered its lobby found a sign directing them to the second floor, where you could buy for three cents an autograph booklet from Morojo. The convention hall seated 200 persons, and possessed a deep red rug that several fans found more useful for sleeping purposes than as a soft object on which to stand. Cover paintings were displayed about the convention hall, until they were sold at auction. Adjoining were the banquet and dressing rooms.

Among the first to arrive were Olon Wiggins and Lew Martin, who made the trip from Denver in thirty hours by courtesy of several boxcars. A fellow traveler failed to complete his journey in a bloody manner, but he wasn't a fan. The longest journeys were those of Paul Freehafer, Acker-

Front: Morojo, Richard Meyer. Back, l. to r.: Erle Korshak, Mark Reinsberg, Forry Ackerman, Paul Freehafer.

man, Morojo, and Pogo, who rode the Santa Fe in more comfortable style from Los Angeles. Art Widner and Earl Singleton persuaded the Skylark of Foo, an ancient auto, to make the trip all the way from Boston. All but two of the Futurians from New York were on hand, surviving an overturned auto with no casualties except a cut over one eye of Robert W. Lowndes. Others hitchhiked, but nobody was prosperous enough to use airplanes as a means of travel. The Literature, Science and Hobbies Club of Decker, Indiana, turned out in full force and brought along Oscar, the skeleton mascot, who was given a chair and a copy of *Amazing Stories* behind the speaker's stand.

E. Everett Evans was there because his son had wanted to go, couldn't make it, and sent his father, with far-reaching effects on fandom's future. Mr. and Mrs. Rich Frank combined a honeymoon with attendance at the worldcon. Lots of pros were on hand, mainly from Chicago and immediate surroundings: Charles Tanner, Ross Rocklynne, David Wright O'Brien, Ralph Milne Farley, Otto Binder, Mort Weisinger, Robert Moore Williams, Don Wilcox, and Jerry Siegel. One count of attendees showed a dozen New Yorkers, five Los Angelenos, three Washingtonians, and three New Englanders. Noticeably absent were two of Chicago's best known fans, Jack Darrow and Trudy Hemkin. It was a fairly good showing, in view of the tender years of many fans, the chronic unemployment of lots of major fans, the distance between Chicago and major fan centers, and the bad taste lingering in many mouths from the Nycon "exclusion act" (by which Wollheim, Lowndes, Kornbluth, Jack Gillespie, Pohl, and Michel were banned from the convention because of their opposition to the Moskowitz-Sykora-Taurasi axis).

Pre-convention activities included much chatter in the Lab, the basement headquarters of Meyer, Reinsberg, and Korshak, and at the YMCA where the thriftier fans stayed. In the hotel itself, Room 689 became the first in an interminable series of famous worldcon hotel rooms to which almost everyone gravitated. It was Morojo's room, Pogo and Gertrude Kuslan helped serve as hostesses, and it reminded one visitor of the famous Marx Brothers stateroom. One count showed fifty fans inside simultaneously. On the other hand, a lost worldcon art is that of greeting visitors from other cities at the terminals. This was done at Chicago's bus depot by up to a dozen local fans, some carrying signs, others experimenting with esp cards while awaiting the arrival of such notables as Ted Dikty and Fred Shroyer. A streetcar rider saw a group of costumed fans parading on Madison Street, jumped off to chat with Ackerman whom he somehow recognized, then dashed away without leaving his name. Reinsberg, Korshak, and Tucker propelled a pushcart several blocks from the Ziff-Davis office to their car, after Palmer gave them more than 200 original illustrations and 300 copies of *Amazing Stories* for convention use. Fans with fancy dress showed no reluctance to wear it outdoors.

Sunday morning has been a dead spot in most recent conventions. The Chicago committee brazenly began the Chicon at that time. No formal events occurred that morning, but fans were told to be in the convention hall for talking, purchasing, and staring. The program itself began at 1:30 p.m. on Sunday, September 1, 1940, with 125 fans registered and a few stowaways. Tucker called the convention to order and welcomed the fans. Meyer gave the report of the convention committee. Then Reinsberg began to read his speech, "One Year of Fan Progress." He became ill midway, a nervous reaction that has kept turning up at opening sessions of worldcons. Korshak took over with a report of the resolutions committee.

2. Edward E. Smith: "What Does This Convention Mean?"

E. E. Smith was the star speaker at this first session. In years to come, he became one of the most familiar and best-loved pros at worldcons. But few fans knew him in 1940 as anything more than a nebulous legend who had written the "Skylark" and "Lensman" novels. He had made his first appearance up in Morojo's room, bringing along his wife Jeannie and daughter Clarrissa. His talk's topic was: "What Does This Convention Mean?" The speech may have had a stronger effect on fan history than generally recognized. He spoke of matters that soon became major forces and chronic points of argument in fandom. Smith asked why fans spend their money to attend their conventions, unlike other convention-goers who have their trips financed, as employees or official delegates of firms or organizations. Then he tussled with the nature and definitions of science fiction: he called it muddy thinking to call science fiction "escape literature," for all literature is escapist, and he denied that it is light literature, for many of its stories require or deserve three or four readings for full value. Smith recognized fantasy fiction as closely akin to science fiction, when stripped of superficial differences. He called Merritt's and Campbell's developments of stories equally logical, given the authors' premises.

"The casual reader does not understand science fiction, does not have sufficient imagination or depth and breadth of vision to grasp it, and hence does not like it," Smith said. "What brings us together and underlies this convention is a fundamental unity of mind. We are imaginative, with a tempered, analytical imaginativeness which fairy tales will not satisfy. We are critical. We are fastidious. We have a mental grasp and scope which do not find sufficient substance in stereotypes, in the cut and dried. Science fiction fans form a group unparalleled in history, in our close-knit although informal organization, in our strong likes and dislikes, in our partisanships and our loyalties. The necessity of possessing what I may call the science-fantasy mind does now and probably always will limit our number to a very small fraction of the total population. In these personal meetings, there is a depth of satisfaction, a height of fellowship which no one who has never experienced it can even partially understand."

He got an ovation from fans unimpaired by any prescience about the purposes to which that philosophy would be put in the decades to come.

Edward E. Smith, Ph.D.

The afternoon session included introduction of fans and an estimate that three-fourths of the attendees had traveled more than a hundred miles to be present. Most of the pros spoke briefly: Farley, Weisinger, Siegel, Binder, Rocklynne, Tanner, Wilcox, O'Brien, and Donald Bern. Palmer described an editor's problems. Reinsberg had recovered and completed his talk. Then Tucker screened *Monsters of the Moon*, a film that he and Roberds had pasted together from various sources. This whacky Martian invasion pastiche was destined to cling tenaciously to its unholy life, bobbing up over the years at the most unexpected times when fans had congregated. A little later, the Indiana Fantasy Association staged a meeting. Ted Dikty was named its director and talked about its history.

3. Masquerade and Banquet

The masquerade Sunday evening contained many fannish props that have survived through the years. Water pistols were unholstered, and weapons described as dart guns—almost certainly primitive plonkers—were in use. "Filksong" was a term that had not yet been invented, but songs were sung that consisted of new lyrics with a science fiction theme set to familiar tunes. And the masquerade didn't start until 9:00 p.m., faithful to the tradition that convention events may not proceed on schedule.

Speer and Rothman were masters of ceremonies. Speer attempted to promote a word game, in which an intelligible sentence was built up by answering correctly a science fiction quiz, but this was too intellectual for the time and place. Costumed fans walked one by one to the dais, and identified the characters they represented. Dave Kyle won first prize as Ming the Merciless, Emperor of Mongo. The adjective recurred to fans in his connection at a much later convention. Lowndes in a pale orange robe took second award, as the Bar Senestro, of *The Blind Spot*. Leslie Perri had originally made the costume for Wollheim. Morojo and Ackerman, dressed as at the Nycon, put on a skit representing people of the future, and placed third. E. E. Smith, Rocklynne, and Tucker were judges.

Others in costume included Kornbluth, as the invisible man; George Tullis as Johnny Black, de Camp's humanized bear; Pogo as the High Priestess of FooFoo, an early manifestation of pure faanishness; Elmer Perdue and Earl Singleton as competing Jurgens; Rothman as a typical scientist; Siegel, in normal garb, representing his famous character not yet stripped down for action; Speer, Korshak, and Reinsberg, all dressed as Buck Rogers; Smith, not competing but in black to represent Northwest Smith; his daughter Honey as Nurse MacDougall, the "Lensman" novel heroine whom she had inspired; Tucker as Hoy Ping Pong; and a late improvisation that was a smash hit, Widner as Giles Habibula, constructed out of Pogo's hat, Trudy Kuslan's pillow, and an anonymous bartender's wine bottle.

Korshak conducted auctioneering that same night. Prices will be hard on the nerves of contemporary collectors. Finlay's "Darkness and Dawn" cover from *Famous Fantastic Mysteries* went for a bit over $5 to Rich Frank. A Paul oil, depicting a Martian, brought about the same price, and his "Cat Women of Ganymede" went for $3.50 to Widner. Tanner got the Paul cover from *Fantastic Adventures* for "Blue Tropics" for only a dollar. The auction netted about $120.

There was also a skit that night, in which Morojo depicted the ingenue, Ackerman was a monster, and Reinsberg was the rescuing hero.

The convention got a good press from Chicago's dailies. Some of the masqueraders had walked en masse to two newspaper offices Saturday night, to encourage the reporters to do their best. But the custom of going outside the hotel in masquerade outfits suffered a blow just after the party that proved fatal. Speer, in a golden radio helmet, flying belt vest, helium gun, and shorts, attracted the attention of a policeman. The officer first threatened to call a patrol wagon, then tossed in a heretical manner several auction originals to the street, and simmered down only when Speer proved his identity and business by means of cards showing him to be a federal employee.

Most of the drinking at this Chicon occurred outside the hotel, in a boite at Eighth and Wabash, close to the YMCA Hotel. The only events that have been preserved for future generations were Ackerman's refusal to drink a bottle of soda pop, on the grounds that it might be a trick to end his career as a teetotaler, and Lowndes somehow managing to get his foot stuck in a spittoon.

The convention's second-day attendance was virtually as large as on opening day. This was a surprise, because only half of the first nighters had had the heart to go back on the second day of the Nycon. The morning's program was devoted mainly to a private meeting of the sponsoring IFF. This group was formally dissolved as a national body, after it had voted to give the profits from the Chicon to the convention committee. The afternoon business session contained much squabbling about the site for the 1941 convention. New York, Cleveland, Chicago, and Denver offered themselves. Los Angeles and Philadelphia were wooed but declined hastily. Jack Chapman Miske, who surprised the convention by being less formidable than his paper personality, said that his hometown, Cleveland, or Cincinnati would host the event, if no other city were found acceptable. Olon F. Wiggins then heard his bid for Denver accepted, after considerable debate. There were warnings that a convention so far west of the frontier wouldn't be well-attended, but the Futurian offer to put on another Nycon seemed to delegates even less likely to draw well.

The banquet that night had food in quantities approximating the cost of the meal. But good fellowship reigned. Korshak was master of ceremonies, reintroducing everyone. E. E. Smith gave an informal and unimportant talk. There were 62 fans around the U-shaped table, with the Smith family at its head. Oscar deadheaded at the meal.

Officially, the convention ended that night. Fans blinked in astonishment as the significance of this conclusion became apparent. There had been no serious fusses at this second worldcon and none of the overt feuding that had spoiled conferences in Philadelphia. Several hatchets were also buried in the course of the Chicon, never again to rise above the surface. Miske, Wollheim's only contemporary rival for getting involved in fannish fusses, marveled: "There seemed to be a strange peace reigning in fandom. Everyone seemed willing to be fair and aboveboard, desiring only to have a good time, so dozens of petty feuds were forgotten forever." Symbolic was the 2 a.m. escort that took Rothman from the YMCA to the railroad station. About fifty fans formed a college-type snakeline, sang everything from "He's a Jolly Good Fellow" to "The Internationale," picked up stragglers from saloons, and enjoyed every step of the fifteen-block trip. But a tradition died on Tuesday, September 3rd. The annual fannish softball game was scheduled for that day, with Chicagoans to battle a team directed by Art Widner. Unpreparedness among the Illini forced its cancellation, and a bunch of fans went instead to Chicago's Field Museum of Natural History.

Left to right: Ross Rocklynne, Dale Tarr, Trudy Kuslan, Bob Tucker, Walt Liebscher, Morojo, Erle Korshak, Forrest J Ackerman, Julius Unger, Bob Madle, Robert Thompson, and the Field Museum.

4. Newarkon

One of the decisive events in fan history occurred between the Chicon and the Denver world convention of 1941, the Denvention. There is no real reason why fandom should have just one worldcon each year. Fraternal orders and trade associations limit themselves to a single national convention because it is a place where officers are chosen, policy is settled, and long trips by delegates aren't a problem because the delegates don't pay their own expenses. Fandom's worldcons are different: primarily social gatherings, with a seasoning of program sprinkled on the surface, and an opportunity for filthy pros to swing a few deals between drinks. There is no compelling reason why fandom should not have two or three worldcons annually, one for each major section of the nation. The loss in attendance at any given con would be minimal, compared with the prospective attendance if a unique worldcon were scheduled there, since ninety per cent or more of a worldcon's attendance normally comes from the host third of the nation, and prominent pros are distributed impartially over the entire nation for use as speakers and guests of honor.

Some of these thoughts may have occurred during the jockeying that went on between the Chicon and the Denvention. There were few active fans within 500 miles of Denver. Some eastern fans couldn't understand why they should travel a long way to the worldcon for the second straight year. So a Newarkon was announced. Olon Wiggins, Denver's best-known fan, immediately accepted the opportunity to indulge in the latest in an interminable series of fusses with an old sparring partner, Sam Moskowitz. This argument failed to survive its birth, when the embarrassed Wiggins learned that James V. Taurasi, not Moskowitz, was pushing a Newarkon.

Typical publicity for the Newarkon revealed the philosophy behind the plan: "Are you from the East? If you are, I doubt if you will ever get together enough money to travel to the Denvention, so for that reason we Eastern fans are planning to have our own convention in Newark. It will be entirely independent of the Denvention, as far as the date goes." Moskowitz was certainly not opposed to this rival convention. At the August 15, 1940, Newark Science Fiction League meeting, before the Chicon, he had urged an effort to obtain the 1941 convention for Newark. After the Chicon, at the September 19th meeting of the NSFL, Moskowitz suggested the issuance of feelers to determine opinions on a Newark convention, despite Denver's successful bid. Less than a month later, Taurasi had proposed calling the Newark event a conference rather than a convention, a semantic formality that helped to persuade Moskowitz of the validity of the idea. News about the competing conventions appeared in the October issue of Gerry de la Ree's *Stf Scout*, and a hundred postal cards were sent out to spread the news. Reaction was violent. The Futurians predicted that prozine editors would not support a Newark convention. At that fall's Phillycon, Rod Gaetz revealed that the Westwood, New Jersey, Solaroids had withdrawn any support from the Newarkon. Moskowitz soon told the NSFL that the Newarkon was cancelled. It was the closest fandom has ever come to getting away from the one worldcon per year schedule.

The Chicago group was solidly behind Denver. New Fandom had been listed as a sponsor for the Newark event, but this group was essentially Moskowitz, Taurasi, and Will Sykora. Some prozine editors were undecided about which event should get publicity. But Palmer threw the support of Ziff-Davis behind Denver. He was still popular enough to make this a significant move. So, only ten months after the Chicon, the Denvention occurred without competition.

5. Denvention, 1941

Denver didn't have a fandom with the manpower and professional resources that Chicago enjoyed. As late as 1940, some prominent fans had been certain that Denver possessed only one or two fans, and charged an attempt at a hoax when *The Alchemist* began to appear with such unknown names as Charles Hansen, Lew Martin, and Roy Hunt as editors, writers, and artists. They were real persons, but the city's fandom was so minute that there was little chance for factionalism to disturb preliminary work on the convention. Denver prepared for the worldcon just as Chicago had done, by organizing a statewide group as official sponsor. The Denver Science Fictioneers had organized in the spring of 1940, held a half-dozen meetings, then dissolved to be succeeded by the sponsoring Colorado Fantasy Society, formed immediately after the Chicon. Olon Wiggins was director, Lew Martin was secretary-treasurer, and Hunt was artist and editor. This group was national until the Denvention, after which it was destined to become a state organization. To keep fandom aware of convention plans, the club published the *CFS Review*, a newszine, and the *Denventioneer*, a combination fanzine that contained special small issues of such major publications as *VOM*, *Snide*, *Alchemist*, and *Fantasite*. Martin made an awesome sacrifice. He quit his job so he could devote his time solely to convention planning.

Lew Martin (left) and Olon Wiggins.

The program didn't begin until Independence Day of 1941, but the fans couldn't wait. By Wednesday, July 2nd, they had already begun to cluster around the Shirley-Savoy Hotel, where Robert A. Heinlein's fourth-floor room was the focal point. For the first time, a worldcon was preserved in more literal form than memories and the printed word. Walter J. Daugherty came from Los Angeles on his honeymoon, and brought both a bride and his disc recording equipment. On 65 records he caught much of the program and some more faanish matters such as chatter from private rooms, an account of experiences by those who lived through the Widneride, and Rothman and Liebscher playing boogie-woogie. Nine of those discs were devoted to Heinlein. He filled exactly the role that Smith had played the previous summer in Chicago. Fans came to marvel at a previously unknown man who was famed as a writer, and they left loving the whole man.

Attendance at convention sessions averaged seventy, better than was to be anticipated from fandom's current size and impoverished condition. Rusty Barron, then unknown to fandom, hitchhiked all the way from California. John Millard found his working hours preventing his attendance, so he quit his job and attended. Al McKeel drove for 22 hours without a break to get there on time. Chet Cohen showed up in a beard, not yet associated with fans. Yerke, Freehafer, and Morojo rotated at the wheel to make the trip from Los Angeles in 36 hours, remarkable for those pre-freeway days. For some reason, two fans unknown before and never heard from again, Elmer Meukel and Dave Dawson, made the long trip from Washington, D.C. There was one special feature to the Denvention: once a fan arrived at it he was likely to stay. Denver's street system made it quite impossible to leave the hotel for any length of time, because a walk of more than two blocks in any direction brought the fan back to the starting point, presumably with the help of a turntable on which this sector of the city was constructed.

After two days of talking and drinking, the convention began early on the afternoon of Friday, July 4th. Martin, Hunt, and Wiggins realized from listening to their own introductory remarks that they were not the sort of fans who should preside over a convention. Walt Daugherty came to the rescue and presided over much of what followed, although Wiggins retained the title of permanent chairman.

6. Robert A. Heinlein: "The Discovery of the Future"

The Guest of Honor was Robert A. Heinlein. His talk was entitled "The Discovery of the Future." He spoke for a significant half hour. "I think I know . . . why it is that we like science fiction primarily. It is not just for the adventure of the story itself . . . It is because science fiction has in it as its strongest factor the single thing that separates the human race from all other animals. . . . I refer to a quality that has been termed 'time-binding.' . . . It is a technical term invented by Alfred Korzybski and it refers to the fact that the human animal lives not only in the present but in the past and in the future. . . . The child-like person lives from day to day. The adult tries to plan for a year or two at least. Statesmen try to plan for maybe twenty years . . . There are a few institutions, longer than the lives of men, . . . who think not in terms of lifetimes, but in centuries. . . . Science fiction fans differ from most of the rest of the race by thinking in terms of racial magnitudes— not even centuries, but thousands of years. . . .

Robert A. Heinlein

"That is what science fiction consists of: Trying to figure out from the past and from the present what the future may be. And in that we are behaving like human beings." Heinlein credited fans with a better than average ability to avoid becoming unsane. And after his talk, he answered written questions. He urged fans to join political clubs, to become involved in community events. Asked about conscientious objectors in these early days of selective service, he declared that the nation is worth fighting for, particularly for its civil liberties. He declined to try to predict the far future on the basis of the safer extrapolations from the present to the near future.

"I've heard Wells, and now I've heard Heinlein," Ackerman said that day. He meant it as a compliment.

The party that evening included a masquerade. E. E. Evans took the first prize of $5.00 as a birdman from Rhea, apparently modeling the costume after a Paul cover. Daugherty was second, winning $3.00 as a Venusian space pilot in an elaborate costume and helmet. Ackerman took third money of $2.00 for his grotesque mask of contorted rubber, and a suggestion of the hunched back possessed by the Notre Dame inhabitant. Ray Harryhausen, a Los Angeles fan who later became famous as a producer of special effects for movies, designed the mask. Other costumes included Damon Knight as a sloppy John Star, complete with junior G-man badge; Bill Deutsch, issuing lifeline prophecies in a French accent; Kornbluth, posing as a mad scientist with a minimum of change in his physical appearance; Lowndes, as a zombie; Chet Cohen, using that beard for his prophet's role; and Mrs. Heinlein, whose semi-oriental dress represented Queen Niphar in Cabell's *Figures of Earth*.

Rothman was master of ceremonies, a duty that he wasn't told about and discovered only when he read his program book. Lowndes, Kornbluth, and Daugherty told stories to provide some entertainment. But many fans seemed content to look at Morojo, wearing an ugly mask as Akka from *The Moon Pool*; Widner, in another smash success, as Old Granny from *Slan*; or Heinlein himself, who claimed that he was Adam Stink, the world's most lifelike robot, in normal flesh and garb. The evening included the screening of the Beery-Love-Stone incarnation of *The Lost World*, accompanied by much kibitzing by the fans. They were marveling over the greater wonders at the convention, such as the fact that Daugherty would have been forced to pay $500 for the glass in his helmet if he hadn't salvaged it from a trash pile at an airplane factory, or the painstaking way in which each feather had been attached to the Evans costume. The Evans costume, with its entrancing cockeyed eyes on stalks, ended up as an auction feature, purchased by Morojo.

The next morning, the Colorado Fantasy Society was to meet. Only one faithful member, Rothman, showed up. The convention's business session had better luck in the afternoon. The convention approved the existence of the British Science Fiction Relief Society, an American organization in spite of its title, intended by John Cunningham to get science fiction publications across the ocean. Widner moved and Martin seconded the proposal that a city bidding for next year's convention should have at least one person of legal age in its sponsoring group. The motion failed. Ackerman gave a little talk to explain why he never gave talks. But he appended a coda to this formal speech, in which he told fans to send their publications to the Library of Amateur Journalism, at Philadelphia's Franklin Institute, and urged fanzine publishers to produce one more issue after a title's final issue, to carry letters of comment on that last one. Walt Liebscher gave a brief talk on falsifications in fandom, the content of which has become one with the song the sirens sang. Rothman got in a commercial for the Fantasy Amateur Press Association and revealed the results of that organization's election. Daugherty, after a talk on the importance of cooperation among fans, presented small engraved medallions that he had made for accomplishments by fans, a procedure that was received quite calmly, in contrast to the death and destruction that ensued when the same thing was proposed by George Willick many years later. Ackerman got one for his interest in and help to fans; Unger, for spreading news about fans; Wiggins, for the consistently best fanzine; Damon Knight, as publisher of the best humorous fanzine; and Roy Hunt, as the best fan artist. Daugherty picked the winners without help from others.

7. Business and Banquet

E. E. Evans gave the second important talk of the convention, one that was destined to have all sorts of alarming consequences and to put him overnight into the forefront of fandom. He said that fandom had emerged from swaddling clothing and should wear in its new adulthood the proper garb of a carefully planned program and cooperative work toward that goal. "Fandom must go ahead or it will retrogress," he asserted, adding that such progress would be best accomplished if fans agreed on a long-range program that they themselves drew up. The goals that Evans envisioned were a mite ambitious. One was to lift mere readers of science fiction from their squalor into the higher glory of fanhood. "Readers are only that. Fans are a higher, more far-looking group," Evans said. "It is up to us to get more readers, and then help turn them into eager, active fans." He thought that by uniting, fans could put sufficient pressure on prozines to cause publishers to abandon the satanic practice of using flash-drying inks on covers. Slow-drying inks, he explained, would not smudge the hands of collectors. Evans cited letters from Unger, Widner, and D. B. Thompson, who had proposed other major projects for fans.

Specifically, Evans proposed the appointment of a committee that would figure out a long-range program and would issue a report at the 1942 worldcon. In the meantime, he exhorted everyone to persuade as many persons as possible to read the prozines and then to transmute these new readers into true fans. He also spoke of the need to organize state federations of fans. Evans then offered a resolution that would cause the chairman of the meeting to appoint a five-member committee for planning. Rothman promptly offered an amendment that would cause the planning to be done by the recently organized National Fantasy Fan Federation. Widner spoke about the NFFF. Korshak countered with an eloquent plea for fannish anarchism. This produced a faint cheer from the back and a futile suggestion by Kornbluth to forget the whole pretentious mess. The resolution was altered by Evans to a motion that would give the NFFF the power to appoint the planning committee. It passed almost unanimously, although there was an undercurrent of dissatisfaction with that organization. Daugherty, for instance, spoke for those who believed that the NFFF should enroll anyone with any interest in science fiction, a major issue of the day. Widner defended the stand of those who would limit membership to fans with long records of active participation in the hobby.

The auction followed. There were fewer items offered than at Chicago, and the advent of war had made good-paying jobs easier to find, so bidding was brisker. A fine Bok interior brought a bit over $9.00, and a Paul cover of secondary merit sold for about the same figure. Finlay seemed to have the greatest favor among the purchasers, with a cover bringing the top price of the auction, $20.00, and an interior going for $10.00. Even the original of the cover for the souvenir booklet, by Hunt, was worth $6.50 to a bidder. Wollheim bristled ferociously when auctioneer Korshak asserted that the purchaser of a *Cosmic Stories* cover had paid more, when he bid $1.50, than the magazine publishers had paid the artist. With Gus Willmorth as the most active bidder, the forty items of art contributed by Wollheim, Lowndes, Fred Pohl, and Mary Gnaedinger brought a total of $110. In a private transaction, Evans paid $15.00 for Finlay's "The Metal Monster" cover. A skull that Korshak had worn to the costume party, and had almost gotten into a brawl over when he ventured onto a street with it in view, was auctioned, resold, and eventually given to the Daughertys as a wedding gift.

The final business session of the Denvention was scheduled for 1 p.m. on July 6th. The convention officials weren't among the ten fans who were on time. Someone remembered a statement in "The Wheels of If" to the effect that any member of a group has authority to call a meeting to order when no officers are in sight. So Kornbluth presided over a fake session. Rothman resolved that Yngvi was a louse, but Kornbluth overruled the motion on the grounds that the business session should not determine personal characteristics. Rothman had better acceptance of his next proposal: himself as winner of the $25.00 offered by *Comet* for the fan who had overcome the greatest hardship in connection with attending. Rothman had sat beside Madle for 1,500 miles. Nominated as the site for the next convention were Baltimore, Piccadilly Bomb Shelter No. Three, and Mariyoupa, the Russian city where Rothman's grandfather lived. The bomb shelter was chosen as the most pleasant of the three alternatives. Just as the group ruled that Rothman was a louse, the real meeting began. Los Angeles' bid to stage the next convention was helped immeasurably by the fine service that Daugherty had provided from the platform during this one. The Futurians praised his skillful guidance of discussions. Joseph J. Fortier brought a message from Mayor Rossi of San Francisco, Madle spoke for Philadelphia, and Rothman offered Washington. But Los Angeles received all but a dozen of the votes. Widner promptly became the first member of the Pacificon Society.

That prize offered by *Comet* embarrassed the convention, because the prozine was in financial trouble and failed to cough up the money. The convention talked over the situation, then voted to wipe this discussion from the official records. Heinlein continued to win friends by donating the money himself. Lowndes, Wiggins, Knight, and Ackerman were named a committee to choose the winner. Allen Class, an Ohioan who is unlikely to reappear in this chronicle, was the recipient. He'd hitchhiked to Denver. His figure is so shadowy that it's not even agreed whether the name was Class or Glass. Fans were so impressed by Heinlein's generosity that they forgot their criticism of the judges' choice for the winner, and started a hat-passing project. It provided enough money to buy eleven books for Heinlein. Franklyn Brady made the presentation on the Monday after the convention, Heinlein's birthday.

During this session, an almost unnoticed incident was important for the excitement it caused in one then-obscure attendee. At 2 p.m., a Western Union messenger brought a sealed envelope to the hotel. Its face said: "Message to the Denvention." Convention officials glanced at its contents, decided that it would be more trouble than entertainment to do anything with, and laid it aside. The only two Indiana fans who attended the convention got hold of it. They were Leonard Marlowe and Claude Degler, who had collaborated on a fairly good fanzine, *Infinite*. "A strange doubt began to dismay our firm convictions," Degler related. "This was no ordinary hoax. If hoax it was, its unknown author had put an enormous amount of work into it." Like Shaverites who had just photographed deros, the pair plotted to force the message onto the banquet. But Degler's attempt to weave the contents of the envelope into his talk after that meal was not sufficiently coherent. Eventually, he published the talk, with Wiggins' permission, in *Infinite*. This message purported to be from Martians who had long been on Earth in small numbers, keeping their presence a secret, while awaiting a great migration to Earth at the next opposition of the two planets. The alleged Martian message said: "Many fans are evolved centuries beyond their times, at least in neuron connections and areas of association mentally." Moreover, the Martian authors claimed they felt "most at home among these cosmic-minded creatures like yourselves." They asked the convention to publish in any prozine three questions about Mars, which they would answer at the next convention, where they also intended to put up an exhibit. In an anticlimactic afterthought, the Martians also promised to annihilate Berlin, Rome, Madrid, and Tokyo, as soon as more of them had reached Earth. The real authorship of the message was never proven. It was obviously written by someone after listening to Heinlein's talk. Dave Elder probably got blamed by more fans than anyone else. It was not the work of Degler, asserted fans who should have known.

There were forty fans on hand for the banquet. After the breaking of bread, there were many informal talks. Willard Hawkins, one of the pros at the convention, made everyone feel fine when he said: "It's the world that's out of step, not the science fiction fans." Daugherty was applauded for his impersonation of Franklin Delano Roosevelt. Heinlein and Unger gave particularly lighthearted talks, Lowndes spoke briefly, and everyone sang "Auld Lang Syne."

Earlier that day, the last fannish softball game had been played, at Lakeside Amusement Park. Evans umpired the four-inning contest that ended in a seven-seven tie. The teams were captained by Widner and Korshak, with Korshak, Daugherty, and Dale Hart as the pitchers.

Fans were on fairly good behavior throughout the Chicon. The presence of a *Time* reporter may have helped to cause this. But in the lighter and freer air of the wild west, they did more merrymaking. There was the occasion when John Michel practised his hypnotism act on Chet Cohen, who went into instant rigidity in an elevator. Alarmed elevator boys carried him to a second-floor couch but couldn't revive him. They called for the assembled might of the Futurians to help. Michel snapped two fingers, uttered the magic word, "Chester!" and Cohen rose and walked among them. There was a night when a group of fans didn't want to have their pleasure curtailed by the conclusion of the hotel's drinking hours. They lay down on a rug in the lobby until they got kicked out. On their departure, they took along the rug and vanished down side streets when sirens sounded in the distance. The exploring minds of fans made the great discovery midway through the convention that it was possible to lock the room doors from the outside, and Widner, Madle, Yerke, and Unger got trapped for a while as a result of a successful experiment based on this hypothesis.

It had been the most faanish worldcon of the three. But fandom never got a chance to make a decision between continuation of this trend toward fan domination and the original concept of a convention that put most of its formal attention on professional aspects of the field and aimed for bigness at all costs. Before the Pacificon could take place, the Japanese bombed Pearl Harbor, and there was a five-year lapse between worldcons.

6. FANDOM IN THE FIGHTING FORTIES

1. Forrest J Ackerman

The fans who won the highest places on popularity polls in the early forties were mostly individuals who had taken little or no part in the fandom of the thirties. But a few top fans bestrode the gap between the two decades, outpacing their contemporaries both before and during World War II.

Forrest J Ackerman had already become an elder god during the early forties, although he had not yet parted company with his twenties. He was born November 24, 1916. His parents named him Forrest James Ackerman, but he spent an appreciable portion of his early fannish years attempting to persuade people that J should be his entire middle name. He confused fans a little more by explaining that this grew out of his fondness for an uncle who was named A and whom everyone called Ed.

It is fascinating to speculate on the course that fandom might have pursued, if Ackerman's mother had chosen some other reward on a day in 1926 when he suffered mildly from constipation. She acceded to his request for a copy of the October issue of *Amazing Stories*, in return for taking a dose of milk of magnesia. The Paul cover for A. Hyatt Verrill's "Beyond the Pole" fascinated the nine-year-old Ackerman. Thus began a lifelong devotion of his time, thoughts, and affections to science fiction. Almost from the start, Ackerman seems to have dedicated his life deliberately and knowingly. Many fans have succumbed helplessly to the mad whirl of fandom, trying in vain to check themselves from getting sucked into its activities. Ackerman has never evidenced the slightest regret over his devotion to science fiction nor has he made any obvious attempt to extricate himself from the commanding place he took almost immediately in its fandom.

Forrest J Ackerman

Ackerman's earliest efforts to become a collecting fan had brought him a library of forty magazines. The elder Ackermans decided that these were too many magazines. They banished his collection. The younger Ackerman immediately languished in such alarming manner that his parents permitted him to buy back the lost treasures.

Ackerman made his first attempt to break into the professional field around 1928. He wrote 10,000 words of a story entitled "The Madman of Mars."

By bogging down at that point, he remained a pure fan for a few more years. Dutifully, he reprinted parts of this story for FAPA some fifteen years later.

Bob Olsen, a frequent contributor to the old *Amazing*, may have been Ackerman's first professional contact. In later years, Olsen swore that Ackerman was a starry-eyed youngster of only eight or ten years the day that the boy rang the author's Beverly Hills doorbell to ask for an autograph. Ackerman not only got an autograph, but also cookies. Long afterward, Olsen decided after a long friendship with Ackerman: "In all my experiences with science fiction, I have never read, seen, or known anything that was so amazing as 4e himself."

The Ackermans lived in Los Angeles till the fan was about eleven, moving to San Francisco around 1927. It was the Staples Avenue address in the northern city that went with his first appearances in print: letters to the prozines. He was first published as a letterhack in the first *Science Wonder Quarterly* in the fall of 1929. That letter began with a phrase that became immortal, and continued in a foreshadowing of an exclamation that *Time* later grafted onto fandom: "Although I am only twelve years old, I have taken a delight in reading the magazines you have published for almost the last four years. Let's give *Science Wonder Stories* a big yell. Hip, hip, hip, hurrayyyyy."

Inexorably, the youthful Ackerman's fannish infancy was shaped. Linus Hogenmiller, a Missouri teenager, saw his name in a prozine and struck up a correspondence. He is remembered today as the first of uncounted thousands of fans with whom Ackerman was to associate by the mails. Ackerman continued to write to the prozines, partly because of his discovery that

Linus Hogenmiller

his parents were more willing to purchase issues that contained a letter from him. By 1930 or 1931, Hogenmiller and Ackerman were corresponding about formation of a Boys' Scientifiction Club, an organization that blundered into the creation of fanzines.

Julius Schwartz and Mort Weisinger, two other fans of tender years and mighty enthusiasm, decided that their original plan to create a magazine for the club by putting eight carbons and second sheets into a typewriter was too much work. There was a search for a more dignified and scientific method of reproducing the written word. *The Time Traveller* was hatched.

Ackerman needed only half of the thirties to attain fabulous status in fandom. In 1935, he admitted that he already owned more magazines and books than he ever hoped to read. A year before that, he had raised eyebrows on many sensitive fannish faces by offering to provide Franklin L. Baldwin with an autographed picture of himself for ten cents. Almost automatically, he became a charter member of the Science Fiction League. That organization tested members' knowledge of science fiction with a questionnaire. To the question asking the names of the nation's two most active fans, Ackerman answered: "Remember our modesty." The club listed it as a correct answer. He had accomplished the difficult feat of upsetting the temper of Howard P. Lovecraft with disparaging remarks about the fiction of C. A. Smith, and the two feuded briefly over the point of literary honor in the pages of *The Fantasy Fan*.

It must be emphasized that Ackerman was a fundamentalist fan. "Science fiction is my god and my religion," he once declared. On another occasion: "I may say I honestly cannot recall ever having been surfeited with science fiction—not once since 1926—not for a moment. Science fiction and its attendant fandom are practically the totality of my interests." Perhaps his closest approach to heresy involved his interest in the movies. He was fascinated by Fritz Lang's *Siegfried* when eight or nine, then "nearly died of ecstasy" over the same producer's *Metropolis* two years later. In 1933 he had "a whole box filled" with clippings and pictures from movie magazines and film companies, the first seeds of a profitable later harvest. In one year he saw 356 movies, another feat that would later pay off. As the thirties progressed, the Ackerman correspondence reached a peak of 115 simultaneously active letter exchanges. He was writing for the leading fanzines, mostly about fantasy movies and their creators. He probably knew personally more pros than fans at this time, although Hogenmiller paid him a surprise visit in mid-1934. And this was the first of the four phases of Ackerman, in which his fanac was more remarkable for its quantity and vigor than for any other attributes.

The second phase of Ackerman in the late thirties and early forties was different. Now he began to associate personally with many fans, he began to take up causes, and he cultivated the eccentricities that masked his true self to so many fans.

Many of the eccentricities were visible only in his letters and publications. His florid handwriting was modeled on that of a favorite movie star, Kay Francis. He affected a green and brown color scheme in all his paper manifestations and the combination was eventually adopted as the official colors of the LASFS. He began to battle for a remarkable offshoot of simplified spelling that quickly got the name of Ackermanese. The abbreviations and neologisms soon dominated his writings until the fascinated reader ignored the message in the game of figuring out the meaning of individual clusters of letters, figures, and symbols. He used "r" for "are," but studiously kept all the silent letters in his own name. To the spelling changes he added a telegraphic style that was further contracted by a Joycean habit of running words together when the terminal and initial letters or syllables happened to be the same. Ackerman's obsession with puns became more prominent. Eventually he came to hate his idiosyncrasies of this period, but one of them persisted and may still be found in an occasional fanzine: nonstoparagraphing, in which the new paragraph begins one line below and one space to the right of the punctuation mark that concluded the previous paragraph.

Ackerman's inability to keep his hands off the language manifested itself in other ways. Even his own improvements on the tongue took a back seat to his enthusiasm for Esperanto, another cause which fandom ignored. But his interest in the artificial language did bring into fandom a few Esperantists almost by accident. He couldn't even be satisfied with his own name, using many pseudonyms that were not intended to deceive anyone: Weaver Wright, Jack Erman, and Claire Voyant, for instance. And to complete the distorted picture of his real self that Ackerman projected outside Los Angeles, he was the victim of a perfectionist fetish at this time that caused him to write inhumanly correct letters. He later confessed to destroying completed letters not only because of a minor typographical error but also because he accidentally folded them for the envelope in such a way that the crease came within a line of type rather than between two lines. Even the act of writing a letter with the paper upside down was cause for the missive's destruction: the uprightness of the paper was determined by holding it to the light and inspecting the faint watermark.

It may be accidental or significant that these alarming habits developed after Ackerman became a charter member of the Los Angeles Science Fiction League in 1934. His Esperanto interest showed up in 1935. As associate editor of *The Time Traveller* in 1932 and as film editor of *Science Fiction Digest* in 1933, his writing style had been tame, showing mostly the influence of the movie fan magazines, but it had all its unique properties by the time he began helping with the Los Angeles club fanzine, *Imagination!*, in 1937.

Ackerman was the inspiring force behind some publications, edited others, angeled more fanzines for other fans than anyone will ever know, and for many years responded to any fanzine editor's request for material. Nor did he escape the aspect of fanac that comes to most of us: the physical labor of publishing a fanzine. Los Angeles fandom had a Civil Service Senior Typist at its service, in Ackerman, and he typed uncounted stencils in his time.

Ackerman never was repressed with any desire to remain a purely amateur fan. He was a merchant in prozines and fanzines almost from the day that the first fanzines began to accept advertisements. For a time, no fanzine was complete without a large list of his offerings in the current bargain sale. He was again trying to sell science fiction stories around 1934, with a collaborator who worked in an Indianapolis bank, the then unknown Catherine L. Moore. Their "Nymph of Darkness" couldn't find a market more profitable than *Fantasy Magazine* until *Weird Tales* published it in expurgated form in 1939. Ackerman first saw his name on a prozine story when *Wonder Stories* published "Earth's Lucky Day" in the April, 1936, issue. It had been written in collaboration with Francis Flagg. Ackerman made a few later sales. But he admitted the possession of "no ambition to write anything long, either complicated and worthwhile or hacky, just for money. I have no patience for anything but the short-short."

A straight-A student, Ackerman finished high school, attended the University of California for one year, then quit college to try to support himself by writing. He soon took his first real job, as a typist. He submitted to standard employment with such firms as the Associated Oil Company, Motion Picture Academy of Arts and Sciences, and Fluor Drafting Company, but didn't forget the delights of self-employment. In February, 1941, he found overtime work cutting into fanac so severely that he quit his regular job and spent nine months with a friend, Ted Emsheimer, running Assorted Services. This did anything for anyone, from borrowing a book to reminding about birthdays. It was immortalized by Heinlein, who adapted the idea for his story, "–We Also Walk Dogs."

In the summer of 1942, selective service got around to Ackerman. Despite a job in a defense industry, in which he operated a machine that nobody else could run, Ackerman was inducted on August 15. He prepared for this event by writing in the blackest possible terms about his probable inability to adapt to army life. He replaced his "green phantom" glasses (the first masculine harlequin style), wrote a will that left $1,000 to establish a science fiction collection foundation, and publicly proclaimed that he wept on the day the induction papers came. These preparations for tragedy proved to be a waste of time. What followed could serve as a symbol of all the fans who have disproven charges of inadequacy to meet the real world, by scoring success therein. Ackerman promptly gained fifteen pounds, and soon found himself at Fort MacArthur, California, editing the base newspaper, which he filled with thinly disguised fannish references. After promotions, he extracted yet another punning pseudonym from his name: Sgt. Ack-Ack. Editing the publication became his full-time army job, providing him with his own office. The Ackerman efforts were so adroit that the publication finished second in a worldwide contest involving 2,000 army post publications that were judged in order of quality.

Fort MacArthur was close enough to Los Angeles to permit Ackerman to attend most LASFS meetings. The club had begun to publish *Imagination!* in 1937 as a group effort. Ackerman gradually took an increasingly large role in the magazine. When it collapsed as a club organ in 1938, he converted its letter section into a non-club successor fanzine, *Voice of the Imagi-Nation*. This survived for some fifty issues, with Morojo providing a lot of help. The magazine became the home of a collection of arguments and discussions on matters with slender or no connection with science fiction. It was famous for such things as the sketches of physiologically unique women on the covers, a strictly sic manner of editing that in the earlier issues reproduced even strikeovers and type size from the original letters, and an interminable barrage of Ackerman puns. Topics of the letters ranged through such matters as child rearing, the black arts, Michelism, religion, and what the postwar era might bring. After 41 issues, someone with too much time to spare counted up and discovered that 687 letters and articles had already been published, from the typewriters of 233 fans and even pros like E. E. Smith and A. Merritt.

This was the last fanzine with which Ackerman had more than a nominal or financial association. Perhaps the termination of his fanzine publishing career was partly the fault of the increased amount of sniping and criticism aimed at him. Fans were by this time putting into print opinions that in an earlier day they restricted to conversation or correspondence. And as the most prominent example of the all-out fan, Ackerman became the inevitable target of anyone who felt impelled to discharge a broadside at fandom in the course of quitting the field. Usually, the departing fan was describing more accurately the attitudes that he himself was attempting to abandon, rather than itemizing accurately the Ackerman shortcomings. But even the rank of Number One Fan couldn't have anesthetized Ackerman completely against the sting of remarks like those of T. Bruce Yerke: "He has refused to take on some of the responsibilities and attitudes of an adult. In ordinary moods he has the happy optimism of Disney's Duckling. He has a faith in things that thinkers are telling us the twentieth century has proved to be undependable." Laney liked Ackerman personally but disapproved of his all-consuming interest in science fiction and wrote: "Here is a man who believed very deeply in the importance of both fandom and science fiction, a generally dignified character with strong convictions. So he filled his fanzines with froth, fake spelling, weird typing, and outré mannerisms generally; rarely getting serious and straightforward about anything unless he was mad at someone." Later there was a change in attitude toward Ackerman; meanwhile, he put it into the simplest and most accurate terms himself: "Being the No. One Fan to me means being the guy who likes science fiction the most."

The 1944 blowup in Los Angeles fandom and the publicity from it that blanketed fandom must have hurt Ackerman deeply. But he contended that two specific affairs only vaguely related to the local schisms broke his fannish heart. First was the poor financial response to the Big Pond Fund, his appeal to fannish altruism which was ahead of its time. He believed that Ted Carnell, the leading British fan, could be imported for the Philcon in 1947 by means of cash donations from American fans. Ackerman was dismayed and unbelieving that it would take three years of campaigning to accomplish the goal. The second heartbreak was the scant continuing enthusiasm and support for the Fantasy Foundation, after diligent lip service given to its introduction. Another factor was his break with Morojo, in 1944; he was now left without a feminine acolyte to lend moral support to his many unconventional convictions. His only brother, Alden Lorraine, was killed in the Battle of the Bulge on New Year's Day, 1945. Ackerman published a memorial booklet in which he spoke with a simple eloquence, like a newly matured person.

When he got his discharge from the service, Ackerman set about the process of making a living out of his favorite field of interest. He rented from his grandmother an apartment and garages. (From that time on, Ackerman without garages would be as unthinkable as Ackerman without a friendly personality. Garages became absolutely essential to his well-being, for reasons we shall soon learn. He needed three of them as early as 1948.) He earned some money through huckstering, made some tentative experiments with the duties of agenting, and kept alive with the help of additional income from the federal government, under a program that helped veterans to enter new occupations after discharge. In 1946, Ackerman announced his decision to concentrate his attention on the field of agenting. Kuttner's persuasion had helped him to make the decision but Ackerman didn't heed advice to move to New York. A gap had opened there when Julius Schwartz gave up his science fiction agency and Fred Pohl became part of a larger agency. This was the start of the third Ackerman.

Ackerman immediately got the right to handle reprint and translation matters for European appearances of writers like van Vogt, Kuttner, and Bloch. Out of respect to the bitter controversy he'd engaged in with Palmer during the Shaver season, he warned that he wouldn't touch anything concerned with Lemuria. He claimed seventy clients for the agency by 1952 and later built the stable of writers to one hundred. The business began meagerly with a gross income of $1,075 and a net income of $50 in its first year. But eventually the agency supported him.

During the later forties, Ackerman's status as a fan altered gradually to that of a kind of elder statesman, one who bordered both fandom and prodom. But his collecting instinct remained intact. His lack of fanac caused him to receive few fanzines. He even thought that the Eaton, Barrett, Doreal, and Shroyer book collections were larger than his at that time. But he continued to amass from all over the world volumes, magazines, pictures, original manuscripts, illustrations, and objets d'art related to science fiction in quantities that far exceeded the cubic footage of any more specialized collection. Nobody knows the exact statistics on the collection, other than the number of garages that it has filled at various eras. He estimated it at 15,000 books and magazines as early as 1947. In 1951, he moved for the last time. His seven-room apartment and adjoining garages had proved too cramped for his expanding holdings. To transfer Ackerman and collection to the South Sherbourne Drive address required six preliminary weekends during which fans helped to sort and pack the collection, then on moving day itself, repeated trips of a two-ton truck and the labor of thirteen fans. By then, Ackerman estimated that the collection contained 25,000 items, worth $150,000.

By now, the house and three garages on South Sherbourne Drive are full. Every few years, Los Angeles fandom is moved by some obscure instinct to undertake to get the stuff into a semblance of order. Normally the driveway is filled with stuff that must be moved outside the garages to provide working room for fans to rearrange the rest. Ackerman is confident that he hasn't failed to acquire a professionally published book or magazine since 1926. He owns the original manuscript of *Fahrenheit 451*, a paperweight made of the Martian flying machine built in miniature for the Pal filming of *The War of the Worlds*, a toy dinosaur that throws plastic balls at visitors. Nothing that Yerke or Laney revealed shocked Los Angeles fandom quite as much as the discovery during the 1962 Westercon that there was a gap in this collection after all: Ackerman did not own the Oz books.

In the fifties, Ackerman attained in the mundane world the authority regarding science fiction that he had long held in fandom. He pinchhit once for Aldous Huxley on a television program. In 1955, he helped to save the existence of a German prozine, *Utopia*. A Bonn committee was considering charges that it glorified atomic war and created too much tension for young readers. Ackerman acted as a correspondence witness for the defense, writing: "If sometimes the authors dip their pens in acid and blood and paint pain-pictures of ghastly atomic horror, it is to crystallize for their perhaps less imaginative brethren the disastrous results of unholy ambition, twisted reasoning, misapplied science." The federal board of examination voted unanimously for *Utopia*.

Many honors have come Ackerman's way. He was the guest of honor at the first international con in London in 1951. Two years later he became the world's first recipient of a Hugo, awarded to him as the leading fan personality. The first Pan-Germanic con in 1957 made him its guest of honor. He can look back on his lasting influences on fandom. He invented con nicknames like Chicon, Nycon, and Philcon. He introduced and popularized Hogenmiller's "stf" as the once most frequently used abbreviation for scientific fiction. He was the first to wear a futuristic costume to a convention, starting the costume ball tradition. At one time or another, he has met most of the important pros. The handshake that he accomplished with H. G. Wells, when the Britisher delivered a lecture in Los Angeles in 1940, impressed Ackerman so deeply that he refrained from Ackermanese when writing about it. A half-dozen years later, he visited Edgar Rice Burroughs, then considered beneath the attention of most fans.

Traditionally, he is the first person every visitor to a worldcon encounters. His birthdays had become occasions celebrated by fans and pros alike from as far away as San Francisco. Shortly before his 50th birthday, following seven evenings and two weekend afternoons of Open House, host Ackerman collapsed of a heart attack. A week after his actual birthday he was able to attend a surprise birthday banquet sponsored by 200 friends. He called it "without doubt" the happiest event of his life. He would never again have huge night after night parties in his home; now they would be spaced perhaps ten a year with invitations limited to about sixty.

There is comparatively little to write about the minute portion of the Ackerman story concerned with mundane matters. His long friendship with Morojo was "a camaraderie based on mutual cultural agreements," he once wrote. After the two split, fandom got excited over a public exchange of what appeared to be proposal correspondence between Ackerman and a semi-fan who hovered over the outskirts of fandom and insisted on being called Tigrina. But Ackerman remained a bachelor until he married Tilly Porjes in May, 1949. She was a native of Frankfurt-am-Main, Germany, had been a nurse in London during the war, loved fantasy, and was working as a Los Angeles department store clerk when they met. She pointed out science fiction book bargains to her future husband. For a brief period prior to the marriage she was known as Wendayne Mondelle, an Ackerman creation. When she became naturalized she officially took the first name of Wendayne. In the eighth year of their marriage, mutually incompatible, they were divorced. Since, Ackerman has said, "we get along better divorced than when we were married," and they have been almost constant companions for approximately twenty years.

Ackerman began his fan career writing about fantasy films. When he finally became editor of a professional magazine, he found himself once more writing about fantasy films, beginning his fourth self. Ackerman came full circle in mid-1959, when he announced at a LASFS meeting that he was retiring as an agent because of the success of *Famous Monsters of Filmland*. This was a professional venture with strong resemblances to a neofan's fanzine which Jim Warren had hired Ackerman to edit. He dusted off that old movie fan magazine writing style, delved into his collection for illustrations, and managed to do his job in ten days of every month, leaving him free to enjoy the remaining two-thirds of his time. Ackerman turned over his agency clients, except for a few favorites, to a New York City firm. At one point, he thought his job as editor was arduous enough to require a secretary. Jacie Astrachan, hired in that capacity, found herself spending much time wrapping duplicates from the garages for shipment to fans all over Europe. The philanthropy that has characterized the entire career of Ackerman even survived his creation of monster fandom.

The Ackerman influence on fandom should outlive him. From a quite early date, Ackerman was obsessed by worries over the fate of his collection, possibly as a result of the loss of those forty prozines before he entered his teens. He even wanted to leave his body to science during his pre-induction despair. "The brain at least ought to be of interest to someone," he wrote puckishly. After writing that thousand-dollar collection fund into his will, he scrupulously insured his life to the limit on every airplane trip, assigning the proceeds to fandom if he should be killed. Elsewhere in this chronicle, we have learned how these collection survival instincts culminated in creation of the Fantasy Foundation and in arrangements to preserve the Sherbourne Drive house as a science fiction museum.

2. Ray Bradbury

Ackerman is a typical fan in a most extreme manner. Another Los Angeles fan came to typify fans in another sense, and briefly participated in LASFS affairs with Ackerman. But Ray Douglas Bradbury typifies the fans who rocketed out of fannish obscurity to professional dignity. His story ends in more money and more prominence than that of most other fans who served their apprenticeship in fanzines before gaining literary masterdom in paying markets.

Bradbury was born in Waukegan, Illinois, on August 22, 1920. He came from a literary family. His great grandfather and grandfather had published magazines, books, and newspapers. His father seems to have had slightly different interests, attending school with Jack Benny and naming his son for Douglas Fairbanks.

Some of the vivid qualities of the imagery in Bradbury's writing may derive from a remarkable if erratic memory. Bradbury claims that he can remember the minor operation that he underwent at the age of one day, and less trying episodes from his first two years of life. Yet he was later to place blossom time for apple trees at the Fourth of July in one famous short story, an occurrence that he didn't remember from the Illinois years.

Bradbury found the prozines when a boarder gave him an issue when he was eight years old. By then, he'd already discovered and learned to love the Oz and Burroughs novels. When he was twelve, two things happened: the Bradburys moved to Arizona, and the boy decided to become a writer. In his new neighborhood he met another youth with a fine prozine collection. Bradbury was inspired to draw comic strips and to collect the Tarzan strips by Hal Foster, a collection that he completed. He also assembled a fine set of Buck Rogers strips, for the befuddlement of those who assume that comics fandom began around 1961. Bradbury was writing unauthorized sequels to the Burroughs Mars novels, on a toy typewriter, when he was thirteen.

In 1934 the family moved to Los Angeles. Ray's writing ambitions were inflamed when he found that the girl next door had a real typewriter and that she was willing to type out the stories as he dictated them. Bradbury saved lunch money during his early teens, and bought a typewriter for himself in 1937. By then, Jeannette Johnson, a teacher at Los Angeles High School, had encouraged his attempts at fiction.

Organized fandom contacted Bradbury three years after he had moved to Los Angeles. An otherwise unremarkable LASFL member named Bob Cumnock gave Bradbury's address to T. Bruce (Tubby) Yerke, who wrote a note on hectographed club stationery, asking the high school boy to drop in to Clifton's Cafeteria, then headquarters of the LASFL. On October 7, 1937, Bradbury took advantage of the invitation. His first words in fandom have been preserved with as scrupulous care as the last words of various other celebrities. They were: "Is Mr. Yerke here?"

Within a week, Ackerman had put Bradbury to work as a writer and artist for *Imagination!*, the clubzine. Up to now, Bradbury had been trying desperately to find the key to the chamber within himself in which good fiction was locked. He'd written twenty stories in one semester of high school, and the senior class annual rejected them all. Fandom provided him with the first real outlet for his imagination. At this time Bradbury was also quite interested in theatricals, as both actor and director. He played the violin poorly, thought *Astounding* was the best prozine, and thought of his own nose as an object that would pass for a cabbage with the light behind him. He was graduated from high school with the class of 1938. Immediately he went to work selling the Los Angeles *Daily News* at street stands, first at Tenth and Normandie, and later at Norton and Olympic. The job brought him $10 weekly.

Futuria Fantasia

Bradbury has named Ackerman as the decisive factor in his fannish career. After he became famous, he described Ackerman as his "editor, publisher, and backer. You kept my spirits up during my 18th, 19th and 20th years while I wrote my pretty terrible short stories and sent them off to be rejected." Besides buying prozines from Bradbury to help him over financial crises, Ackerman angeled publication of *Futuria Fantasia*. This was a fanzine that Bradbury began to plan in 1938 and started to publish in 1939. "It was the real start of my career," Bradbury acknowledged two decades later. It contained his first published story. In its four issues, material by big-name pros like Kuttner, Heinlein, Petaja, and Haggard associated with Bok covers and Bradbury's own fiction under a variety of pennames. He used green mimeograph ink, out of respect for the patron colors of Technocracy. Why did he publish it, beyond the fiction-outlet function? "*Futuria Fantasia* hypoed into life mainly because of the crying need for more staunch Technocrats, mainly because of the New York convention, and mainly because it's been a helluva long time since a large-size mag came from out LASFS way," he said. *Futuria Fantasia* was a very well-edited publication that was outstanding for its lack of bad material and for the editor's inability to spell correctly the name of the thoroughfare on which he lived, Manhattan Place.

Bradbury used "Hollerbochen" as the penname under which he attempted to emulate Jack Benny in his published efforts at humor. They were quite bad. Ron Reynolds, Guy Amory, Doug Rogers, E. Cunningham, Brian Eldred, and Cecil Claybourne Cunningham were other pennames that he used during a brief time when he inundated fanzines, principally in Los Angeles, with contributions. He still had earned nothing for his stories, but his style was shaping up. "The Piper," in *Futuria Fantasia*, has clear foreshadowings of his later writing: "Stars shuddered. Winds stilled. Nightbirds sang no songs. Echoes murmured only the voices of the ones who advanced, bringing new understanding. The old man, caught in the whirlpool of ebon, was swept down, screaming."

Ackerman also made it possible for Bradbury to go to the first Nycon, lending him the fare. While in New York, Bradbury plugged the art of Hannes Bok with professional people, almost got ejected from a hamburger establishment when he mixed his famous Ghoul's Broth, and sang so loudly while riding a boat in Central Park that authorities intervened. He also saw the World's Fair, hardly imagining that he would help to arrange the United States exhibit in the next World's Fair in New York under a commission from the federal government. He managed to repay the money to Ackerman in the course of the following year.

Around this time, Bradbury liked to loaf at the Brown Derby, but dined at the less famous Hugo's Hot Dog Stand across the street. His particular brand of humor during club meetings got on Russ Hodgkins' nerves. But Yerke found underneath the outer shell of bacchic extroversion a deep core of understanding of humanity and a great ability to see through the political shams that were leading the world to join in Europe's war. Bradbury liked to impersonate Franklin Delano Roosevelt, W. C. Fields, and Fred Allen, and he also liked to tell people he was on speaking terms with Jack Benny. He frightened the wits out of an unidentified girl by wearing a weird mask to the Halloween showing of *The Cat and the Canary* at the Paramount Theater in 1939. He spent a year with a little theater group piloted by Laraine Day, writing some plays and doing some acting. He was turning out 1,000 words of fiction every day and selling nothing. He once estimated that he burned almost three million words of fiction written up to the age of twenty.

Then, in 1941, Bradbury made his first sale. It was hardly a spectacular breakthrough. "Pendulum" was a collaboration with Henry Hasse that sold to *Super Science Stories*. He made three sales that year. With the help of various friendly pros and his agent, Julius Schwartz, he sold a half-dozen stories in 1942, a dozen in 1943, and he had sold his last newspapers. Bradbury was no longer a reader of the prozines by the end of 1944. By now he was on his way, along a route that led to better markets than the wretched pay rates of the prozines. In his first two decades as a professional author, he sold some 300 stories. He quickly discovered that his reputation as a pulp hack was harming his chances for selling to the slicks, so he used a penname to sell almost simultaneously to *Collier's*, *Mademoiselle*, and *Charm*. The big money began to roll in. His short stories began to appear in collections in book form. He had the distinction of having one novel, *Fahrenheit 451*, banned in Russia because it denounced thought suppression. It promptly enjoyed a brisk black market sale in the U.S.S.R. Ilya Ehrenburg rated him as one of the four most popular American writers in Russia. Faulkner, Steinbeck, and Hemingway were his formidable rivals. Bradbury did the screenplays for *Moby Dick* and a variety of lesser movies, and four scripts for Alfred Hitchcock's television program. In one fantastic three-week period of 1950, he hit the *Saturday Evening Post*, *Collier's*, *Coronet*, and *Esquire*, and sold a novel and a book of short stories to Doubleday. Silly disputes popped up in the fanzines over his literary origins. It's hard to say who cited the more impossible models in this dispute: Damon Knight's Robert Nathan and J. D. Salinger, or Sam Moskowitz' Thomas Wolfe and Ernest Hemingway.

Bradbury was different from some other fans who turned into prosperous pros. Palmer turned on fandom violently, and Charles Nutt tried to forget and conceal his literary babyhood and became Charles Beaumont. But Bradbury has shown himself fully willing to acknowledge and assist the womb of his authorship. E. Everett Evans testified to Bradbury's page-by-page dissection of a story that he was trying to sell, involving long pages of criticism that took as much time and trouble as a new Bradbury short story might have consumed. He could write a kind letter of acknowledgment to an obscure fan's mediocre new publication, William E. Neumann's *Realm of Fantasy*. He helped out with a fanzine tribute to Ackerman with neofannish enthusiasm late in 1960.

In 1942 Bradbury had moved from Los Angeles to a beach town and had dropped his membership in the LASFS. He married Marguerite McClure in 1948. The Bradburys and their four daughters now live in Cheviot Hills, while he maintains an office in Beverly Hills.

Bradbury became almost as famous for anti-machinery statements as for his fiction. There were few signs of this attitude during his years in fandom. Allegedly, he still doesn't know how to drive an automobile, but rides a bicycle when he wants to provide his own power, and uses an airplane in case of necessity. Happy-go-lucky in appearance, and still possessed of an ample sense of humor, he has been credited with believing that the human race is as bad as he pictures it in his stories. (He had given ample warning to fandom, as early as the first Westercon in 1948, that he wanted to scare the dickens out of everyone with his stories.)

As usual, Walter A. Willis sums up the individual superbly. "Young, friendly, talkative, confident, and looks a bit like a boxer," Willis wrote about Bradbury. "He may be a little pleased with himself, but then he has a great deal to be pleased about and there is nothing bumptious about him. If there was a poetic genius who could survive among businessmen, it is Ray Bradbury."

3. Bob Tucker

Bob Tucker was Ackerman's only rival for the rating of Number One Fan during the first half of World War II. Like Ackerman, Tucker has maintained some kind of tie with fandom over an inconceivably long span of years, despite the handicaps imposed by professional success. But similarities between the two end almost completely with those generalities.

He was born Arthur Wilson Tucker on November 23, 1914, on a farm at Deer Creek, Illinois, a village near Peoria. He grew up in an orphanage and on farms around Bloomington and Normal, Illinois. In his teens, he journeyed forth from the orphanage aboard a boxcar, got a job as a printer's devil, then in 1931 found his true trade by becoming an apprentice projectionist at a movie theater.

Tucker had already found science fiction and fantasy. In 1929 he discovered in a closet a stack of *Argosy* that contained Ray Cummings' "Brand New World." Traveling theatrical troupes in 1929 and 1930 left behind occasional issues of *Weird Tales*. He discovered fantasy movies around this time, then read his first science fiction prozine in the form of the June, 1931, *Astounding* that featured Burks' "Manape the Mighty." The letter section fascinated him at once. He began corresponding with fans whose names he found in the readers' columns, starting with one Ted Lutwiniak, of whom we know only the fact that he later became a reporter in Jersey City. Tucker's name burst into print in the June, 1932, *Astounding*, where he was mentioned among those who had also written letters of comment. Already he was neither Arthur nor Wilson, but Bob. This was a corruption of Bub, the nickname given him by a younger brother or sister.

Tucker discovered fanzines almost as soon as they came into being. He was a charter subscriber to *The Time Traveller*. Affluent with his first $6.00 per week job, he issued his own four-page fanzine in November, 1932. It was *The Planetoid*, whose first two issues were so crammed with scientific facts that the reaction from readers destroyed any possibility of a third issue. As a writer, Tucker hit the fannish prints first in the September, 1933, issue of *The Fantasy Fan*, with a serious dissertation on science fiction in England. But two months later "How to Write a Stf Story" in the same publication introduced Tucker as a humorist and gave the first glimpse of the most celebrated penname in fandom, Hoy Ping Pong. As Hoy, Tucker wrote a fake convention report for *Wonder Stories* in 1934 and organized the Society for the Prevention of Wire Staples in Scientifiction Magazines. The mock controversy on which it fed resulted in some genuinely hurt feelings. The SPWSSTFM first emerged in the first issue of *D'Journal*, which George Gordon Clark mimeographed from Tucker's editing in the spring of 1935. (Incredible though it may seem to think of Tucker with a street address, he had one in those years. He got his mail at 304 West Market Street in Bloomington until a nosy landlady caused him to rent the legendary Box 260. It didn't wear out but was abandoned when it became too small for the quantities of fanzines and bricks in Tucker's mail.)

The staple annihilation movement had 45 members and *D'Journal* was in its second issue when Tucker's first gafiation occurred. The report of his death that appeared in *Astounding Stories* in 1936 was not revenge by a jilted girl, as a persistent rumor asserts, but a sick joke that backfired, perpetrated by a young lady. Tremaine, then editing *Astounding*, learned of the falsity of the report too late to keep the obituary out of print. Tucker immediately dropped his fanac. I like to think that my unrestrained enthusiasm over plans to publish a fanzine and the hysterical delight with which I welcomed manuscripts for it helped cause Tucker to resume his fannish career late in 1938. He joined FAPA and almost immediately began publishing again. But it was a new writer and a different Tucker. Something had happened in those two years to put a bit of Tucker into Hoy and something of Hoy into Tucker. Previously, his writings under his own name had been embarrassingly solemn and sercon, and Hoy often wrote ridiculously rather than with humor. Now, whichever name the writings carried, the humor had an undertone of a serious message and the non-humorous manuscripts did not take themselves and the world too gravely. Tuckeriana began to show up in many leading fanzines by 1939. He published around this time a wide assortment of fanzines: there were several issues of *Science Fiction Variety*, seven *Le Zombies*, three *D'Journals* in a new series, a yearbook, an *Invisible Stories*, and several *Science-Fantasy Advertisers*, all in 1938 and 1939.

During his first career in fandom, Tucker had done most of his fanning by mail. He had seen Hornig once, in 1934, and the following year he'd met a Chicago Science Fiction League member, Bill Dillenback. His third fannish visitor arrived one day in 1937, borrowed money, and departed. The experience persuaded Tucker to keep his home address out of circulation, a persuasion that he has never abandoned. Personal contacts began to grow more frequent on his return to fandom. Wollheim, Michel, and Wilson visited him in 1938. His close contacts with Chicago fandom began the next year. Tucker played a major role in planning the first Chicon, and he helped prevent that city's fandom from destroying itself in a feud before the convention.

Le Zombie was Tucker's most celebrated fanzine. "The original reason for its existence was to wash some of the starch from the stuffed shirts of fandom," Tucker remembers. Its first issue was dated December, 1938, was intended principally as an advertising medium, and was mailed as a free supplement to *Fantasy News*. This mutated into a free rider leaflet of humor and comment, later turning into an independent subscription fanzine, always written mostly by Tucker. The first nine issues went with Taurasi's news weekly. It became independent with its tenth issue, in August, 1939. The magazine appeared so frequently that its 59th issue is dated November, 1944. But the next issue was nearly a year late, another year elapsed before the 61st was published; the 63rd was intended as the last issue, produced for the Torcon, but an absolutely last issue bobbed up in the Autumn, 1954, FAPA mailing, commemorating the 25th anniversary of the first known fanzine. Like a diva with her farewell recitals, *Le Zombie* resumed its existence yet another time, with a June, 1958, issue distributed with *Fanac*.

Tucker's writing was so prolific and possessed an atmosphere of such informality and improvisation that it may have helped to encourage overproduction and careless composition by less talented fans. But Tucker's creative methods, whether in *Le Zombie* or an article submitted elsewhere, differed sharply from those of most fans. As a result his writings stand the tests of rereading and time better than all but a tiny fraction of the better fanzine material of the day. He rewrote and revised, often as frequently as a half-dozen times, and sometimes even sent manuscripts to other fans for advice before permitting them to see print. This care, so different from the first draft publishing habits of most fans, may have helped to prepare him to be a professional writer. By 1940, Tucker had become senior projectionist at the newest movie theater in Bloomington and had moved from his apartment to an eight-room country home at Downs, Illinois, with a room of his own. He didn't turn into a pro for lack of fannish duties; on one day, he received 62 pieces of mail, including 21 replies to a poll.

He'd begun efforts to sell as early as 1931, when *Argosy* rejected a story. His first success came in 1941, when Fred Pohl purchased "The Interstellar Way-Station" for *Super Science Novels* at one-half cent per word. Another story about the same characters, "The Princess of Detroit," sold to Lowndes the next summer for *Future Fiction*. His third sale, also to Lowndes, was notable for the manner in which he slipped references to fans like E. E. Evans and H. C. Koenig into the story, "Gentlemen—the Queen." He had also sold shorts to *Planet Stories* and *Astonishing Stories* by 1943, but it was clear that he did not have exceptional talent for the short story form. He found his medium later—the novel. In 1946 Rinehart published *The Chinese Doll*, a murder mystery. The critics praised the novelty of its plot gimmicks, and didn't realize that some of these gimmicks were real. Into the novel Tucker stirred references to fandom, to amateur journals called *Le Zombie* and *Rosebud*, and to characters named Ashley, Burbee, Kennedy, and Evans. Science fiction was an element of the plot. It smacked of in-group humor but didn't harm the book's success with the public.

In the dozen years that followed, he sold fourteen books and a dozen short stories. Hollywood bought one novel for filming, and a short story was sold to television. *The Long, Loud Silence* was his most talked-about science fiction novel. He'd based it partly on an aborted short story, "The Very Old Badger Game," partly on a short that sold to Boucher, "To a Ripe Old Age." Only the novel's rapid sales rate could console Tucker for the publisher's insistence that he change the ending to omit an episode of cannibalism.

Tucker remained part of fandom while selling novels. He created one legend with his quest for black wallpaper decorated with grinning octopi, inspired by one of the treasures of an eccentric wallpaper fan. He finally was forced to decorate his room with paper containing fire engines, horses, and racing dogs on a cream background for the walls, blue paper with white and gold stars on the ceiling, and a sign over the door: "Please, Lord, help me to keep my damn nose out of other people's business." When *Le Zombie* sickened, Tucker began to publish *The Bloomington News Letter*. This emphasized journalistic material dealing mostly with the professional field. He later changed its title to *Science Fiction News Letter*, in order to get on book publishers' review-copy lists, and it became the only fanzine listed in the *Literary Market Place*. But free books from a score of publishers failed to compensate for the financial loss on the newszine with its lithographed format and large circulation. It saw 28 issues altogether, and was as close an equivalent for science fiction to *TV Guide*'s place in the television world as fandom has produced. Tucker may have been the first fan to seek political office. He was a write-in candidate for the lower house of the Illinois state legislature on November 7, 1944. Friends gave him nine and one-half votes, not sufficient for the purpose. Tucker believed fans are well-equipped for politics, because both fans and politicians can frequently be defined as big blows. "The bird with the biggest mouth and the fanciest promises usually wins. That's fandom, brother," the defeated candidate said.

Older fans got the sensation that "this is where we came in," when Tucker was reported dead for the second time in 1949. A Detroit fan, Ben Singer, had spent a weekend with Tucker. After enjoying the hospitality, Singer sent out word to fandom that Tucker had died in a theater fire. Singer related that Tucker had reported for work in a dazed condition because the completed manuscript of a novel had been lost, had dozed off while smoking, and the blaze had resulted. Sometimes described as a hoax, this was also categorized as a lie. Singer still contends that he thought Tucker had known Singer's intentions. But the episode was more unsavory than the first death report, because Tucker's theater boss believed that Tucker had inspired the report to publicize a new book. Police investigated, and only his union's intervention made it possible for Tucker to preserve his job as a projectionist.

Tucker's only extended absence from the Midwest occurred in 1946. He worked in Hollywood for 20th Century-Fox for three months, as an electrician. When a television station presents *The Late George Apley* and the street lights come on in the winter park scene, that's Tucker.

In 1955 he moved to a new home a dozen miles outside Bloomington. Its address is one of the most determinedly preserved secrets in fandom. During recent years, Tucker has contributed occasionally to fanzines, provides periodic articles in impeccably polished prose in FAPA publications, and helps in both official and unofficial capacities to keep Midwestcons and worldcons alive and happy. It would be hard to find any sane fan who wouldn't agree that he could have been one of the nation's wealthiest, best-known humorists if he'd tried harder in a different literary direction. He achieved in a humane way for all fandom what Laney did some years later for the Los Angeles fans with a sledgehammer. Describing his early days in fandom, Tucker wrote of himself: "He had received a few of those 90-day wonders, the fan magazines, and he saw people's names in them over material they had composed. He also noted that the fantastic magazines which printed stories of atom bombs would also print letters from readers; these two facts being quite consistent, what should he do but promptly make an ass of himself? Exactly what made Pong tick is something this Illinois fan cannot yet explain, unless it was that all other fans were as stupid." Then, as early as 1939, he described his deliberate purpose in these words: "I am doing my darndest to provide fandom with a big bucketful of that humor it so sorely needs, and above all, I am not trying to bait, tease, ridicule or besmirch anybody." Bob Bloch diagnosed the success of *Le Zombie* as due to "the thread of candor and common sense readily apparent in its pages. Tucker is the kind of guy who would have delighted Diogenes. He is an honest man. He has always gone his own way, governing his life-pattern with the same quiet determination which marks his progress as a professional writer. He is neither a blatant exhibitionist nor a timid conformist."

Bloch, who claimed that he'd never found a purpose in life until he met Tucker at the 1946 Pacificon (the goal thereupon became the kidding of Tucker), said on another occasion: "He has become a legend in his own time and it would be impossible to imagine the curious microcosm, science fiction fandom, as it might have evolved without his influence. Tucker is a writer, and a considerable one. Tucker offers, with disarming simplicity and direct narration, a clean and lucid narrative approach. He writes fluently and forthrightly, employing few polysyllables and avoiding terminological trickery in an effort to dazzle or display specious erudition. His characterization is completely honest; his human beings are human throughout. Tucker's work is to science fiction what Graham Greene's 'entertainments' are in relation to the average whodunit."

Tucker didn't write an *Ah! Sweet Idiocy!* He could have done so, but he summarized his progress through fandom in a single sentence: "I've never found science fiction or fandom a way of life, but there were times when I came perilously close to it."

4. Jack Speer

It is hard to decide which role in fandom was the most important one, of the many that Jack Speer played. Innovator might be a proper description of him. He invented many of the bits of business and family traditions that make fandom the distinctive and mysterious hobby that it has become. Chronicler would be an equally accurate title. Speer was one of the pioneer historians of fandom, and the first to stress its subcultural aspects. Singlehandedly, he made fandom's ayjays something entirely different from the mundane amateur journalism groups. His voice emerged loudly from the wilderness periodically over the years, reminding fans that there is reason to pay some attention to literacy in fan writings. Methuselah would be no exaggeration for Speer. Nobody unsullied by the taints of prodom has been so consistently active in fandom over such a long span of years.

Jack Speer

John Bristol Speer was born August 9, 1920, in Comanche, Oklahoma. His earliest fannish manifestations have been preserved and described in rare detail, because of twin impulses that manifested themselves early: to write down things and to throw away nothing that has been written down. So we know that Speer read the September, 1927, *Amazing Stories* before he had accomplished his seventh birthday, a precociousness that no other major fan can claim. He'd read nineteen volumes of the *Book of Knowledge* before he reached his teens, skipping the twentieth not for lack of interest but because it had been lost. There is reason to believe that he has forgotten nothing that he has ever read, then or since. He was

groping vaguely toward the fannish destinies that awaited him when, in 1931, he did some writing for a carbon-copied amateur publication produced by a brother's friends. He was also a collecting fan by then, saving faithfully each day's panels from the new daily comic strip, *Buck Rogers*.

In 1934, Speer and fandom united. There were forebodings of this event, such as his production of Buck Rogers flying belts out of cardboard, his trade of a rocket pistol for a decayed typewriter, and his inclusion of poems from *Wonder Stories* in a booklet of poetry that was a school project. He had also spent part of a scout hike thinking out a space opera. Then he saw a mention of *Fantasy Magazine* in *Astounding*, obtained the issue of the fanzine devoted to that prozine in October, and he hasn't really been out of fandom since. Those who think comics fandom is a recent invention might like to know that Speer's main fanac at the start was the trading of comic strips. One deal has been recorded in detail: Speer sent Wollheim a Buck Rogers Big Little Book, got back ten Buddy Deering pages, and was slightly frightened at the discovery that he was negotiating with a grown-up man of twenty years. By 1935, Speer was corresponding with another pioneer Oklahoma fan, Dan McPhail. Almost immediately, Speer became a columnist for McPhail's newszine, *Science Fiction News*, then helped to form the Oklahoma Stf Association in 1936.

"An observer would have guessed I was headed for being one of those inadequate, extreme-introverted droops." Speer recalled, looking back on those days. But the teenager kept enough contact with the real world to use ingredients from it in 1937 for the successful manufacture of a hectograph. With this he formed the Institute of Public Opinion, the first formal poll-taking project in fandom. He got out into the genuine world immediately upon completing high school. After some business college in Oklahoma City, he went to Washington, D.C., to work for the federal government by day, to attend school by night, and to devote the rest of the time to an all-out plunge into fandom whose ripples still are visible. In 1938, he began *Sustaining Program*, the publication that turned FAPA from a political tool and an indifferently successful attempt to transplant a mundane ayjay into fandom, into an organization that was unique in and out of fandom. He was a stenographer for the Public Building Administration while he worked for his B.A. degree at George Washington University, where he majored in American thought and civilization. Later, he switched jobs to become a confidential file clerk for the War Department.

Most of Speer's influences on fandom stem from those years in Washington. Many of his deeds were the transplantation of mundane techniques or procedures into fandom, with such modifications as the hobby required. He circulated through FAPA in 1939 the first extensive history of fandom, *Up to Now*. It was mainly concerned with fandom as a political power struggle, a conception which later disastrously influenced Moskowitz' longer historical project. But it was a breakthrough for the manner in which it showed fans that they were active in a group that was old and large enough to be the topic for a historian. Speer made the first practical attempts to determine the real nature and ability of fans, by administering intelligence tests to them at every opportunity. He shares with McPhail the honor of introducing mailing comments into FAPA. Mundane ayjays had reviews of amateur magazines, but not the discussion-pregnant mailing comments that Speer created. He worked out the first practical indexing system for science fiction and fantasy stories, a variant of the Dewey decimal system for libraries that permitted each story to be assigned one or more numbers as a description of its basic plot. He was already hinting at a theory that he later developed more fully, one that explained fandom as completely as Einstein's unified field theory of relativity explained the remainder of the universe. (Nobody really understands it except Speer, who claims that all fans are handicapped and that there is a connection between their handicap and their activities in fandom.) Early in his Washington stay, Speer created the first genuine hoax in fandom, as distinguished from the simple lie. He used a different writing style, typewriter, address, and set of opinions to create the alter ego of John Bristol. Nobody guessed the deception before he revealed the truth deliberately. On Thanksgiving Day of 1938 he made one of the pioneering long trips intended solely to visit other fans, collided with a utility pole near the West Haven, Connecticut, home of Louis and Gertrude Kuslan, and escaped with minor injuries when the transformer atop the pole landed a couple of feet away from his auto. This event caused him to cut down on his fanac for a few months.

At this time, Speer found six personalities in himself: the man who appreciates art without expressing himself, the high school youth who grew desperate over man's stupidities, the fellow who spends his time worrying about the world war, the person of indeterminate age who is accepted by adults as an adult, the former radical, and the confirmed atheist who became a church-goer for social reasons. He made a totally unsuccessful attempt to break loose from fandom's ties in 1940. After Washington's fandom had dispersed, Speer plunged into another major lonewolf project, the first *Fancyclopedia*. It did for fandom's traditions, language, and mores what *Up to Now* had done for its history. When the manuscript was virtually complete in 1943, Speer made a famous tour of fandom in the last rides of his notorious auto, the Spirit of FooFoo. This was the journey on which he wrote the famous postal cards about the Cosmic Circle from unlikely towns, including the most celebrated of all, mailed to Degler from Utah: "I have a Cosmic Mind. What do I do now?" After breaking bread with the fannish outposts in Los Angeles and Battle Creek, Speer returned to Washington, hitchhiked to New York City, visited Gettysburg, spent a night in a haymow, attended the Michicon, and found himself prepared for a change in his way of life.

He had resigned from his War Department job, in anticipation of overseas civilian duty. Early in 1944, he was still sweating out the journey's start, meanwhile working for the Office of Lend-Lease Administration. The previous July he had completed the work for his B.A. degree. Speer explained his reasons with his usual impartiality: "I don't want to feel shut out when men of my generation get to talking about their war experience," and "My age, education, and marital status are such that I can profit especially from living a while in a foreign country at this time." Besides, it would help to earn money with which to pursue his law school studies. As an administrative aide for the American Food Mission to French North Africa, he spent a year in Algiers. After failing to get the transfer that he wanted to another American agency in Europe, Speer returned to this country as the war was ending.

A young Chicago labor lawyer spoke so glowingly of Seattle, Washington, at the Army Educational Center that Speer chose the Northwest as his new base of operations. Simultaneously, he enrolled in the law school of the University of Washington and exploded in his greatest outburst of fanac. Quickly, he became official editor of the NFFF, got the same duties in FAPA, began publishing a newszine, *Stefnews*, that ran for 53 issues in 1945 and 1946, and engaged in a stupendous feud with Walt Dunkelberger. This originated in an NFFF quarrel and eventually engulfed the Pacificon, FAPA, and many contemporary fanzines. Dunkelberger finally asked for a truce, suspecting that Laney was enjoying the feud so much that he was keeping it in existence. This explosion of fanac reached brennschluss after a year. Speer nearly dropped out of sight by 1948, confining himself to FAPA and local fan club activity while completing law school. Armed with his law degree, he was admitted to the Washington state bar in 1949, and began the practice of law in North Bend.

Speer married Myrtle Ruth Cox, then an airport management student, on June 2, 1951. They have two children. With the advent of the fifties, Speer also began to do something about his long-standing love for politics. He had become president of the Young Democrats of King County by 1953, and four years later he was executive director of the Young Democrats of Washington. He was an alternate to the Democratic national convention in 1956. After serving in 1957 as clerk to the Democratic caucus in the Washington house of representatives, Speer made a successful race for election as representative in the 47th District of Washington in 1958. He lost his bid for re-election two years later, and blamed his defeat on habits acquired in fandom.

Like any number of other antiquated fans, Speer put most of his fannish energies into FAPA during his declining years with a series of publications that carried on the individzine tradition that he had created in the long-dead *Sustaining Program*. He has published well over 2,000 fanzine pages, a remarkable record for a fan who doesn't get help with the writing, editing, or reproduction.

In 1962 Speer moved to Santa Fe, New Mexico. He concealed this fact for a while in an effort to create another hoax fan, June Bonefas. She published one fanzine that was so scholarly that nobody could believe it was created in the lovely head shown in a tipped-in photograph. Speer has not formally acknowledged the hoax, but it was revealed by fan sleuths who spotted telltale address similarities.

"He was one of the few great fans who was able to synthesize in himself the sercon and the fannish attitudes," Willis said. His use of the past tense was premature, but the statement is otherwise completely accurate.

5. Francis T. Laney

Francis Towner Laney was a combination of Jonathan Swift, Clarence Day's father, H. L. Mencken, your high school principal, Job, and a bank clerk. He was damned as a muckraker and lamented as a peer of Voltaire. Entering fandom in later life than most fans, he died after a lingering withdrawal from fandom. The contradictions between his actions and his writings, the ambiguities in his personality, have created arguments that still live. He was quite possibly the most brilliant nonfiction writer ever to be a big name fan.

Laney was born in Denver on March 11, 1914, the only child of a rock-ribbed DAR member and a university professor who was important enough to appear in *Who's Who in America* and *Burke's Landed Gentry*. Laney lived as a child in Berkeley, California, and Salt Lake City, then was graduated from Moscow, Idaho, High School, and in 1935 received his bachelor's degree in education from the University of Idaho. He had a four-year scholastic average of 5.03, against the 6.00 that meant straight A. He claimed later to have disliked college as much as he had been dissatisfied in Moscow, but considered his life's turning point the fact that he did not obtain a teaching certificate upon being graduated from the university. His father was head of the geology department at the University of Idaho, and Laney lived at home until three months after he had completed college. "I weighed my life up to that time, decided that it had been largely dross, and insofar as I could, cast it from me," he recalled.

This transformation first assumed the form of a year of business college in Spokane, Washington. Laney then worked for Weyerhaeuser, shuttling between Clarkston, Washington, and Lewiston, Idaho.

Fandom was not Laney's first hobby. The printed page had attracted his attention early in other forms. He edited his high school newspaper, ran a linotype for a while for a daily newspaper, and as early as 1923 was a stamp collector. He ran a "museum of mineralogical and Indian" items from the ages of eleven to fifteen,

Francis T. Laney

presumably an outgrowth of his father's field of education. From 1926 to 1930, Laney was deeply interested in entomology. In 1935 he began the phonograph record collecting, with emphasis on hot jazz and swing, that survived his entrance into fandom (he'd sold the stamp collection in 1936, after it had reached major proportions). He was an avid reader of books about faraway places. Unexpectedly, carpentry was another major interest.

Perhaps significantly, Laney did not add women to his list of hobbies until he was twenty. Later he was to criticize much younger fans for ignoring women in favor of a hobby.

Music brought Laney into fandom. He and Duane Rimel were tight at a jazz session that has been variously described as occurring in 1936 and 1937.

This began an acquaintance that increased to friendship in 1939. Laney, who had written for stamp collectors' publications, didn't know that Rimel was a professional writer and a fan until 1940, when Rimel gave him a Lovecraft collection or Laney bought one—he told the event in both ways, years later. Laney ignored this book for several days, then began to skim through "Pickman's Model." The denouement excited him enormously. He read half of that volume before going to bed and he was now a Lovecraft fan. The following year, he discovered the writings of Merritt under different conditions. On this occasion, he was seated on the toilet, read the entire "Snake Mother" there, then found himself on the verge of complete paralysis when he tried to rise. In 1942, Laney abruptly became a fanzine publisher. With Rimel's aid, he produced the first issue of *The Acolyte*, running off 120 copies on Labor Day weekend, and locating only thirteen names for a mailing list. Les Crouch and H. C. Koenig each disposed of 33 copies of that first issue.

Laney always insisted that *The Acolyte* was proof that the first fanzine fandom had not been buried under the ruins when *Fantasy Magazine* col-

lapsed. He pointed out that he had gotten ideas and help from the old publications and old-time fans. At the outset, *The Acolyte* was not intended as the glorification organ for HPL that it later was reputed to be. And a paragraph from an early issue makes odd reading of another kind today, in the light of future events: "What peanut minds these Martins and McCoys of the fan world expose when they cut loose! Just a bunch of cheap exhibitionists on the rampage, immature children mentally regardless of the age on their birth certificates. Stow it, fellows, it does make dreadfully dull reading." That first issue was dated Fall, 1942, hectographed in Clarkston, and dedicated "to the memory of the late HPL

The Acolyte

by two of his sincere acolytes." Laney's boss unwittingly lent the duplicating facilities. The magazine became almost at once the rallying point of the cult of devotees and profiteers who had sprung up around the memory of Lovecraft, now dead long enough for the first grief to subside and for a host of new fans to grow curious about his personality and writings. *The Acolyte* survived regular publication for almost four years, paying for itself and even showing a profit part of the time.

In 1942 Selective Service removed Laney's job at Clarkston from the deferrable category. This inspired him to make the fateful move to Los

Angeles, preceded by a trip to look for work that could keep him out of the service. The change in draft status occurred October 3, 1943. Laney resigned his job immediately, took his wife and small children to her parents' home, found $385 in paper money in a gutter, and entered Los Angeles on November 4, 1943, a date that is the fannish equivalent of the night that Martin Luther threw an inkpot at the devil. Almost immediately, Laney attended his first LASFS meeting. On his first day in Los Angeles, he walked diffidently into the clubroom from the cold afternoon air. He found Merlin Brown, Mike Fern, and Lora Crozetti loafing there.

They saw a man with weird green-brown eyes, brown hair, sallow complexion, awkward body, and tremendous feet. He reminded one fan of a newly painted totem pole that had been out in a hailstorm. "He frightens you, and then he smiles," was a typical reaction. The Laney laugh was compared with the cry of a frustrated cow elephant during a monsoon. His thick glasses kept sliding down his nose. Laney, who had met few fans until then and who may have taken too literally the fanzine references to Shangri-LA and the city of the angels, found himself in a storeroom in the Wellmant Apartments that impressed him as a merger of a pigsty and a monk's cell. He looked at naked light bulbs, a worn-out rug, and a filthy couch. The die was cast.

Before Laney began to write literally about Los Angeles fandom, fanzines had soft-pedaled the less savory aspects of fans. Uncomplimentary remarks had generally involved the fan's writing ability, political ideas, or collecting abilities, rather than his real faults. Most fanzines were as free from impartial and complete description of evil as well as good as a church bulletin. In no fan center was this policy as determined as in Los Angeles, where Ackerman was in a puritanical mood and anxious to keep before the public eye a united front of apparent good will and good fellowship.

Nobody has explained completely why Laney became the force that caused fans to look at their personalities, actions, and motives more frankly. Psychiatric analyses of Laney's crusade have been attempted. They have as much validity as any attempts of the like made without the active presence and cooperation of the subject and by an individual with no training or experience in the field. It is impossible to be sure if Laney feuded with Los Angeles fans because he tried to reform them, or if he tried to reform fans as a result of a feud with them. Particularly perplexing is the extreme violence of Laney's harping on homosexuality in Los Angeles fandom. There is no reason why he should have expected the club to be any more free from fairies than the average boy scout troop or Sunday School class. More confusing yet is the fact that Laney always took a double attitude toward Los Angeles fandom as an abstract whole and its fans as real individuals. Like Frederic, he liked almost all of them individually, and hated them only in a collective sense. Alva Rogers, a survivor of those days who is still able to review them calmly, thinks that there were such factors as a deep-seated strain of puritanism in Laney's own makeup, a chronic inability to understand other persons' convictions, and a desire for power.

Whatever the inward events in the Laney mind, the outward events in Los Angeles fandom began quite soon. As early as January, 1944, he engaged in open warfare with Ackerman and Daugherty, who objected when Laney used the clubroom as a studio for teaching Pogo how to dance. There were political repercussions in Los

Pogo (Patti Gray)

Angeles fandom that Laney later related in all their tedious detail. They are summarized elsewhere in this document. Essentially, an Ackerman-Daugherty-Morojo bloc opposed a clique that grew up around Laney and became known at varied times as the Knanves and the Outsiders. There were frequent truces, when everyone went on a publishing binge or played miniature golf in the best of spirits and friendship. Changes of allegiance among the factions were frequent among the other Los Angeles fans. Laney was without question the best party-giver in the club. When he brought his wife and children to Los Angeles, late in 1944, there was a memorable housewarming where A. E. van Vogt made his debut among fans and Ackerman did the only surprising thing imaginable: he got drunk, completely and deliberately. In general, Laney acted somewhat like a sophisticated playground leader. He wanted fans to be less introverted, to go out more regularly with members of the opposite sex, to indulge in wine and song (preferably accompanied by a good jazz band) in addition to women.

Speaking of those years, Laney said: "Fandom's chief attraction for me was that it furnished me with a quasi-success which somehow compensated for the fact that I was not especially successful otherwise. I am disgusted to find out how I kidded myself for a while. I actually believed all the high-sounding things I used to say about fandom as a hobby." Laney thought that he'd had it as an active fan by the end of 1946, when a job promotion cut down on his spare time. Samuel J. Russell had been helping him with *The Acolyte*, as well as rocking the small Laney children to sleep by chanting Lovecraftian invocations to them until they got drowsy. Laney decided to let the Fantasy Foundation continue publication of *The Acolyte*, amputated most of his correspondence, and announced his intention to stop his NFFF activities. He sold off most of his collection in 1947, although he retained his fanzines at this time. The events during this leavetaking were hardly calculated to improve his temper. The foundation got *The Acolyte* with enough material for three more issues, 200 on the mailing list, and $90 in the kitty. Nobody ever put out another issue. In the end, Laney turned the material over to Helen Wesson, abandoned all claim to the money, and proclaimed his delight in not feeling obligated to answer letters and be at the clubroom on Thursday nights. He didn't attend LASFS meetings after 1947, pointing out in summary: "I had the motivation of cleaning up the group. My aim was to make the club such that one could belong to it with pride and take his wife or sweetheart there without shame." Rogers suspected that Laney failed in his endeavor through impatience to let things work out gradually and through his uncanny ability to coalesce a cluster of followers around himself.

Laney had become active in FAPA quite early in his fannish career. His first mailing as a member, June, 1943, contained a single-sheet first issue of *Fan-Dango*. This publication appeared quite regularly through the remainder of the forties, representing the best example of the wide range of Laney's interests, abilities, and temper. He began to plan his fannish memoirs in mid-1947, a time when he retained enough faanishness to have devoted thirty hours to talking over ways to escape nuclear bombs with Al Ashley. Under the title of *Ah! Sweet Idiocy!* the giant work appeared in FAPA in 1948. Incredibly, Laney had originally persuaded Ackerman to provide Fantasy Foundation money to finance the bombshell, promising in return to give the profits to the organization. Ackerman took one look at the contents, refused to get the foundation involved in it, but typically offered to pay the costs himself. Laney eventually paid the bill himself. If legend is correct, he never owned a complete copy of it.

ASI does not quite equal the *Confessions* of St. Augustine in depth of thought and it has not gained the international fame of the older work, despite its reprinting in 1962 by Richard H. Eney, who used most of the original stencils that had somehow survived death and destruction. But any fan who has read Laney first and St. Augustine later has found the saint's work somewhat the more pallid of the two. Laney said that he wrote it "to try to explain to myself the inexplicable, to resolve if possible in my own mind the reasons which caused me to get so deeply involved in the amazing happenings which this book chronicles." Nothing else written in fandom has produced so many and varied reactions. Tucker immediately likened Laney to the man who blames liquor for his shortcomings because he can't stop drinking. Beak Taylor quit fandom after reading it. Boggs claimed that Laney told only the seamy side of the LASFS. Rothman hopefully suggested that the club wasn't typical of fandom. Rusty Hevelin found little gross exaggeration in the work. One Los Angeles fan who was implicated as a queer indignantly denied this definition, amending it to explain that he was actually a sex maniac. Certain other fans were allegedly mirthful because Laney had not spotted their own tendency to fairy status. Laney much later became his own critic, blaming himself for being too hard on Evans and too easy on Ashley. Rogers pointed out that Laney had once laughed about some of the events that he was bitter about in *ASI*. Rogers described it as "the product of a sour and embittered man who pulled out all the stops, lost all sense of balance and restraint, and forgot that he ever had a sense of humor by the time he got around to writing it. It is not the true measure of the man." Laney didn't allow its reprinting during his lifetime, fearing that his mysterious immunity from lawsuits wouldn't be shared by any future publisher. Vernon L. McCain may have given the most succinct description of what influence the work created in fandom: "The new fan instinctively feels and in some cases attempts to emulate without knowing what he is imitating. Much of the boorishness of some of the youngest fans is traceable to this. Laney brought to boorishness a class and elegance beyond the ken of the current practitioners. The legacy of Laney remains with us. And part of that legacy is the near-ostracism suffered by the earnest young fan who wants to devote his life to science fiction and fandom."

At least part of Laney's behavior may have been the simple result of wife problems. He married four times. His first wife is a shadowy individual about whom we know about as much as we know about Romeo's girl friend before Juliet. This marriage ended in divorce around 1939. In that year, Laney moved to Clarkston and married for the second time. To this second wife, Jackie, the two Laney children were born. They were Sandra Rae, born April 8, 1940, and Sonya Lynn, born November 11, 1942, mentioned in a thousand fanzine pages as Sandy and Quiggy. Both became pets, mascots, and the favorite people of the entire LASFS. Sandy cranked the club mimeograph many a time. Jackie did not look kindly on Laney's intensive fanac. There was a separation in October, 1946, just about the time Laney proclaimed his fannish career at an end, followed by divorce the following February. On February 14, 1948, in Las Vegas, Laney married Cecile Barham, who died on August 26, 1950. He married his final wife, Edith, in or around 1957.

During the long afterglow following 1947, when Laney was trying to persuade everyone that he had gafiated, he claimed to be interested mostly in fandom's FAPA manifestation. "Otherwise, I was writing almost entirely for the titillation and edification of Charles E. Burbee and to a much lesser extent to amuse Rotsler and Dewey and one or two others."

A home workshop that he used for hobby purposes had given Laney skills that he borrowed to obtain work in a machine shop. The Laney-Burbee symbiosis of fanning occurred when they worked in this factory from 1946 to 1952. Their writing styles interacted, and when they finally drifted apart, neither retained quite the brilliance as a writer he'd possessed during and before their friendship. Laney retained enough of the old fire in 1949 to introduce fuggheadedness certificates, the first of which went to Russ H. Woodman for a pair of feats. He'd resigned from the FAPA waiting list so he would have enough money to buy his aunt a Christmas present and he had predicted that the first artificial satellite would come to a bad end by falling to Earth faster than the Earth receded from it.

A curious episode began in 1950 when Laney plunged into Dianetics almost as violently as he had entered fandom. Just after Cele's death he was deeply absorbed in the new discipline, although besieged with misgivings about the eccentrics who were epidemic in the field. When he needed $500 to pay for training as a professional auditor, he simply advertised in the Los Angeles *Daily Mirror* for a young lady to serve as his sponsor. He finally lost interest in Dianetics around the end of 1951.

Burbee reported in 1956 that "the Laney of today is much like the Laney of yesteryear, except that his fine mind dwells on other topics." Laney himself insisted that he had dropped FAPA in part because "for a variety of reasons such minor writing ability as I had left me completely." He vanished from all fannish contacts in March, 1957. The circumstances of his final months of life remain mysterious. His few remaining correspondents were required to send letters to him in care of Edith, who remailed them from Altadena to his undisclosed address, once described as "as far east as I can get without taking a boat." Edith insists that Laney got religion a few months before his death, after mighty efforts by a preacher. "This is a lot of crap," Elmer Perdue said. "Laney and God never did see eye to eye," Burbee commented doubtfully. Other Los Angeles fans remembered how Cele had forced Laney to take her to church because she was a schoolteacher and this helped her to present a fine public character. Laney told friends that during these hours on Sunday, he played jazz records in his head, and that even the scratch from the needle was audible during the sermons.

Laney died Sunday morning, June 8, 1958, at Webster Groves, Missouri. There is no more known explanation of how he ended there than there is for the presence of that leopard's body atop Kilimanjaro. Burbee and others expressed disbelief at the news, but other fans saw the death certificate. Cancer of the bones and lungs had apparently affected his health for several years. He had worked in agony until February 21, and his final six weeks of life were a horror. Laney dedicated his body to the medical school of Washington University for cancer research. There was no funeral, but a memorial service was held at the First Congregational Church of Webster Groves.

It would be hard to imagine a set of more varied reactions than those provoked by Laney's death. Several Los Angeles fans first made certain that he was really dead, then hastily began to claim for the first time that all the things he had said about the city's fandom were wrong. Redd Boggs compared Laney's writing with that of Dean Swift, although Laney reputedly modeled his style on that of William Cowper Brann, an obscure late nineteenth century Texan editor and publisher. "If most present-day fans take a saner, more realistic view of fandom, it is largely because of Laney," Boggs said. Burbee wrote: "When I heard the news that F. Towner Laney had gone off and died somewhere, I was shocked. It didn't seem the thing to do. In short, it seemed so unLaneylike." Bloch declared: "Laney was a person I'd enjoy having for a friend. Laney was one of the rare spirits, one of the few whose abilities were so great that his influence survived for a dozen years after he ceased activity." And Speer: "I was always a little uneasy at Laney's careless destructive approach to things. But I liked him. In respect to his famous attitudes toward sex and the serious side of life, by the end Laney had rejected what he had tried to live by." One of the fans whom Laney most admired, Alva Rogers, summed him up: "He was a good friend and stimulating companion, a man with a crazy sense of humor, and a perceptive if impatient understanding of the shortcomings of fandom and fans, himself included. He was probably more conscious of his own deficiencies than most of his critics ever were."

I did not know Laney personally, but as a magnificently gifted correspondent. Instead of trying to proclaim the truth about this paradoxical and mysterious fan, I'll settle for a few final random quotations from the enormous treasure trove of Laneyana:

"I've been unable to find a single advantage I've gotten out of fandom, except an increased skill in written self-expression and greater manual dexterity with a typewriter." "My better than average mind does me absolutely no good because other phases of my personality are inadequate; I have little or no ambition, no particular desire for money, and would much rather go out on a drunken party with some hyper-babe than spend my evenings in self-improvement." "I have never intended to claim, either directly or through inference, that I am a great, big, strong, well-developed, virile he-man. I'm still willing to bet that I come nearer to being normal than a lot of you." "A neurotic bunch of apes like us should hide away individually in private padded cells, instead of harrowing each other's nerves with our utterly crapped-up personalities." "Like most fans, I tend to be introverted, but unlike many of them I tend to put on an act of extroversion. As a result, I am annoying to the more retiring fans. I take a sadistic joy in saying things that make people squirm and am thoroughly disgusting when I find a chink in some poor knight's armor."

6. Claude Degler

Like Christ and Shakespeare, Claude Degler is a shadowy figure in his earliest life and a meticulously annotated personality later on. We know that he—Degler, that is—was born on May 19, 1920, at Poplar Bluff, Missouri, and that he first walked the streets of New Castle, Indiana, in 1925. He once claimed to

The shadowy figure of Claude Degler

have spent most of his life, up to the forties, away from New Castle. He had been in Los Angeles in 1937 and 1938, according to his own testimony, had worked in New York City and in Florida, had lived somewhere in the South; and despite the fact that he moved about so much, he was on the honor roll of at least one school. In a fannish sense, Degler began to exist about 1940. He was then head of the Cosmic Club of New Castle, which lasted three or four years. Before that, however, he had been associated with something called the Buck Rogers Club. And at this point we must advise ourselves at regular intervals that from now on it is almost impossible to separate fact from legend, reality from apocrypha. Degler frequently used his imagination when writing about his activities, and his adversaries adopted the same tactics and occasionally improved on them.

We are told, then, that the New Castle club's first major activity consisted of digging a hole in the ground because Degler had a "radio tube device" that had detected metal below. Club members thought they might uncover an underground city. They put up a sign with a downward-pointing arrow and the legend, "Hell, 12 Feet." By the time the pit was 23 feet in depth the neighborhood was quite perturbed. This was an emotion that frequently permeated Degler's environment in the years that followed.

Degler said that he formed the Cosmic Circle on February 22, 1940, and the group remained confined to Indiana for several years. Degler attended the first Chicon in 1940, giving fandom its first look at and knowledge of him. He evidenced nothing more unusual than any other neofan. He was a quiet, good-humored youth who spent much of the convention engaged in hero worship of Ackerman. The next year, Degler went to the Denvention. There he did nothing to arouse attention, except when he believed or purported to believe that there might be some basis of truth behind a message from a Martian that the convention committee received but refused to dignify with notice from the chair. He seems to have had nothing to do with the creation of this document. Phil Bronson commented in 1942: "This

Indiana fellow's drawl fascinates me. I like to hear him talk. He's a rather tall chap, enthusiastic about it all, and has nice plans for Indiana fandom and their fan magazine, *Infinite*. I met him at Denver last year; I liked him then and like him more yet now."

Degler's first traceable fanzine appearance is in the April, 1941, issue of *Voice of the Imagi-Nation*. He had learned a great deal about fanzines at Chicago from Ackerman and this letter showed him already ambitious to take part in fannish controversies: "Down with the hordes of ghu. Hail, Foo! Fight to make the world safe for science fiction. We will not accept any peace dictated by ghu! We are united solidly behind a common effort. Fooism shall not perish from the Earth!" In later years, he switched allegiance to Ghu.

With Leonard Marlowe, another Indianan, Degler published the first issue of his first fanzine, *Infinite*, dating it September, 1941. It was a fairly normal fanzine, a trifle more juvenile in tone than most of its contemporaries. The first issue contained the complete text of that Denvention message from Mars and an extended commentary on it by Degler. He said: "We are thinking of forming a group to help promote publicity and discussion of the message."

Several other things made 1941 significant for Degler's entrance into fandom. The year marked the first fanzine appearance of the totally enigmatic Helen Bradleigh. She defies all efforts to deduce the facts about her existence. The name had been associated with the old Cosmic Club. In *Infinite*, her byline accompanied poetry and nonfiction too well done to be reconciled with the individual whom Degler introduced as bearing that name at later fannish events. *Infinite* claimed that she had conducted a "private feud of long standing with Mr. Degler" despite the tender years possessed by the Helen Bradleigh whom fans saw. Helen Bradleigh may have been a house name, a penname that someone else later borrowed, or an individual unaffected by the normal restrictions of space and time.

Degler seems to have traveled a great deal in 1941, although fans were not often the objects of his trips. He had suffered extensively from low temperature and wet precipitation during a hitchhiking trip to Michigan in September that involved the help of some thirty motorists. Much later, he recalled a dangerous adventure during the winter of 1941, when he went to Windsor, Ontario, to visit one Suzette de Frontenac, somehow lost his way in the wilderness, and was snowbound for three weeks in a primitive cabin.

Degler's whereabouts and activities during 1942 are obscure. The year produced few large fan gatherings to attract him, because the nation had just involved itself in war and travel was discouraged. It is conceivable that Degler was simply storing up energy in a deliberate manner for the future. There is no other logical explanation for the flooding vigor that he poured out almost as soon as the 1943 calendars went onto the walls. He held at least briefly the presidency of the Indiana Fantasy Association around this time, appointed by Ted Dikty upon the latter's departure from fandom. Degler apparently practised his organizational tactics during that period, forming several local clubs under the state body and changing its name to Indiana Futurian Association.

But starting February 20, 1943, Degler's life is fully chronicled. He began on that notable occasion to hitchhike from New Castle to the Boskone in Boston, assuming that he could cover the 1,000 miles in three wartime days. He didn't get to Philadelphia until the fourth day. He contacted John Baltadonis and Ossie Train there, went to Brooklyn and stopped long enough to converse with Julie Unger. He finally reached Boston on February 27, under the assumption that he had missed the Boskone and further handicapped by the fact that he depended on a Daugherty directory to locate Art Widner, and that publication put Widner in a nonexistent city.

What happened next might have convinced Degler that he had superfannish blood. He tried another fan listed in the directory, Harold Keating. Keating was away at the war. But by coincidence, Widner's in-laws not only lived across the street from Keating, but Widner's wife was visiting her parents at that moment. She delighted Claude with the news that he was also misinformed about the date of the Boskone. It was not four days ago but was in progress at that very moment. Degler plunged into Boston's subway and re-emerged at the Ritz-Plaza, to the great amazement of all the fans assembled.

Someone in Boston stole Degler's baggage, leaving him with only the clothing on his back. But he bored undiscouraged deeper into the New England wilderness. There was a 31-mile hike to locate an unidentified old-time fan in "the remote mountains of New Hampshire." Degler considered it worth the trouble when this fan promised to organize a state subsidiary of a group that Degler had begun to talk about, the Cosmic Circle. With somewhat less difficulty, Degler located Jim Avery and Norm Stanley in Maine. Then he crossed into Canada, where he claimed to have rescued one Jodine Fear, "a girl from Frankfort, Indiana, who was in some minor trouble with the Canadian authorities."

Next, Degler headed south where he visited at length with Raymond Washington in Live Oak, Florida, later to become second in command of the Cosmic Circle. Of Degler's further actions in Florida, we know only that he got lost in the Everglades and was chased up a tree by an alligator. By early summer, he was back in Indianapolis where he found work and for two months saved money to finance another trip.

On this second trip, many exciting things happened. In anxiety to be on time for the Schenectacon, Degler aroused, at 6 a.m., a proprietor of a dress shop whose establishment he mistook for the conference site. Degler got chased. He spent several months in New York City, working in the Unger grocery store, staying at Little Jarnevon, and reputedly nourishing himself almost solely with hotdogs and grape juice that he manufactured from a glass of grape jelly.

On this trip, he penetrated as far south as Charlotte, North Carolina, and visited the site of the prospective Cosmic Camp in the Ozarks. Then, by way of Oklahoma, Degler followed the precedent set by many other celebrated men by turning to the West. On one leg of this journey, he learned to drive an auto under difficult circumstances, when the lieutenant with whom he'd hitched a ride fell asleep at the wheel while crossing the desert. This decisive spot is identified only as in the vicinity of Yuma, Arizona, "near a sharp turn in the road around a deep canyon." Degler wandered in this very same desert for two days between rides. The date on which he entered Los Angeles has been lost to history, or at the very least, to this historian. He moved in with James Kepner, and immediately began to emit prodigious quantities of Cosmic Circle publications on the LASFS mimeograph.

The tenor of these publications and Claude's personal characteristics began to alienate some LASFS members quite promptly. The publications were on the verge of hysteria in general tone. In general, they proclaimed that fans were practically a new and superior breed of humanity. The beliefs and program of the Cosmic Circle will be considered in more detail in Chapter Eight. Degler's interminable visits to fans' houses, his frequent use of pennames, the superfan connotations that surrounded him, and the contacts that he made with the prozines did not endear him to more conservative fans. T. Bruce Yerke suffered a genuine heart attack during one attempt to dislodge Degler from the clubroom. The club changed its constitution to attempt to avoid recruiting new members in the future. But it is difficult to be certain how much fault was Degler's and how much the situation arose from the propensity of the Los Angeles fans to bicker about anything handy. On one occasion, for example, Phil Bronson and Walt Daugherty were getting angry at one another because each claimed the right to throw out Degler, while the subject of the controversy was handing ten dollars to Morojo for a life membership in the club.

Some of the uproar developed when New York fans charged that Degler had walked off with part of their collections. These charges were never substantiated and they lost their effectiveness when one of the complaining fans himself vanished with everything that FAPA possessed. Norm Stanley testified publicly that he had given Degler certain fanzines that others had assumed to be stolen. Degler retorted that he was only one of many fans who had access to the collections while he was in New York City, and the charges were not made until months after he left that city.

Ackerman and Morojo continued to stick up for Degler after most of the club had turned against him. They blocked his formal expulsion from the club, and this attitude helped to precipitate the formation of the Knanves and Outsiders. Degler finally lost his membership on charges that he failed to pay his dues. Previously, he'd been helping to pay the rent on the clubroom, something that certain of his severest critics in the club neglected to do. Degler never delivered a speech he had prepared for his last meeting, late in 1943. "It is a sorry and black day for all of us when it comes to the point that the director of the Planet Fan Federation, president of the Indiana Fantasy Association, and representative of the Dixie Fan Federation, on tour of fandom as an ambassador in Los Angeles, is to be brutally kicked out," he intended to say resoundingly. It was at this moment that he added his famous warning that this might be the eve of the day "when perhaps all fandom will be plunged into a war that will parallel the war in the outside world."

While in the West, Claude claimed the nation of Mexico for fandom. He told of a Cosmic Circle member named Chiquita Domingo who either resided in or managed an orphanage at Nogales, Sonora. She was identified as founder of the Mañana Fantasy Society of Sonora and as the stenciler of the first Mexican fanzine, *Mañana*. Degler also made a pilgrimage to San Francisco in the company of Kepner. There he met Bill Watson, George Ebey, and Harry Honig, and made a quite good impression. Now at the height of both his fame and his mobility, Degler next struck to the Northeast. He found Alfred Maxwell, a Louisiana fan in the service, at his Salt Lake City base, paid a hurried call on Canada, and passing through Casper, Wyoming, made famous as the erstwhile home of Elmer Perdue, he proceeded to Chicago, then to the 1943 Michicon, in Battle Creek. At least part of fandom immediately was plunged into war, when they wouldn't let Degler attend it.

The Michicon was to begin on October 30, 1943. Al Ashley claimed later that the event had been canceled for the year, because of wartime conditions, and that what actually occurred was basically a housewarming for the newly opened Slan Shack. The semantic confusion was sufficient for Tucker to publicize it as a Michicon and for Degler, in a hungry and tired condition, to arrive at the same moment as three moving vans. Degler claimed he'd been invited, and was ordered not to come back until the next afternoon. When he reappeared instead the next morning, Abby Lu Ashley made a similar afternoon appointment. Then Al Ashley, Walt Liebscher, and Jack Wiedenbeck formed a united front with a policy of lending no money to Degler, out of respect to his ability to live indefinitely on the slenderest means and the high probability that any support would make him at least a semi-permanent Battle Creek citizen. This treatment was not perceptibly worse than the rebuffs that Degler had met in other cities. But something in it caused Degler to erupt in a previously unparalleled manner. He went storming back to New

Castle, where he claimed that he was immediately honored by fourteen fans and eight mundanes at a banquet staged for him by the Oak Grove Science Fiction Society. This honor was particularly welcome because he had not eaten for the past 22 hours. Somewhere on the later stages of his journey, he had caught cold, and Cosmic Circle publications publicized for weeks the Ashley atrocity that had caused Degler to be "sick with a heavy chest cold and fever, sometimes in delirium. It may seriously impair his health for a long time." Despite illness, Degler declared formal war on virtually all aspects of fandom, particularly the NFFF and LASFS. He was well enough by November 14th to go to Muncie, Indiana, for what was publicized as a combined conference and council meeting of solidarity with the Muncie Mutants.

About this time, Degler began to use quite regularly the name Don Rogers in references to himself. He had adopted it as a pseudonym in efforts to sell professionally and was thinking of turning it into his legal name. Cosmic Circle publications were frequently credited to other new names, never known to have edited or published anything before or after, all of them using the same syntax and typewriter.

Another trip occurred late in 1943, details of which weren't widely publicized. It culminated in another visit to Suzette, at the Chatham, Ontario, home of her parents. She was now described as a French girl who had left her native land just before it fell. The two claimed to have "run around with" the only known Chinese fan, an individual named Mei-Lee. Then the December 18, 1943, issue of the *Cosmic Circle Commentator* announced several new developments. Degler had resigned from the Cosmic Circle. He issued a disclaimer to charges that he created the group. And he retracted everything in the fanzine's first ten issues: "Not because there was anything untrue in them, but because too many fans were against some of the ideas expressed in them."

It must be remembered that today's image of Degler as a clown whom fandom universally despised and ridiculed is not at all accurate. Degler's supporters were very much in the minority, but they included some of the most prominent and intelligent fans. This minority's attitude ranged from simple tolerance to qualified backing. Even a few of his devout enemies could see both sides of the Degler character. After Degler had finally been dispatched from Los Angeles, Yerke wrote that he "is not guilty of deliberately trying to perpetuate a fraud on the science fiction field. He doesn't know what he is doing. He is sincere in his endeavor, but lacks the training and awareness to realize the complications he is running into." Don Wollheim was quoted in a Cosmic Circle publication like this, in April, 1944: "However impractical some may feel your projects are, there isn't one I disagree with. While I feel you're being utopian, you're still talking some great dreams, the sort of dreams that rightfully should come out of science fiction. And I like it." The mature, wise Norm Stanley got along well with Degler. Ackerman admired him for the singleminded devotion to science fiction fandom that overshadowed any minor defects that Degler might possess. Perdue testified that Degler paid back a $5 debt in only two months, without being dunned, an unprecedented act for any fan. These and others may have felt at least subconsciously what Wollheim put into words: "Degler saw more of the inevitable and ultimately logical outcome of fan trends than any of the more sanely minded fans who were later to foreswear him. There is nothing in Degler's program, no matter how fantastic it may seem, that is not properly and directly derived from fandom and its own previously mentioned ideas and notions." We shall see how each of the Cosmic Circle's tenets came from an accepted fannish or professional belief, in the section of this narrative that considers the Cosmic Circle itself.

But there was also language referring to Degler that was hardly matched by any of the tirades that Degler put into his own publications toward the end. Laney described his magazines as bowel movements with New Castle postmarks. Rothman marveled with reference to Degler's writings: "What I was reading was so monstrously evil, so enormously wrong in its concept that I could not think of words sufficiently expressive to show my opinion." Walt Liebscher proclaimed his intention to cut all correspondence and friendship with "any fan even remotely connected with the Cosmic Circle." Bob Tucker took a humorous attitude toward the situation for a considerable while, but finally wrote as 1944 started: "In one way, at least, fandom displays a shade more intelligence than the outside world. Out there, rabble rousers often succeed. In fandom, they are met and defeated, or are absorbed or ignored. We see no reason why this one will not." The Futurian Society of New York showed perhaps the greatest ingenuity. It announced its support of Degler, with the proviso that this support would·end if he should visit Greater New York.

I could never get rid of a nagging suspicion that Degler somewhere along the line became aware that his ideas and actions were causing fandom to twitch and quiver out of all proportion to his real importance, and that he then proceeded to exaggerate and strengthen those stimuli out of the entertainment that he derived from teasing and harassing, rather than from any continued belief in himself as a superfan with a mission. He visited Hagerstown in August, 1943, in dead center of the most turbulent Cosmic Circle maelstrom. I found him no more wildeyed or enthusiastic about his ideas than a number of other highly respected fans. He behaved like a gentleman and showed none of the unpleasant characteristics of which he was accused after other visits. He left Hagerstown without getting into my home, an accomplishment for which I have never been sufficiently recognized.

Or at worst, there were two Claude Deglers: one who wrote wildly and emotionally while under stress, another who could see humor in situations of his own doing. He produced one set of mailing comments for FAPA in 1944 that might serve as a model of what good mailing comments should be. Nobody struck a more deadly blow at Raymond A. Palmer than Degler on the occasion when Palmer was uttering diatribes at fans and their ideas, and Degler headlined the news about them in a Cosmic Circle publication this way: "PALMER QUITS FANDOM!" After Speer published a report on his investigation into Degler's background in New Castle, Degler published a shrewdly intelligent reply that unerringly attacked the weakest points in Speer's line of attack; he charged Speer with "the malicious distortion of history to his own ends, the semantic prostitution or employing of words cunningly calculated to work on the reader's emotion; the attempt to give a seeming authority to what he says by claiming that what he states is on the part of several hundred devotees of science fiction, whereas he alone is doing the writing." Degler did not lose the opportunity to point to humorously intended statements in Speer's past as evidence that a fan mustn't be taken seriously in everything he writes.

Speer had done his investigating in New Castle during the Easter holiday of 1944. He talked with law enforcement authorities, welfare workers, courthouse personnel, and innocent bystanders. He found no evidence of the existence of most of the Oak Grove and New Castle individuals mentioned in Cosmic Circle publications. He found law enforcement agencies ignorant of the existence of gang warfare in the area that Degler had described. He located one girl whom Len Marlowe had identified as the sole, genuine Helen Bradleigh but she denied possessing the name. The report went out in the June, 1944, FAPA mailing. A petition to suspend Degler from membership in FAPA went around. The membership apparently failed to give sufficient support to expel him, but Lowndes managed to make it valid on a technicality.

As has happened so frequently, FAPA was the harbinger of a general fandom trend. Degler's star was sinking rapidly in the west, although it lingered longer above the horizon than most of us expected. Degler suddenly apologized to the objects of his attacks during the spring of 1944, declared a no-feud policy, and turned the leadership of the Cosmic Circle over to Raymond Washington. Although he had already logged 13,000 miles of hitchhiking in the interest of fandom, Degler went traveling again. He visited the new director, stopped in St. Louis, and perhaps appeared in other cities. Cosmic Circle publications bearing Deglerian traits continued to appear through the first half of 1944. One of these charged that someone had stolen many of the organization's records from New Castle. The ageless Miss Bradleigh announced the celebration of her eighteenth birthday. Degler was blaming the

long-gafiated Marlowe for starting the report that Degler claimed status as a
superfan. He retracted his statement that fans are "actual mutations of the
species." Raymond Washington saw him for the last time in August, 1944,
only a month after a previous visit to Live Oak. Washington said: "With
him was a girl he led me to assume was Helen Bradleigh. They departed via
thumb for Jacksonville, to find work for a while, then migrate to California
and the LASFS."

Degler's spoor vanishes at this point for several years, because a thumb
does not leave a fingerprint when waving in the air. Somehow and sometime,
he got to Philadelphia. Using the name of John Chrisman, he settled there
for a while and grew acquainted with fans who were unaware of the celebrity
in their midst. He was so quiet and mild-mannered at PSFS meetings that he
impressed Joe Kennedy as one of the best behaved of the town's fans. One
of the greatest sensations since the walk to Emmaus occurred when Tucker
at the Philcon in the fall of 1947 recognized Degler and spoke to him by that
name. Degler even displayed good humor at his unmasking. He immediately
donned a button that said: "I am Richard S. Shaver, who are you?" Rumors
flew that he was attempting to organize a new Cosmic Circle secretly among
younger fans. Vague reports bobbed up that he had visited fan centers on
the West Coast. But specific information is scanty. Under yet another name,
John York, he was in New York City in 1949. The next year found him at
Portland's Norwescon, where he presided at long tables of books and magazines for sale. He was on good behavior and did not give the appearance of
irresponsibility that so many fans had previously found. The only noteworthy thing he did at the worldcon was to sponsor a resolution that called
for fans to outlaw Communism. Feeling that this was a bit too large a job
for fandom to accomplish without help, the convention turned down the
proposal unanimously. Also in 1950, Degler mailed out from New Castle
a catalog of fantasy items for sale. He used his own name, and called his
business the Futurian Book Service.

There was definitely a West Coast visit in 1951. He introduced himself to
John Van Couvering as Don Rogers, said he wanted to see San Francisco's
fans, and borrowed fifty cents for transportation purposes. In Los Angeles,
Dennis Lynch fed him, Freddie Hershey refused to let him in the house, and
Anna Sinclare convinced him that she wasn't home. He left the city, listing
as cause that his mother had died. In 1954, someone reported him alive,
married, sick, and holding a job somewhere in California, completely out
of touch with fandom. Recent reports of dubious accuracy have had him
burned to death in a fire, and residing in the Ozarks with a hard core of followers. His active career in fandom lasted only a couple of years and he has
already been a living legend for a couple of decades. More information about
Degler may be found in the section "The Cosmic Circle" in Chapter Eight.

7. THE WAR HITS FANDOM

1. Fans as Pacifists

Fandom had several reasons for paying some attention to the Second World War. For one thing, it was science fiction turning into reality. Wells' *The Shape of Things to Come* had been the longest and most celebrated of a profusion of stories based on probabilities of the form that would be taken by the successor to the First World War. The public feared that the new war would cause suffering and death beyond imagination, but fans could imagine those results through long experience with stories about them. It made a genuine difference in outlook. A second reason for the war's particular importance to fandom was the fact that most fans were of an age to be eligible immediately or very shortly for selective service. There were fears that all fandom might be wiped out by a couple of months' conscription. There was the additional point: how would fans react to the war as individuals who were mostly committed to world brotherhood and to fighting nothing less exotic than Martians?

Wartime effects are woven all through the story of fandom of the first half of the forties. But let's take a preliminary general view of how fandom entered war, reserving until later many additional less-direct influences.

Apparently, only one fan of any consequence had been in a war before Germany moved into Poland. He was Clifton Amsbury, a founder of the pioneer Science Correspondence Club. This group, claimed as the first fan organization, later became the International Scientific Association. Amsbury had been a member of the International Brigade that fought for Loyalist Spain.

Not all fans were sure that they were willing to fight. American fans spoke much about the larger responsibility to humanity. Then most of them followed obediently the orders of selective service. British fans, always more thoughtful and mature, had more courage of these convictions. Quite a few of them became conscientious objectors. To be fair, the differing regulations in the two countries may have prevented a number of sincerely pacifist American fans from claiming the status, for only religious grounds were acceptable in the United States.

Typical of the reactions of many American fans to the war were the emotions of Ackerman. "Until 1941, I was passively pacifistic in thought." he wrote, midway through the war. "I always had supposed that if invited to be inducted, the CO stand would be the one I chose. I found to my surprise, that rather than having the hard row to hoe of the CO, I'd go along docilely with the draft if and when it ever caught up with me, because I had no objection to killing anybody who had intentions of bothering me. So I've gone to war in the capacity the local authorities seem to think I'm best fitted for; but I'm not proud of engaging in what Dr. Stapledon described as 'the most shattering and degrading of all human experiences.' "

Before Pearl Harbor, the New York Futurians were the most vocal group in expressing fears of the results if the war should engulf the United States. Wollheim warned that if the nation became involved, "It will be the end of science fiction as we know it." Lowndes agreed that "The entrance of the United States into the war would mean the end of science fiction and fandom here." However, the Futurians threw their full resources into the world struggle, standing beside Roosevelt and Churchill after Pearl Harbor. Ending any national suspense that may have existed, Michel proclaimed: "The Futurian Society appeals to all science fiction clubs, publications and readers to issue similar declarations and to do all in their power to help the United States to absolute victory."

Charles D. Hornig, by now more a pro than a fan, was the most prominent American science fiction figure who became a conscientious objector in fact rather than in idle thinking. He refused all military service and war work of every kind. In 1942, he went to a CO camp, left it in 1943, and entered prison later in the same year as an absolute objector to all forms of wartime service. Later he seems to have regretted only the fact that he did not refuse to register for the draft. A New York fan, Abe Oshinsky, failed to receive the CO classification that he requested. An old timer, Arthur Berkowitz, was first jailed for refusal to fight, then was assigned to a CO camp.

2. British Fandom Feels the First Blow

But more active British fans had stormier experiences. J. Michael Rosenblum was the most prominent among those who refused to help kill their fellow men. Fandom came into the situation when a government inspector who knew of his pacifist tendencies queried him thoroughly in 1940 about fans and fanzines. "He went away with the impression that the field was harmless," Mike said. Rosenblum was assigned, after a difficult inquisition, to farm work near his Leeds home. He rose at 5 a.m., spent all day in the fields, received next to no pay, but still managed to keep British fandom alive. Other British fans who acted on their pacifist beliefs included R. G. Medhurst, who went before a tribunal at Cambridge in 1941 and was permitted to continue his

J. Michael Rosenblum

studies for a while; Walter Gillings, whose request for CO classification was denied by two tribunals and who finally entered the service only to prevent his wife and child from starving; Doug Webster, a Scot who got assigned to farm work; Jack Banks, who spent six months in prison in 1942 when he refused to submit to a medical examination for service in the armed forces; Ron Holmes, C. S. Youd, Dave McIlwain, and John F. Burke—almost a listing of Britain's most gifted and active fans of the day.

It might not seem likely that anyone's fanac could affect adversely the cause of the Allies in the war. But some fans demonstrated a guilt complex about continuing activity in their hobby. Speer tried to bring them to reason: "Sully Roberds wondered how fans could placidly continue their activities while the world is blowing up. The answer is that, much as the issue of that conflict may influence our lives, there are a lot of other things that also influence it—whether we hold our job, whether our wife quits us, whether we learn anything more in math than grade school gave us; and to devote all time to contemplation of just one influence is foolish, especially when it's a thing we can change so little as the course of the European War."

Hardcore fandom existed only in English-speaking countries at this time. Britishers felt the effects of war on fandom before Americans, partly because they began to fight two years earlier, partly because they were closer to the enemy and got directly clobbered. In the first few months of the conflict, portents occurred. Maurice K. Hanson and James Rathbone were called up for service, Youd was assigned to CO work, the same happened for Harold Gottcliffe, Science Fiction Service found its operations severely hampered, *The Futurian* abandoned a regular schedule and letterpress in favor of an irregular mimeo format, Science Fiction Association suspended, and The Flat in London became a legend of the past.

British fandom suffered from the war in a shortage of reading matter that had no real parallel in the United States. During the fire-blitz on London in January, 1941, some six million books went up in flames, including the warehouses of half of the city's publishing industry. Reading matter also vanished from circulation through giant paper collections. In 1943, for instance, Liverpool residents gave more than 100,000 volumes to such a drive, of which hardly one out of five survived: 17,407 went to the troops and were undoubtedly lost in the end; 2,060 were assigned to schools; libraries got 1,705; and most of the rest were condemned to salvage purposes. The two British prozines fell victim to paper shortages. Both *Tales of Wonder* and *Fantasy* had vanished from the newsstands by the summer of 1942.

More important to the fans was the loss of American prozines. Most of them had always reached Great Britain in the undignified status of ballast. On arrival, they were sold for a fraction of the American price. When war came, east-bound ships needed the cargo space for merchandise. British readers were forced to get along with reprint editions of American prozines, starting around the middle of 1939. These contained an average of seventy pages, few illustrations, and no departments. The lack of letter sections meant the disappearance of a favorite recruitment station for new fans. *Astounding*, *Unknown*, and *Science Fiction* were the first titles to appear as reprints, lacking some of the fiction from the American guise. But some American fans actually preferred the British reprint editions, on the grounds that they were not cluttered up by advertising, their edges were trimmed, and the covers contained better color reproduction.

The collapse of the SFA was the first big change for British fandom. Internal difficulties not connected with the world conflict helped to hasten its end. A month before the war broke out, the organization found itself unable to finance regular publication of *The Satellite*. Its last issue as the SFA organ was dated November, 1939, and appeared after the SFA committee had met in mid-September and voted to follow the lead of the British Interplanetary Society and freeze. However, *The Satellite* struggled along as an independent fanzine until the issue of August, 1940, when it folded on the grounds of rising costs and lowering fanac. It had begun life as a hectographed official organ of the Liverpool branch of the SFA early in 1938. The SFA did not die completely at once. Some persistent members insisted that it lived, and held weekly meetings at 88 Gray's Inn Road until Christmas, shifting the gatherings to the Red Bull in 1940 until the blitz stopped travel and the meetings ended in September, 1940. George Medhurst and Sid Birchby claimed that they were the only participants in the group's last official meeting. The group revived for a shadowy kind of life in mid-1941, when a half-dozen or more old and new fans were claiming to represent the organization with meetings at the Anthrosophical Society headquarters. By

now, fans no longer talked much about science fiction when they got together. Ted Carnell estimated that nine-tenths of their time was spent talking
about the rest of the topics known to mankind. "There are too many other
things to talk about—life in the forces, leave, friends and fans in remote
spots and how they are doing. Friendship is strengthened, not fandom."

Ron Holmes of Liverpool seems to have been the next British fan to convert his publishing to wartime conditions. He began late in 1939 a single-
sheet news publication, *War Digest*, to take the place of his *Science-Fantasy
Review*. Holmes was out of fandom less than two years later, and fandom
in Great Britain was almost vanished by that time. The Germans did their
best to destroy it literally. Bill Temple's home at Wembley was damaged by
enemy action late in 1940, while he was stationed at Whalley, Lancashire.
Eric Needham's typewriter got into the path of a shell splinter during a raid.
Ken Bulmer was bombed out. Liverpool fandom suffered a critical blow in
1941 when the blitz got the famous mimeograph that had published Youd's
The Fantast and Rathbone's *Moonshine*. The pros were not immune, either.
John Russell Fearn had plaster in his Blackpool garden and shrapnel just
missed his coffee. Sid Birchby's home was demolished by a direct hit that
destroyed his correspondence files, much SFA material, and most of his
collection. Sid spent three days scouring the neighborhood for the fragments of precious issues of *Weird Tales*, tracking down about one-third of
his original possessions. But only one British fan was killed in the early
stages of the war and he was not a widely known one. Ted Wade of Leeds
was fatally injured in 1940, while serving in the RAF.

Fanac in the British Isles might have ended if Rosenblum hadn't come to
the fore. He was a Leeds resident who had been active in the city's chapter
of the Science Fiction League and in publishing *The Futurian*, a club organ.
In October, 1940, Rosenblum published the first issue of its wartime successor, *Futurian War Digest*. The title saw 39 issues that appeared through
March, 1945, produced under almost impossible personal and national conditions. Money, publishing materials, and time were virtually impossible to
find. But Rosenblum's titanic accomplishment spurred other British fans
to continue a semblance of fanzine publishing. Many of them issued small
magazines that went out as riders with *FWD*. One collector has calculated
that 21 fans distributed more than a hundred issues in this manner. Rosenblum, describing his feat modestly as an intellectual outlet from the strain of
manual labor, got some help from various sources. Doug Webster helped
to cut stencils. Americans like Ackerman, Daugherty, Tucker, and John
Cunningham provided precious paper. John Burke, Eric Hopkins, Harry
Turner, and C. S. Youd were among the first to distribute publications regularly with the magazine. A couple of years later, names like Ken Bulmer,
George Medhurst, and Art Williams had come to the fore. There were various

crises. Once the authorities decided that Rosenblum was publishing seditious material, and put him under police study for a time. Rosenblum was forced to act as censor once, when a contributor's rider spoke so frankly about sex that the parents of subscribers might complain. And as if he didn't have enough to do, Rosenblum suddenly decided in mid-1941 that British fandom should again be formally organized. He feared that he might find it impossible at any time to continue its last cohesive force, *Futurian War Digest*. The British Fantasy Society evolved from this suggestion by July, 1942. Carnell was its president. D. R. Smith was secretary, Rosenblum served as director, and he distributed the BFS *Bulletin* with *FWD*. As if to prove that fans are everywhere and everywhen the same, several Britishers immediately abstained and pronounced themselves fanarchists. It was probably the first organized use of that term. Turner and Webster were prominent in this attempt to become known as non-organization men.

The BFS prospectus described its objective: "To bring together for their common good persons interested in scientific or weird fantasy." Its activities centered on the *Bulletin*, a library which Jack Gibson headed at the start, provision of a list of current addresses of fans, assistance with starting correspondence, an information bureau, agenting service for stories aimed at professional publications, and maintenance of contact with American fandom. The first *Bulletin* appeared in July, 1942. The group had a score of members, listed an obscure fan named A. V. Busby as treasurer, and had appointed Webster as coordinator of the advisory board despite his opinions. Among the group's possessions was a catalog of prozines, authors, and stories that the Stoke-on-Trent Science Fiction Club had put together in a dozen folders in the late thirties.

Rosenblum must have done most of the organizing. Carnell was too busy with the war to provide much more than ample enthusiasm and a store of experience. Within a year he resigned as president because he faced a long overseas assignment. Illness forced Gibson to resign as librarian. J. P. Doyle and Fred Goodier took over for him. Kenneth Chadwick operated magazine chains for a time, permitting many persons to read scarce prozines, and retaining some control over their distribution. There was even a belief that the group's success might cause revival of the SFA. But the advisory board decided in mid-1943 not to disturb the mouldering corpse of the older group. The board even announced that the BFS would continue after the war as the new name for the old idea. The *Bulletin* was a small mimeographed sheet, and the big publishing activity of the BFS used carbon paper for duplication. It was *Beyond*, a magazine that circulated members' stories for comments and criticism by recipients. Under the editorial guidance of E. Frank Parker, the first issue appeared around the end of 1942, circulating five yarns and offering distribution to stories as long as 20,000 words.

The organization had grown to 87 members by the fall of 1943. It had formed a sub-group devoted to weird fiction, under the direction of Terence Overton. Incredibly, it even dabbled in cons. A proposed general convention covering the entire British Isles was voted down in 1943, out of respect to wartime conditions. But Roy Johnson and Arthur Gardner helped to arrange more realistic small conferences that were practical among transportation problems and armed service duties. A BFS Pendle Expedition on Whitsunday of 1943 descended upon Avalon, a bungalow at Highford, Lancashire, owned by Rosenblum's mother. Such now forgotten fans as Roy and Joy Johnson, Ron Bradbury, George Ellis, and Don Houston climbed Pendle Hill, which they compared unfavorably with Martian landscapes, and decided that there should be a British Amateur Press Association. A more elaborate fannish conclave was dubbed the Midvention. Scheduled for Birmingham, it was switched to Leicester, where it lasted from April 23rd to 26th, 1943. With fourteen fans on hand, there was an auction cried by Ron Holmes, a debate between Lewis and Overton on the difference between science fiction and fantasy, some fencing, and a questionnaire to fill out. The committee making the arrangements included Johnson, director, aided by Houston, Art Williams, Ralph E. Orme, A. W. Gardner, Rosenblum, and a subcommittee from Birmingham composed of Tom Hughes and Art Busby. The next year, a Midventionette was staged from September 1st to 3rd. Only six fans, two musicians, and one fencer were on hand, but they included an American, Gus Willmorth. There were an auction, jazz, and fencing.

In the middle of 1943, the BFS owned several hundred prozines in its lending library. It had established a branch to handle the sale of magazines. A batch of helpful American fans had been named honorary members, including Ackerman, Cunningham, Bill Evans, Joe Gibson, Morojo, Rothman, Paul J. Searles, and Tucker. But the awful nuisance of trying to hold an election cost the group as much woe as the process has inflicted on many other groups. An attempt to stage an advisory board election late in 1943 almost aborted. The only candidate who got a unanimous vote, J. E. Rennison, resigned. But somehow, a board finally got elected, composed of W. R. Gibson, Donald Houston, Terence Overton, R. Silburn, Dennis Tucker, and Edwin MacDonald.

3. American Fandom Fills the Gap

But this excursion that began with an explanation of how Rosenblum prevented the death of a fandom has carried us far too deep into the war years. Let's backtrack, and alternate between American and British events that occurred earlier in the conflict.

American fandom's first major wartime decision after Pearl Harbor was the cancellation of the Pacificon. When the United States entered the conflict, travel became so difficult and Los Angeles seemed so imperiled by Japanese attackers that convention enthusiasm evaporated. The Pacificon committee distributed a letter dated January 11, 1942, asking fans to decide the Pacificon's fate. The letter listed these possibilities: hold the convention as planned, transfer it to a less exposed city, postpone it for the duration, or cancel it completely. The letter pointed out the nationwide conditions that hampered conventions: blackouts without warning, the possibility that almost everyone might be drafted if the war went wrong, the danger that the government might prohibit all gatherings. The count in this vote does not seem to have been made public. But the committee decided to postpone the convention until peace returned.

Patriotism in fandom appeared in such projects as Fanzine Service for Fans in Service, a title that may have made permanent the new name that Louis Russell Chauvenet had devised for fan magazines. Tucker's *Le Zombie* and my *Spaceways* sponsored it, starting in mid-1942. Publishers got a leaflet listing the names and addresses of some thirty fans in the armed forces, and were asked to mail to them free copies of every issue. This was a hasty revision of the original plan to ask fanzine editors to send bundles of free copies to Hagerstown for distribution in packages like apa mailings; the postage bill was too high. This entire scheme crashed and burned when the United States Office of Censorship told periodicals to stop publishing lists of servicemen's addresses, and grumbled about this matter in a letter to Tucker. He tried to salvage the idea by urging fanzine editors to send free copies to the home addresses of fans for forwarding by relatives, but that was the last that anyone heard of this particular morale booster.

Somewhat more effective was the Science Fiction War Relief Society created by John Cunningham of Beaumont, Texas, who occasionally prefixed its title with the additional adjective, British. He aimed at British fans who couldn't get American prozines readily. His project made it possible for British fans to subscribe to the American prozines at wholesale rates. Moreover, Cunningham plunked a quantity of his own dollars down every week to buy magazines for those who could not afford to send cash. Alden H. Norton assisted with free copies of his magazines, *Astonishing Stories* and *Super Science Stories*. It was pretty much a one-fan effort for Cunningham, who got little help from American fans and introduced the purchase plan only when he found himself unable to buy magazines fast enough to fill the British prozine vacuum. Cunningham got drafted late in 1942. After the war, Frank Parker told him: "You have made friends here who will forever remember your exceeding kindness to us at a time when we were otherwise simply cut off from the world science-fictional."

Fanews published a British edition for a brief time. Editor Walt Dunkelberger sent the stencils to Ron Holmes, after finishing the American edition. Once again the mundane world broke up a fannish expedient. Postal authorities demanded first-class postage, mailing tubes, and a half-pound per parcel maximum for the shipments of stencils for the British edition. This may have been inspired partly by the fact that there was never any certainty that overseas copies of a fanzine would arrive. Submarines were even harder on fanac than Washington bureaucrats. Only two copies of the second annish of *Spaceways* were known to have lived through their trips to destinations in Europe and Australia. Canada's small fandom found itself powerless to help British fans when in late 1942 Canadian authorities put a ban on mailing complete newspapers or magazines to many destinations elsewhere in the British Empire, to conserve shipping space. But Canada had already undergone its own catastrophe in February, 1941, when all pulp magazines containing non-serious material from the United States were banned from the newsstands. Canadian presses immediately began to publish in vast quantities reprint editions of *Astonishing Stories* and *Super Science Stories*, as well as several titles of the dominion's own, like *Uncanny Tales*. Australia lost its supply of prozines and also cut off most fanzine publishing because of the paper shortage. But that continent's fandom was so much a world of its own that its story will be narrated separately.

4. Fans in Service

The identity of the first fully active United States fan to enter military service has not been determined. Taurasi was supposed to hold the distinction, getting blazing headlines when he passed his pre-induction physical examination as early as December, 1940. But he got deferred and did not serve until a bit later. In actuality, fans did not enter the service in the United States as speedily as expected. Someone studied FAPA's roster in 1940, for instance, and found that 31 of the 60 members were draft bait, but four years later, only 18 members were in the service, one had served but had received an honorable discharge, 12 were physically disqualified, and the rest had been otherwise deferred or simply hadn't been called. This was a slightly higher rate of rejection for physical reasons than the national average, but not spectacularly so. Not until late in 1943 did the number of fans in the service go over the 100 mark. There was little to confirm theories that fans are slans or misfits in the rate at which they advanced in rank. When 100 were serving, seven were commissioned officers, not remarkably high or low a proportion. The lieutenants were Donn Brazier, Charles Chandler, Ralph Hamilton, David Kyle, Grady McMurty, Fred Shroyer, and Steve Takacs.

5. Fannish Casualties

A. E. Astad, a little-known fan from Berkeley, California, was apparently the first war casualty in American fandom. He was taken hostage while living in Japan and went to a concentration camp soon after Pearl Harbor. Nothing more was ever heard from him by fans.

During the first months after Pearl Harbor, American fans began to wonder if they had a survival genius, for lack of injuries and deaths involving members of fandom. And American fandom continued to publish fanzines and squabble over organizations much more energetically than their British brethren had done during the early period of that nation's involvement in the conflict. The British Isles had possessed six fanzines when war broke out—Youd's *The Fantast*, Rathbone's new *Macabre*, Carnell's tiny newszine *Postal Preview*, Burke's *The Satellite*, L. V. Heald's *Science-Fantasy Review*, and Rosenblum's *The Futurian*. They were all gone in little more than a year, and only Rosenblum kept the fanzine tradition alive over there.

Great Britain had also lost to the conflict its most famous fannish dwelling, The Flat. This was 88 Gray's Inn Road, where William F. Temple and Arthur C. Clarke had resided for eighteen months. It resulted in an endless series of legends and anecdotes. The pair once were visited by a German journalist, later found to be a spy, who wanted clippings about rockets. Gillings announced the first true British prozine, *Tales of Wonder*, in these sacred walls. Maurice Hanson nearly lost his life while walking to visit The Flat, when a tram swooped down on a typewriter ribbon he was absent-mindedly trailing behind him, and he almost forgot to let go in time. Tourists were particularly fond of looking at the overflowing condition of the bathroom, which had Clarke's nearly complete collection of bottles, syringes, and drugs; at twenty shelves of books and magazines that awed all fans but the all-out collector, Rosenblum, who was disappointed; at the table tennis room, whose ceiling was too low to permit playing the game in an upright position, and whose door knocked down one competitor whenever anyone entered. Professor A. M. Low once visited The Flat. John Beynon Harris enjoyed a fish and chip supper there. "Ego" Clarke suffered one of the few defeats of his life, at the hands of a mimeograph there. The BBC and newspapers sent representatives there, every time they were in the mood for a feature about science fiction and its adherents. It was the scene of many a BIS and SFA meeting. The BIS *Bulletin* and *Novae Terrae* were published there.

The first fully active fans in the British Isles were the men who started the SFA. Most of them became professionals of one sort or another eventually, like Carnell, Chapman, Gillings, Temple, Clarke, and Russell. By the start of the war they were mostly in their late twenties, much given to beer, songs, and merriment; opposed to fighting and harsh words. Webster found that they "regard science fiction as a sort of ritual rather than as bedtime reading or comic relief." Most of these men were suspicious of poetry and were not completely comfortable in the vicinity of art. They displayed comparatively little of the political consciousness that was later so obvious in British fandom. The SFA had had its finest period in 1937. In that year it had organized its first foreign branch, in Los Angeles where Russ Hodgkins was chairman of ten California members. Its Leeds branch was enthusiastic enough to meet weekly, on Saturdays. There was a Nuneaton branch that met tri-weekly, had its own library, and conducted formal readings of prepared papers under the chairmanship of M. K. Hanson. H. Warnes was the chairman at Leeds, where the branch published *Tomorrow* and discussed many serious subjects. Eric Williams was working on the formation of a London branch at the end of 1937, aided by Chapman, Carnell, Clarke, Gillings, and Hanson. The SFA had to its credit the publication of a bibliography of science fiction. Williams operated a book lending library. It issued a fanzine, *Amateur Science Stories*, whose nature was implied by the title.

Its decline had begun in 1938. Two members, Reginald Stevens of London and J. T. Greenwood of Birmingham, had saddened the group by dying. The club got much of the material in their collections. When Gillings became busy with *Tales of Wonder*, *Scientifiction* and *Tomorrow* were amalgamated, cutting into the small total of British fanzine titles. There was still enough goodwill and liveliness to bring out 43 persons at the second convention and annual meeting in London on April 10, 1938, and Harry Turner was attempting to start a Manchester branch. But rumblings were booming underground. The old fannish problem of lively youngsters and staid elders bothering one another caused difficulties. Charges that Carnell and Chapman were running the club as a means of boosting their Science Fiction Service were published in fanzines in 1939. SFS was a Carnell project that traded British fan and pro publications for American prozines with the same face value. Frank Edward Arnold urged an end to schoolboy-type squabbles, but without success.

The younger element heralded the second fan wave in England. It was already active by the start of the war. Individuals like Webster, Youd, Burke, McIlwain, Hopkins, Medhurst, Rathbone, Turner, Smith, and Needham had some common factors. These included introversion, hot tempers, good command of English, fire in the pens, firm belief in their talents, great interest in music, and love of intellectual-type books. Most of these were quite unknown qualities to the older fans. They averaged perhaps a half-dozen years younger than the old guard, although many had first found fandom through the SFA as early as 1936 and 1937. Webster even found a third fandom emerging under the second fandom during the early war years, resembling first fandom despite the fact that some were as young as Don Houston, at fourteen. Webster predicted accurately that they wouldn't write novels and wouldn't carry on the SFA. Certain mavericks were unclassifiable: Rosenblum, Hanson, Birchby, and Clarke, in particular, possessed both serious and lightweight elements. Years later, Turner summarized British fandom before and after the early war years: "Unlike U.S. fandom which gradually changed from a dead serious absorption with science fiction to the lighter approach we find today, British fandom went from serious to faanish in the early forties, then back to serious again, only to emerge into the present-day British fandom we know and love."

The British Interplanetary Society (BIS) does not properly belong in a fan history, although a few prominent British fans were influential in it. It went into cold storage at about the same time as the SFA, at the war's start.

Apart from general depression over the war and the threat of direct enemy attack, economic conditions were making quite difficult any hobby that involved corresponding and publishing. The war doubled U.S. postage on printed matter and the letter rate went up two cents.

The high survival rate of fans during World War II occasioned much comment. A variety of factors must have operated to produce this phenomenon, rather than any mystical special attribute possessed by fans. The induction rate for fans was slightly lower than that of the general public, because the sedentary nature of fandom attracted a fair proportion of physical wrecks. The particular interests and skills that a fan was most likely to possess were not usually those that would induce the military to send him to the front for combat duty immediately. There was also the obvious fact that most fans who entered the field after the mid-thirties were young and apt to receive deferments though enrollment in high school or college.

None of fandom's strongest pillars lost his life during the war. But a number of quite active fans did, and by some grim chance, almost every fatality involved a fan whom everyone had liked and admired for both intelligence and character. Typical was Walter Sullivan, who had somehow remained on good terms with everyone despite holding membership in the Queens Science Fiction League, normally a situation that precluded universal popularity. He was an Oklahoman who was fandom's earliest traveling giant, and a frequent contributor to fanzines until his entry into the service. He died in an airplane crash while on duty on May 28, 1944. For six months, he had been flying the Hump between India and China as a radio operator with the Army Air Transport Command.

Blaine Dunmire of Charleroi, Pennsylvania, a private first class in the Army Air Force, was aboard a transport that went down in the Mediterranean without survivors in the spring of 1944. He was assistant director of the Western Pennsylvania Science Fictioneers, had attended LASFS meetings, and published *Stellar Tales* and *The Ghoul* before entering the service.

A less active New York City fan, Arthur Kimball, died in the Pacific in 1942 to become the first known fannish death for the nation. Lawrence Lambert, known locally as a member of the Cincinnati Fantasy Group, died during the Battle of the Bulge. PFC Orville Karkow, once head of the Minn-Dak Fantasy Society and an SFL member, was reported killed in action in early 1945 in Germany, after going on the missing list the previous November. Edward Wade, once a member of the Leeds SFL and the twelfth member of the SFA, was killed in action while on duty with the RAF in 1940. Less than a week after he received the Silver Star for outstanding bravery, Sgt. Harvey Greenblatt was killed in action in France, on August 5, 1944. He had been an active PSFS member. The Silver Star had been his reward for a single-handed capture of an enemy tank, and he had received a Purple Heart for two wounds the month before his death.

Another wartime death that was not directly connected with membership in the armed forces was that of Lt. Mike Lord, a member of the British Fantasy Society. He had completed training as an officer in the Fleet Air Arm in 1944 when he slipped and fell to his death while attempting to photograph a kestrel's nest under a cliff on Norfolk Mountain. Earl Kay, who provided a lot of help to Walt Dunkelberger with *Fanews*, while stationed in the United States, was apparently the last fan who lost his life in wartime service. He was reported missing in southern Germany on May 2, 1945. Dunkelberger learned that he had been captured and executed when the war had only hours remaining before the cease-fire.

6. Georges H. Gallet

Continental Europe had no fandom such as it now possesses, at the time of World War II. But many American fannish eyes were on France in 1939, because a science fiction enthusiast with fannish contacts was about to start a prozine that could have created a fandom in his native land. Georges H. Gallet, a mature individual with numerous professional literary accomplishments, had produced the advance copies of the first issue of his magazine, *Conquêtes*, at the worst imaginable time: August, 1939. This publication laid more stress on speculative and fact articles than the American prozines of the day, but Gallet explained this: "It is the first attempt in a long while to build up a field in France for science fiction. One has to begin slowly to accustom one's audience to quite a new climate." It was to appear weekly, selling for a franc. The few specimen copies that found their way to the United States promised good things to come, for the editorial urged readers to write letters of comment, in the *Amazing* and *Wonder* tradition.

Yvonne and Georges Gallet

Gallet, who had already served in the French army in the Rhineland in 1922 and in the Ruhr in 1923-4, entered active duty when the war began, and postponed publication plans. He saw action in Flanders and at Dunkirk as Germany swept across Europe. The vessel that rescued him from Dunkirk sank in the North Sea when attacked by German planes, but an English coast guard ship rescued him. At the age of 37, Gallet was back on duty at Cherbourg only three days later, and continued to fight until the fall of the nation. Upon demobilization in August, 1940, he found himself in Paris. There he refused to accept his former job with *Le Petit Parisien*, a newspaper, because it had come under Nazi control. Propaganda authorities demanded an explanation for this action. On Christmas night, Gallet and his wife Yvonne walked fifteen miles through the snow with a resistance guide and escaped into unoccupied France. At Marseilles he accepted work as a censor of press information.

Around the end of the war, Donald Wollheim charged that Gallet through a fanzine letter "clearly reveals himself as a Vichyite and as one of those Frenchmen able to reconcile himself completely with the fascistic, democrat-persecuting, pro-Hitler regime of Marshal Pétain and Pierre Laval." Gallet had been co-editing *V*, a magazine associated with the Mouvement de Liberation Nationale, and working for the press service of the National Council of the Resistance at Basle. Gallet won full clearance by the French, British, and United States departments of military investigation at the end of the war. Rothman visited Gallet at Marseilles in 1945 and discovered that Gallet had immortalized a VOMaiden as the cover of a French publication he was currently editing. Somehow, Gallet managed even to preserve part of his prewar collection of professional and fannish material. But as late as 1958, we find him still lamenting the disappearance of his April, 1935, issue of *Fantasy Magazine*.

7. Herbert Häussler

Like France, Germany had only one fan of any prominence before the start of the war, as distinguished from the readers of science fiction who later became known as professional writers and scientists. Herbert Häussler was born in 1912, and discovered fandom through Esperanto. While he was corresponding in that tongue with Americans, an Oregonian sent him a copy of *Astounding Stories* in 1933 or 1934. The Science Fiction League department of *Wonder Stories* provided him with the knowledge that Ackerman was also an Esperanto enthusiast. After the two got into contact, Häussler bobbed up occasionally in Los Angeles fanzines. All contact with him was cut during the war years. He had been drafted in June, 1940, and served with the occupation forces in Poland, then went to the Russian front in 1941. Frozen feet resulted in two years of hospitalization. Häussler then became a prisoner of war in 1944, and was incarcerated for the next two years in France. During his imprisonment, his seven-year-old son, Wolfgang, died. Many years later Häussler resumed as much fanac as a German living in the Russian zone can manage, principally correspondence and attendance at a few German conventions.

But the conditions that cut off English-language fandom from fans on the continent made possible the first personal contacts of any extent between North American and British fans. Gus Willmorth, the Los Angeles fan, was the first big name who visited British fandom. While serving with the armed forces in England, he met nine members of the Cosmos Club at Teddington, in August, 1943. A little later, John Millard of Jackson, Michigan, spent a weekend in Leeds with Rosenblum and Gillings. Bob Gibson, a Canadian fan whose activities did not survive the war, was in England and meeting fans as early as December, 1942. There was little traffic in the other direction. A Scot, Edwin MacDonald, was the first British Isles fan to come to North America for wartime duty. But his arrival in Canada was almost synchronous with his disappearance from fandom. Little or nothing was heard from him, after he entered training with the Royal Canadian Air Force. A borderline case was that of A. Bertram Chandler, the Englishman, later transplanted to Australia, who hovered in a condition of delicate balance between prodom and fandom for a while before collapsing into the former condition. He was in New York City at least twice as a ship's officer during World War II, visiting Unger and Campbell. Another special case was Malcolm Ferguson, an American who had shown no fannish inclinations until he was given duty in England. He immediately became known as a writer of scholarly articles in a few fanzines and as a bookplate collector. On his return to the United States and civilian status, he vanished as abruptly as he had materialized.

8. Canadian Fandom

There was little fandom in Canada for the war to affect at the outset. The dominion's population was only one-third that of Great Britain, one-tenth that of the United States, and most of its residents were so widely scattered that there was less chance for little clusters of fans to form in specific areas. Before the war, it had been to blame for few fanzines. Nils Helmer Frome was a pioneer fan in Canada, writing and drawing for American publications under his own name and with the penname of Herkanos. He published a couple of issues of *Supramundane Stories* in the late thirties, combining hectography and multigraphy. He had quite a lineup of writers for his second issue: Lovecraft, Rimel, Haggard, and C. A. Smith. Although Allis Villete of Alberta had turned up in the letter section of *Fantasy Magazine* as early as 1934, Frome was the first Canadian to publish a general circulation fanzine and to make himself prominent. He had gafiated by the time World War II grew intense. The second Canadian fanzine, however, had begun by then a career that was to exceed a quarter-century in various guises. Leslie A. Croutch of Parry Sound, Ontario, had begun publishing a carbonzine during the late thirties, *Croutch Magazine Mart News*. This contained mainly lists of magazines he wanted to trade, but news items and other fillers padded it out. Croutch didn't save a complete file, but he had issued 92 of those leaflets by early 1941, when he changed the title to *Croutch News*. Its circulation now was up from five to ten copies. After some experiments with a hectograph, Croutch turned it into a real fanzine, retitled *Light*, with the 108th issue in 1941. The following year, he obtained a mimeograph by mail order, and the magazine didn't die until he dropped from FAPA in 1963.

Leslie Croutch

Wartime troubles woke up fandom in Canada. The ban on importation of American prozines soon after Pearl Harbor and the embargo on subscriptions to American magazines caused the dominion to get its own prozines. *Uncanny Tales* was not permitted to pay Americans for fiction, but it picked up some reprint rights, and philanthropic writers donated other stories. Soon there were lots of Canadian publications, many with such familiar titles as *Weird Tales*, *Astonishing Stories*, and *Science Fiction*. As if a law of contagion were operating, fans also began to materialize. There were enough of them in Canada to put seventeen names into a Canadian fan directory around the time of Pearl Harbor, and a count a year later showed 22 names. Ted White was president of the Ontario Science Fictioneers, a group that disappeared soon after he entered the Army Medical Corps in 1941. Bob Gibson was a silent fan in Canada. But when he went to England with the armed forces, he added 500 books to his collection and helped to establish the British Fantasy Society, serving on its advisory board. Another obscure Canadian, Ron Conium, became an object of wonder in 1942 when he was found to own every prozine published in North America.

Canadian fans got into the service faster than their southern cousins. A tabulation in 1944 showed that 21 Canadian fans consisted of 14 still in the nation and seven on duty elsewhere with the armed forces. The only casualty that I have traced was James W. Lauder, Windsor, Ontario. As a member of the Essex Scottish Regiment, he vanished during the raid on Dieppe, and later was found in a German prison camp with the grisly duty of painting the names of the dead on crosses over the graves of Canadians. His postwar life didn't cross fandom.

Fred Hurter is generally credited with publishing the third native Canadian fanzine and the first to appear in any ayjay mailing. He called his project *Rocket*, ran off a cover with that title in 1941, learned that Daugherty had already published a fanzine with that name, and lettered "CENSORED" over the title. That became its new name. Beak Taylor helped him. Hurter also made an abortive attempt in 1942 to form a Canadian Amateur Fantasy Press to unite and promote fanzines in the dominion. By the fall of 1942, John Hollis Mason of Toronto and Gordon L. Peck were planning fanzines, and Alan Child was giving birth to *Mephisto*, which emphasized weird fiction. Taylor had begun publishing *Eight Ball*. This surge soon yielded to the effects of the draft and enlistments. By 1944, Hurter was in St. Andrew's College, Croutch was publishing for FAPA, and Canada was down to one subscription fanzine. This was *Canadian Fandom*, which Taylor was publishing in Aurora, Ontario. It was a title that was destined to hold a persistent existence under various publishers for decades to come.

9. Australian Fandom

Australia had the most stringent regulations against the importation of professional publications from the United States, and there was next to no native professional publishing in this field on the island. So here was the world's first test of a question that fans have long argued about: can fandom survive without prodom? The wartime events in Australia indicated that fandom can live with no magazines and with only an imperceptible trickle of books, and that fandom left to itself in this manner is quite likely to create a prodom for itself. The Australian government imposed the ban on importing prozines in the spring of 1940, the last shipment from the United States arriving in May. This embargo did not lift for eleven years, and even in 1951 *Weird Tales* was still excluded. To complicate matters, the Australian government demanded at the start of 1943 a license for each fanzine. One or two editors applied for licenses, but hastily abandoned the efforts when they learned how much red tape was involved. The paper shortage was probably the cause of this government action, or at least the excuse for it. Australian fans had no illusions about the test that was to come. *Futurian Observer*, which advertised itself as "the magazine of scoops," had a big one in its issue of December 14, 1941, with this headline: "War Declared!" The magazine explained: "We in Australia have never had war so close. And the very fact that it is so close will bring about circumstances which will inevitably enforce much less activity among fans. Science fiction is now meeting its second rough time. The first was the depression, which it weathered despite much battering. This is a much sterner test." At the time of the prozine ban, there were some thirty active fans in Australia. SFL chapters had existed at Sydney and Melbourne. Except for tiny-circulation ephemerae, Australia's first fanzines appeared in 1939. They multiplied fast until eight were alive in 1941. The decline began before the license provision. Paper was scarce and service inroads were severe despite the phenomenally youthful condition of Australia's fans. By early 1941, Bill Veney, Kenneth Dwyer, and Bert Castellari were only seventeen, Ron Levy was still only sixteen, and they represented perhaps half of Australia's major fanac strength. The war was also blamed for the club breakups in Australia, but mightier forces may have been at work from within. Feuding was endemic. The Futurian Society of Sydney, for instance, stopped and started nervously under a variety of names until it was suspended at the start of 1943, ostensibly because of the war. Pearl Harbor was blamed for the cancellation of a proposed third Sydney Conference. The Futurian Society of Melbourne declared itself extinct because of war work. It had been the only fan club in Australia outside Sydney. Australia didn't have its own reprint publications, like those in England and Canada, until after the war. Gayle Publications was once said to have planned to issue a prozine during the war, but reneged because of difficulties in obtaining paper. The first real science fiction produced on that island continent was believed to be a dingy six-penny booklet issued in January of 1942, *The Living Dead*, written by J. W. Heming and published by Currawong Publications.

10. Fandom and the Increasing Cost of Living

Fandom, which occasionally admits to some dependence on the professional field of science fiction, is accustomed to think of the great national boom in science fiction as beginning soon after World War II and exhibiting its most violent manifestations in the early fifties. But the prozines had enjoyed their first real prosperity a decade earlier. Statistics tell the story: exclusive of *Weird Tales*, there were never more than three or four prozine titles alive during the depression years, producing among them fewer than three dozen issues per year. But in 1939, when the European phase of the war began, there were a dozen titles with 66 issues. By 1941, the year of Pearl Harbor, 18 prozines published 99 issues, still not counting *Weird Tales*. There was gradual subsidence after this, as customers went into the armed forces and production costs rose, until seven titles and 37 issues were tabulated in 1945, the year that saw the end of the war. The effects on fandom had been cataclysmic. Fandom grew both in numbers and in independence from old fannish traditions. Many of the new magazines had catered to fans quite diligently, with fanzine review columns, chaotically informal letter sections, and departments in which the fans themselves wrote the articles. These features, unknown in the Gernsback- and Sloane-dominated years, were inspired at least in part by the way former fans began to be hired more and more often to edit new prozine projects.

The war years also brought the first intimations of the later orgy of science fiction book publishing. Phil Stong's *The Other Worlds*, generally looked upon as the first anthology with contemporary science fiction, was published in 1941. The next year, Pocket Books brought out the first soft-bound anthology, *The Pocket Book of Science Fiction*, edited by Donald Wollheim. Wollheim also edited the *Portable Novels of Science* volume in the Viking hardcover reprint series in 1945. Without the success of these three volumes, the postwar outburst of anthologies, novel reprints, author collections, and sundry other publishing ventures might have been delayed or modified.

Another important influence on fandom was the goosing the war gave to prices. The cost-of-living increase throughout the conflict had a dismal effect on fanzine publishing supplies. Scrap paper drives and dislocation of fans from their homes had removed much printed matter from circulation, sending the cost of collectors' items ever higher. The increased quantities of fans resulted in bigger press runs for fanzines and greater competition for rarities. Fans were more likely to find jobs that paid good salaries during the war than in the old depression years that spawned fandom, while servicemen were quite apt to blow all their small salaries on such things as hobbies, not knowing if they'd survive long enough to use the money for something useful. Additionally, it must be remembered that the war lasted six years, equal to almost half of the entire time that had elapsed from the start of prozines until the start of the war: that is, from 1939 to 1945, the age of the oldest prozines increased by fifty per cent, causing proportionate and sometimes out-of-all-proportion increases in the cost of back issues.

Some idea of the cost of fanning as the war began may be found in calculations made by Jim Avery of Skowhegan, Maine, who was a medium-active fan in 1939. He found that he spent $66 per year on his hobby. This included $14.60 for prozines, $2.50 for fanzines, $5.00 for stationery and stickers, $12.00 for postage, $4.50 for back issues, $4.50 for books, and $5.00 for a half-interest in a mimeograph. The absence of a budget for fanzine publishing in this particular list does not make it untypical, because the small fanzines of the day cost next to nothing to produce and the big ones nearly or completely paid their own way. There is no expense for transportation, but in that day the fan who spent money to visit other fans or attend cons was the exception, not the norm. Fanzine publishing was quite simple in those wartime days. Before prices rose so sharply, you could pull off your hectograph a 24-page issue and distribute it to most of the prominent fans for as little as $5.00, then you would get a substantial portion of that back in subscriptions, and you broke even if you calculated the saving on fanzines for which you traded instead of purchasing. This was long before it became common practice for fanzine editors to send free copies to fans for letters of comment or as plain tokens of friendship. Even the fan who mimeographed didn't spend a lot. Stencils cost $2.50 per quire from standard sources, less if you hunted bargains. If your mimeograph didn't wrinkle second sheets, paper cost 25¢ per ream; otherwise you spent 60¢ for 500 sheets of paper. Postage was one cent per copy, you might put 50¢ worth of ink into an issue, and you could buy a stapler from Woolworth's for a quarter, complete with enough staples to turn out an issue. A collector's expenses depended mainly on how close he lived to back-issue and second-hand book stores that hadn't been raided by other collectors. But in 1940, one dealer estimated that a fan could quickly assemble a complete set of the science fiction prozines, including the quarterlies and the annual, for only $90.

In contrast, by the time the war was near its end, Unger was forced to pour $77 per month into his newszine, *Fantasy Fiction Field*, for four four-page issues. When the war ended, the collector's $90 might have bought him the first fifty issues of *Amazing Stories*, nothing more, because those prozines of the twenties were selling for figures as high as $2.00 to $8.00 apiece.

Despite these rising costs, fanzine publishing thrived mightily in the United States during the war years. The growth of apa popularity, a trend toward larger issues, and other factors make it hard to determine the exact rate of increase. Limited help comes from Tucker's habit of keeping track of the number of general-circulation fanzine titles alive during the years the United States was in the war. From 81 titles in 1941, the number dropped to 61 in 1942 and to 49 in 1943, but rose to 106 in 1944 and 95 in 1945. Before the United States entered the war, the number had been only 47 in 1940. These figures do not include FAPA publications. Moreover, they ignore altogether the size of issues and frequency of publication. My impression is that a greater proportion of fanzines were larger and there were more titles that appeared frequently, later in the war years. There can't be much doubt that the quality in 1945 was better, on the average, than in 1940.

8. "AH! SWEET IDIOCY!"

1. The National Fantasy Fan Federation

Three major events of the forties can be grouped conveniently for consideration. They cast flickering gleams on one another, although they differ widely in nature and fate. The National Fantasy Fan Federation became, during the fifties, something more respectable than its first decade promised. The Cosmic Circle was a phenomenon that attracted much more permanent attention than its brief lifetime could have foretold. The Shaver Mystery was not properly a fan matter of mainstream nature, but its effects on fandom were important enough to cause its intrusion into this narrative.

Damon Knight wasn't a fan very long, because his writing ability propelled him into prodom rapidly. But he was a fan long enough to write an article that resulted in a national organization which outlived all the pro-sponsored bodies: the National Fantasy Fan Federation. In a sense, I lay modest claim to the role of the first in a long line of critics involving this organization. I rejected the article by Knight that told of the need for such a group. I didn't object to the quality of the writing but to the presence of a message in the essay. I feared that it might conflict with a no-controversy policy that I maintained for *Spaceways*, the fanzine to which it was submitted. This is the only authenticated example of my possession of a gift for prophecy.

"Unite or Die" was the title of the article that soon found a foster home, in Art Widner's *Fanfare*. Widner published it in the October, 1940, issue. Fans read there Damon's message: "A successful national fantasy association is possible, it could offer a needed service to every fan, and it could be established today. The association would be organized with one purpose only: to supply the fantasy fans of America with those services with which they cannot supply themselves singly or in local groups." Knight suggested such

possible functions for a new national fan group as public relations with the
mundane world, production of a handbook of fandom, distribution services
for fanzine subscriptions, regular fanzine reviews in an official organ, awards
to the best fanzines, and information on the whereabouts of collectors' items.

To understand the atmosphere surrounding this proposition, it is important to remember that a vacuum awaited a chance to escape its abhorred
status. Professionally-sponsored national fan clubs had proven useless for
fan purposes, aside from inspiring the formation of a few local clubs and
helping to publicize them. The early fannish attempts to form national
groups unadulterated by professionals had failed uniformly and completely.
But lots of new fans had arrived on the scene too late to know much about
the factionalism and bitterness that the old organisms had achieved. Both of
the New York area cliques were anxious to extend their influence nationally,
with New Fandom and a generous supply of Futurian organizations, but
they caused little stir. Here and there an isolated fan was thinking that an
organization might spur more cooperation among fans. Widner sensed this
and stressed the importance of the Knight article in these words: "The crying
need is cooperation among all fans and this seems an impossible situation
at present. Fandom should have some sort of united front to put toward
the rest of the world, or it will continue to be regarded as just the juvenile,
goshwowboyoboy gang." But I had company in opposition to the article
even before that issue of *Fanfare* reached subscribers. Knight seconded my
premonitions. He said he'd dashed off the article on a sudden impulse and
realized almost immediately "that I had made a colossal error in supposing all
fans would be able to forget petty differences in a program of such obvious
benefit to all concerned as I have outlined. Fans in large numbers are the
most uncooperative group in the world. The article was originally written
as a sort of feeler."

Widner liked the idea so much that he put more
concrete proposals into that same fateful issue of
Fanfare. Widner asked fans to promise their help to
the concept. Fans who would be willing to serve as
officers were asked to get nomination papers signed
by ten top fans. This was the first ominous hint of
the enormous bureaucracy and wasted motion in the
form of useless ritual that the organization featured
for years to come. "We could expand to a thousand
or more during the next decade," Widner predicted.

Like American liberty, the National Fantasy Fan
Federation was born in New England. The parturition
could be pinpointed at a meeting at the home of
R. D. Swisher in April, 1941. The Strangers, Boston's

Art Widner

fan group, nine Futurians from New York, and an assortment of independent New Englanders whipped the organization into existence, putting into the batter mainly the Knight article and a proposed constitution that Widner had inserted into the December, 1940, *Fanfare*. Much of this meeting went to talking over ways to avoid splits in the new group like the one that had fractured the New York chapter of the Science Fiction League.

Widner's constitution cited as the group's purpose: "To unite all existing fan organizations that are willing to cooperate with other fan organizations into a federation which can be recognized as the official organization of fandom, representative of the majority of fans. It shall set about bettering the conditions within fandom itself, and those of science and fantasy fiction in general. It shall endeavor to keep the peace in fandom." Those modest goals were to be achieved without the nuisance of dues-paying. The NFFF was conceived as a selective group whose expenses would be met by volunteer donations. It borrowed an SFL idea by proposing examinations that would test the knowledge of science fiction fandom possessed by those who sought

Louis Russell Chauvenet

admission. Widner handled applications for membership and office from fans east of the Mississippi. Knight, living in Salem, Oregon, took over the same chore for the rest of the continent, apparently unconcerned over the sea change that his original concept had already undergone.

Louis Russell Chauvenet became the group's first president. His platform had stated that fans proselytizing prospective readers of science fiction "will receive better hearing if backed by a responsible group of fans with an adult outlook." Chauvenet believed that no individual associated with feuding should hold important NFFF office. He urged freedom for the organization from control by any individual or clique. The emphasis on these points and the success of his candidacy suggest that the fusses did not interest contemporary fans nearly as much as later fan historians. Chauvenet, despite his total deafness, conceived the brilliant name for the official organ, *Bonfire*, derived from "Bulletin of the National Fantasy Fan Federation." Its first issue went into the mails in mid-1941. The group had 64 charter members, and the constitution after revision had been adopted by a 52-1 majority. Lou Goldstone had circulated a two-pager that inspired the revision. The major change involved scrapping the radical method that was originally set up to finance the group: a tax on each fan, its size determined by his amount of fanac, in parallel with the governmental custom of asking

little or nothing from the lazy or idle.
The NFFF didn't do much for a while except publish
its official organ. Moreover, it reverted to this behavior
with remarkable frequency throughout the following
years. I published the first *Bonfire*, Tom Studley issued
the second, Widner produced the third issue, and Harry
Jenkins was editor of the fourth. This simple record
provides evidence of the state of confusion. Studley was
the first vice-president. Named to the advisory board
were Milt Rothman as chairman, Joe Gilbert, Robert W.

*Joe Gilbert (left)
and Harry Jenkins*

Lowndes, Phil Bronson, and Joe Fortier. The unsuccessful candidates were
Tom Wright for president, Pogo for vice-president, and Louis Kuslan, Jack
Speer, and Dale Tarr for the board. Most of them had more experience in
fandom than the successful candidates, another unsubtle hint that fans were
tired of the old order's poli-
ticking.

Joe Fortier (left) and Tom Wright

By the end of the year, only
eight of those charter members
had paid a 25¢ fee that was imposed to pay operating costs
and called a "tax," a survival
of the rejected proposal. Despite this lethargy, the NFFF
officers had blithely drawn up
a fifty-question examination to determine if prospective members were
learned enough to join, had appointed E. E. Evans as chairman of a planning
committee, and had gone to work on the pastime that was to recur as the
NFFF's main function, that of rewriting the constitution. This new version
was accepted, 29-5, when it came up for vote, undoubtedly encouraging
many later players at the game. It didn't take long for another matter long
associated with the NFFF to materialize: impossibly grandiose projects. The
planning committee set quite quickly such goals as publication of a history
of fandom, creation of a fan annual, formation of sectional federations and
local clubs under NFFF sponsorship, and responsibility for the system of
choosing the next convention's site annually. Only one of these pipe dreams
ever amounted to anything under the NFFF. It was a primeval form of the
welcoming committee. Meanwhile, evidence was growing that the flaming
idealism of the Chauvenet platform had not completely purified the minds
of officers of the slag remaining from past troubles. First-rate fans who got
along with virtually anyone, like Len Moffatt and J. Michael Rosenblum,
received an opposing vote when they came up for admission to the group.
Speer's complex taxation system was permanently junked early in 1942,

when Chauvenet recommended an equal levy. And after his year as president, Chauvenet could safely prophesy in September, 1942, that the next president could "guide the NFFF to the accomplishment of even more important and valuable aims than have been attained up to now." By now, Jenkins had quit as *Bonfire* editor. E. Everett Evans took over the duties with the November, 1942, issue, at about the time that he was elected the group's second president. He had no real opposition and he became the first all-out NFFFer as the term was later understood. Bob Tucker defeated two oddly assorted competitors, Joe Fortier and H. C. Koenig, for the vice-presidency. Speer and Chauvenet got the same number of votes for the office of secretary-treasurer. The latter got the job, because Speer had overlooked the formality of filing as a candidate. The advisory board for this second year had Widner as chairman, and Phil Bronson, D. B. Thompson, Morojo, and me as members.

The NFFF was taking on recognizable form by now. The welcoming committee ("welcom") had sliced the nation into seven sections for functional convenience. The advisory board had approved Speer's proposed encyclopedia of fandom. (After many adventures, this turned into the *Fancyclopedia* in 1944, with only financial assistance from the organization.) The establishment of multiple bureaus became another obsession within the NFFF. Evans appointed Morojo to have charge of feminine fans, although it isn't clear what she was expected to do with them. Widner was named polltaker, Thompson was head of the welcom, Tucker was assigned to a committee to provide not one but two free copies of each fanzine for fans in the armed services, one to read now and another to go to his home for his collection, and I got the congenial duty of revising the constitution.

Evans began the second change in the original scope and purpose of the NFFF when he said that the organization should be "almost entirely coordinative. Its function is to assist in the upbuilding of fan groups. It is my earnest desire to see fandom so well organized and so smoothly functioning that whenever something comes up that fans want done, we will have the machinery ready and working to handle the work." He proposed sectional groups under the NFFF: one in New England, with the Strangers-Boskone group as nucleus, others for the eastern, Dixie, midwest, western, and Pacific areas. Evans was overly optimistic about the ability of fans to be active regionally, because he lived in Battle Creek, Michigan, and happened to have a bunch of active fans situated within a compact area and without enough experience in the field to begin fussing and feuding among themselves. What worked well in Michigan was not appropriate for fans located hundreds of miles apart in geography and three ideologies distant in thinking.

It must be remembered that Evans was different in background and age from almost all fans of the day. He was on the brink of his fiftieth birthday

E. Everett Evans

when he became president of the NFFF, double and triple the ages of most fans. He had had an adventurous life that apparently contained disappointments which fandom helped to assuage. He wrote seriously about many important topics, fandom accepted him as a wise and experienced philosopher-friend, and permitted him to run things for a while. When Evans' deficiencies as a thinker and as an organizer became obvious, the effects on both fandom and Evans as a fan were quite large.

Several exciting things happened late in 1942. Evans didn't like the revision of the constitution that I submitted. Undaunted, he revised it himself, sent it to the directors for comments, and at this instant vanished instantaneously in magical manner from fandom. A cryptic statement whose origin still is disputed led astonished fans to believe Evans had been called into the navy for wartime duty of unspecified but important nature. On November 25th, Tucker assumed the presidency of the NFFF just long enough to appoint Ashley as acting president. Instantly, the siren call of constitutional revision took exclusive possession of the thoughts of the acting president. Ashley first of all proposed to offer both the Evans and Warner revisions for vote. Only the small formality of producing an issue of *Bonfire* held up a decision on these documents.

Ashley issued, at the start of 1943, a report that defined himself as "the best placed to carry on the plans outlined and started by EEE." This, Ashley said, caused his appointment to the acting presidency. Ashley pointed out that the original NFFF was supposed to deny membership to new, unproven fans, causing it to reach a condition of hobby incest. He described the Evans constitution as the sole salvation for the club, in a chain of logic that might have been accurate if the NFFF had at any time in actuality failed to snatch the opportunity to enroll even the most obscure fan as a member, despite ideals. In line with the Evans concept of the NFFF as a coordinative body, Ashley said that "it is necessary for all fandom to become members of the NFFF." Nothing else in particular happened for the better part of the year that followed. Finally, in October, 1943, Ashley came to the conclusion that when in doubt, write a new constitution. He drew up an emergency constitution of his own. It appeared in the December, 1943, *Bonfire*, just as Evans returned to our midst, although unable to participate in much fanac for more months to come through unspecified hindrances. By now, one NFFF officer had recommended disbanding the organization. Another had proposed mothballing it until some future epoch. The fanzine supply arrangements for service fans had crashed and burned. But the organization staggered on in its paper existence. It even managed to issue laureate awards. Winners in 1943 were *Le Zombie*, as best fanzine; *Fanewscard*, newszine; Duane Rimel, author; Jack Wiedenbeck, artist; Walt Liebscher, poet; Tucker, article writer; Walt Dunkelberger, new fan; Ashley, fan who did the most; and Tucker, highest score for everything.

The fumbling continued during the early part of 1944. At one time, Sam Russell and Chauvenet were the only members of the organization in good standing. But Evans resumed fanac in the spring, writing a presidential message that thanked Ashley for splendid work as acting president "during my unavoidable absence." Dunkelberger was appointed secretary-treasurer, to succeed the resigned Chauvenet. Evans' leadership was powerful enough to cause membership to zoom to 110 by the end of 1944. That emergency constitution had passed by a 32-4 vote, but finally someone noticed a minor defect in it. It provided no mechanism for obtaining officers for the NFFF. So Evans took it upon himself to schedule an election for the start of the coming year. It was just one additional bundle in an already enormous burden for Evans. He reckoned up his duties for one period of less than three months duration: they included writing nearly 100 letters and postal cards and three monthly reports, and stenciling two issues of *Bonfire*. Meanwhile, Rosenblum had been elected an honorary member for wartime services to fandom and Evans appointed Art Sehnert to replace another defection, the resigned director Thompson.

The organization had spent $3.49 per member during the year, but contributions made up the difference between the costs and the $1.00 in dues. The spending included an advance of $25.00 for publication of the *Fancyclopedia*. Members were allowed to purchase the thick publication for 50¢, in return for providing this aid. The welcom had issued a 41-page booklet, *What Is Science Fiction Fandom?* It was quite well printed professionally and fairly well written by Rothman, Ackerman, Tucker, Wollheim, Ashley, and me. Giddy with elation over these modest achievements, the NFFF was considering by the end of the year: a who's who of fandom, a chainzine of long stories by fans, a collection of recorded talks by professionals on their work, an advertising magazine, and a manuscript bureau. But for some members, these plans didn't compensate for the change in title for the official organ. *Bonfire*, the only touch of poetry in the club and the only thing that had been impregnable to the sercon philosophy, turned into the dismal *The National Fantasy Fan*.

As 1945 got under way, the organization could have expected progress. Membership was still growing and those accomplishments were nice to talk about. The annual laureate awards covering 1944 activities resulted from 57 ballots. They showed Tucker as the favorite fan author of fiction and non-fiction; J. Russell Gray, best poet; Wiedenbeck, best artist; *Fanewscard*, best newszine; *Acolyte*, best general fanzine; and Dunkelberger, best fan. Lou Smith won a promise of help with his proposed great bibliography of fandom. ("It will be a work that will almost never be done," Evans wrote, accurately.) There was even talk of publishing the legendary treatise on time travel that R. D. Swisher worked on for so many years. Evans was still president; Tucker, vice-president; Dunkelberger, secretary-treasurer; and the board consisted of me as chairman, Widner, Leslie A. Croutch, Sehnert, and Dale Tarr. The welcom made a weighty decision: it would not send its booklets to letterhacks in *Amazing Stories* who seemed to be interested mainly in Shaverian caves. The official organ was running regular articles on how to do better mimeographing. The war in Europe and the Pacific was nearing its end and hostilities were about to transfer to the NFFF.

There may be no surviving fan who remembers all the causes of the midsummer crisis. That old tool of the Devil, a new constitution, was mixed up in it. Evans' long-incubated constitution finally came up for a vote. It got 43 votes to accept as a whole, 32 votes to reject as a whole, and 24 votes for acceptance in part. The result was retention of the club's original name; rejection of a proposed set of judges, appointed for life, who would settle fannish disputes; and the resignation on August 4th of Evans as president. He claimed that the organization needed "another type of man" at its head. He'd had a fuss with Ashley, who had shared Speer's viewpoint on the constitution while sharing the Battle Creek house with Evans. Evans did not argue the matter in print, saying publicly only: "I did my durndest, and if it was not good enough, I'm truly sorry." Dunkelberger claimed that only one or two fans had caused Evans' resignation. Evans said nobody influenced it. Tucker was condemned to serve the remainder of Evans' term. The new constitution had remembered to provide for elections, although it had overlooked provision for amendments, and what was described as "the most screwed-up election in NFFF," a really impressive claim, followed. All the petitions for candidacy arrived too late and the ballot contained no names except those of proposed write-in candidates. Somehow or other, Dunkelberger became president; K. Martin Carlson, vice-president; Widner, secretary-treasurer; and the directors were myself as chairman, Fortier, James Hevelin, Francis T. Laney, and Dale Tarr.

Dunkelberger was younger than Evans, equally willing to work for the NFFF, and much more excitable. His reign was turbulent in the extreme, constantly threatened by real or imagined revolution or treason within and without the NFFF. He was president in 1946 when the NFFF had the most distinguished of its long list of authors of proposed constitutions, Burton Crane, a New York *Times* reporter. Speer kept in practice by producing a proposed new constitution, too. Confusion arose when Charles Tanner resigned as official editor while an economy committee was trying to figure out how to make the income provide for expenses other than those of the official organ. The archives had been sent to Ackerman, to dispose of as he thought best. The NFFF possessed a lending library, which consisted of six batches of pamphlets given away by manufacturers of duplicating equipment. The laureate report for the year listed Tucker as the best fan author; Dunkelberger, fan of the year; *Fanews*, best fanzine; and Carlson, best new fan. Membership stood at 169, one of whom was Redd Boggs, who paid his dollar for dues only once but didn't escape captivity for six long years. He ignored duns for more dues, wrote a formal letter of resignation without result, and did not become a free man until G. M. Carr took pity. This seems to mark a dividing point in the group's history, because just before he joined, 43 members had been suspended for nonpayment of dues.

This was the year when someone at the Pacificon sent a telegram to Dunkelberger that announced a convention decision to disband the NFFF and to send its treasury to the atomic scientists for undisclosed purposes. Dunkel-

Walter Dunkelberger

berger contacted an attorney, drew up legal papers to salvage the money, and instigated a Western Union investigation into use of its wires for fraudulent purposes, before the mess died down. Dunkelberger might not have reacted so violently to that fake telegram if he hadn't perpetually feared a palace revolution. Half-accurate rumors about the undercover formation of the Fantasy Foundation had reached him in sufficiently distorted form to cause him to think this was to become a direct competitor club. Rothman tried to make peace by explaining the lack of conflict between the purposes of the two groups. I even attempted to be Machiavellian by a proposal to reorganize or disband the NFFF, in the hope that this would drag into the open any genuine plot that might have the same intention. Dunkelberger finally proclaimed an emergency condition to freeze the treasury and to prevent the transaction of any but routine business. Laney promptly asked Dunkelberger to resign, on the grounds of unfitness to hold his exalted office. Laney admitted that he himself had sown the seed of the treason suspicion through an unfortunate statement in a board letter. Laney, the most unlikely officer the NFFF ever had, entered the board through appointment to the planning and publicity committee, after he had been challenged to do something about the welcom booklet which he had blasted.

The mess culminated in an election of normally severe confusion at the end of 1946. For president, Widner nosed out Tarr, who had also been a Laney target, 48-42. Walter A. Coslet was elected vice-president, Carlson became secretary-treasurer, and placed on the board of directors were Else Janda, James Hevelin, Leslie Croutch, Benson Perry, and Phil Schuman. Impeachment of Fortier for some forgotten transgression was favored in most of the ninety valid ballots. The outgoing officers looked ruefully back on a year that contained only one genuine accomplishment. The NFFF had published an eight-drawing Finlay portfolio that flabbergasted everyone by looking handsome, selling more than 200 copies, and producing a profit. In return, the official organ appeared only on the rarest occasions.

"As 1946 ended on a note of confusion and disunity, I hope to start 1947 on the theme of harmony and cooperation. So far, the prospects look good." That was Widner's message for the new year. *The National Fantasy Fan* kept up the best traditions by publishing a proposed new constitution that had been drawn up by Hevelin and Tarr on the skeleton of Speer's brief proposed constitution, which in turn had been written as a contrast to Evans' long constitution, after that had been amended. Dunkelberger had resigned without attracting as much attention as Evans had done, and blamed the trouble of 1946 on "the reaction at the end of the war which has caused considerable unrest." The NFFF had $100 in its treasury and it had acquired the emblem

NFFF emblem

that survives to this day. Jack Sloan drew it with a symbolism intended like this: a blue field to represent the sky into which spaceships head, crosses to symbolize leadership by an analogy that is lost upon me, buds to stand for growth, and a skull as proof that the organization contains fans of weird fiction. Somehow, even though the NFFF had published only one *TNFF* in the first two-thirds of 1947, even though the incoming treasurer hadn't yet received the treasury, and even though the Pacificon had coughed up only $5.00 from the $47.80 it had voted to the NFFF, the laureate awards were processed. Moskowitz was named best author; Boggs, poet; Kennedy, editor; *Vampire*, fanzine; *Fanews*, newszine; *Fantasy Advertiser*, specialist fanzine; Kennedy, fan of the year; Tom Jewett, new fan; Bradbury, professional ex-fan; John Cockroft, artist; Tucker, humorist; and *Astounding*, prozine.

The success of the Finlay portfolio had hinted that major projects might succeed better than the easy ones. So now the NFFF tried something elaborate, and won again. With Paul Spencer in charge, its book committee obtained rights to produce the first American edition of Dr. David H. Keller's *The Sign of the Burning Hart*. This short novel had previously appeared only in a 100-copy edition issued in 1938 in France. The NFFF arranged a 250-copy edition that sold out at $1.75 a throw by the end of 1948, before publication. Publication was considerably delayed by opposing fates that caused the printer to go bankrupt and Frank Wilimczyk's jacket drawing to get lost. Around this time, the NFFF began to break definitely from general fandom, with no apparent intent. Perhaps the clearest evidence of the cleavage came from the experiences of Charles Burbee, whose fannish career had reached its peak and shifted to the decline. Early in 1948, when he was near gafiation, he was notified that he had won a year's membership in the NFFF for excellence as a fan. Almost simultaneously, W. Leslie Hudson wrote to him, asking if he thought he could write well enough to contribute to the organization's publications. He also received a welcom letter from the legendary Zeda P. Mishler that went like this: "Chas do you have fireflys or lightning bugs (as we call them here) out there? The other night I had a fan here & he had never seen them before. Chas I always did think Religion & Science could go hand in hand & they have finally got together. This Continent is what's left of Biblical Land of Eden. & in Missouri around Independence was the site of the Garden of Eden." By now, Tarr was president; Henry Georgi, of whom nobody had heard before or has known about since, was vice-president; Carlson, secretary-treasurer; Stan Mullen, chairman; Rick Sneary, Ray Higgs, Andy Lyon, and Benson Perry, board members. They'd been elected at the end of 1947. The organization distributed, in March, a proposed new constitution which the vice-president hadn't seen, but it didn't matter because he wasn't sure what a fanzine was like.

Carlson got credit for holding the group together in 1947. It grew remarkably, under the circumstances. There were 151 ballots in the election at the end of that year, and there were 98 new NFFF members during 1947, not to mention the $175 in the treasury. Indeed, the organization grew steadily after the war: from 124 members at the end of 1944, it bloated to 169 members as 1946 began, by the end of 1948 the roster had risen to 319 names, a year later there were 373 NFFF members, and that approximate level held steady as the new decade arrived. This growth was all the more remarkable because *The National Fantasy Fan* failed to materialize into a new issue from February through October, 1947. Carlson finally got out election ballots after the secretary-treasurer failed to do anything about them, near the end of the year. It was about this time that the last of the original NFFF members, myself, dropped active participation.

Dale Tarr was re-elected president at the end of 1948, when a respectable total of 184 fans voted. Leslie Hudson became secretary-treasurer. Names that indicated the arrival of a new generation of fans were on the board of directors: Sneary, Darrell C. Richardson, Higgs, Art Rapp, and Ed Cox. They caused the club to prosper so well during 1949 that Sneary could announce, on assuming the presidency at the start of 1950, that the NFFF was ready to form a book club. It was to operate much like the Book-of-the-Month

Club with a four-man review panel for potential science fiction hardcover choices. Reduced prices and book dividends were to be part of the scheme. Ralph Fluette was named book distributor. It didn't pan out but the scope of this project was evidence that the club was strong enough to think of major matters rather than small mimeographed publications, and that there were enough new members to dilute the memories of past failures. Another clue to changes in the club occurs in the laureate awards for 1950. The ballots had formerly been almost completely fan-centered. Now professionals got most of the attention. Horace Gold was named the best prozine editor; *Galaxy*, best prozine; Bradbury, best filthy pro; Cartier, best artist; and curiously, Lee Hoffman was voted best fan editor but Don Day's *Fanscient*, already extinct, was named the best fanzine. The club still had an active welcom and its main fannish activity was the encouragement of fanzines sponsored or published by the club in one way or another. Higgs was again editing *The National Fantasy Fan*, after brilliant Rapp-edited issues. *Postwarp*, the publication devoted to letters, was edited successively by Rapp, Bob Johnson, Doug Fisher, and Higgs. Boggs started *Futurist*, but this ended up in the all-encompassing maw of Higgs, too. Bill Venable began *Aleph Null*. Before it could encounter the same fate, the NFFF cut it off without a penny because of its free-thinking contents. The club's dissociation from general fandom can be considered complete by now, because Roy Lavender, who had done next to nothing outside the organization, was voted the top fan.

2. The Shaver Mystery

Richard S. Shaver was a professional phenomenon who did not graduate from fandom and had no success at all with his repeated attempts to become a neofan. It is quite impossible to determine if Shaver or Ray Palmer had any genuine belief in the theories that they publicized at any stage of the improbable proceedings. Some published evidence seems to say that Palmer acquired the faith while Shaver was losing it. An almost unknown scrap of evidence to confirm an originally serious intent on Shaver's part is a tiny advertisement in the October, 1943, issue of *Writer's Digest*. It said "Antique language, newly discovered, needs scholars' care, advice." The address was "Shaver, Barto, Pa." It must be noted that this same name and address was appended in the same issue to another small advertisement proclaiming that an "attractive single male, 35, wishes friendly feminine correspondence." Another advertisement may be a coincidence, rather than an influence on the happenings. *Amazing Stories* had published, in 1940, several advertisements for a Lemurian Fellowship that promised to give data about lost continents. It had elements of the Rosicrucians, Col. Churchward's Mu theories, and myths. Readers were offered the chance to become members of the ruling class of the next society of mankind, by obtaining immediately full Lemurian citizenship.

Shaver first showed up in *Amazing*'s letter column in the January, 1944, issue. Immediately we run into conflicting legends. One school of thought asserts that this letter instigated a considerable correspondence between Shaver and Palmer. A conflicting tradition is that Palmer first became fully aware of Shaver when Palmer was glancing over the stacks of manuscripts his first reader, Howard Browne, had rejected, and found there "I Remember Lemuria." Whatever the circumstances, Palmer published it, later claiming that his superiors objected to the story on the grounds that it was over the head of the average *Amazing* reader.

It is not even possible to be sure how much writing Palmer, Browne, and W. Lawrence Hamling did in the stories published under Shaver's by-line. Palmer once claimed that he personally put the early stories into the traditional pulp fiction style. But careful readers have found the Shaver series too radically different from Palmer's hackneyed pulp narratives to admit this as reliable evidence. Someone even found a similarity between the style of Shaver and that of E. R. Eddison, whom Shaver once identified as his literary idol. Whatever the full facts, the Shaver Mystery was first hinted at in the December, 1944, *Amazing*, and "I Remember Lemuria" was published in the March, 1945, edition.

The entire Shaver mythos is so obviously derived from the Lovecraftian fictional background that it is hard today to imagine that it impressed any experienced readers. The first Shaver story told how the people of ancient Earth were endangered by a degenerated elder, how the hero and his followers learned of the danger, and how escape was achieved with the help of immortal elder gods. In June, "Thought Records of Lemuria" tried to present the fiction as fact more boldly. It told how Shaver had entered caverns in which he listened to thought records that enabled him to relive past lives. One of these thought record stories was retold, involving a wise worm that grew big enough to extend all around the Earth and to crowd things considerably for humans. December presented "Quest of Brail," which featured machines that enslaved women, and a hero who fought the evil with brains and science rather than fists.

Essentially, Shaver's long series of stories offered this set of modest claims, presented as truth: that the author had discovered in those caves an alphabet from which all present languages derive; that these caves are miles deep, carved thousands of years ago, and full of wonderful machines as well as degenerate humans known as deros; that originally the caves were tenanted by elder gods, more advanced mentally and spiritually than present men;

that after these elders left Earth for other planets, men found their way into the caves and degenerated because they operated the machinery in such a clumsy way that harmful rays came forth; that to date these deros have been fighting among themselves too much to cooperate in an attack on mankind; and that mankind is in double trouble because the sun emits detrimental rays causing old age and death, the cause of the elders' climbing down into the caves in the first place.

Fans were already in insurrection against the Shaver stories by the summer of 1945, both because they were so sensationally publicized that they threatened to come to public attention as examples of the finest science fiction, and because of the insinuations that they were dramatically presented fragments of a great truth. Tom Gardner cited the scientific absurdity of the elders moving to a larger, denser planet when they sought a new residence because of an increase in their size. He found the voices and imaginary events in early Shaveriana too similar to schizophrenic phenomena to make good reading. "From just a publicity stunt, this hoax is rapidly becoming psychopathic," he wrote in *Fantasy Commentator.* "Were public opinion to crystallize against the Lemuria-Mu bunk in *Amazing Stories,* it might spread to a denunciation of the better fantasy publications as well. And a blanket ban of this entire segment of the pulp field would not be out of the question." Dunkelberger found it hard to refrain from voicing doubts about the reliability of the Shaver material, after *Amazing* published a letter that solemnly discussed various volumes from the collection of the Miskatonic University. Ackerman was the most prominent fan who got really angry over the situation, striving to persuade fandom to cut all ties with Palmer and *Amazing.* By 1946 the condemnation was general throughout fandom, causing Palmer to explain late in that year what was happening: "The latest attack on your editor by dero is the hypnotic ray attack on a group of fans." The Eastern Science Fiction Association voted 21-4 to go on record as opposed to the presentation of Shaver stories as fact instead of fiction. Members booed Shaver loudly when he showed up at a meeting. Here and there, fans gave Palmer and Shaver some support, usually on the grounds that a free-press principle was involved. Dunkelberger broke with Ackerman on the question, citing the loss of life in the Second World War that "you and I, Ackerman, Palmer, Degler, all of us, might think as we please without let or hindrance. Now Ackerman denies me all that. Denies Palmer all that. Denies all fandom that right. Did these, our brothers and fans, die in vain?" Years later, Eva Firestone recalled her own tolerance that might have been typical of that of many non-fan readers of *Amazing*: "We were thrilled with Shaver's stuff even though we screamed at him for the sexy slant to much of it. We didn't care two hoots whether his theory was true or imagination. Some of my correspondents did believe the story true and some still do."

It's impossible to be sure what Palmer really thought, from his contradictory writings, reactions to the fan press, and interviews. His opinion of fans seemed to veer erratically from disdain through condemnation to a wheedling humility. At the start of 1947, we find him writing to Taurasi, identifying himself as a newly resuscitated fan, who wants to subscribe to all fanzines and would like to write reviews of his own prozines in Taurasi's *Fantasy Times*. A little earlier, he wrote in *Cepheid*: "It has been my fondest hope that the fans would begin to see that I'm serious about this Shaver business, and that I do believe in it implicitly. I went to visit Mr. Shaver and heard the voices myself. I've thousands of letters from people who have had similar experiences. Soon I hope to be able to solve the whole mystery." The quality of Palmer's research into the mystery may be guessed from his remark in a 1948 issue of *Amazing*: "In order to study a language based on something before the birth of this planet, we must discard the books that have been written on language, and approach the study with a completely blank mind." But in the mid-fifties, we find him quoted in *Dream Quest* in utterly different words: "Why did we ever fool with Shaver? One thing only, his unusual imagination. His strange sense of the unusual, his feeling for emotion, his sense of the beautiful and his sense of the outré." The safest conclusion to draw from at least one aspect of the whole enigma is that Palmer shared with almost every prozine editor in history the unshakable certainty that fans were too few numerically to be important, too eccentric in their opinions to be reliable guides to how to edit a professional magazine, and too much of a nuisance to be ignored.

Typical of Shaver's repeated wooing of fandom was his contact with Joe Kennedy, whose *Vampire* had reviewed unfavorably a Lemurian fanzine and *Startling Stories* had publicized that fact. Kennedy found Shaver anxious for a chance to blast someone for fandom's opposition to Shaverism. Kennedy rejected a four-page "prose poem" submitted to *Vampire* by Shaver. Kennedy described it as beginning with a blank verse discussion of Palmer and deros, then shifting into straight prose as more appropriate to its consideration of the dero-controlled fans, finally assuming the guise of an ordinary letter, and ending without the least warning. Kennedy also got into correspondence with Rog Phillips, who was conducting a fan column in *Amazing*. Phillips wanted an advance look at an article that Vaughn Greene had written for *Vampire* about Palmer's letterhacks, explaining that there was no reason to worsen the Palmer-fandom vendetta through publication of erroneous information. Phillips dutifully corrected several minor errors in the manuscript and seemed satisfied for it to be published.

W. Lawrence Hamling, a former fan, revealed himself as an agnostic in regard to the Shaver Mystery. There was a letter that Hamling wrote in an effort to explain away as a hoax the report that a nervous breakdown had happened to Palmer: "The greatest mistake the fans ever made with their dealings with a professional house, they made with Ray Palmer and *Amazing Stories*. *Amazing Stories* and its companion, *Fantastic Adventures*, are the leaders in the field today. The Shaver mystery, true or untrue—and what difference it makes I fail to see—will continue to go on, more and more. This is only the beginning. As usual, the fans and the minority they represent have missed the boat." The hoax, Hamling claimed, had been instigated by Palmer himself to have some fun at fandom's expense. Much excitement was raised when Ackerman told the LASFS about the letter from Hamling at the June 20, 1946, meeting.

If general fandom showed such small respect for Shaver, a subfandom decided to spring up about this topic. Shaver claimed in *Vampire* that he regretted support from occultists and denied all communications with spirits. The first real Shaver fanzine was *Maxin-96*, a "magazine of occult research" that David D. Dagmar, Hollywood, began to produce in 1945. It boasted forty printed pages. Kennedy described its contents as "a pathetic mixture of fact and fancy, no proof whatsoever being offered for any of the statements." Other Shaver fanzines followed, receiving much publicity in Ziff-Davis magazines. Meanwhile, yet another defector from fandom, Chet Geier, became a major force in formation of the Shaver Mystery Club. He claimed that Shaver had donated $1,000 and that Ziff-Davis had tossed $250 into the kitty for the club and its 64-page monthly magazine. Geier formed the club and became its first president in 1946. The first thing the club intended to do was to begin publishing a 300,000-word Shaver novel, "Mandark," that told what the caves revealed about the life of Christ. By 1949 there was an American Shaver Mystery Club that claimed more than 2,000 members and published for 50¢ per copy a bimonthly *Shaver Mystery Magazine*. There were those who thought that the thing could become as large and as near respectability as that Madame Blavatsky cult.

In June, 1947, Palmer proudly turned an entire issue of *Amazing* over to Shaver material. Circulation had grown memorably since Lemuria came to attention. Palmer claimed it had risen from 27,000 to 185,000. Then something happened. Palmer was no longer editor of any Ziff-Davis magazines. The full story has never been told in an authorized published version. Palmer once referred to the episode as "a terrible accident." Shaver claimed that Ziff had ordered Shaverism killed in the magazines when a reader's letter pointed out that the theories did not fit into Einstein's general theory of relativity. Whatever the events, Palmer soon began to publish a series of new magazines with less substantial financial backing and somewhat modified public acceptance. They veered far enough from fandom to be worthy of ignoring, although we must return briefly to consideration of Palmer when we arrive at the fifties.

If it did nothing else, the Shaver Mystery indirectly helped to create a major recruiting ground for fandom. Palmer or someone at Ziff-Davis became sufficiently alarmed at the bad press in fandom to create "The Club House" in *Amazing Stories* as a new reader section devoted to organized fandom and to hire Rog Phillips to conduct it. Vernon L. McCain summarized the overall importance of this feature like this: " 'The Club House' had done more to make fandom grow than any other single force in history, and it altered the whole character of fandom by bringing in a different type person. Not that this new type was in any way superior or inferior to the old type, but they were different and they changed fandom. Many of us preferred the old type to the new, which somewhat resembled a combination of the American Legion and the Housewives' Thursday Knitting and Tea Auxiliary. Less publicity is what fandom needs."

3. The Cosmic Circle

The Cosmic Circle claimed at various times too many goals and purposes to list. It is so inextricably bound up with the adventures of Claude Degler that a month-by-month account would repeat the biographical material on that gentleman needlessly. At the start, it claimed ideals no more alarming than those of fan clubs sponsored by prozines and the NFFF. Things took a change for the worse quite promptly.

The group apparently originated as a local activity in Indiana in 1940. It didn't come to fandom's attention until 1943, when Degler's ideas became inescapable through his liberal patronage of the postal service. Aside from generalities borrowed from previous clubs, like a united fandom for accomplishment of fan projects, Degler believed that fans could become a force operative outside themselves. He sought increased membership for the CC not for delight in large numbers on the roster but "so that cosmic fandom will actually be some sort of power or influence in the postwar world of the near future." The very first *Cosmic Circle Commentator*, dated September, 1943, contained the fateful statement on which opponents soon pounced: "Declaration of existence: of a new race or group of cosmic-thinking people, a new way of life, a cosmology of all things. Cosmen, the cosmic men, will appear. We believe that we are actual mutations of the species." Pending the full realization by the world of this situation, the CC intended to help fans plan tours, to promote the artwork of Hannes Bok, to set up Cosmic Camp in the mountains of Van Buren County of northwestern Arkansas, to use an unidentified Arizona ranch for rocketry experiments, and after the war to purchase a tract of land where futuristic homes and a beautiful park would be constructed for fans.

In all justice, it must be emphasized that little or nothing in the CC program lacked a parallel in general fandom. Degler and whatever real fans he may have possessed as his local lieutenants served as a sort of trick mirror for fandom. The mirror was misshapen sufficiently to cause the CC version of each item to be difficult to recognize., But the mirror lacked the power to create without something which it could reflect. Thus, the futuristic homes and the park could be traced back to the half-serious talk of Los Angeles and Michigan fans, about a cooperative housing project they imagined evolving from the apartments and houses they shared during the war. Cosmic Camp must have derived from this or that weekend when a few fans had a get-together in a non-metropolitan area. Rocketry experiments were an old fannish tradition, still remembered from the years when a fan was in disgrace if he wasn't also an amateur scientist. Campbell had been harping on mutations in *Astounding* almost as steadily as he later preached about psi. There were some parallels between the CC and the prozines, too. The first issue of *Cosmic Digest*, in the spring of 1943, contained remarks that are interesting in the light of those in *Amazing* in 1945. The CC statement, presumably by Degler: "Man is still evolving toward a higher form of life. A new figure is climbing upon the stage. Homo Cosmen, the cosmic men, will appear. We believe that we are mutations of that species. We are convinced that there are a considerable number of people like ourselves on this planet, if only we could locate and get in touch with them. Someday we will find most of them, and then we will do great things together." The relevant passage from the prozine: "And indications are that when all these people are united they will make an organization which not only will have an expert on every subject, trade, and profession, but that their pooled knowledge will be far in advance of anything that has been developed on earth to the present day! Thus, we urge every reader . . . who believes he has a work of some far-reaching scope to perform, who believes he is part of a great plan, and who is convinced that he knows things today unknown to science, to write to your editor, who is one of those people! The time has come for action!"

It must also be remembered that science fiction put great stress on the superman story in those days. Possibly because of the Hitler master race theory, fans were reading and talking about several popular novels centered around supermen: Stapledon's *Odd John*, much of which was devoted to the search for the mutants mentioned by Degler; van Vogt's *Slan*, whose title was close enough to "fan" to be symbolic in sound; Weinbaum's *The New Adam*; and Beresford's *The Hampdenshire Wonder*.

Two other quotations might be apropos. Both reflect attitudes expressed by individuals more dignified than Degler. He did not hear the first when originally spoken but he must have encountered the thinking that it caused in fandom: "There is something in each and every one of you fans which places him automatically above the level of the average person; which, in short, gives him a vastly broadened view of things in general." That was John B. Michel in his celebrated "Mutation or Death!" read by Wollheim at the 1937 Phillycon. And: "Science fiction fans differ from most of the rest of the race by thinking in terms of racial magnitudes—not even centuries but thousands of years. . . . I think the corniest tripe published in a science fiction magazine beats all the *Anthony Adverses* and *Gone With the Winds* that were ever published." Robert A. Heinlein should have known better than to say that at the Denvention. If the audiences had interrupted both talks with laughter suitable to the occasion, the Cosmic Circle might have adopted less alarming goals. But fans and pros devoutly rephrased and rehashed those ideas from time to time. Then they blamed Degler when he was naive enough to attempt to take action based on the ideas to which the others had given mere lip service. The Cosmic Circle did fandom its greatest service by exaggerating the idea that fans are slans. The absurdity of the proposition that others had hinted at so delicately became quite obvious when Degler spoke it out boldly. The question has never seriously arisen since.

The Cosmic Circle program was too many-faceted to allow even its most violent opponents to claim that all of the numerous ideas were equally bad. T. Bruce Yerke of Los Angeles worked himself up severely enough over Degler to suffer a heart attack, but admitted fondness for the CC proposal to abandon "fan" as a name of hobbyists of science fiction. He also approved the suggested central purchasing agency that would make fanac materials available at near-wholesale prices to all fans, through quantity purchases. Larry Shaw, after resigning all connection with the CC, reconsidered in early 1944 and hinted that he might be willing to rejoin. Joe J. Fortier thought that the most shattering suggestion of all, a merger of the CC and the NFFF, would be "wonderful."

Degler was so anxious for the CC to take over fandom that he didn't waste time on technicalities normally associated with organizing and recruiting. A fan could join the CC without payment of dues, simply by asking to become a member, assuming that Degler had not already listed him unbidden on the roster. However, payment of 95¢ enabled the fan to become an inner circle member, entitled to certain improbable-sounding privileges. Degler didn't always ask a fan if it would be satisfactory to make him an official of some suborganization of the CC. Thus, after Degler's visit to Hagerstown, I discovered in a CC publication the news that I had been for some weeks the chairman of the Maryland, Delaware, and District of Columbia Regional Federation of the CC. Alfred Maxwell, a Louisiana fan, became director of the Southwest Fantasy Unit despite the fact that he was stationed at Salt Lake City in the armed forces. Julie Unger never ceased to mourn the generous impulse that had caused him to loosen consequences like these upon fandom. He'd given Degler permission to copy a 700-name mailing list that Unger had compiled for his dealership and newszine. However, Degler did not stop at the names on this list. One CC member's last name is unknown to history. She is identified only as one Gloria, who entered the Unger grocery store with the goal of purchasing garlic, admitted to Degler that her brother had once looked through an issue of *Amazing Stories*, and found herself enrolled in the Cosmic Circle.

The most mysterious thing about the CC is the question of the fans and organizations alleged to exist around Degler's New Castle, Indiana, home. Speer and other iconoclasts flatly denied the existence of any fans in New Castle outside the confines of Degler's skull. It is a cynicism that circumstantial evidence makes dubious. The consistency with which Degler drew on outside inspiration for so much of his material makes it improbable that he created the whole elaborate series of cliques, personalities, and events around New Castle out of the whole cloth. It is even less likely that all these fans and their clubs existed as CC publications described them. Another fragment of evidence is the fact that Len Marlowe before breaking with Degler described the reality of certain science fiction readers around New Castle who were good friends of Degler although unknown to fandom as a whole. On purely stylistic grounds, I am convinced that someone else wrote most of the CC material that appeared under the name of Frank N. Stein. The typewriter that cut the stencils is Degler's but it is hard to believe that the sharply different prose was his. Stein was described as hailing from Haiti, Miami, and Greenwich Village, making most of his trips by airplane, and possessed of considerable quantities of money. Degler never went to the extreme of claiming the latter attribute for anyone else connected with the CC. The most likely guess is that Degler had cronies in the vicinity of New Castle, some of whom may have belonged to mundane juvenile gangs, a few of whom read science fiction occasionally, and the lurid fan clubs described in CC publications may be transfigured and embellished versions of these individuals, their outings, and their squabbles.

A sample of what fans were told by the CC appeared late in 1943 in *Fanews Analyzer*. This CC publication asserted that twenty ghuists had gone to jail in the first actual fan war, fought with "fists, brickbats, slingshots, sabotage, and actual force of numbers." This was said to have occurred after a complex series of events in the old Cosmic Club of New Castle caused creation of a new Oak Grove Fantasy Society and a Rose City Science Circle, from which subgroups emerged like the Legions of the Damned and the Sisters of Tanit, as well as black masses and eventual violence. Degler was careful to point out that no CC members had been among those jailed. The Oak Grove Fantasy Society is described as strong enough to stage a big banquet for Degler when he returned in tattered triumph from one good-

will tour of fandom, and to have possessed enough knowledge of fandom
to stage a Halloween party that included a photograph of Wollheim over the
speaker's platform and one member dressed up in tail and horns to symbolize
Yerke. Early in 1944, we are asked to believe, a local group honored Degler
with a parade in New Castle followed by a picnic where the town band provided music.

Of all the projects that the CC claimed to accomplish or predicted as imminent, the production of fanzines was the only visible evidence. These
fanzines billowed forth in unceasing, overwhelming quantities for many
months. Usually, three or four titles arrived simultaneously to those still
on good terms with Degler, each title averaging four to eight pages, each
page tightly packed with CC propaganda and the news of fandom through
Degler's eyes. Degler apparently financed all this publishing with little or
no help from general fandom. He claimed in late 1943 that he had already
spent over $400 on the CC, a large sum for a period when postage, paper,
and ink were cheap. Degler even tried to be a CC equivalent of FAPA all by
himself. The Cosmic Circle Amateur Publishers Alliance had its first mailing
in September, 1943. This consisted of seven sheets of paper stapled together,
all containing symptoms of deriving from the same mind, typewriter, and
mimeograph. Degler claimed that distribution would reach 500 copies and
that dues would be 60¢ annually for non-members of the CC, with free membership to CC members.

By the end of 1943, Degler claimed for the Cosmic Circle twenty-two state
organizations, ten local groups, and fifteen sectional bodies. Most of these
amounted to nothing more imposing than the fact that someone in a state or
city had been civil with Degler and had been rewarded with the presidency
of a newly colonized CC territory. At one time, Degler claimed "more members than any other fan organization that has ever existed," strong language
in view of the numbers that the Science Fiction League once counted. Unlike other world leaders, Degler never claimed the status of god, although he
did accomplish an occasional miracle of medium stature, if we believe the
claims of such deeds as cornering the mimeograph paper stock in Indianapolis. He did tinker with religious matters at the height of the CC. Somehow, he started to associate the mock fannish religion of ghughu with devil
worship and even hinted that this combination might help to save the world
from Catholicism. Sex was not completely forgotten in the CC. A one-
sheeter entitled *Ghu* explained the situation: "The human body is sacred to
Ghu—it is in all cosmos, infinitely beautiful. Sex is the most wonderful,
beautiful, powerful, uplifting force for good in the universe." But Degler
may have feared that a conflict between sex and slannish qualities might con-
fuse his followers, and little more was heard about the advantages of the
physical self.

For all the commotion that it aroused, the CC had a remarkably brief lifespan. Little was heard about it in general fandom until the early part of 1943; by the end of that year Degler was frantically attempting to salvage something from the ruins by recanting statements and dissociating himself from the CC; and in the spring of 1944, Jack Speer conducted the investigation in New Castle that ended neutrality among any fans who tried to keep an open mind. Speer leafed through telephone and city directories, conferred with law enforcement and welfare authorities, and visited addresses found in New Castle references in the CC publications. He could locate no evidence of the existence of the area fans about whom Degler wrote, although a welfare worker knew Joan Dominick under another name. Joan, traced down, denied membership in the old Cosmic Club and said she wasn't Helen Bradleigh, the most famous of the Degler friends. Newspapers gave no evidence of the fights and jailings that were reported at Oak Grove. A post office box that was Stein's mailing address was rented to one Vergie Degler, presumably Degler's mother.

Degler's final efforts to salvage something from the wreckage started with a strong hint that Speer had stolen priceless CC records while in New Castle, followed by the sudden springing up, on Independence Day of 1944, of the World Science-Fantasy Association, proclaiming itself free from all ties with prozines, fandom, "and any other groups." Raymond Washington, Jr., a young Florida fan, officially became head of the CC at the start of March, 1944. Degler was still recruiting for undetermined purposes, possibly out of sheer habit, a month later when he formed the Futurian Society of Alabama

and placed Julian Williamson and Tom Pace at its head. The name derived from yet another new universal CC group, the Young Futurian League, and that in turn was an affiliate of the Planet Fantasy Federation. But the CC was dead, having failed to go over with a bang, and with nobody to whimper over it. Washington did nothing either to keep it alive or to hasten its dissolution. The Cosmic Circle and all its sub- and super-organizations got only this valedictory from Washington in the middle of 1945: "I think the CC would have done more good than harm had I been in control from the start. People are still asking me what became of Degler, and I am still telling them I do not know. I last saw him in August, 1944 and have not heard from him since."

Raymond Washington, Jr.

9. FORTRESSES OF FANDOM: The Amateur Press Associations

1. The Fantasy Amateur Press Association

It's always hard to determine the motives behind the organization of an amateur press association. The founding fathers have a habit of giving one set of reasons while in the process of creation, and then frequently revealing entirely different sets of reasons in retrospect years later, and from these it is necessary to attempt to determine the real reasons why they formed the groups.

The Fantasy Amateur Press Association was the first fannish equivalent of the mundane ayjay groups. In the first FAPA mailing, in July, 1937, Donald A. Wollheim gave an explanation of his motives. There were 27 fanzines extant; they had circulations ranging from 20 to 35 copies; all of them lost money, despite receiving some subscriptions, because of the many exchanges with other fanzines. "Measures are needed badly to preserve the individual publications and to place the entire field of fan magazines upon a more friendly, less commercial and more solid foundation," Wollheim wrote. "There are many fans desiring to put out a voice who dare not, for fear of being obliged to keep it up, and for the worry and time taken by subscriptions and advertising. It is for them and for the fan who admits it is his hobby and not his business that we formed the FAPA." A year later, Wollheim described a slightly different attitude toward the organization on behalf of some of its members: "FAPA was formed for those fans who have outgrown the idea of trying to sell their magazines and now recognize their sincere interest in publishing and writing as a hobby. That is its purpose: to provide a vehicle for those who wish to publish but feel no desire to be tied down by strings of commercial obligation. It has to have a membership interested in doing, not in getting." Robert W. Lowndes described an unpublicized portion of the motives behind the founding: "While there was no intention to drive the subscription magazines out of business, we reasoned that, if the new organization clicked, FAPA would absorb all the fan publishers. The idea was that, for a modest membership fee which would cover mailing costs, we would be sure of getting all the fan magazines published. We mustn't overlook the fact that part of the motive in organizing FAPA was prestige-building on the part of the organizers and the heavy contributors. Finally, there was the hope that through the media of publishing and criticizing in FAPA, some fans could be helped to attain the status of professional authors."

Whatever the complete list of purposes, the sequence of events that led to organization for FAPA is known. Wollheim was present at an International Scientific Association meeting in 1936 where complaints were sounded about the large number of fanzines and the difficulty of keeping up with exchange obligations. Wollheim knew little or nothing of the mundane apas. But he conceived the theory of publications intended solely for exchanges, all mailed from a central source to cut mailing expenses. From Lovecraft, he learned about the mundane ayjays, joined the National and United APAs, and talked the matter over with other fans. During a talk in the spring of 1937 with Jim Blish and Bill Miller, the name and some of the operating details were chosen for FAPA. Wollheim looked over constitutions of mundane ayjay organizations, and modeled FAPA's first constitution after that of the New England Amateur Press Club. He and John Michel signed that constitution on May 19, 1937. Wollheim named Michel editor of the new group. Miller became its secretary, the only officer in FAPA's history who was not a member. He lost interest in September and quit fandom before joining the new group. Dan McPhail received the vice-presidency and the task of recruiting members. Morris Dollens provided three designs for selection of an emblem. Michel and Wollheim picked the one that was used on membership cards. Fred Pohl became the first fan to pay dues and receive one of those cards. Others who joined before the first mailing went out were Ted Carnell, Harry Dockweiler, J. Michael Rosenblum, Robert Madle, Robert Lowndes, James Taurasi, John Baltadonis, H. C. Koenig, Dave Kyle, Sam Moskowitz, Alex Osheroff, Vodoso (Virgil Douglas Smith), Jack Speer, Julius Schwartz, Robert G. Thompson, Thomas Whiteside, Olon Wiggins, and Dick Wilson.

The first mailing in July contained thirteen items, seven of them printed and all of them tiny, containing only 42 pages among them. The bundle cost only three cents in postage and was unthinkably different from the FAPA mailings that evolved within a few years. An alarmingly large proportion of it consisted of leftovers of previously circulated fanzines, an indication that already the announced purpose was being sidestepped. Many of the 21 charter members had little or no fanzine publishing experience. Represented as publishers in the first bundle were Carnell, Willis Conover, Taurasi, Michel, Baltadonis, Wollheim, and Will Sykora. But it didn't take long for the distinctive aspects of FAPA to make their appearance. In the next organizational mailing, out in October, the first mailing comments appeared. McPhail conceived of them, described his inspiration to Speer, and both had them in that mailing. In this primitive form, they resembled letters of comment to prozines, mainly listing likes. But they started a tradition that quickly became the new group's selling point and its greatest difference from mundane apas, providing a genuine continuity between bundles and inspiring members to think about what they read in place of simply reacting to the magazines.

Wiggins provided the first postmailing in FAPA's history with the Winter, 1937, issue of *Galaxy*; this indirectly served as a basis for a later decision that also distinguished FAPA from the older groups. It is standard operating practice for mundane amateur journalists to distribute some of their best publications only to inner circle members and close friends, rather than the full membership. The postmailings, by going to everyone on the membership list, solidified the tendency of FAPA to remain as one bundle, equal for everyone. The first mention of a waiting list occurred in the third issue of *The Fantasy Amateur*. (This official organ first appeared in the May, 1938, bundle, succeeding the semi-official *The FAPA Fan* published by Wollheim.) Taurasi, the secretary-treasurer, put Edgar Allan Martin, Millie Taurasi, Bob Tucker, and Willard Dewey on a list, and said that they would "be allowed to join as soon as some of the present members quit." This was heretical from the standpoint of amateur journalists outside fandom, whose organizations had no upper limit on membership. FAPA originally operated with a fifty-member limit, to permit the use of the hectograph by members. The decision to retain an upper limit and to force excess applicants to wait had tremendous consequences in later years.

The organization started with fanzines that were just like those circulated in the rest of fandom. In the first few years, FAPA seems to have interested leading fans more as another excuse for power politics and a medium for exchange of insults than for the noble purpose that had caused its foundation. As if by unwritten agreement, the nature of the bundles changed near the end of the thirties. The publications grew larger. Fewer of them came from the mimeographs of New York fandom. There was more inclination to publish material that dealt neither with fantasy fiction nor with the prevaricating habits of the editor's current opponents. Discussions sprang up unpredictably on a variety of subjects and continued through many mailings. The organization showed no inclination to collapse after a couple of years, as every respectable fan organization did in those early times. Speer was more responsible than any other single fan for the changes in FAPA. He provided a couple of decades later a good summary of what FAPA evolved into: "Some innocents think that FAPAzines should be science fiction fan magazines. Maybe they should be, but they aren't. Our organization can be what we wish it to be, and we wish it to be a medium in which we consider a great range of subjects, in many of which scientifantasy is not even a flavoring. Some think the Fantasy APA is just another ayjay organization. They observe no preponderance of material pertaining to fantasy and they conclude that we're mundane. We're not. Nearly all FAPAns served at least an apprenticeship in science fiction fandom. This both became a part of us, and selected us out of the general literate population, for whatever qualities they are that orient a person toward stf and incline him to the discussion of it."

FAPA's first year produced mailings that contained 348 pages, of which 125 pages came from the Futurian group around New York City. At first, FAPA had official critics, who reminded Norm Stanley of something out of *The Mikado*. They published a couple of phrases about each publication and decided on winners of laureate certificates. These first honors went to

Taurasi as publisher, Baltadonis as editor, Walter E. Marconette as artist, and Lowndes as poet and literary man in general. The following year, Michel won as publisher, Swisher as editor, Marconette as artist, Lowndes as poet, and Jack Chapman Miske for literary qualities. During the second year, FAPA's mailings were only one-half or one-third the size that they were to average a little later, but already they were astonishing mundane apa members for their size in proportion to membership. The 300-member NAPA, for instance, distributed only nineteen items in what was considered a big bundle, and the 200 AAPA members put only 23 items into a mailing around the same time.

Jack Chapman Miske

The tendency of fandom in general and FAPA in particular away from domination by New York City's cliques and politics became obvious in the fall of 1939. Milton Rothman defeated Taurasi for president, Speer beat Pohl for the vice-presidency, Madle bested the Futurian-oriented Wiggins for secretary-treasurer, and isolated Marconette became editor, besting Philadelphian Jack Agnew. Proud of his 28 known members, Rothman said in a presidential message: "The FAPA has expanded in size about as much as it can." There were a few stray problems, to be sure. Agnew became official editor after all, when it was discovered that Marconette hadn't been a candidate. Madle didn't get the organization's money and records until the president made a trip to New York City to dislodge them from Taurasi's grasp. Wollheim claimed that the whole election was illegal anyway because Taurasi had sent ballots to inactive members. But in compensation the members got genuine photographs as illustrations in the March, 1940, bundle: Speer put a 1939 convention scene and a Buck Rogers Sunday page into the pages of his *Sustaining Program*.

FAPA took a significant step toward permanence in the summer of 1940 that is hard to describe today with the effectiveness that it possessed in fandom when it happened. The June bundle failed to appear. Speer, Rothman, and Elmer Perdue drove from Washington to Philadelphia to determine what was wrong and to rectify the situation. This seems today like a normal course of procedure. But in fandom of that time, it was an inconceivable amount of trouble to take. It was the sort of situation in which everyone just stood around and let the organization collapse, under the traditions of the day. Besides, a three-fan trip between cities 150 miles apart was headline news in that day, no matter what the provocation. The Washington group couldn't find Baltadonis at all. They ran down Madle. He sicced them onto Agnew, who was attending a church camp, of all things, at Beaver College outside town. With his permission, the Washington group staged a raid at the Agnew home the next day, got the publications, wormed the records out of Madle, went back to Washington, produced the mailing, and issued a one-shot, *Blitzkrieg*, to commemorate the whole thing. FAPA gained enormous prestige because three fans had considered it worth all that time and trouble.

In the fall of 1940, FAPA elected Tucker as president, me as vice-president, Rothman as secretary-treasurer, and Perdue as editor: four fans who were not only free from feuds but also from interest in feuds. The group now had 46 members. A new constitution proposed by Speer, Rothman, Perdue, and Baltadonis passed by a 22-1 vote. It discarded the less satisfactory borrowings from the mundane ayjay traditions. The official critics, somewhat handicapped by recent troubles, resumed their function. Speer lost some of their report but from memory he announced that they had chosen Freehafer the best publisher, Speer the best editor, Michel the best artist, and Rothman the best writer. By the time the March, 1941, mailing appeared, the New York City contingent had almost completely vanished as publishers, Philadelphia fandom was also quite inconspicuous, and still there was enough publishing activity to encourage an increase in dues from 50 to 75 cents. The Futurians made one final effort in the summer of 1941 to stir up the old spirit. They emitted an assortment of small publications that repeated in various degrees of loudness and seriousness their election cry, "Turn the Rascals Out." Simultaneously, Tucker suggested another reversion to type, enlargement of FAPA so it could cover all fandom. Both projects failed, and were never again taken seriously. I got elected president, Rothman became vice-president, Perdue, secretary-treasurer, and Louis Russell Chauvenet, official editor. The group now had a genuine waiting list, in addition to 51 members, one too many. The extra fan got in because of a mixup. The increased popularity of mailing comments was causing alarm and a prediction that has turned up at least once each year ever since. In *The Damn Thing*, someone wrote: "If this goes on, it won't be long before the entire FAPA mailing will consist of reviews upon the reviews of the reviews of the reviews of the last mailing." A laureate report at the end of 1941 produced awards to Koenig as writer, Chauvenet as poet, Speer as editor, Freehafer as publisher, Harry Jenkins as artist, and Speer as photographer.

The mailings began to bulge impressively in size in 1942. They were full of such lively chatter as a statement that Bill Groveman was a stooge and the unconfirmed report that Rothman had had a brainstorm. By now the braintrusters were becoming a fixed part of the organization. The term was more a compliment than an insult, applied to a half-dozen or so who wrote in more intellectual manner than the others and dealt with the major issues of the world. *En Garde* had been started by Ashley as the year began, D. B. Thompson had joined late in 1941, Norm Stanley made his first appearance, Chauvenet was enough of a fan to have mis-numbered several issues of the official organ, and old-timers like Speer and Rothman joined them in that braintrust category.

In the election in the fall of 1942, Speer defeated Lowndes for the presidency, Perdue became vice-president, Chauvenet nosed out Widner as secretary-treasurer, and Ashley defeated Jenkins for the job of official editor. (In those years, the constitution forbade the secretary-treasurer and official editor to return to office within five years, accounting for the consistency with which the really hard jobs changed hands.) Koenig again took laureate honors for editing and publishing, in a laureate report issued in mid-1942. Chauvenet was first as both writer and poet. The waiting list was up to six by the end of that year, and some of that half-dozen had waited during several mailings. Life became considerably easier for historians at this time, too. Koenig made a suggestion so simple that nobody else had thought of it: inclusion of a list of the contents of the bundle in the official organ. Up to then, you just hoped that the official editor had sent you a complete mailing. The trend toward literary matters continued, with such manifestations as publication of Chauvenet's collected verse, a wordy debate on the usefulness of the current war by the braintrusters, and a Faulkner-like genealogy of the Futurians' penname family, the Conways.

Laney made his significant first FAPA appearance in the June, 1943, mailing. He proposed a 200-page fanzine anthology, exactly the sort of idea that he later called a Daugherty project. Perdue experienced the first in a series of thrilling escapes from expulsion from FAPA. These suspense-filled adventures enlivened the organization for two decades. This time, he was on his way out for failure to pay dues, when Chauvenet found a lost letter that contained the money. In the fall of 1943, Ashley became president after a triangular contest with Lowndes and Unger. Chauvenet became vice-president, Stanley defeated E. E. Evans and Michel for secretary-treasurer, and Swisher became official editor. The first issue of Degler's *Cosmic Circle Commentator* went out with the September mailing. The final mailing of that year was the biggest in the organization's history, containing 41 items. It also was one of the most significant of all mailings because of several publications: the first issue of Les Croutch's *Light*; Widner's reprint of "Alicia in Blunderland," the P. S. Miller parody from *Science Fiction Digest*; the *Lovecraft Bibliography* directed by Laney; and the first issue of Langley Searles' scholarly and literate *Fantasy Commentator*. Wallowing in these delights, the membership took calmly the bulletin announcing the disappearance of the precious official emblem. The first genuine popularity vote in FAPA's history occurred in 1944, when Widner took a poll to which 23 responded. *Fan-Tods* of Stanley, *Sustaining Program* of Speer, and *Yhos* of Widner were voted the best fanzines; Jack Wiedenbeck, Rosco Wright, and Ronald Clyne, best artists; Speer, Stanley, and Chauvenet, writers; Speer, Ashley, and Widner, fans.

The Degler situation neared a climax in the March, 1944, mailing. Vice-president Chauvenet studied charges against him, found him guilty of using the names of fans without their permission, but not guilty of antagonizing prozine editors. Chauvenet left it up to the members to decide if they wanted to take action. The organization could afford to lose a member, because by June it had a waiting list of record size, seventeen strong, despite the recent lengthening of the membership list to 65 names, and its bundles had been virtually twice as heavy during the seventh year since founding as during the sixth FAPA year. The election that fall produced a comeback for the Futurian forces that almost had disastrous consequences. Lowndes defeated Chauvenet for the presidency; Suddsy Schwartz beat Tucker for secretary-treasurer; Ashley nosed out Stanley for the vice-presidency; and Larry Shaw was elected official editor. Dues were raised to $1.00. A petition to suspend Degler apparently failed to pass but Lowndes found a technicality that made it effective. Lowndes put another Futurian, Wollheim, into an official capacity, as historical coordinator. This post was supposed to provide for preservation of the FAPA archives. Despite the discovery of the fan poll, the laureate machinery was retained, and the worthies found for Bill Watson, editing and publishing; Chauvenet, non-fiction; Wiedenbeck, art; Lowndes, humor; and Stanley, best in the mailing.

FAPA had another decisive crisis at the end of that year. The Futurians had sponsored an amendment that changed the mailing date from December to January. Nevertheless, they issued a small bundle in December and called it a November mailing. A tremendous semantic war began instantly over whether this was a mailing in itself or part of a split mailing. Perplexity over the reason for this mailing, which contained nothing urgent, was soon replaced by concern when January passed without any additional bundle. Mike Fern, obscure in FAPA before and after, now had his great solo scene. He began to ask about the missing bundle. On January 28th, Shaw told him it was assembled. But on or about this date, Fern blundered into a discussion in Lowndes' apartment. He was allowed to know that the formation of a new ayjay group was the subject and he was told to keep this matter a secret. On January 30th, Shaw resigned his office. The next day, Lowndes followed suit. Their duties were conferred on Watson and Ashley, respectively. Still there was no mailing, as two weeks elapsed. Schwartz had become unobtainable and Shaw claimed that he had no spare cash of his own available for putting out the bundles, because of illness. On February 10th, Evans as president of the NFFF mailed $10.00 to Shaw to bail out the FAPA bundle. It stayed in seclusion. On February 17th, Ashley wrote to Fern, telling of his vain efforts to set Lowndes and Shaw into motion. The pair alleged in turn that they had originally begun to wait for the arrival of some Slan Shack publications before sending out the bundle. On the same night, Fern went in search of Schwartz, and found that he had left town.

With the support of Tucker, Koenig, Kepner, Searles, and Evans, Fern got busy. One of the tremendous documents in FAPA history boiled out of his typewriter. Entitled *Neither Blind Nor Idiot*, it charged: "The Futurians, while neglecting the affairs of the APA of which they were elected officers, busied themselves with the organization of another similar and partly competitive group. They tried to keep these activities a secret from the rest of the FAPA membership. I must consider them guilty of attempting to destroy FAPA." The Futurians denied the last sentence. Wollheim insisted that the Futurians were really anxious to put out the mailing, so that they could turn their full attention to the new ayjay group. To counter the charge that they had refused Unger's offer to bail out the organization, the Futurians cited an apparent epidemic running through their midst: Michel claimed that he'd been sick like Shaw, Lowndes said he had a broken rib, and Wollheim simply said he was too overwhelmed with literary work to help. Lowndes' reason for resigning from the FAPA presidency was explained: "He felt it unbecoming that he function as chief of both organizations and he frankly found the new club more worth his while." The mailing finally reached members near the end of February, the confusion over officialdom compounded by an unrelated imbroglio, censorship efforts by Searles. It finally went down in FAPA history as section B of the thirtieth mailing. We shall hear more soon of the new group, the Vanguard Amateur Press Association.

Loss of interest and members to VAPA and reaction from the mess were responsible for a lot of turnover in membership during the second half of the decade. FAPA had admitted 71 new members from 1941 through 1945. There were 104 admissions in the following five years. The group even lost momentarily its guardian angel, Speer, who managed to rejoin before anyone noticed that he was gone. He has been the only original member who has received every bundle from start to present. President Ashley revealed another problem in the July, 1945, mailing: money. Expenses were twenty per cent or more above income. Ashley announced a 50¢ assessment, the first time that FAPA had ever invoked this escape clause in its constitution. Stanley also noticed that the trend was still toward mundane matters. In the summer, 1945, mailing, 31 per cent of the pages dealt with non-fantasy material, compared with a 25 per cent content three years earlier. Stanley was elected president in the fall of 1945, Tucker became vice-president, Ashley was the new secretary-treasurer, and Speer became editor. The new president finally buried permanently the official critics as well as the historical coordinator. Schwartz failed to turn over the records, holding up the mailing until December.

Nothing in particular happened in the next few mailings, which were slender. The waiting list withered to a half-dozen individuals. But things perked up in the spring, 1946, mailing, which featured two large issues of Koenig's *Reader and Collector* and Speer's return to full productivity. In that fall, Rothman was elected president; Stanley, vice-president; Widner, secretary-treasurer; and Perdue, official editor. Lowndes belatedly apologized for what had happened two years before, claiming that "I was a party to what has turned out to be a raw deal." The tradition of trouble with outgoing secretary-treasurers was perpetuated. This time, Ashley held up the autumn mailing. The mailing was finally distributed by guesswork about the proper recipients. Censorship also came to the fore again at the start of 1947. A cover for Evans' *The Time Binder* was approved by Rothman after a complaint. The president pointed out that the questionable gentleman on the front cover was fully clothed. However, he banned *Light*, on the grounds that a flying pig in a picture was relieving itself. Mailing production problems continued. The spring mailing of 1947 didn't arrive until June. Perdue blamed his marriage in early April for the delay. Such celebrities as Larry Farsace, Taurasi, Sam Youd, and Swisher were dropped for nonpayment of dues around this time, and membership fell to 58 persons. Speer offered a proposed new constitution. The general environment was so confused that nobody could locate amendments made some years back to the present constitution, for comparison purposes.

It took another blitzkrieg to extricate the summer mailing. Perdue claimed that his failure to receive a mailing list was his principal trouble, but he admitted that a publication from F. R. Burgess had vanished in a box that had contained a wedding present. Rothman authorized the worried Laney and Charles Burbee to take action. On August 9th, the pair confronted Perdue with the letter providing authority. They gave him a few days of grace. They were preparing to take action after the following week produced no bundles, but the LASFS got evicted from its clubroom on August 19th, upsetting their schedule. On August 21st, Perdue told Burbee that his mother-in-law had died, and asked for help in getting out the mailing. Burbee turned the magazines over to Laney and tried to get money for postage out of Ackerman from Fantasy Foundation funds. Ackerman turned down the suggestion on the grounds that FAPA had done nothing for the Foundation. Laney exploded over this attitude toward the $400 in the FF's treasury and over the condition of the partially assembled bundles that he'd acquired. Laney wrote to Rothman, who forwarded the money. The bundles went out on September 2nd. Laney made a remark that somehow has failed to become a fannish classic: "If you ever conduct a blitz, don't be a gentleman." Burbee wrote his greatest article about the blitz. Little more than a month after the summer mailing, the fall bundle arrived on time. Records held by Widner were still missing and funds were in short supply, but the organization now had an all-LA officialdom. Perdue won the presidency, Laney was vice-president, Ackerman became secretary-treasurer, and Burbee was official editor. The new constitution had passed, by a 13-1 majority.

The winter mailing of 1948 was a remarkably fat 296 pages, considering that membership was understrength by seven and there was a bitter fuss over bundles for review in *Amazing Stories*. This mailing contained the first official FAPA egoboo poll. It produced 35 votes and the results were announced in the spring mailing. *Plenum* was the best publication, the work of Rothman. Rothman also won for writing articles, Speer for mailing comments, Burbee for humor, Dale Hart for poetry, Burbee for fiction, and Bill Rotsler for art. Speer was voted top FAPA member overall. Complementing this demonstration of democracy was the fact that the bundle contained the first half of Laney's *Ah! Sweet Idiocy!* The remainder appeared in the summer mailing.

The bundle also had another significant item. This was a drawing on the back cover of Len Moffatt's *Moonshine*. It depicted a winged reptile and the cryptic statement: "I can hardly wait till South Gate in '58." Rick Sneary, whom the slogan made famous and vice versa, became president at the end of 1948. Immediately he began to worry about postmailings, which represented one-third of the FAPA output over the past year. Uncertainty over the probability of bundles appearing may have caused some members to think it safer to do their own mailing. Laney, who thought postmailings were good as a moneysaving device, was the new official editor. Boggs was secretary-treasurer and Burbee became vice-president. A strange intruder in this mailing was a fanzine published by a pro, Fritz Leiber's *New Purposes*. FAPA officialdom agreed to give him a free mailing in return for the supply of copies of this avant garde item. The second official poll named Boggs' *Skyhook* as the best publication; Speer won for mailing comments, Rothman for humor and fiction, Boggs for poetry, Rotsler for art, and Rothman headed the top ten on an overall basis. Thanks to recruiting led by Laney, the roster was again full, and nearly a dozen were on the waiting list. Bundles grew fat enough to force an increase in dues to $1.50 before 1949 was half complete, but a proposal to raise the membership limit to 75 was defeated at that time. Another borderline censorship case occurred. Laney refused to circulate a booklet because he feared legal action over its juxtaposition of a picture of Dr. David Keller and an article on racial prejudice.

The Los Angeles stranglehold on officialdom was broken at the end of 1949. Boggs became president; Henry M. Spelman III, vice-president; Walter A. Coslet, editor; and I took the secretary-treasurership. One of the biggest FAPA publications was postmailed, an 88-page issue of Rotsler's *Masque*. The poll results: *Skyhook*, best publication; Rothman, articles; non-member Al Laney, poetry; Burbee, humor; me for mailing comments; and Boggs was top pointgetter overall. With this fiftieth mailing, we have reached a convenient stopping point for the time being, both for its roundness of number and for the fact that it went out in February, 1950. We can wait a while before we consider the fifties.

2. The Vanguard Amateur Press Association

The founders of the Vanguard Amateur Press Association started out by imitating FAPA, later tried to dissociate the new group from fandom, and eventually saw it become one of the first fannish ayjay groups to collapse and die. It's still difficult to understand why the VAPA founders went to all that trouble, instead of attempting to raise the quality of FAPA mailings by distributing their best work there. The suspicion that they wanted to pretend they controlled something cannot be chased from the mind.

Lowndes got the inspiration for the group. He wanted to call it the Gothic APA. Meeting first at Waverley Inn, then at the Emden flat, he talked over the idea with Michel, Shaw, and the Wollheims, and drew up a constitution on January 13, 1945. The first word in the name gave all sorts of trouble. "Cooperative" and "Modern" were considered. Wollheim even published a small magazine called the *GAPA Vanguard*, and Jim Blish's first issue of *Tumbrils* referred to the MAPA. The group made some effort to be different from FAPA in unimportant ways. It had the same four offices, for instance, but preferred to refer to the official editor as the manager and to designate the other officers as numbered advisors. Retiring managers were automatically placed on the list of advisors in theory, although in sad practice the group never had three surviving retired advisors. Lowndes was the first manager. Wollheim was named first advisor, Shaw was the second, and Virginia Kidd Emden became the third.

Around the end of winter, Lowndes ended the secrecy by circulating an announcement, "Here's VAPA." He wrote: "We believe FAPA to be a fine club, one which is still in the process of evolving and maturing, and we further believe that a friendly rivalry between the two organizations will be of mutual benefit. Certainly there is room for two apas whose base is fantasy in literature." Long afterward, Lowndes recited an entirely different story: "Vanguard was formed by a group who were dissatisfied with FAPA, and tried to profit by the experience of what we thought were weaknesses in FAPA: the deadhead members and the semi-illiterate who flooded mailings with trivia, often atrociously reproduced to boot. Vanguard was supposed to be sercon." Wollheim betrayed at a later date evidence of a leftout feeling that the Futurians must have felt, now that FAPA failed to get excited over the Futurians' jeremiads and politics: "We felt that the FAPA was somehow not fulfilling our desires. It just didn't seem to quite satisfy us. Somehow the greater part of the FAPA seemed rather unpleasantly busy with self-analysis. I would like to think that my writings would be appreciated by VAPA. Certainly the FAPA tends to blur one's worth."

A clue to the real flaw in VAPA might be found in the dreadful pretentiousness and bombast of its constitution: "Its purpose shall be to provide for the mutual exchange of opinions and publications of interest through the medium of mailings. While such opinions and/or publications shall be largely pertaining to fantasy in literature and/or concepts derived therefrom, it is not expected that such opinions and/or publications shall be exclusively devoted to such subjects and/or conceptions and derivatives."

There was supposed to be a fifty-member limit, with subscriptions available to anyone when the roster was not full, just another way of stating the FAPA procedure that permitted a non-active member to rejoin after expulsion for lack of activity, if there was no waiting list. When the first mailing went out in March, 1945, there were fifteen members: James Blish, George Ebey, Virginia Emden, Jim Kepner, Damon Knight, Robert Lowndes, John Michel, Boff Perry, Larry Shaw, Bill Watson, Russ Wilsey, the Wollheims, and Dan and Judy Zissman (who later became more celebrated as Judith Merril). Four subscribers were listed: F. Lee Baldwin, Capt. Jack Emden, Dr. C. L. Barrett, and Graph Waldeyer.

All fourteen publications in the first mailing were the work of the New York City area members. They contained poetry like:

> see, a shiny handle,
> you turn it on, and you turn it off,
> look at the water gush out; see how
> it runs down the bowl.

V-R Record Review announced plans to issue a six-record album of fantasy music composed by fans. Membership rose to 23 and subscribers multiplied to seven by the second mailing at the end of May. Its biggest item, Norm Stanley's 28-page *Fan-Tods*, was straight out of FAPA, containing no mention of VAPA and with mailing reviews dealing with the older group. But a real novelty was Blish's musical setting of a Cyril Kornbluth poem, "Cry in the Night." The third mailing in July was notable for distributing the first fanzine by a convert from mundane ayjaydom: Bill Danner's *A Dangerous Thing* had sixteen tiny mimeographed pages inside a printed cover. Stanley had an ominous judgment on the VAPA material that he had read: "I found it a little dull." Blish and Lowndes announced in *Renascence* the formation of an Usher Society as "a foundation for the practising artist, whatever the specific nature of his endeavors; its purpose is to encourage, through study, publication, and (whenever possible) endowment the proliferation of all serious art-forms." This seemed quite unremarkable in the general environment. A revised constitution that limited the powers of the manager was approved when it went up for vote with the fourth mailing in September. This had eighteen items, most of them slender. The thicker ones were made that way by mimeographing on only one side of the page. Wollheim disposed of the end of World War II in one-half page, and Joe Kennedy was represented for the first time in VAPA.

In the fifth mailing, in November, Knight enlivened things by slashing out at A. E. van Vogt, much as he later did in professional surroundings. Virginia Emden laconically announced in *Futuria*: "Donald Wollheim has placed within the jurisdiction of the Supreme Court of the State of New York a personal dispute involving a fan publication and the zest has pretty well gone out of amateur publishing for me."

Fifteen of the twenty members decided to renew membership with the sixth mailing in January, 1946. Lowndes revealed a totally different policy for VAPA: "The intent of the organization now is to provide an interested and appreciative audience for the amateur publisher or writer who has something to say, either in the way of opinions or in the way of attempts of creativity in any publishable and mailable form. It can and will offer itself as an experimental lab for writers, artists and poets, but that is not the sole aim. Material of general interest will always be the backbone." More practically, Danner pointed out that many members didn't know how to run a mimeograph. Wollheim had vanished from the organization. Stanley was third advisor. In a poll tabulation covering the first year, Lowndes' *Agenbite of Inwit* was listed as the best publication; Lowndes, best writer; Andy Lyon, best fiction; Lowndes, best poetry; Knight, best artist; Danner, best humorist; Blish, best article writer; and Lowndes, best editor. The February mailing contained only four items, one of which was the official organ and another a leftover that had come too late for the sixth mailing.

Signs of trouble continued to show up with the eighth mailing in May. Larry Shaw announced himself in the merchant marine and ready to discontinue activity. The group abandoned the effort to produce mailings bimonthly. But the August mailing, the ninth, was the fattest so far, with thirteen publications. Included was the third constitution proposed in less than two years. Virginia Emden announced that the Wollheim suit had been thrown out of court. Danner was the latest to jump on van Vogt and stamp down hard, this time over the professional writer's bungling of steel mill color.

In the November bundle Lowndes gave the 22 members his farewell message as manager. The fourth constitution was proposed by Blish. It was the shortest so far: "The name of this organization shall be the VAPA. Its purpose shall be to circulate constitutions."

With the February, 1947, mailing, discussion of *Finnegans Wake* began to take up the space formerly devoted to criticizing van Vogt. Blish was elected official manager, leaving Lowndes, Shaw, and Virginia Emden as advisors. VAPA demonstrated its first genuine difference from FAPA by possessing such a surplus in the treasury that $33.50 was donated to the Committee for American Remittances to Europe. The poll declared that Danner's *Stefantasy* was the best publication; Blish, writer; Lowndes, poet; Danner, humorist and editor. The twelfth mailing, dated May, didn't arrive until June. The next, dated July, was slender and Lowndes produced three-fourths of its contents. Mailing comments and reprints were now taking up most of the space in VAPA publications, a far cry from the original material that had once dominated. I found little support for a proposal to merge VAPA with FAPA. Blish said it would ruin VAPA's "smooth-running, virtually effortless administrative machinery." Virginia, whose last name had become Blish, said that half of FAPA's members couldn't reach VAPA standards. Lowndes said that he liked VAPA "the way it is" and that he was thinking of forming a new apa. There was a loud squeak in that smooth-running machinery at the year's end when C. Burton Stevenson committed the heresy of postmailing a publication. Lowndes promptly ruled that this couldn't be done without the manager's permission and tried to enforce the rule by imposing complete secrecy over the names and addresses on the mailing list. Lowndes also pronounced the first three years of VAPA experimental. The group would now enter a new phase, marked by no compromise of standards to meet mailing deadlines, he said.

Those standards quivered slightly at the start of 1948, when Ray C. Higgs, as president of the Lone Indian Fraternity, announced free membership in that group for six VAPA members for their publishing accomplishments. In the election at the year's start, Virginia Blish became manager, leaving Jim Blish as first advisor, Lowndes as second advisor, and Chandler Davis as third advisor. Another new constitution was proposed. Poll results were announced in the April mailing: Virginia Blish swept almost everything, winning for reviews, publication, editing, and poetry. Her husband was named the best writer and Danner the best humorist. Lowndes proposed constitional amendments.

D. B. Thompson shook up the eighteenth mailing with this assertion: "I've found nothing in VAPA that would be out of place in FAPA." Ray Higgs was about to be bounced, for failure to meet those standards, whatever they may have been. Activity slumped again later in the year. Lowndes got married and began the Spectator Club, slowing down one of the major enthusiasts, and leaving hardly anyone with all-out interest except the Blishes. Another new constitution was adopted with the 21st mailing, in February, 1949. It tried to improve things by renaming the "subscribers" as "associates" and reducing the number of mailings to five each year. Only fourteen members and seven associates existed. Jim Blish was elected manager. Virginia Blish became first advisor; C. B. Stevenson, second; and Lowndes, third. There was the rare spectacle of a pro acting fannish in the April mailing, containing an issue of *Knight's Mare*, published by Norman L. Knight. More organizational changes were considered in June, such as wiping out the board of advisors and giving the manager an aide. The Blishes were doing most of the publishing by now, so it didn't really matter. The approach of the end became apparent with the 26th mailing, dated February, 1950. There were only eleven members, five associates, six publications in the bundle, and no election because of projected constitutional changes. The activity declined further in the 27th mailing, with only four publications in addition to the official organ and the ominous word from Jim Blish that he was too busy to be manager any longer.

The 28th mailing consisted of two pages in the July, 1950, issue of Danner's *Stef*, labeled "The Vanguard Amateur." Danner said he'd been railroaded into serving as manager, but he had nothing to manage and no magazines to distribute. "Unless I get prompt and concrete evidence to the contrary, Vanguard is dead!" he declared, setting August 1st as a deadline for a mailing. Danner also conducted the wake, in the form of a one-page *The Vanguard Pallbearer*, mailed December 9, 1950. Headlined "I give up," it declared that only five of the 24 members had responded to his proposal

to salvage something from the wreck and form a simplified group. Blish
refused to answer his letters, the culminating blow. A pathetic one-sheeter
called *This* from George Milwee, Jr., a Nashvillean who was one of the few
non-fans who ever did anything in VAPA, accompanied the *Pallbearer* to
carry VAPA to oblivion.

3. The Spectator Club

The Spectator Club can be dismissed more briefly, because it had vaguer
connections with fandom and because its history was that of VAPA, only
more so, and faster. The first issue of *The Amateur Spectator* was dated
March, distributed in April, but said the club was founded on January 1st,
in 1948. Lowndes, the individual mainly responsible, was custodian. This
was the newest name for the fellow who sends out the bundles. The new
group named its other officials "electors" and the first holders of the posts
were Charles Dye, Rita Dragonette-Dye, Lester del Rey, Philip Klass, and
Frederik Pohl. Membership was by invitation only, subscriptions to the
mailings could be bought for 75¢ per year, bimonthly mailings were planned,
and the club was intended for those with "interest in some aspect of amateur
publishing in general and compatibility with the Spectator Club's temper in
particular."

The first mailing, in April, 1948, contained three publications besides the
official organ. They contained such arty things as a reprint about music, by
Tovey, another reprint from Hayakawa on general semantics, the blankest
verse you ever saw, and a description of an imaginary country called Valdivia.
The group's intent changed quite fast. The third mailing's *Amateur Spectator* had comments by such notables as Nat Schachner and H. Beam Piper,
together with this announcement by Lowndes: "The appeal of the Spectator
Club is largely to professional and/or semi-professional writers; most of the
names you see in our publications are the names of persons who either make
their living through commercial writing, supplement their income with sales
to newsstand magazines, or are interested in reaching the point where they
will be in one of the aforementioned groups."

The group proved that such people who are interested in writing for the
money it produces are not often willing to devote their output to non-profit
writing that will be read by only a dozen or so individuals. The group contained at various times such notables as Isaac Asimov, L. Ron Hubbard, Ted
Sturgeon, Frank Belknap Long, and Bea Mahaffey. But it survived only a
dozen mailings, and many of those mailings were given the name only for
politeness' sake: five of the alleged bundles contained nothing but the official
organ. The club produced only about 260 pages in its lifetime, Lowndes

contributing about three-fifths of the whole. The last mailing in 1950 was a single-sheeted *Amateur Spectator* in which Lowndes announced unconditional surrender to such overwhelming odds as lack of activity by members, lack of members, and lack of a mimeograph in operating condition.

4. The Spectator Amateur Press Society

There was a conflict in name but not in intent between the Spectator Club and the Spectator Amateur Press Society. The SAPS had squatter's rights on the common word. SAPS can trace back its ancestry to a letter that Joe Kennedy wrote to Sneary in August, 1946. This described a new group, the Comet APA, that Kennedy had just about decided not to form. The discarded ideas included some later used by SAPS, like one-officer operation and the general atmosphere: "The concept of a brand new apa which would throw its gates wide open to the new fans is an idea with intriguing possibilities. It might not be literary, it might not be intellectual, two-thirds of its publications might stink to high heaven, but it would probably be a heck of a lot of fun." This inspired prophet did not keep his intention to forget the plan completely. A year later, a clique of New York and New Jersey fans who called themselves the Spectators were meeting at Kennedy's home and complaining about the difficulty of getting into FAPA, then bearing its intellectual burden, once joined. The Spectators, who were already planning a newszine and a book-publishing venture, felt ambitious. Present for this portentous meeting in February, 1947, were Kennedy, Lloyd Alpaugh, Ron Christensen, Ron Maddox, George Fox, and Lee Budoff. Maddox suggested Spectator Amateur Press Association as the name, Budoff then had the inspiration to change the last word to Society, and the group's initials set the tone for its starting attitude.

Details of the new group were carefully tailored to the circumstances. Membership was limited to 25, to permit easy use of the economical hectograph. Dues were set at 25¢ for six months, easy enough a sum for the younger fans to scrape together. There was to be no constitution, presumably in an effort to avoid the threat of stuffiness. Long after, Alpaugh remembered the atmosphere this way: "SAPS was begun as a joke. It was intended to be a sort of parody of the FAPA. We felt that FAPA was stuffy, self-centered, self-important, and dictatorial. There is also a possibility that we were mad because we couldn't get into it." True to these forgetful founding fathers' traditions, Alpaugh also remembered things differently at a different date: "We weren't bored with FAPA. How could we be? Only one of us was a member. He remained in FAPA until a couple of months ago, long after he dropped out of SAPS. SAPS came into being simply because we had nothing better to do. Can you think of a better reason? We once made a rule that the organization could never be disbanded." Kennedy took a more philosophical outlook: "I felt a tweak of conscience for helping launch a club which conceivably might drain some of the lifeblood away from FAPA. But possibly SAPS could serve as a field for fledgling fan editors to flutter their wings."

Maddox was appointed official editor. But true to the tradition of new apas, nothing happened for a while. The Spectators didn't publicize their intentions widely. The notices that did appear were carefully slanted to appeal to the right instincts, like this one: "Young fans! Do you find yourself developing an inferiority complex when you peruse the productions of FAPA's braintrust? Then you'll enjoy the Spectator Amateur Press Society." But some of the day's prominent fans were charter members: Alpaugh, Fred Burgess, Christensen, John Cockroft, Coslet, Fox, Kennedy, Maddox, Sneary, Telis Streiff, Redd Boggs, Van Splawn, Harold Cheney, Jr., Tom Jewett, Andy Lyon, and one other. It was quite typical of the group that it knew one charter member only by his last name, Tullis, possessing no clues to either his first name or his address. The first mailing was due in March, 1947, but Maddox did nothing about putting it out for six months or so. At that fall's Philcon, violent pressure was put to bear on him. With Alpaugh doing most of the work, he got the bundle out pretty soon after that, then had a good excuse for giving up the duties: he was asked to do so, and besides, his father got a job with Haile Selassie and took him to Ethiopia.

The mailing, distributed in September, contained 52 pages and a warning: "Any letters of complaint will be completely ignored." The sixteen members had produced ten publications, extremely in keeping with the anti-intellectual, lighthearted principles. Alpaugh put out the second mailing, having become editor, on the second day of 1948. There were now 24 members, 19 magazines, and 65 pages in the bundle. The group kept up the pretense of not having a constitution, but there was a list of rules and regulations to follow. There were two major differences from the FAPA rules: a ban on reprinted material in mailings and a prohibition on postmailings, in an effort to secure fat bundles of original stuff. The organization was creating a greater stir in fandom than its founders might have expected, thanks to the vigorous good humor and enthralling hints of illiteracy that it evidenced. Sam Merwin filled two columns in *Startling Stories* with comments on it. Moskowitz joined and tried to get into the spirit by reprinting old articles he'd written when he was young like these fans. Some critics pronounced Alpaugh's publication, *Sun Shine*, equal to the best things in FAPA. A real scoop for SAPS occurred when Harold Cheney distributed a small but genuine book in an early mailing, a bound collection of good amateur fiction, 32 pages of ozaloid reproduction, *The Hands and Others*.

The membership limit went up to thirty with the third mailing, whose envelope swelled with the pride of 164 pages. Such prosperity in activity caused a crisis in the treasury, so dues were raised to 70¢ annually with the fourth mailing. That New Jersey faction and spirit dominated the first half-dozen mailings. The sixth and last under Alpaugh contained such interesting things as a completely illegible issue of Charles Henderson's *Moon Blurps*, a noisy argument over Negroes that had Paul Cox in the middle, and a FAPA publication that Dave MacInnes got into SAPS by penciling the four magic letters onto the cover.

Not because of any particular interest in extending democracy to their own group, but because Alpaugh was tired of doing the work, the SAPS members had an election then. The original Spectators claimed that they arranged this election because they were getting annoyed at the fine acceptance for something that had been intended at least partly as a jest. They picked the almost unknown Phil Froeder to run for the editorship and voted for Henry Spelman. Spelman lasted three mailings, starting with the seventh bundle, dated April, 1949, in which Coslet announced the formation of the Galactic Amateur Press Association, Cox continued to argue over Negroes, and the largest magazine was a 13-pager, *Sun Shine*. Coslet announced in a single-sheeter that VAPA had kicked him out. The old Spectator circle declined and fell about this time. Most of them shook off the adolescent shenanigans and became quite successful in the outer world. Kennedy taught school and published a book of poems, Christensen taught English in a secondary school, Fox became an editor for Fawcett Publications, Alpaugh became a technical writer for an Albuquerque firm dealing in atomic ordnance, and Budoff sold art professionally.

The eighth mailing was notable mainly for Kennedy's three fine publications, and then in the ninth bundle, in October, SAPS members found that Higgs had provided 56 of the 134 pages in the bundle. Spelman turned the official editorship over to Art Rapp before his year was gone. Rapp immediately set a new record with a 190-page bundle, although 76 pages were in retroactively illegal subzines. The mailing was notable for copies of the *Cinvention Daily* of Rapp and the first SAPS poll, which was handicapped by the failure of anyone to vote. By the eleventh mailing, Rapp had been confirmed as editor unanimously and the group had a six-member waiting list. But Rapp decided to return to the armed forces, midway in the occupation of publishing the official organ for the twelfth mailing, dated July, 1950. He turned the 34 members over to the tender mercies of Coslet, who was designated official interim official editor. The first dozen mailings had contained 1,522 pages in the form of 221 magazines.

Coslet got the thirteenth mailing out in October, 1950, although only fourteen members published, in the wake of the confusion over Rapp's sudden defection. Coslet ruled that there should be an election and gave thirteen inactive members a spell of grace. Richard H. Eney, who had produced his first SAPS publication only a few months previously, was casting about for a way to make himself known in fandom, and did it by running for the editorship. We are on the verge of penetrating too far into the fifties at this point, but one disclosure is justified before a temporary curtain lowers. Eney became the first official editor of SAPS to get out four mailings as he was supposed to do.

5. The Galactic Amateur Press Association

Coslet thought up projects too frequently for any fan historian to trace down the facts on whether any of them amounted to something. His Galactic Amateur Press Association sounds so much like general fandom that it could hardly have been distinguishable as an entity if it did exist briefly. There was "practically unlimited" membership, people could get the publications by subscribing if they didn't care to contribute, and mailings were planned every month. Wallace Shore of Billings, Montana, was once listed as an official editor pro tem. The first mailing was promised in July, 1949, but I cannot guarantee that it ever emerged. Any enthusiasm that Coslet may have aroused must have subsided when he disclosed that activity credit would be given only to material that was about fantasy fiction. Coslet also started a group called the Christian Amateur Press Association that was as unconcerned with fandom as the Spectator Club tried to be. It had a mailing in the middle of 1948, claiming 102 pages in seventeen publications, four of them the work of Coslet and his wife, Dorothy.

10. FANS AROUND THE NATION

1. A Decade of Local Fans

Geography meant a trifle more in fandom during the forties than it does today. Fans were less prosperous, the war made travel difficult during half of the decade, and the prozines were urging fans to form local clubs. Many more local fan clubs, confined to a city and its immediate environs, existed in those days, usually for a brief time with insignificant results. The popularity of local clubs must have helped to encourage the delusion that something could be gained by formation of regional clubs, covering a state or a batch of states.

Today, most fans belong to the nation rather than to some particular region. But it might be instructive and useful to survey the decade by roaming up and down the nation, pausing briefly wherever enough fans were active to justify some description.

By the most curious and inexplicable coincidence, a remarkable number of local fan cultures underwent sweeping changes around 1949 or 1950, as if the new decade were bringing in a new generation of fans and sweeping much of the debris of the previous ten years into gafiation. So consideration of the fannish culture on a local and regional basis within this decade will not be quite as arbitrary as such neat divisions of time in history normally become. Obviously, there is no point in detailing the date of organization and the officers of every evanescent and forgotten chapter of the Science Fiction League, Science Fictioneers, Cosmians, and *Weird Tales* Club. We'll inspect only the groups that had some real contact with fandom in general.

2. Jim Avery

In Maine, the roots of fandom went back at least to
1936 in an organized sense.
The Skowhegan Junior Astro-
nomical and Rocket Society
wasn't quite as big as its name,
but 75 per cent of its four
members were science fiction
fans. Besides surviving experiments with mixtures of salt-
peter, carbon, and sulfur, the

Jim Avery

schoolboys reviewed science fiction stories for one another and corresponded with a British rocket group. The only member who became an
active fan was Jim Avery. He worked with me to start *Spaceways* in 1938,
then in August, 1939, formed the Maine Scientifiction Association with the
help of Jerry Clarke and Eddie Smart, during the Skowhegan Fair. Rum-
ford's Jerry Meader published the *MSA Bulletin*, starting in September, and
the group reached a membership peak of fourteen. Norm Stanley, a powerful force in FAPA a few years later, made the club quite attractive when he
offered to lend the seventy bound volumes in his science fiction library to
members. Youngsters predominated in the group, although Eddie Smart was
an antiquated 33, a Mt. Vernon resident who had been collecting so long
that he had lost a valuable collection to the depression. The club was prosperous enough to buy a mimeograph by the end of 1939. But in the next
year, Avery rashly published an item about financial problems of Street &
Smith, then publishing *Astounding Science Fiction*. It produced a threat
of legal action from that firm that inspired his parents to extract him from
most fannish pursuits. Clarke resigned as president of the MSA around the
same time, for other reasons. Not much more was heard out of Maine after
that until Ed Cox began to make noise out of Lubec around 1947, joining
Russ Woodman of Portland as one of the state's two most prominent fans.

3. The Stranger Club

Massachusetts' fandom during World War II centered around the Stranger
Club, more frequently called the Strangers. This group formed under the
impetus of Art Widner as the Nameless Ones on February 18, 1940, at the
Cambridge home of Louis Russell Chauvenet. Widner, Francis Paro, William

Schrange, John Ferrari, and the R. D. Swishers indulged in a discussion of science fiction and chess. The next meeting, a month later, resulted in the election of Widner as director, a duty which grew almost chronic for him, and Paro as secretary-treasurer. The group changed its name to Eastern Massachusetts Fantasy Society, and decided to publish a fanzine, *Fanfare*. A third meeting at the Massachusetts Institute of Technology saw the acquisition of more members and the name Strangers. The name came from the Stranger Club stories that Laurence Manning used to write for *Wonder Stories*. By the fourth meeting, at the MIT grad house, there were fifteen members. Territorial rights were rather vague, but the Strangers were proud to call themselves a Boston organization without a member who lived in that city. It had no formal organizational framework, officers had little to do, and there was next to no operating expense, a far cry from most fan groups of the period.

The Strangers acquired a library, starting with the gift of 250 prozines, a fair quantity of mature and intelligent members, and some big shots as visiting celebrities. On July 19, 1942, it scored a genuine coup at the Swisher home, where John W. Campbell, Jr. came visiting and L. Ron Hubbard, pre-Dianetics, also made his first appearance at an organized fan event, while his ship was being outfitted at an Atlantic port. Tom Gardner, a fan who had made pro sales and had become a scientist, began to attend meetings in 1941, then moved the next year to Tennessee. Earl Singleton, soon to gain renown for his dramatic method of gafiating, was elected treasurer near the end of 1940. Meetings were held on schedules varying from biweekly to monthly for the next year or two, at the homes of members and at MIT. By 1942, fourteen of Massachusetts' 22 known fans were members and five fanzines were emanating from Strangers. But wartime attrition soon caused the group to suspend operations. It revived in Cambridge in the fall of 1946, by when most of the old members were out of fandom or elsewhere. Widner was the only important holdover. Timothy Orrok and Chan Davis took the lead in the renewal of activity. Harry Stubbs, Dave Thomas, Boff Perry, Bill Mason, and John Pomeroy were among the others who frequented meetings at members' homes on a monthly basis during the following year. But it was another decade before MIT students caused the area to resume strenuous fanac.

4. Boskones

New England discharged its fannish energy annually at regional conferences that were known as Boskones, a pun that equated *Bos*ton *Con*ference with *Boskone*, the villainous culture in E. E. Smith's famous Lensman series.

The first of them occurred in late February, 1941, at the Swisher home. About 25 adults, mainly from New York and Boston, were on hand for an event that was so informal that it cost nothing to stage. The assemblage talked at considerable length about the NFFF, played a Christmas message on a recording from Los Angeles fans, spent much time poring over the legendary Swisher files, and ate. Widner was informally in charge, with Swisher the sergeant-at-arms. Widner announced that the formal program originally scheduled had been scrapped, announced results of his latest poll, and tried to guide a discussion of how the NFFF could be prevented from falling into heresy and schisms.

The next year the Boskone was on February 22nd, at Boston's Ritz-Plaza. Once again, about 25 fans showed up. But this time they came from points as remote as Columbia, South Carolina, in the form of the majority of that city's fandom, and Columbus, Ohio, from which Bob Jones derived. The Strangers presented a skit, "Legions of Legions." It was a theater-in-the-round parody of Jack Williamson's novel. The audience received copies of the script, to make sure that there would be plenty of prompters for the shakily memoried cast members. Widner welcomed the group, announced his marriage, and added the equally exciting news of his first sale to *Weird Tales*. The group discussed the possibility of sponsoring a big fan gathering in Philadelphia, if the war caused Los Angeles fandom to postpone the Pacificon. Local club affiliation in the NFFF was also talked over. John Campbell, Mary Gnaedinger, and Robert W. Lowndes provided original illustrations for an auction. Suddsy Schwartz impressed many when he lavished $5.25, half of his worldly wealth, on a Finlay cover.

The 1943 Boskone was the one that was spiced by the arrival of Degler after nine days of hitchhiking and by his ignorance of the correct date and location of the event. It was held on February 28th. Attendance fell to fourteen, including five Strangers and one or two fans from the other large cities of the Northeast. Schwartz called the meeting to order. To preserve a tradition, the group talked over the NFFF. The new fannish game of "Interplanetary" was played to determine the winner of a Finlay original: it went to Jules Lazar.

A fourth Boskone occurred over the weekend of February 3rd and 4th, 1945, but few of its happenings have been preserved during the passage of fannish civilizations. It occurred at the Swisher home, where only a handful were on hand: Milt Rothman, Jack Riggs, Widner, Stanley, and the host. The event was not revived until the sixties. Presumably, the area's few fans found it simpler to go a little further and attend meetings in New York City and Philadelphia. However, there was a conference on V-J Day that was billed as the North East Science Fiction Convention. Nine fans showed up on September 2, 1945, in Hotel Hawthorne, Salem, Massachusetts. Doris

Currier served as master of ceremonies. The best-known fans on hand were Jack Riggs, whose home was in San Francisco, Perry, Widner, Gerry de la Ree, and Sam Moskowitz. The day consisted of informal discussions and a long walk to the Willows, an amusement park. The original intention to continue the con into a second day was abandoned, when hotel space was not available.

5. New Jersey

New Jersey's fandom was obviously dominated by the bulk of its fans residing so close to New York. But the state had a most curious fannish center during the early forties in the town of Westwood, with ten active fans among its 5,000 residents, some sort of record. Gerry de la Ree was the most active of the batch and helped to organize the local group, the Solaroids. Roderick Gaetz, a reformed Canadian, and Roy Plotkin, just arrived from England, were his co-founders on July 25, 1939. The group, composed mostly of high school boys, were enthusiastic enough to meet twice weekly for many months. They published a fanzine, *Sun Spots*, and in 1940 opened membership to the entire universe.

Also active around Westwood were Joseph J. Millard, a professional writer who had been introduced to science fiction by Ray Palmer; Manly Wade Wellman, the prolific fantasy pro; his wife, Frances Garfield, also a professional writer; and Charles A. Beling, who published his own fanzine, *Fan-atic*, for a while. *Sun Spots*, which began as a single typewritten page in February, 1940, went to mimeography after its first year, later used letterpress for reproduction, and survived temporary catalepsy and changes in editorship for some five years. By the end of that span, Westwood had returned pretty much to normal, although de la Ree remained known to fandom long after, for his activities as a dealer.

6. Newark SFL Chapter

The Newark chapter of the Science Fiction League staged its first meeting in April, 1940, with ten persons on hand. Moskowitz was elected its first director, Richard B. Crain became secretary-treasurer, and Allen Moss, editor. In an effort to prevent hostilities with the Queens SFL chapter, the new group was restricted to Jersey inhabitants. By July, it had 65 persons attending a meeting at the Bergen Street School. (Giant crowds at fan gatherings in the New York area around this time must be qualified with the reminder that fans in the area were generously equipped with sisters and girl friends, and were in the habit of dragging at least one of each type of female to a meeting.) Ray Van Houten told at this meeting about his new Brother-hood of Pro-Scientists. The Newark club cooperated for a while with the Queens group on a project to stage a major conference or convention on May 4, 1941, in Newark. When fandom elsewhere began to charge that it was an effort to stage direct competition to the Denvention, everyone in the New York area said that he wasn't responsible for the idea, and it was dropped.

New York City's fandom has had one reliable characteristic down through the decades. Its most prominent fans are invariably split into at least two or three camps, each of these camps is seething with internal problems, and at least annually there is enough disruption to make it obvious that fandom has collapsed in the metropolitan area. In addition, most fans in New York City move to other parts of the nation in the course of any given year. It apparently is mixed up with hyperspace or a timewarp or something, because this keeps going on and on as the century progresses.

7. Queens SFL Chapter

The Queens SFL Chapter behaved remarkably like a Roman candle during the early part of World War II. At periodic intervals, a fireball in the form of a new fan club would whiz out of the organization and would have a fiery existence of its own for at least a little while. This operation repeated itself time after time, and years later the Queens SFL chapter was to all outward appearances as unchanged as the exterior of a burned-out Roman candle. Will Sykora, Sam Moskowitz, Jimmy Taurasi, and Mario Racic had been the principal creators of the Queens chapter, with the blessings of Leo Margulies. The *Thrilling Wonder Stories* executive thought that forming a chapter in Queens would end the problems that the old Greater New York SFL chapter had encountered. "There is no reason why New York City can't have several individual chapters, each headed by an enthusiastic follower of science fiction, each composed of a group of individuals whose interests and relations are both mutual and compatible," were his famous last words.

The Queens chapter promptly acquired one of the largest memberships and most potent drawing power at meetings of any fan club in history. At a typical meeting in December, 1940, the members and guests gazed simultaneously upon such pros as Arthur J. Burks, Isaac Asimov, L. Sprague de Camp, Malcolm Jameson, Frank Belknap Long, and Leo Morey. Moreover, most of them gave talks. Asimov condemned the mixture of politics into science fiction, Burks said that fans influence prozine editors, and de Camp revealed that prozine writers consider their work art but not so much so that it doesn't help to pay the rent. The following month, the club did it again at a meeting that attracted fifty persons and a mostly new assortment of pros like H. L. Gold, Willy Ley, Hannes Bok, Charles Schneeman, Alfred Bester, and Julius Schwartz. This meeting was enlivened by first the ejection of Dick Wilson and Dan Burford, at the hands of Sykora and Taurasi, then the loss of the hall as a meeting place when the manager got angry at such goings on. An innocent bystander was the only person who suffered permanent loss in the fray. Mrs. Sykora ruined the strap on a perfectly good purse when she used it to speed the parting guests.

The club's first annual social and dance, at Bagley's Hall in Astoria, attracted 45 fans and friends who saw live entertainment by the Three Dark Clouds, a song and dance team, and consumed 24 pitchers of beer and two bottles of soda. This was in 1940, when the club claimed to be the largest in the world. Heinlein had just attended a meeting, talking about his new story, "If This Goes On—." A meeting in April marveled at the novelty of fans from far away: three from Philadelphia and one from Washington, D.C. Then the draft began to create problems for the QSFL, Taurasi quit fandom several times, and Sykora moved to Baltimore, while other prime movers began to show more interest in prodom than in fandom. It survived the war in one way or another. A pre-Thanksgiving meeting in 1946 at Astoria's Bohemian Hall saw Jerome Stanton, associate editor of *Astounding*, speak to 26 persons. In 1948 it had attendance varying from ten to thirty at its monthly meetings, and helped to bring about a conclave on September 12th in Manhattan attended by more than 130 persons, largely lured by a screening of *The Cabinet of Dr. Caligari* and an auction. The first genuine social meeting since the war occurred on April 17, 1949. In that year, the club rented a room at 31-51 41st Street in Long Island City, putting its charters, trophies, and other spoils of war on display. The group crawled off somewhere to die almost unnoticed after a feud a year or two later.

8. The Futurians

The Futurians, like the Newark SFL, contained many former members of the Queens SFL's hard core. The Futurians had the advantage of somewhat more mental maturity and considerably better spelling ability than the other New York fan groups. Their principal disadvantages involved quarrelsome tendencies and chronic inability to operate a mimeograph skillfully. They chose their club name "because it describes an attitude of fans" who "have a dynamic conception of the future, one whose concepts extend to everything and not limited by his reading." The reasons were presumably thought up after the group had failed in an effort to become the Kings Science Fiction League chapter.

The role of Futurians in general fandom has been somewhat overplayed. The wordiest fan historians, Speer and Moskowitz, were constantly engaged in fusses with them and suffered from the human tendency to write most about the most familiar topics. "Futurians have gotten a hearty laugh out of the *Fancyclopedia*," Lowndes said of Speer's original volume. "To read its pages, one would think that Wollheim and the other Futurian Society of New Yorkers were the axis around which fandom revolved. We know we weren't that important."

The group formed in 1938, calling itself at first the Futurian Science-Literary Society, and borrowing its distinctive adjective from the name of the Leeds club's fanzine. John Michel, Don Wollheim, Fred Pohl, and Bob Lowndes, who also called themselves Michelists, were joined by Bob Studley, Hannes Bok, Dave Kyle, and Dick Wilson. They promptly formed the Futurian Federation of the World in April, 1939, claiming a score of members in five states and two foreign lands, and planning to charter branches in other cities. This was presumably an attempt to provide a counterweight to New Fandom, and possessed as brief a life and eventless a career as the competing group.

The New York Futurians presented a united front to fandom, but they had private problems. There was a semi-serious split in 1941, when Pohl, Leslie Perri, and Wilson wanted to grow big and compete with the QSFL, while Wollheim, Michel, Lowndes, and Cyril Kornbluth wanted to retain the status of a semi-closed group. There were thirteen members at the time. Pohl and Jack Gillespie suffered formal censure later that year for describing a small fanzine, *Futurian Review*, as the club's official organ. At the start of 1943, the club officially closed membership ranks, after suspending Perri, Robert G. Thompson, and Isaac Asimov. Membership was down to nine active members in the following year. The real explosion waited until 1945. Kornbluth and Harry Dockweiler had been ejected from the Futurians for vaguely defined reasons. Wollheim and Michel wanted to give the same treatment to Lowndes, Jim Blish, and perhaps others. The latter group retaliated by announcing that they represented the Futurian Society of New York, and proclaiming the ejection of Wollheim and Michel. Their description of Wollheim and Michel in a fanzine angered Wollheim, who began $25,000 worth of libel proceedings against Blish, Larry Shaw, Chet Cohen, Damon Knight, Lowndes, Judy Zissman, and Virginia Emden. The case was settled before it reached a full-scale trial, with no judgment for Wollheim but a $700 bill for the defendants for attorney's fees.

Today, the political and splintering disagreements of the Futurians make dull reading but the accounts of their cooperative living experiments are as

delightful as when they were contemporary. The Futurians were accustomed to settling down in apartment
houses, usually three or four members together, to cut
expenses while they were trying to become professional
writers and editors. Futurian House was perhaps the
most famous of these dwellings. It was a Brooklyn
house at 2574 Bedford Avenue. The line of demarcation
between residents and freeloaders was never completely
distinct, but in theory at least, Wilson, Dirk Wylie, Wollheim, and Michel lived there in 1939. Futurian House
was frequently visited by police for reasons somewhat
associated with fandom. Some neighbors saw the print-

Cyril Kornbluth

ing press and told United States Treasury agents that counterfeiters were at
work there. On another occasion, the Futurians performed too loudly the
Wilson-Kornbluth production of *The Mikado*.

Ivory Tower was inhabited during parts of 1939 and 1940. It was a Brooklyn tenement flat. Wollheim once said that the most valuable lesson it taught
was the importance of being firm about who should wash the dishes. Walter
Sullivan on a visit was awed at the Wylie collection of weapons that made up
its arsenal. Kornbluth published in Latin a little fanzine intended solely for
the residents and guests, *Tabula Futuriana*. Futurian Embassy flourished in
1941, when it was the home of Lowndes, Michel, and Dan Burford; it was
the successor to yet another establishment, Prime Base, where Lowndes,
Cohen, and Burford had lived. Michel, who suffered from various physical
problems, nevertheless was the sturdiest when it came to cooperative living,
for as late as 1945, we find him lending his name to Michel Manor, where
Larry Shaw and Russ Wilsey also stayed. Also known as Station X, it was
an apartment at 313 West Fourth Street in Brooklyn, tastefully decorated
with red walls, blue rugs, and a green bathtub.

Some sort of Futurian organization apparently survived the lawsuit, for in
1946, we find Lowndes denying stoutly that he is still a member of it. But
by then, most of the old guard had either gafiated or had acquired enough
writing and editing experience to be more immersed in the professional side
of science fiction.

They weren't the only fans who were trying to profit by their hobby.
The Cometeers organized on October 14, 1940, at the home of John Giunta,
with Taurasi and Moskowitz as the other founders. It was a group for fans
who had turned professional and planned fanzines only for their own amusement, according to early announcements. Later, its purpose was described
as "a fan-author-artist-editor cooperation club in which every member tries
to help his fellow member sell to the pros." It recruited a few more fans,
like Ray Van Houten and John Peterson, and some professionals who hardly

needed this assistance, such as Elliott Dold and F. Orlin Tremaine. Membership was by invitation only, and eventually the group either became so exclusive that it lost all contact with civilization, or it disintegrated; the last positive evidence of its survival is at the start of 1944.

9. The Eastern Science Fiction Association

After World War II, various other groups sprang up in the New York area to attempt to fill the unnerving peace and quiet left from the cessation of hostilities between the Futurians and the QSFL. The Eastern Science Fiction Association turned out to be the longest-lived and most prominent of the postwar groups. It had a complicated origin. The younger generation of New Jersey fans had formed in December, 1945, a new group, the Null-A Men, in the same historic Slovak Sokol Hall in Newark where a convention had been held in 1938. Sam Moskowitz, Julius Unger, Joe Kennedy, and George Fox immediately began to plan a conference that turned into the first Newarkon on March 3, 1946. Despite the lack of time to get ready and to publicize the event, it was a tremendous success as the first big postwar fan gathering. It has even been credited with inspiring Philadelphia to resume the tradition of the Phillycon. A few belligerent fans hinted at competition for the Pacificon, just as they had done in connection with a proposed Newarkon four years ago, but there was no fuss this time.

Some 107 fans attended from the New England and Mid-Atlantic areas. Abe Oshinsky proved that the future had arrived by becoming the first fan to fly to a meeting, taking a plane from Hartford, Connecticut. Moskowitz as chairman introduced everyone, even the Futurians after Mrs. Wollheim insisted. He paid tribute to Walter Sullivan, the most prominent fan who had been killed during World War II. Will Sykora recalled events at the first Newark convention. L. Sprague de Camp spoke about lost continents and announced that he didn't read Shaver's stories. Langley Searles expressed a fear that science had overtaken science fiction. Sam Merwin received a two-gallon jug of zeno from fandom and heard the convention urge him to retire "Sgt. Saturn," who conducted a letter column. The 75-year-old C. A. Brandt, survivor of the Teck *Amazing Stories*, was introduced and said that he intended to publish a new prozine. F. Orlin Tremaine predicted that science fiction stories in the future would put more stress on psychological aspects of scientific living. Manly Wade Wellman said there was need for adjustments in human relations. A new magazine, to publish offtrail stories, was announced by Robert Arthur. Mrs. Doris A. Currier reviewed plans of the Buffalo Book Company. An old-time filthy pro, David M. Speaker, said that science fiction was keeping far ahead of science, citing television as an example. Taurasi was shouted down when he tried to propose revival of the Science Fiction League. Ron Clyne asked the group to try to find him an apartment. There was a successful auction, whose size may be guessed from the fact that one individual alone, Tom Hadley, contributed more than 200 items. Moskowitz as auctioneer did such a fine job that the convention showed a profit of $50, with no other source of revenue.

Having proven that there was lots of fan interest, the Null-A Men then decided to wrestle with parliamentary procedure for three hours on April 28th in good old Slovak Sokol Hall. (To end the suspense, this is a good place to explain that fandom's history is so linked with this structure because there was a bar downstairs and the proprietor rented the meeting place for pittances to any group that might be likely to patronize his liquid refreshments before and after.) The Eastern Science Fiction Association was the result. Moskowitz was elected as director, de la Ree as treasurer, and Ricky Slavin as secretary. The ESFA's first decision was on its meeting place, and that $3.00 rental fee for Slovak Sokol Hall settled the matter instantly. The club prospered from the start, despite minor gripes that meetings were more like sales headquarters for dealers. By its fourth meeting, there were nineteen on hand, seven newly joined members, and it claimed to be the third largest fan group in the nation. A bit later in the year, 53 persons turned out to hear Dr. David Keller tell about his 51-year writing career. Max J. Hertzberg, literary editor of the Newark *Evening News*, attracted visitors from points as remote as New Haven, Connecticut, and Bridgeport, Pennsylvania, for his talk. At the meeting of September 7th, when August Derleth was the visiting celebrity, 75 were present.

The ESFA began in 1948 its tradition of a whopping big general meeting each spring. There were 85 on hand for the first, where the stars were Sam Merwin, Ted Sturgeon, and George O. Smith. This was the famous meeting at which fans and pros tested their ability to survive atmospheric conditions that might be experienced on other planets. Two enterprising fans, Ron Christensen and Bob Gaulin, had shinnied up to the rafters and unleashed ammonium sulfide there. When it turned into hydrogen sulfide, the ESFA learned a valuable scientific fact: opening the windows makes the stuff even more potent. The next spring, Moskowitz almost nabbed Olaf Stapledon as a speaker, but conflicting dates forced the writer to be in Boston and fandom lost its only chance to meet him. The annual meeting was held on March 6th, with 41 items in the auction bringing $47.80. Moskowitz spoke on the prophetic nature of science fiction. Thomas Gardner became director of the group that spring, with Sam Bowne, Jr., named secretary, and Allan Howard, treasurer.

But the ESFA also drew components from smaller, quite different fan groups. Starting in March, 1944, Wollheim locked up his fanzines and held an otherwise open house for a selected group of fans at his Forest Hills apartment every other Sunday. Bill Stoy suggested the name, the Arisians. Someone objected that it sounded too much like a well, but it permitted naming the official organ *La Vie Arisienne*. These fans were mostly younger, obscure chaps. Wollheim found some of them by contacting prozine letterhacks. Austin Hamel would be completely forgotten today if it weren't for one inspired remark: "What am I doing here when I could be playing baseball?" (Despite this unpromising start, he grew up to become a public relations man.) Wollheim apparently formed the group partly for the sake of the mentor sensation, partly for the old thrill of being part of a fan group, now that only Michel remained of the old crowd as a good friend. But the Arisians waned within a year, as the older Futurians began to take more interest in VAPA. The group was dead in 1945, with some of its membership gravitating to the ESFA.

George R. Fox of Rahway, New Jersey, had formed the Null-A Men. The name was chosen despite the fact that no member liked the van Vogt story that inspired it. Some ten fans joined in December, 1945. The following March it had sponsored the Newarkon and by the summer of 1946 it had been gobbled up by the ESFA. Some of its members took part in the formation of the Spectators around the start of 1947. This was intended as "an informal metropolitan-area science fiction discussion group." Energetic youngsters like Christensen, Maddox, Fox, Alpaugh, Ricky Gaulin, Lee Budoff, Phil Froeder, and Joe Kennedy planned such projects as a biweekly newszine, a book-publishing firm, and a collection of pictures. SAPS was its only lasting accomplishment.

10. New York Fandom

Meanwhile, several noteworthy events were occurring in New York fandom that involved individuals rather than organizations. On March 19, 1944, Moskowitz and the Futurians came face to face for the first time in years. The High Noon moment occurred in the Unger apartment, and it was such a critical occasion that the very words have been recorded for posterity. When Michel entered, Moskowitz cried: "Hiya, John, you're looking great!" This was not only relief to peace-loving fans but also accurate, because the sickly Michel had been in much better health of late. Wollheim entered with considerably more caution, Moskowitz hesitated for a moment, and then said decisively: "Well, hello, Don." Later Moskowitz explained: "The old feuds, while not as foolish and unnecessary as they might superficially seem, were years away—and time mellows all things." Moskowitz was later involved in another fateful event. After some sort of an argument between him and

Ricky Slavin, she resorted to the most awful reprisal that the mind of fan could conceive. She tore up the dust jacket of the Arkham House *The Outsider and Others*. Seconds later she went whizzing down the stairs and out of the building, impelled by the outraged collector. Ricky disappeared from fandom almost immediately and is presumably wandering through the pages of legendary lore with whatever vandal put the torch to the library at Alexandria. Somewhat less harrowing was the action of Steve Takacs who, in 1948, opened a new science fiction book store at 45 Fourth Avenue in Manhattan. Many fans had flatly refused to venture into the wilds of Brooklyn to ferret out his former shop.

Sam Moskowitz

Many lesser groups floated through the fannish atmosphere of New York in the forties. For a while during the war, something called the Stforum was meeting at monthly intervals, starting in mid-1942. Professional editors, writers, and artists, some of them of such stature as Malcolm Jameson, Frank Paul, and Frank Belknap Long, mingled with newly professionalized fans and fans who hoped to become professional soon. A meeting in the following January brought out nearly twenty persons, who were despondent over the failure of fans to give pros sufficient respect. This may or may not have been a group that was forming in mid-1942 and getting mysterious allusions in fanzines, claiming such celebrities as Catherine Moore and Henry Kuttner. The Hydra Club sprang up later, with even stronger professional coloration. Fred Pohl and Lester del Rey claim that they founded it late in 1947 at the Pohl apartment, despite persistent reports of events years earlier involving the group. Its Christmas party in 1947 attracted thirty persons, ranging from Fletcher Pratt and Sam Merwin to Bob Tucker and Ron Clyne.

A sercon group called the Centaurian League happened around 1948. Walter R. Cole was president, Ricky Slavin was secretary, and Alan M. Gordon was treasurer, for at least a dozen members. The purposes were defined as criticism of science fiction and speculative science. It seems to have had something to do with the Brooklyn Fufen, and may have been another name for that even more obscure group. Helena Schwinner and Marcia John were organizing around the same time a Bronx Science Fiction League as an informal discussion group for younger fans. Little was ever heard of it, so the discussions must have been extremely informal. Strong enough to publish a fanzine was the Mid-Manhattan Science Fiction Society, which started to issue *Etaoin Shrdlu* in 1949. It was undoubtedly cradled in a high school, because of the unknown nature of all the names on the editorial staff: Siguar Larsen, editor; Morton Sternheim, assistant editor; Gary Feinberg, Peter Schwartzberg, Morton Isaacs, Selwyn Rosenthal, Sheldon Glashow, Stanley Nathanson, Menasha Tausner, Stephen Taller, and Ezra Shahn were all staff members for the puny little publication. The Brooklyn Futuremen organized in 1945 without awareness of the existence of fandom or other clubs. Only one member admitted that he read *Astounding*, and the Standard magazines were the real literature to these youngsters. Fred Goldberg was probably the only semi-known member in general fandom.

By the time the new decade arrived, New York area fans could choose to pledge allegiance to any of a wide variety of loyalties: the ESFA, where Moskowitz remained in control; Cole's Eastern Telescope Makers Association; Taller's Mid-Manhattan group and his Science Fiction Society of the Bronx High School of Science; the moribund QSFL; and Ken Beale's new Scifans. The names of the clubs were mostly new and many strange names appeared on their membership rosters, but reassurance that New York fandom hadn't really changed came when the ESFA and the Hydra Club sponsored a three-day conference centering around Independence Day, 1950. Sykora began kicking up a storm in advance with complaints that this was a full-scale competition to the worldcon. At the conference, he distributed a leaflet denouncing the ESFA. Finally he was bounced in the middle of someone's speech. Ken Beale came to his defence, alleging that the Sykora contingent was well-behaved and did not distribute the booklet while talks were in progress, much the same arguments that had been used for the banished Futurians after the first worldcon. This is where we came in.

Elsewhere in New York state, Rochester had the most active local fandom. Bernard A. Seufert had been active in the earliest stages of organized fandom and Elmer E. Weinman had begun collecting in 1929. Larry B. Farsace became prominent in the late thirties, issuing the city's first fanzine, *Fantastic*, for the first worldcon. Seufert produced the first issue of *The Asteroid* a month later, but it was one of those non-reproduced publications done by a typewriter and ink. Francis J. Litz began *Scenes of Fantasy* the next year, and continued it for a while. October, 1939, saw the first issue of Farsace's *Golden Atom*, which was a stronghold of collecting fandom for the next couple of years, and still emerges with a new issue once every five or ten years. The collecting side of fandom predominated in Rochester in those early years. Both Farsace and Weinman had collections that were among the largest of the day.

11. Pennsylvania Fandom

Pennsylvania's fandom has been dominated by Philadelphia. But there was one regional group, the Western Pennsylvania Science Fictioneers, which Len Moffatt formed after he joined the Science Fictioneers in 1942. He found support from such as Blaine R. Dunmire of Charleroi, who surprised Moffatt with the news that Ed Hamilton resided only ten miles from Moffatt's New Castle home. Dunmire put Moffatt into touch with Springsboro's Basil and Margaret Wells. They turned up a couple of other interested youngsters in Charleroi, and recruited a few pioneers in Pittsburgh like Jack Daley, Jack Gilbert, and Dave Elder. An intended con in Pittsburgh's Kennywood Park brought out a group of most modest size. Five members managed to attend an eight-hour session in Charleroi on January 10, 1943. But correspondence was the main link, rather than personal contact. Dunmire joined the army and marched away to meet his death. Moffatt joined the navy and nothing more was heard of the group.

Pittsburgh itself had three obscure, short-lived fan groups in the thirties and forties. The city's real civilization and worldcon belong to a later stage in this narrative.

Recognizable Philadelphia fandom dates to the organization of the Philadelphia Science Fiction Society in October, 1935. Milt Rothman, Robert Madle, John Baltadonis, Ossie Train, and Ray Mariella were present for the first meeting. Jack Agnew and Harvey Greenblatt showed up for the second. Charles Bert became another prominent early figure. But Train claims that the core of the group had existed since 1933, merely attaining a paper

Milton Rothman

existence two years later. Before the thirties ended, Philadelphia fandom had acquired additional strength: Dr. John D. Clark, who sold occasionally to the prozines; Helen Cloukey, who inherited the collection of her late brother, Charles, who had also sold to the prozines; Bernhard Larsen, much-envied for a complete prozine collection; and Bernard Quinn, an early FAPA member. The comparative maturity of its membership may have helped to prevent Philadelphia fandom from bogging down into the fusses that overtook New York's fans. One-third of its members were already in their middle or late twenties when World War II began, genuine maturity for fans in those years.

Philadelphia was not only the scene of the first major fan get-togethers, but also an early source of fanzines. They started with a club publication, *Fantasy Fiction Telegram*, progressed through the excellent *Science Fiction*

Collector of Baltadonis and *Fantascience Digest* of Madle, and multiplied until sixteen titles were alive at one time. But the draft made its cleanest sweep in fandom in Philadelphia. By the end of 1942, Train blinked and found himself the only PSFS member still a civilian residing in the Philadelphia area. Fifteen members were in the service, and the others were civilians who'd gone elsewhere. Singlehandedly, Train kept the dismembered club alive during the war years. Meetings of a sort were kept up through the spring of 1943, but the real cohesive force was his correspondence and his publication of the *PSFS News* among members and general fandom.

Meanwhile, a competing group arose in Philadelphia, consisting of younger and livelier fans. They called themselves the Philadelphia Futurians, and claimed twenty to thirty members. Sam Mason, who had been a bete noire in the minds of most PSFS members at one time or another, was president. The new group had as its secretary Jean Bogert, who was to become a fixture in Philadelphia fandom. This insurgent group disclaimed any connection with the New York Futurians, doing so by going to the extreme length of fining any member who discussed politics during or after meetings. An even more phenomenal club rule prohibited the presence of intoxicating beverages at meetings. Mason resigned in the middle of 1944, and a merger of the two groups was proposed almost at once. Albert Pepper, a former PSFS member, became head of the Philadelphia Futurians, and James Hevelin, who had been PSFS president when the club suspended activities, suggested to the scattered membership that it wasn't right to have a club with only one member in the city for which it was named. The two groups merged on October 8, 1944, retaining the PSFS name and keeping in office the incumbent Futurian officials. Joseph Selinger, the secretary, and Guyon L. Kendter seem to have done the most to close the split in the city's fandom.

With the return of peace, some of the old group reassembled. Alexander Phillips was the first member to come back from overseas. He brought along a gavel for the club, constructed from material quarried under the walls of Jerusalem. L. Sprague de Camp attended his first meeting, and became an honorary member. Baltadonis got back safely from the Aleutians but never resumed full fanac. Harry Altshuler, then a reporter for the Philadelphia *Record*, became a recruit who was important to the professional side of science fiction a little later, agenting under his own name and writing as Alexander Faust. Madle attended his first postwar meeting on January 20, 1946, when Train was elected president; Pepper, vice-president; Madle, secretary; and Bogert, treasurer. With the ship home safely, Train turned over the *PSFS News* to Allison Williams in late 1946.

In its infancy the club had met in members' homes, then had concentrated sessions in the tavern run by Baltadonis' father at Frankford and Columbia Avenues. In mid-1946, the dozen members imitated the Los Angeles rent-payers and obtained their own clubroom. This was in a semi-residential section, under a dentist's office at 56th and Pine Streets. Walls were covered with original illustrations, books, and magazines. Across the hall, there was living space for two individuals. The clubroom inspired membership to boom. Attendance reached thirty at some meetings, and George O. Smith added himself to the already impressive list of professional adjuncts.

In addition to its distinction as the cradle of liberty, Philadelphia holds a slightly less supernal distinction as the host city for the earliest big inter-city fan meetings. The first of these occurred in October, 1936, when the New York branch of the International Scientific Association, consisting of a half-dozen fans, chatted with Philadelphia fans in Rothman's home. A year later, the next meeting was principally notable for the Futurians' "Mutation or Death" speech attributed to Michel. In October, 1938, the event was attended by 35 persons, despite the Michelists' boycott. Coincidentally or intentionally, members saw instead of Michelists a marionette show provided by Rothman. The 1939 gathering was full of high-sounding idiocy about the way in which all fandom's fate depended on backing either New Fandom or the Futurian ideals. Fandom, as it turned out, ignored both. All these get-togethers are described at incredible length in *The Immortal Storm*.

The next Phillycon, and the last for the duration, was on November 10, 1940, in a hall where the German-American Bund also met. The Bund's rifles alarmed some fans considerably. About 33 were on hand, mainly from the New York and Philadelphia areas, with a scattering of Washingtonians. The Futurians did not attend, but Baltadonis had created a splendid ash tray in the form of a Wollheim caricature, to keep them fresh in memory. Alexander Phillips was chairman and Rothman was secretary. Most of the afternoon was squandered in bickering over the proposed conference in Newark. The matter was finally tabled by a 22-5 vote. Van Houten had better luck with a resolution condemning anti-science slants to science fiction. It passed after some changes. The conference either favored or tabled a motion that profits from conventions be given to the committee of the next convention; contemporary reports differ. The topic derived from the fact that the fans who had done the work on the Chicon kept the leftover money. Rothman tried to whip up enthusiasm for a committee's formation to classify all science fiction stories by the nature of their predictions of the future. An auction not only paid the expenses of the gathering but provided some real bargains. Rothman got the first *Amazing* for 50¢ and Bob Studley purchased all three "Skylark of Space" issues for $1.05.

War preparations forced the cancellation of the gathering planned in 1941. And five years later, the names, attitudes, and topics had changed significantly at the Phillycon on October 27, 1946. There were some 65 on hand. Bob Sheridan provided signs for the ESFA, QSFL, and PSFS members to waggle in political convention manner. Rothman, as chairman, introduced such new notables as Lloyd Eshbach, George O. Smith, L. Sprague de Camp, Isaac Asimov, and Damon Knight, little known or completely unknown before the war. Smith told the meeting that he had started to write science fiction because the stories were more believable than the actual work he was doing in electronics. Samuel Loveman read a prepared speech on Lovecraft and exhibited souvenirs of him. There was a whole series of reports about fan groups. Hevelin told about the LASFS and NFFF; Rothman, FAPA; Sykora, QSFL; and Moskowitz, ESFA. Rothman described Ackerman's plot to import a fan from England. The business session featured a big hassle about Palmer and Shaver. Sykora wanted fans to go on record in opposition to Lemurian stories as antisocial and dangerous to sanity. He advocated turning over magazines containing them to the Society for the Suppression of Vice. Gardner supported the theory that this fiction could drive people insane. The audience immediately objected, on the premises that a sane person wouldn't read the stories to begin with and that efforts at suppression would be equivalent to book-burning. A motion to condemn Shaverism was defeated, 28-26. Rothman received from Moskowitz thirty memberships in the Philcon Society for members of the ESFA and QSFL. Moskowitz conducted the auction, with prices that were quite different from those before the war. A Cartier cover for "Lest Darkness Fall," for instance, brought $29. A pleasant prewar custom, that of preparing special issues of fanzines for cons, was revived, with distribution of copies of the *PSFS News* and the QSFL *Vadjong*. Ricky Slavin, who had not yet had her big moment in fandom, shook up a number of fans by showing how she wore a dagger strapped to her hip.

The Phillycon in 1948 was an anticlimax to the previous year's worldcon in that city. With A. E. Waldo as chairman, the event attracted only a score of persons on November 21st. De Camp spoke about time travel and the fourth dimension. Lester del Rey described interplanetary frontiers. Rothman provided phonograph music as accompaniment to a silent film version of *Fall of the House of Usher*.

Baltimore's fandom has risen and fallen mildly over the years. Its major flowering during the forties occurred at the start of that decade. Frederic Arnold Kummer, Jr. was selling to Palmer's magazines at a great rate, and the Baltimore chapter of the SFL was meeting at his home monthly, with upward of ten members. Virginia Kidd, later to become Jim Blish's wife, was a member. So was George Wetzel, whose Lovecraft research and feuds had not yet begun. The only other member of that era who became known in general fandom was Henry Andrew Ackermann, and his fame was due principally to being mixed up with the more celebrated fan with a similar surname.

12. Washington, D.C., Fandom

World War II brought many fans from various areas to Washington. Those who didn't lose their fannishness when transplanted organized loosely as the Washington Worry-Warts. The immigrants were principally Wyoming's Elmer Perdue, Oklahoma's Jack Speer, and Philadelphia's Rothman, augmented by a delegation from the Los Angeles area such as Helen Finn, Barbara Bovard, and Henry Hasse. The natives showed little or no fannish activity and the visitors went away after the war.

A new and truly indigenous generation appeared around the start of 1946. Chick Derry had begun to contact fans the previous year, then met Bob Pavlat in mid-1947. Their joint attendance at two conventions helped to arouse enthusiasm for a real Washington fandom. Louis Garner, who soon got lost to non-science fiction prodom, Bob Briggs, and Frank Kerkhof materialized. Meetings in Kerkhof's home, the Coal Bin, in September and October of 1946 culminated in formation of the Washington Science Fiction Association, née Washington Science Fiction Society. Derry, Pavlat, Kerkhof, Briggs, and Russell Swanson were its official founders. The group held meetings in the Transportation Building, because of such attractions as lots of space and pictures of nude women. There was also duplicating equipment, which the group ignored for a while in favor of talk and conventioning. After the Torcon, Pavlat drew up a constitution and the group elected Garner as its first president. Briggs was the first vice-president, Roy W. Loan, Jr. became secretary, and Kerkhof was named treasurer. A year later, meetings had twenty or more present, thanks largely to a letter in *Time* that brought lots of inquiries. There was a medium-size squabble around the end of 1948, inspiring Derry to invent a sort of insurgent group, the Elders, to discourage too-elaborate organization in the parent body. Briggs and Pavlat joined him in this rebellion. Already there was thought about winning a worldcon for Washington, with 1950 as target date.

The first fanzine published in Washington in years was *Quanta*, produced in November, 1948, by Kerkhof and Miles Davis. Fanzines almost immediately began to spew forth. Briggs produced the next spring a *Washington News Release*, followed in summer by Kerkhof's *Changeling* and the Derry-Briggs-Pavlat *Hazing Stories*. Pavlat began to issue *Contour* in 1950. In the same year, two major figures who were later to be apa mainstays began to publish: Bill Evans, an old Oregon friend of Damon Knight, and Dick Eney. But more important than the fanzines in lasting effect on fans was the WSFA's publicizing of the nuclear fizz. This was discovered at the 1947 Philcon, when Derry and Pavlat heard Tom Hadley recite to a bartender a formula consisting of one-half shot of gin, one shot of cointreau, one shot of lemon juice, two shots of soda, and a couple of drops of bitters. Derry and Pavlat drank models based on this prototype without great publicity during the next couple of years. The drink became known only when they fed one to Redd Boggs at the Cinvention in 1949. He named it. A Cincinnati bartender was so impressed that a year later he asked Kerkhof to refresh his memory about the recipe. Lee Jacobs created the complementary fannish tradition of silping, best defined as how you consume liquids which you neither drink, sip, nor slurp.

13. Southern Fandom

Further south, big cities had no enormous fannish groups or activities in the forties. But occasionally a small city owned several fans simultaneously and they made more commotion than anyone could logically expect. The best example was Columbia, South Carolina, whose Columbia Camp virtually dominated fandom for a few giddy months. It started in September, 1940, when Harry Jenkins found a letter from his fellow townsman, Joe Gilbert, in *Super Science Stories*. Jenkins, who had become a collecting fan by investing $1.50 in 250 prozines, wrote to Gilbert. The two corresponded on an intra-city basis for a while, and finally Gilbert went calling on Jenkins, bearing fanzines, a novelty to the latter. Meanwhile, Lee Eastman lived in the same block as Gilbert. Gilbert turned him into a fan promptly, after learning that he read science fiction. The trio traced down an older fan, W. B. McQueen, whose home became the site for meetings. This quartet met weekly and informally. Soon they were publishing fanzines at an incredible rate: six FAPA titles were emerging from Columbia, there were eight general fanzines topped by the excellent *Southern Star*, and even a newszine and the NFFF's official organ owed their existence briefly to Columbia. These happy days soon ended. The Columbia Camp last met in December, 1942, because Eastman and Jenkins entered the army and Gilbert went into the merchant marine. When the war ended, the city was as bare of fans as it had been in prewar days.

Despite the hectic fan life in Columbia, Gilbert himself was justifiably pessimistic about prospects for fannish civilization in the South as a whole. "The South is backward, conventional," he lamented. "The states are afraid of progress, regarding any unusual thing as anarchic. The nature of the people is probably the biggest obstacle. Outside of the bitterness and suspicion toward the North, there is another side of the Southerner's character which does not make for the perfect science fiction fan. He is unimaginative. Science fiction is an object of derision to your Southerner. He's too busy trying to beat the wolf to his front door."

Gilbert proved his estimate when he helped to attempt to organize the South through the Dixie Fantasy Federation. It was introduced in 1941 as "an exclusively southern organization, embracing the entire South." It offered such useless attractions as membership cards and stickers, plus practical items like a half-price subscription rate on *The Southern Star* and a chance to participate in a projected group journey to the Denvention. In the early flurry of enthusiasm, the group dreamed of having the worldcon in the South in 1942. The DFF claimed as its territory the entire nation south of the Mason-Dixon line. President pro tem was Erle Barr Hanson, a Floridian who was a big shot in a musicians' union and mainly a collecting fan. He wrote things like: "Our motto, 'Tolerance and Vision,' should reveal the democratic ideals and purposes of the constitution and the colors, blue and gray, contain the essence of the liberal understanding and civilization of the new South." Other officers at the outset were Jenkins, treasurer; Gilbert, secretary; and an advisory board composed of Fred W. Fischer, Art Sehnert, McQueen, Speer, and me. The DFF claimed credit for a number of Columbia fanzines that would undoubtedly have appeared without its existence, and it was abandoned during the winter of 1942-43. A plan to kill it brilliantly through a final 100-page issue of *Southern Star* aborted.

Even earlier, Sehnert and Bill Dubrucq had announced something called the Dixie American Federation of Science Fictionists. But this had even less luck than the DFF. The South didn't inspire enough territorial enthusiasm to hold a big regional conference of its own until the Independence Day weekend of 1950 brought about twenty fans from three states to Lynn Haven, Florida. An auction produced $85 worth of purchases, *Things to Come* was screened, and fans played with a wire recorder.

Florida fandom didn't amount to much until the fifties. The most prominent fan there after Hanson was Raymond Washington, Jr. He lived in Live Oak, shook nuts down from pecan trees to pay for the expenses of publishing his first fanzine, and had brief notoriety as the sole heir to the Cosmic Circle. He was one of the first to praise fandom after abandoning his hobby. In a time when many fans blasphemed at the hobby when they tired of it, Washington remembered in mundania: "I would have been an even shyer and more maladjusted young ignoramus when at last I ventured forth into the tough, uncaring world, if I had not had my gestation period in fandom's womb."

14. Ohio Fandom

There was a mighty urge to organize large geographical areas for fandom during World War II. Ohio did not escape. The Ohio Fantasy Association was organized by Joseph M. Lewandowski in 1940, when a dozen fans were known in the state, most of them in comatose condition. Lewandowski got at least five members and published an official organ, *The Ohio Fan*. He wanted "to attract the adult fantasy readers as well as the younger readers." He didn't.

Jack Chapman Miske was the first fan to make Cleveland famous. He wrote like a young Voltaire from 1938 until around 1943, and got involved in several costly fanzine projects. It was not until Christmas of 1950 that Harlan Ellison was discovered in that city, so its fannish history can be deferred until later.

Cincinnati fandom, on the contrary, has a long history, and a rather quiet one. It dates back to a dreary Sunday afternoon in December, 1935, when Dale Tarr found in *Astounding*'s "Brass Tacks" column the address of Ross Rocklynne, who had just made his first prozine sale. They quickly contacted another filthy pro, Charles R. Tanner. The three began to attend meetings of a mundane club that got together weekly for bull-shooting, and found one of its members, Phil Stevenson, interested in science fiction. When Tarr settled down permanently in Cincinnati in 1941, he and Tanner found enough new readers of science fiction through prozine letter columns and at the University of Cincinnati to turn the discussion group into a semi-fan club. They named it the Hell-Pavers and had a dozen members by the end of the year. Nelson Bond attended during a brief stay in the city. Creighton Buck, who wrote for *Unknown*, was another member. Most of the group were men in their twenties, more mature than the youngsters who created more of a ruckus in other cities. But marriages, the draft, and jobs in other cities scattered the group so completely that only Tanner remained in 1945. Then Tarr returned to Cincinnati, and helped Tanner to issue *Science Fiction World*, Don Ford and Stan Skirvin came back from service, and the discussion group resumed meetings in 1946.

Lou Tabakow was somehow identified as a fan while he was delivering dry cleaning to the Ford home. The group adopted a rule against officiating and parliamentary proceedings, and named itself the Cincinnati Fantasy Group. At the Torcon, Ford was talked into making a successful bid for the 1949 worldcon. By then, the club had attained its numerical peak, with big new names like Bea Mahaffey and Darrell C. Richardson on its roster. Fanac took up the time that had once been occupied by discussions. With $300 in Convention profits, the club acquired a meeting room in the downtown section, where as many as thirty fans crowded into 100 square feet of floor space on occasion. This club room attracted so many juveniles that the meetings retreated to members' homes. The group's second big decimation followed the Cinvention. Tanner dropped out after a spat. He led a clique of his own for a while. Mahaffey left to help with *Other Worlds*. Richardson was sent overseas as an army chaplain, and Wanda Stephenson married Bill Funk. The Midwestcons were closely connected with this group from the outset, but they belong to the fifties.

15. Indiana Fandom

Indiana organized as a state more successfully than Ohio. Ted Dikty of Fort Wayne proposed a state club as a means of turning inactive fans into active ones and to interest them in the approaching Chicon. The group published the *Indiana Fantasy Association Review* as an official organ, and built up a library of books and magazines that members could read for a small rental fee. A half-dozen members had a get-together at the Marion home of Ed Harriman on November 3, 1940, and the special IFA meeting at the Chicon had eight on hand. Dikty served as director, Fred Shroyer as public relations manager, Marvis and Vincent Manning as editors, and Mel Schmidt as librarian. The war and gafiation ate up the IFA after the Chicon.

Indiana had a very special situation, never repeated in the years since anywhere in the world: the Decker Dillies. These were five fans who lived around the microscopic town of Decker, previously celebrated only for possession of the largest sweet potato storage facilities in the world. Before they knew of fandom, the five had banded together as the Literature, Science and Hobbies Club. In a remote corner of the great Indiana wheat desert, they built a two-room cabin. They filled it with such lures as Oscar, a skeleton who lived in a tall glass case; a chemical laboratory; many books; and a batch of safety boxes from some forgotten bank that held correspondence in order. Marvis Manning was a licensed pilot, Vincent Manning, his brother, was a radio ham and collector of Indian relics, William Sisson collected and dealt in stamps, Maurice Paul was scientifically inclined, and Claude E. Davis, Jr. had the special qualification of knowing how to get results from a hectograph. Two wives provided various sorts of help with their hobbies. The first hectoed issue of their fanzine, *Pluto*, burst unheralded upon fandom in the spring of 1940. The second issue was an even greater stunner: not only were there five previously unsuspected fans in such a tiny village, but they had introduced in this issue three-color mimeography. The first fannish dissertation on the zapgun went almost unnoticed in the sensation that raced through fandom at the knowledge that the last reason for using a hectograph, its ability to do colorful artwork, had been disproved by use of multiple inkpads. The third issue boasted five colors, but took so much work to get out that Marvis's wife was forced to call five times to the clubhouse with the news that dinner was ready, almost every evening. This fanac explosion burned out almost as rapidly as it had ignited. Vincent Manning got classified 1-A, Davis got married, most of the other Dillies entered the service, and the first anniversary issue of *Pluto* has not appeared to this day. But the last issue, January, 1941, had been enough to prove to fandom that attention to format, color ink, and imaginative layout could remove the crude and ugly connotations from the concept of mimeography. Fandom had responded by providing a paid circulation of more than 100 to *Pluto*. The Decker Dillies never returned to fandom, although Tarr paid a call on some of them in 1963 and found they had faithfully kept a book he'd lent them, ready to return it at this first opportunity.

16. Michigan Fandom

Michigan made up for any deficiencies in fan organizations in neighboring states, with room to spare. As early as 1939, Martin Alger had formed in Mackinaw City a Society for the Prevention of Bug Eyed Monsters on the Covers of Science Fiction Publications. It was an obvious imitation of Bob Tucker's anti-staple group but it had a more lasting effect on the English language. It helped to call attention to the term bug-eyed as applied to extraterrestrial creatures on prozine covers. As one word, bugeyed entered the dictionary. There had been some sort of small local club all through the late thirties in Mackinaw City, and the Detroit Science Fictioneers began activities in 1939. But general fandom became aware of the state only when the Galactic Roamers formed over its southern part. At the start of 1941, the GR formed when delegations from Jackson, Battle Creek, and Detroit

Walter Liebscher

broke bread in Jackson. John Millard of Jackson became the president and E. E. Evans of Battle Creek was named secretary. There were thirty known fans in the state around this time, quite a few of them out of their teens. By fall, the Galactic Roamers were plotting a Michifans federation, planning a state conference, and claiming that fannish civilization had expanded in less than a year to sixty known individuals. Slan Shack was the third or fourth fannish wonder of the world. Then Evans, Jack Wiedenbeck, Al Ashley, and Walt Liebscher moved to California, and that particular complex dissolved.

But a group known as the Detroit Hyperborian Society formed during the war years, under the leadership of Richard Kuhn. This survived until 1948, when it dissolved over Technocracy arguments. Survivors, including Ben Singer, Fred Reich, Erwin Stirnweis, and George Young then launched the Michigan Science-Fantasy Society, which was to produce fannish legends and excitement replacing the old and now moribund sources in New York City. The club averaged ten members at early meetings. Alger used an enormous Packard to gather up fans. Singer was apparently the first president; Ed Kuss, vice-president; Art Rapp, secretary; Young, director of publications; and Bill Groover, editor. The group was statewide, in theory at least, with meetings alternating biweekly between Detroit and Rapp's home in Saginaw.

The club, quickly dubbed the Misfits, became distinguished because almost every member was either colorful or extremely capable or both. Alger, for instance, had been an NFFF member and Michicon attendee as early as 1941, and a science fiction reader since 1934. Big-hearted Howard De Vore began to read *Wonder Stories* in the mid-thirties, was an ardent collector almost at once, and learned about fandom only through a chance encounter with Arnim Seilstad in a bookstore after World War II. Almost instantly, he sold some British *Unknowns* to Stewart Metchette, instituting a legend about his favorite type of fanac. In truth he has been a most valuable collaborator in indexing and bibliographical projects.

Ray Nelson founded a fan group in Cadillac among high school classmates, before he knew about general fandom. In its brief lifespan, this group produced fantasy dramas on the local radio station, got science fiction into the school publication, then dispersed to the draft and college. Cadillac was the city where George Young purchased the first known helicopter beanie during a visit to Nelson. A dramatic demonstration of the strength of the personalities of the Misfits occurred in Cadillac, where a promising feminine fan not only gafiated but suffered a nervous breakdown, by incautiously meeting Singer and Hal Shapiro in too rapid succession. Shapiro, however, came along too late to belong in this decade's chronicles.

Ben Singer was Detroit's most written-about fan. He published an issue or two of *Mutant* and turned it over to the Detroit club as its official organ, but fandom persisted in giving him credit for succeeding issues on which Young, Alger, Nelson, Rapp, and Metchette did the work. After feuding with the older guard of Detroit's fandom, Singer either got expelled or resigned from the group and began a new club for neofans. This new group had the distinction of entering the official blacklist of the City of Detroit, after Singer left atheistic pamphlets behind after a meeting in a park department building. The Misfits obtained a certain amount of revenge on society, when Alger sold his old Packard to the State of Michigan, which immediately put it to use for hauling patients to the state insane asylum at Ypsilanti. Singer, who had played truant from school so he could run a three-wheel ice cream wagon for financing his early fanzines, calmed down in later years in the manner of most violent fans. We last hear of him reduced to the condition of ordering a Coke in a jazz boite on Paris' Left Bank.

Art Rapp became the best known of Michigan's fans, without sharing the eccentricity that afflicted most other fans in the state. He was a Chicagoan who had lived in Saginaw since he was a dozen years old. Rapp began reading science fiction around the time he was graduated from high school in 1942, but he was drafted in late 1943 and did not become a fan in the active sense until 1947. When he began to publish *Spacewarp* in that year as a handwritten, hectographed publication, he had seen only one issue of one fanzine. *Spacewarp* became quickly one of fandom's favorites, after its conversion to mimeography in 1948. It disclosed Roscoe as a new fannish deity the following year. Rapp was the main force behind the Misfits' biggest publishing project, a 100-copy edition of fiction by William James, *Dark Wisdom and Other Stories*, issued with Nelson illustrations in 1949.

Several exciting things brought Michigan fans to the attention of mundane authorities in the late forties. At a Misfits meeting in 1948, Norman Kossuth thoughtlessly remarked that his neighbors were touchy. Someone immediately proved the truth of this statement by setting off a dago bomb, a device that explodes on the ground and sends another piece of explosive into the air to go off. On another occasion, a group of Detroit Science Fiction League members were picked up for violating a teen-agers' curfew. At the police station, they told the desk sergeant that they had been attending a science fiction club meeting. "Christ, you look it," the officer said, "Go on home." Somehow, a copy of the publication of the Misfits, *The Michifan*, crawled into an abandoned car. The Royal Oak police went calling on Alger, the publisher, when they found it there. The FBI discovered fandom in an odd way. Kossuth was contacted by an agent in a routine check on a non-fan friend. Singer picked this particular time to shake up Kossuth, a Shaver and saucer fan, with a handprinted note of a disturbing nature that ended with a warning not to contact authorities. Kossuth assumed it had something to do with the FBI agent's visit, turned it over to him, and it went to the Washington laboratory of the FBI. Kossuth discovered the note's author before the FBI did, because Singer started to needle him about it. The FBI proceeded to pay Singer a call, and after he provided the names of officers of the Misfits, the thorough agent paid another call on its president, Bennett Sims. Sims père got his son out of fandom quick.

Alger thought that "Join the MSFS and go places" would be the best slogan for the club, after reviewing the travels taken by various members at public expense after involvement in such adventures as possession of machine guns, felonious assault, kidnaping, pornography, dope peddling, and forgery. However, the most publicized brush with the law came on the day the bomb went off, November 13, 1949. The place was the front lawn of the home of

Rapp, 2120 Bay Street, and the occasion was the conclusion of a meeting of the Misfits in that large house. The blast was loud enough to make people jump two blocks away, and it had enough power to break two Rapp windows. Police, firemen, gas company workers, reporters, and assorted bystanders quickly loomed up. Left to greet them were only two blameless fans, the host and Bill Groover, because the remaining members had left rapidly. Groover's last act as a fan was to help Rapp board up the windows. Rapp resigned as secretary and member of the Misfits, after publishing a bulletin which defined the bombers as "juvenile jerks." He estimated that the explosive possessed the kick of an army concussion grenade. R. J. Fluette also thought this was a good time to quit the club. Two Pontiac fans, Fred Reich and Eugene Seger, have never denied publicly the charges that they were responsible. Seger, the alleged bombardier, was a Buck Rogers collector who claimed that he had helped Bok learn to be an artist, while Reich, the presumed manufacturer of the bomb, was principally distinguished in fandom for having spent most of the Cinvention in the snake house at the zoo. The Detroit element in Michigan's fandom decided to form a new group from which bombers would be excluded, and appropriated money from the treasury to help pay for the damage.

17. Chicago Fandom

Illinois fandom was dominated by Chicago. The only state-wide federation, the Illini Fantasy Fictioneers, survived only long enough to sponsor the first Chicon. It was organized in Bloomington in the middle of 1939, and seems to have failed to do anything in particular after holding a meeting during that convention. Chicago's fandom is also closely identified with the first Chicon, in these early days, because the convention was a Frankenstein's monster that obsessed its creators, then put them into suspended animation. The city was almost barren in the fannish sense in 1937, when Mark Reinsberg and Dick Meyer felt an impulse. They unearthed Jack Darrow, the legendary prozine letterhack. He reacted to stimuli sufficiently to show that he was alive but had little interest in general fandom. Nevertheless, Reinsberg and Meyer found younger and enthusiastic readers of science fiction conveniently situated in their own high school, Lane Tech. These included Erle Korshak, W. Lawrence Hamling, and Chet Geier, all of whom were active by 1939. Korshak, Reinsberg, and Darrow attended the Nycon. Reinsberg's *Ad Astra* claimed rank as the first big fanzine out of Chicago. Hamling, after friction developed within the city, countered with the much more ambitious *Stardust*. By 1941, most of the city's fans were either gafiated or obsessed with efforts to earn money out of science fiction.

Before the first Chicon, Chicago had had several small get-togethers, designated Chicago Science Fiction Conferences. The manner in which "conference" could mean almost anything can be understood when we learn that the third of these events, in April, 1940, brought only four fans to Bloomington. It is only just to point out that Korshak, Reinsberg, Bob Tucker, and Willard Roberts kept this conference alive for four days. A Little Chicon that ran from October 7th to 9th, 1944, brought a new generation of fans together: Walt Dunkelberger, Frank Robinson, E. E. Evans, and some lesser lights joined Tucker and two pros, Dr. E. E. Smith and Ray Palmer. Palmer was so friendly toward fandom at that time that he joined the NFFF. The city's next conference seems to have been the First Post-Radar-Contact-With-the-Moon Con at the Fort Dearborn Hotel on April 6th and 7th, 1946. There were sixteen fans and semi-fans on hand, four of them from Chicago, and most of the rest from Milwaukee and Battle Creek. Later that year, a Centracon was staged on November 9th and 10th, with some 25 fans and pros hearing about Smith's new novels and criticizing the NFFF at Korshak's home and the Atlantic Hotel. The professional participation was quite impressive: C. M. Kornbluth, E. E. Smith, Bob Tucker, Bob Bloch, Fritz Leiber, and Oliver Saari.

18. Milwaukee Fandom

Wisconsin experienced the curious condition of pros who acted like fans before there were many fans who tried to act like pros. The Milwaukee Fictioneers were active by the middle of the thirties. They met at members' homes, mostly to talk over their vocation as writers. Associated with the group were such familiar names as Palmer, Bloch, Stanley Weinbaum, and Ralph Milne Farley. The group published the first big semi-pro fantasy volume, the Weinbaum memorial of 1936. A little later, August Derleth in Sauk City began to display limited evidence of fannish instincts that have never quite gained control over his professional impulses.

Only with the start of the forties did a few undiluted fans begin to emerge in Wisconsin. Milwaukee's Donn Brazier published a different kind of fanzine, *Frontier*, a specialized publication that tried to emphasize the borderlines of science. He also organized the Frontier Society, dedicated to similar purposes. Nothing that the club did approached in sensationalism the original accomplishment of the publishers of *Frontier*: they ran off the cover of the first issue on a hectograph created mostly from a box of orange Jell-O. Fandom could count ten members in Wisconsin during the war years, but by 1946 the first wave of Milwaukeeans had dispersed and a new club had formed at Bob Stein's home. It called itself the Neoterics, from Sturgeon's

"Microcosmic God," only four persons were on hand to found it, and not much more was heard about it. Stein managed to promote a conference in Milwaukee over Labor Day of 1948. Eleven persons showed up, five from Milwaukee, to attend a UAPA convention, roast marshmallows, and think about a new midwestern fan group.

19. Minneapolis Fandom

Minneapolis fandom had a consecutive existence and produced outstanding fans and pros in proportions not to be foreseen from the size of the city. Morris Scott Dollens had published, in 1936, the first Minnesota fanzine, *Science Fiction Collector*, which lasted thirteen issues under his editorship. The following year, the original Science Fiction League chapter got started. Oliver Saari, a native of Finland who had been in this country only a decade and was about ready to start selling to *Astounding*, became director. Despite attractions like talks by Don Wandrei and Carl Jacobi, the group collapsed almost at once as a formal organization. But Saari, John L. Chapman, Doug Blakely, Arden Benson, and Robert Madsen liked one another enough to stage informal meetings from time to time in three succeeding years. They reverted to a regular club in 1940, when Clifford Simak arrived in town. The first meeting of the Minneapolis Fantasy Society occurred at his home on November 29th. Simak, already well known as a filthy pro, became director with Saari as his assistant. The group met biweekly and acquired a prodigious assortment of later greats in fandom and prodom. Phil Bronson, whose *Scienti-Comics* had been the first fanzine in the state since Dollens', began to commute from Hastings, and founded *The Fantasite*, one of the best fanzines of the war years. Redd Boggs, whose literacy kept fandom's standards up for decades to come, attended his first meetings late in 1941. Gordon R. Dickson heard about the club in 1942 from a college friend, Manse Brackney, and was active before turning professional. Sam Russell was a director in 1942, later moving to Los Angeles and becoming co-editor of Laney's *Acolyte*, and still later engaging in even more exciting activities in intelligence work. John L. Chapman was another member who soon began to sell professionally. At its peak, the group had nineteen members, many of them publishing fanzines.

The draft and enlistments began to remove members faster than new ones were acquired. After half the membership was lost, there was a brief suspension of the group on May 8, 1942. The MFS resumed activity two weeks later, upon word that Russell and Dollens had failed to pass physical examinations for the service and Saari had degafiated. Bronson moved to Los Angeles late that year, an event that was marked by a titanic eating jag at a farewell party. Meetings became more informal in 1943, usually at the home of John Gergen, who helped to hold the remnants of the club together. Russell and Benson joined the western migrations. Even the informal meetings became extremely infrequent by 1944, when the MFS finally disbanded.

After the war, the MFS was almost immediately revived under a new name. It was Tomorrow, Inc., with the intent "to keep abreast of advancements in all phases of science," with science fiction relegated to an occasional "point of departure." Despite the prominence of the reorganizers, Simak and Chapman, the renamed group met the same fate as every other club that sought to turn science fiction fans into science fans. The revival occurred in 1946. The next that we hear of organized activity in Minneapolis is the reactivation of the MFS under its old name, two days after Christmas of 1947. Back from the old club were such as Gergen, Dickson, Brackney, Bronson, Chapman, Simak, and Jacobi. The most lastingly prominent of the new breed was Poul Anderson. But the MFS was no longer anxious to make itself famous throughout fandom, and it seems to have acquired much of the characteristics of the thirties. Labor Day of 1948 saw Minneapolis play host to a conference at Saari's home, attended by sixteen people, mostly local fans. The Geeps beat the Nanks twice in a double-header that revived the old fannish custom of a baseball game at gatherings. Saari introduced out-staters to such local phenomena as spring-fed lake swimming and night clubs.

20. Fans in Kansas, North Dakota, and Montana

Telis Streiff headed most of the efforts to organize Kansas for fandom. In Wichita, in 1945, he headed Local 0 of the Martian Union, which claimed a dozen fans. A year later he tried again, this time with the help of Norman Storer of Lawrence, with the Junior Bems. This group was aimed at both teen-age fans of any degree of experience and new fans of any age. It published *Adonis* as a club organ, established a library, and died.

North Dakota was briefly prominent in fandom while Fargo's Walt Dunkelberger was publishing, officiating, feuding, and otherwise fanacking at a rate seldom equaled during World War II. He even staged a little conference in that distant territory early in September, 1944, when some non-fan recipients of his mundane publication for servicemen got simultaneous furloughs. He got original illustrations and manuscripts from several prozines for auctioning purposes, sacrificed himself as defendant in a mock trial about funds of the Minn-Dak Fantasy Society, and used the profits of the event to improve his clubroom in his attic. The Minn-Dak Fantasy Society was one of the few groups to make a splash when it disintegrated, for it sold hundreds of fanzines, books, and magazines in 1945.

The equally improbable state of Montana had flurries of activity during the later forties, when K. Martin Carlson was publishing his *Kaymar Trader* and taking much interest in the NFFF, in Great Falls, while Helena's Walter Coslet was becoming known as one of the hardest-working collectors. Another Great Falls resident, R. Vernon Cook, who had started to buy *Weird Tales* in 1923, even showed mild interest in fandom for a time.

21. The Michicons

Claude Degler and E. E. Smith

The entire Midwest threatened to become unified through creation of the Midwest Fantasy Fan Federation on November 16, 1941, at the Michigan First Annual Science Fiction and Fantasy Conference. It was held in a Jackson hotel so unaccustomed to large accumulations of fans that a bed collapsed. Directors were named for each of the states represented: E. E. Evans for Michigan, Tucker for Illinois, Degler for Indiana, and Dr. C. L. Barrett for Ohio. John Millard was chairman of the Michicon, which saw covers from Ziff-Davis bring $3.00 to $5.00 at an auction. There was much audible worry over what would happen to fandom if the prozines all vanished, a potentiality that seemed genuinely dangerous at the time. Later, the group went to the home of Dr. E. E. Smith for a bull session.

A second Michicon was held in the Otsego Hotel in Jackson on September 27, 1942. About 25 persons were on hand, and Phil Bronson rated it as better than the Denvention. Palmer, announced as guest of honor, never showed up. The MFS got admitted formally to the MFFF. Liebscher auctioned off artwork from Ziff-Davis, *Future*, and *Famous Fantastic Mysteries*. Unger shook up the event by writing a special delivery letter about the sale of Munsey to Popular Publications, interpreted as dooming the Munsey reprint magazines. There were minute-long speeches at the opening session, with Degler and Liebscher judged as the best orators. A Chicon record was threatened when eighteen fans crowded into Evans' room. Dr. Becker, a completely obscure gentleman, was elected president of the MFFF, which was soon to be even more obscure. State groups failed to have elections, for lack of representation, but Iowa and Minnesota joined the MFFF and Tucker was named its coordinator. Tarr and Speer discovered that they were simultaneously planning a dictionary of fandom on which the MFS was also working. The MFS agreed to work with them, and this was an early in-fluence on the eventual *Fancyclopedia*. Dinner at the Tommy Tomkins home followed the con. Fans left believing it would be the last con for the duration, because of scarcities of gasoline ration coupons, tires, and fans.

However, the third Michicon occurred in 1943 under conditions of un-precedented splendor: the opening of Battle Creek's Slan Shack. It began on October 30th, when the Ashleys, Jack Wiedenbeck, and Walt Liebscher had just moved into the building. Some 22 persons drifted in and out over the weekend, although Tucker failed to drift out until the following Thursday and Degler wasn't allowed to drift in at all. There was a dinner at a local restaurant. This was the occasion when Speer administered to many fans the mental alertness test from George Washington University. Many fans assumed it was an IQ test and the above-average scores that they achieved caused conjectures about genius in fandom for years to come. A lot of faanism was evident during this event. For instance, a *Science Fiction Song Sheet* was published, containing fan parodies suitable for group singing. Speer blew up black balloons to commemorate the sixth anniversary of Michelism. Saari and Speer disputed at such length that there was talk about sponsoring a nationwide debating tour in which they would star. Liebscher auctioned off artwork from Gnaedinger and Palmer.

The last two Michicons are less well documented. We know that the fourth was held at Slan Shack from June 17th to 19th, 1944. It had a candlelight auction when a thunderstorm disrupted Battle Creek's electricity supply while Liebscher was disposing of a hundred original items donated by prozines. There was a swim on Sunday afternoon. Frank Robinson showed extreme valor by publishing two issues of *Fanewscard* during the con. Some 23 fans were there, including travelers Lynn Bridges of Florida and Ken Krueger of Buffalo.

The final gathering occurred July 7th and 8th, 1945, again at Slan Shack, soon to disintegrate amid the westward movement of its occupants. A dozen Michiganders, the Wollheims from New York, Cincinnati's Tanner, Tucker, and a motley group of wives were on hand. More evidence of how fans were becoming faans can be deduced from the activities. The first day consisted of playing records, listening to Liebscher play the piano, playing games, and talking until 4 a.m. In those years, fans didn't stay up very late. On Sunday there was much picture-taking. Tucker told of his recent experiences as a masseur, and Liebscher obtained prices ranging from one cent to five dollars for 78 originals. One pleasant side effect of these Michicons ended with the last one: beautiful program booklets, perfectly mimeographed, usually with a fine Wiedenbeck cover airbrushed in full color, and plenty of space for autographs inside. Worldcon program books are ugly and ungainly things in comparison.

22. Fans in Tennessee, Texas, and Oklahoma

Tennessee's state-wide fandom had a momentary and unhappy existence. The Tennessee Fictioneers were destroyed soon after organization, when a controversy over a fanzine that Art Sehnert and Joe Gilbert were to edit jointly caused forty minutes of bitter argument. Sehnert and Bill Dubrucq immediately organized a new group whose name is lost in the mists that envelop far-off fannish days.

Texas fandom became nationally celebrated through the lurid anecdotes written by those who escaped sane and alive from the state's fandom of the fifties. But at this earlier period, Texas was quite inactive and what fans it had were reasonably sedate. The Tri-City Chapter of the Science Fiction League had flourished around 1938 and 1939, claiming more than a dozen members in the metropolitan areas of Baytown, Pelley, and Goose Creek. Only one of them, Dale Hart, attained any lasting prominence in general fandom. The last that we hear of this group, it was hoping to raise enough money to buy a duplicator. There were isolated individuals in Texas during the forties who occasionally came to the notice of fandom through such curious ways as Frank Autry's claim of cousinship with Gene.

Oklahoma also waited until the fifties for its fannish convulsions. Before then, however, it produced several small fan groups and a couple of extraordinarily long-lived fannish careers. There was a Science Fiction League chapter in Muskogee as early as 1935, the year when the two eternals, Speer of Comanche and Dan McPhail of Oklahoma City, began to correspond. McPhail formed an Oklahoma City SFL chapter and published the first fanish newszine. Edgar A. Hirdler became director of this group, and his carbonzine was the state's second fannish publication. Louis Watts Clark, a pioneer Oklahoma collecting fan, did so little in general fandom that he'd be forgotten without Speer's frequent references to him. In this early time, an Oklahoma Scientifiction Association existed. It planned something called a Southwestern Fantasy Conference. This had no relationship to the Southwestcons of later years, and it should be noted that occasional references in World War II fanzines to Midwestcons mean the Michicons, not the Midwestcons that began in Ohio in the fifties.

23. Colorado Fandom

Between the Midwest and the Pacific Coast states, Colorado held the most prominent place in the fandom of the forties. When the Denver Science Fictioneers formed during the spring of 1940, Olon Wiggins was suspected of a triple hoax in the persons of the previously unknown Chuck Hansen,

Lew Martin, and Roy Hunt. Wiggins, the only prominent Denver fan until this time, was already on the road to gafia. The DSF dissolved after only a half-dozen meetings, giving way to the Colorado Fantasy Society, which formed in the fall of 1940 to sponsor the next year's Denvention. Worldcons frequently destroyed fandom in the host city, but in this case the fans and the club survived to become one of the oldest organizations and most feud-free groups anywhere. When D. B. Thompson visited Denver for a week in the middle forties, he decided that this was the closest thing to a desirable local club in fandom. It seems to have survived two decades without a genuine feud, possibly because it used some selectivity in choice of members. While sponsoring the Denvention, the CFS had Wiggins as director, Martin as secretary-treasurer, and Hunt as artist and editor. Like the Illinois group the previous year, it reverted to statewide status after having a national nature for con purposes, and in practical use, it was a local Denver club. *The Alchemist* was a celebrated Denver fanzine for a while, after which the CFS made less noise in fandom than some other clubs that were doing no more.

Wiggins attended its meetings as late as 1948, but no longer had fannish prominence after the Denvention. As the forties continued, members like Roy Hunt and Stan Mullen continued fanac despite making money from artistic and writing ability. There were temporary recruits when fans in the armed forces were stationed at bases in the Denver area. Paul O'Connor settled in Denver in 1948 with his publishing business and his Bizarre Bazaar book stock. Charles Schneeman, the once-famous prozine artist, got a job with a Denver newspaper, moved to that city, and the CFS met at his home on occasion. The CFS seems to have met weekly during most of the many years that followed, holding card parties, trips into the mountains, picture-taking excursions, serious discussions of science and literature, and an imposing New Year's party. One thing that the club did not do was lure into membership the mysterious M. Doreal. He would not be more than a dream-like legend, if fans hadn't actually seen him at the Denvention. Hardly anyone has seen what has been described as one of the greatest fantasy collections in the world, in his possession. Reportedly, he invested $150,000 in a shelter in which he hoped to survive atomic war, shortly after Hiroshima.

24. Washington and Oregon Fandom

Fandom in the state of Washington centers around Seattle and it is hardly noticeable until the end of the forties. When Loren Sinn, Charles McNutt, and Jack Speer got together after Speer had moved to that city, on June 10, 1945, in the Speer home, the event was officially described as the first Seattle confabulation. It took the extreme stimulus of a worldcon to get

Seattle fandom into real motion. When Portland won the worldcon in 1949, Don Day's *Fanscient* as a promotional measure ordered Seattle fans to contact Miles Eaton or Bill Austin. By September, the known fans in that city had received a postal card, announcing the first meeting of a new fan club at Pike Street's Wolf Den Book Shop. Austin ran it, and even before the convention hoopla began, he had been thinking about a club for the strange individuals who asked for the science fiction books in his shop, which he'd purchased only the previous February. The Wolf Den Book Shop, having fulfilled its destiny in the development of Seattle's fandom, soon vanished because Austin took out his own collection, sold the rest of the business, and married a local fan, Delcie Arlen Stuart. Royal Drummond became a member of the new group through the accident of walking into the store while a meeting was in progress. He didn't get out again until 2 a.m. the following day. Most of the other early members were associated with the University of Washington, where a combination chess and science fiction club called the Changelings had existed the previous year. Most of the members were students, but Alderson Fry, the medical librarian, and a teacher, Dr. Hatch, helped to arrange for the club to meet on campus. The new group found such interesting new recruits as the widow of Farnsworth Wright and Mrs. G. M. Carr, who was soon to take up the fannish role that Wollheim had dropped. The group called itself the Nameless, because members could not agree on an official name. Its first burst of activity produced as many as forty persons at meetings. Fanzine publishing boiled up almost at once. Mrs. Carr was largely responsible for *Cry of the Nameless*, first a small bulletin containing club news. The elaborate club publication at the outset was *Sinisterra*, edited mainly by Richard Frahm and Mrs. Carr.

Oregon is another state whose fandom is mainly in one city. Portland was headquarters in 1942 for something called the Progressive Fantasy Fan Federation. It had the vaguely Futurian purpose of "social promotion of fandom and for doing something about this better world instead of reading about it." The officers were mainly obscure individuals. The vice-president, Tom Ludowitz, published a fanzine that was famous because it was so terrible, but the president, Sid Dean, the secretary, Mrs. Edith Brown, and the treasurer, Mrs. Ethel Grow, were and are mostly just names in fandom. The group claimed a library with 700 magazines, and a separate chapter in Hillsboro. Simultaneously, Portland had a Stardust Society with sixteen members and equally unheralded officers: a president named Joe Salta and a vice-president called Chet Evans. Fans in Eugene were more active in the early fifties, although Rosco Wright and the name of the group, the Eugene Science Fantasy Artisans, were known before the decade started.

Portland's next go at fan fame had jackpot results. The Portland Science Fantasy Society formed in 1947. By 1949 it was strong enough to sponsor a Northwest Fantasy Conference that was attended by 24 fans from three West Coast states, on April 23rd at Day's home. John de Courcy introduced to the world his celebrated matter transmitter, and got a Venusian monster from it on the first test. After a buffet supper, a business session dealt with the formation of science fiction groups in Oregon and Washington. Forrest J Ackerman talked about the history of *Amazing Stories*. Day conducted an auction in which a Bok original brought $15 and less glamorous original artwork sold for 15¢. Dancing and an unsuccessful attempt to transmit matter followed.

The troubles that Portland's fandom suffered while preparing to produce the 1950 Norwescon will fit more conveniently into the section dealing with that worldcon. But fans there were having miseries even before they won the convention. Just before the 1949 Cinvention, for instance, Day as treasurer suspended half of the membership for failure to pay dues, de Courcy resigned, then became temporary chairman of an open meeting that produced a new constitution, and after that the club's officers fell into the habit of handing in resignations at each meeting, abolishing both the club and constitutions on special occasions. Once Dale Donaldson found himself holding all offices in a club which had just been put out of existence. De Courcy came very near going to law in the dissension and turmoil that followed. The club had become quite famous in fandom through its publication, *The Fanscient*, although Day was later considered its guiding spirit because of his assumption of the editorship when the internal fusses broke out.

25. Bay Area Fandom

California's fandom produced so many colorful characters, popular fans, superb fanzine writers, and bloodcurdling fusses that it would be easy to let it get too much attention in this history, just as similar considerations have caused New York City's fandom to receive far more attention than its true importance justifies from the typewriters of other historians. It wouldn't be hard to assemble enough facts and lies about Los Angeles fandom alone to fill a substantial volume. But first, let's look at the Bay Area complex, to get that out of the way before a sturdy effort to give Los Angeles only slightly more space than it deserves.

San Francisco has ecological interest as the boyhood home of Ackerman. If he hadn't moved away, it might have had as spectacular a fandom as Los Angeles. For instance, when Ackerman paid a brief visit back to his former 530 Staples Avenue address in 1939, where his parents lived, he could meet such members of the San Francisco Science Fictioneers Society as Lou Goldstone, Jr., who published indexes and a fine fanzine; Tom Wright, living forty miles away at Martinez and contributing artwork to most fanzines of the day; R. H. Barlow, a survivor of Lovecraft fandom; Joe Fortier, of Oakland, who was to Laney as John the Baptist was to St. Paul; but without Ackerman's permanent presence, there was no all-out, all-consuming fanac in the city. A few years later, the area's fans organized into the Golden Gate Fantasy Society, which a little later substituted Futurian for Fantasy in the name. This group had all sorts of troubles. Once it suspended during the war, after its president, Louis Smith, moved into a relative's home where he wasn't allowed to indulge in fanac, and many other members went into the service. James L. Kepner, who lived in both San Francisco and Los Angeles, considered the GGFS more cynical and less mature than the LASFS. Bill Watson's *Diablerie* was a fanzine that must have helped to create this former impression. By the time the fifties and the *Rhodomagnetic Digest* arrived, an almost completely new set of fans were active in the club.

The Elves, Gnomes and Little Men's Science Fiction, Chowder, and Marching Society formed toward the end of the decade, deriving its name from the short-lived and literate comic strip, *Barnaby*. It first attracted attention by sponsoring *Rhodomagnetic Digest* from 1949 to 1952. The group had originally formed around Tom Quinn, D. B. Moore, and Pete Finigan. They didn't get along together very long. Dissension plagued the Little Men for years to come. But the fanzine, edited by Don Fabun, has received credit for holding the club together at the shaky start.

San Francisco's first big fan gatherings may have been the Staplecons that Ackerman sponsored twice at his old address. He devoted part of his first furlough to this cause on May 16, 1943. About a dozen people were on hand, including Tony Boucher, then little-known. Ackerman held a second Staplecon on another furlough, but an extensive search of War Department records might be required to locate its approximate date. The third Staplecon was on May 28, 1944, but it did not occur on Staples Avenue. Nine persons put out a one-shot at the Alameda home of Lou and Larry Smith.

26. Los Angeles Fandom: Tenacity Exemplified

Organized fandom in Los Angeles dates back to formation in late 1934 of a Science Fiction League chapter. This seems to have been a sercon, dull group for the first few years. Names of members are just names, except for Ackerman. The secretaries' reports make dull reading, as written by such as Wanda E. Test, K. E. F. van Lutz, and Perry L. Lewis. The club began to coalesce as an active entity with fans known beyond the city limits around 1937. It was meeting then at Clifton's Cafeteria, a downtown eatery at 648 South Broadway. A typical meeting had a score of fans on hand. Their

Pogo (Patti Gray)

average age was in the early twenties and they were well-behaved at the meetings. These fans ran heavily to intelligent readers and collectors who were innocent enough to keep scrapbooks on the march of science but relaxed enough to loaf at Shep's Shop, a Hollywood Boulevard store run by Lucille B. Sheppard that sold prozines, fanzines, Esperanto literature, and less important printed matter. During his Esperanto enthusiasm in 1937, Ackerman discovered Myrtle R. Douglas, at a world language meeting. She promptly became known as Morojo, an Esperantization of her initials. She was a mainstay of the club for years to come, and contributed two relatives to its membership: a son, Virgil, known as Vodoso, and a cousin, Patti Gray, called Pogo in those days before Walt Kelly. Paul Freehafer, another decisive influence on the next few years of Los Angeles fandom, joined the group around this time. He was a Payette, Idaho, correspondent of Ackerman who moved to attend California Institute of Technology.

The most decisive event in the club's history may have been the decision of T. Bruce Yerke, then the secretary, to the effect that he wanted to publish a fanzine. Ackerman agreed to co-edit it, principally through financial assistance. But the club voted to spend $7.50 from its treasury for a hectograph on which the fanzine could be published. It thus became a club project. Instantly it became a magnet to draw together members frequently for long periods of time, in a way that formal meetings and informal get-togethers did not do. So there was soon a more active, more faanish, club and a fanzine, *Imagination!* Before long, the club bought a mimeograph on the installment plan, storing it at the home of one of the more dependable members, Russ Hodgkins. Meanwhile, famous pros like Dr. David Keller, Arthur Barnes, Henry Kuttner, Bob Olsen, and Emil Petaja were turning up at meetings. A vaguely competing group, the Glendale SFL chapter 25 miles away, withered and died under the strain of such white-hot fanac. There were occasional social events, too. A Christmas party in 1937 saw the members unbend sufficiently to put together a grab-bag from science fiction items. The tradition of an annual beach party began the following August 13th. The next year's beach party must have had the most imposing list of seashore visitors in history: Ackerman, Eando Binder, Julius Schwartz, Ray Bradbury, and Kuttner. Bradbury, joining in late 1937, had become the

Dennis the Menace of the group with a love for pranks and anything else that might create a disturbance.

Yerke had assumed his duties in May, 1938, when old-timer Roy Squires quit the secretaryship and the club. The group adopted a constitution that was to last for six years. Charles Hornig paid his first extended visit to California in the same year, further pepping up the club. Another sort of windfall was the donation to the club by Lew Torrance of his 200-pound collection of more than 400 magazines, including complete sets of the already rare pioneer fanzines, *Science Fiction Digest* and *Fantasy Magazine*. But later in 1938, the club took a stunning blow: Ackerman left school and went to work, resulting in retrenchment of the projects in which he took a major part. The resulting club depression was so severe that Clifton's fussed about the dwindling amount of eating with which the club paid for its free meeting room. Nevertheless, Yerke later remembered this era with nostalgia. "The old LASFL was perhaps the ideal fan organization," he said, "because each member had an earnest, sincere interest in science fiction and its hobby aspects. The activity was undiluted with the cynicism, vicarious motivation, and petty jealousy which later wrecked the LASFS."

The club abandoned its name late in 1939, but didn't adopt a new one until March 27, 1940. It chose Los Angeles Science Fantasy Society to avoid favoring either the Science Fiction League or the Science Fictioneers, while retaining affiliation with both groups. There was a big Easter party that year, when a dozen persons chased each other around a planetarium, visited the zoo, and watched Bradbury eat a half-dozen hotdogs, one after the other.

The cast of characters for the later conflict continued to assemble with the new prominence of Walter J. Daugherty in 1940. He was elected director when Hodgkins refused to retain the office, and immediately perked up things. Daugherty got prominent people like high school teachers, college professors, and aircraft industry technicians to speak, located a lot of new members, and inspired so much publishing interest that seven fanzine titles were quickly emerging from Los Angeles. (It should be remembered that "Daugherty project" as a synonym for a wildly visionary idea that never gets beyond the talking stage is the result of brilliant polemics by his enemies, but an inaccurate definition. Without Daugherty, half of the LASFS accomplishments in the forties would not have occurred, the club itself would almost certainly have disbanded, at least one and possibly two worldcons would

Walter J. Daugherty

have turned into fiascos, and three or four other fans would have had to pitch in and help with the mimeo crank-turning, landlord-placating, feud-calming, and fund-raising activities. Exactly the same reversal of reputation was accomplished by the same methods on behalf of Al Ashley, who ended his fannish career in Los Angeles. His actual fan record is the furthest imaginable removed from the fumbling and ineffectual pipsqueak braggart that he was made out to be, after he'd lost so much interest in fandom that he didn't bother to refute the charges.)

The Halloween party tradition sprang up. For three months, 628 West 9th Street became another focal point, where Hornig set up an office to work on his prozines, Bill Crawford operated a candid camera business, Morojo offered her services as a notary public, and other fans loafed. In 1941, the club moved out of Clifton's for a more fashionable Wilshire Boulevard address. This meeting room once had fifty persons on hand, when the California Rocket Society showed up. Los Angeles made history in the same year by electing Helen Finn as director. It was apparently the first time that a woman had headed a major fan club. She wasn't in fandom long, but while on hand she became a mother-in-law to two fans. Her daughters married Bill Crawford and Henry Hasse, another first.

The club had always presented a tranquil public image during its big and little internal problems. Ackerman's urging kept out of print and minimized in correspondence references to cases in which members quit in the highest dudgeon, the fuss over censorship of controversial material in *Imagination!*, the group who attempted to wipe out Ackerman's simplified spelling, and the time of troubles in 1941 when Yerke and Daugherty resigned at successive meetings as secretary and director. Some evidence of the fact that the club was not a place where everyone remained permanently bound by blissful happiness can be deduced from the 217 names of persons who had been on the membership roster at one time or another up to 1942.

The club moved into its celebrated soundproof clubroom at 637 South Bixel Street in April, 1943, holding its first meeting there on April 29th. This sanctified site resembled to the passerby a second-rate apartment. Inside, its 20 x 30 feet of floor space was principally remarkable for its large collection of cigarette butts, the outcome of Ackerman's ban on ashtrays in his effort to halt smoking in the clubroom. Almost every type of fannish spoor could be found in the clubroom, even unto a printing press. Across the street was 628, Téndril Towers, a boardinghouse much favored by fans for its nearness to the clubroom, its lenient landlady (who once, when charged with being a Communist, retorted: "I can prove it!"), and its modest $6.00 per week rental. Mel Brown, Jimmy Kepner, Niesen Himmel, Gus Willmorth, Lou Goldstone, Art Joquel, E. E. Evans, his daughter Jonie, Art Saha, and Alva Rogers were among those who lived there at various times.

Morojo lived in the same block at 643, an address that was later occupied by the Ashleys, Wiedenbeck, and Liebscher after Slan Shack closed down.

Fandom didn't learn of the tremendous events in this one block of Bixel Street until Jules Lazar spilled the beans in a letter published in Unger's *Fantasy Fiction Field*, dated March 11, 1944. Lazar revealed that he, Pogo, Laney, Bronson, Mike Fern, and Brown had resigned from the club the previous night. He had called the Ackerman-Morojo-Daugherty combine "horrible saboteurs and malingerers of fandom," and he openly identified two other club members as homosexuals. In the same issue of the newszine appeared an open letter, signed by much the same group, that censured Ackerman for his efforts to keep mundane activities from defiling the clubroom. The fuss went on for months, with a new episode or individual invariably turning up in time to keep it going, every time the participants seemed to be losing material to argue about. Thus, we find at various times such topics of contention as whether Ackerman's honorary membership

should be cancelled; someone's insertion of a tribute to the late Paul Freehafer in the club publication without first asking permission of the editor, Arthur Joquel; Laney's habit of slipping out for drinks in the course of a meeting; and the same individual's insistence on use of profanity when addressing the mimeograph. As direct repercussions, the battle drove out of fandom most of the active LASFS members, either immediately or after a brief effort to keep going; Ackerman's leadership in fandom was lost forever and his attention turned

Arthur Joquel increasingly toward the professional aspect of science fiction after this; and it brought out the best writing abilities of such fans as Laney and a bit later Charles Burbee. Indirectly, it caused all fandom to fall into the habit of writing frankly, settling forever the old question of whether fanzines should publish material about the seamier side of fanac and fans.

The LASFS survived despite losing eighteen members to the armed forces and many others to the nearer conflict. In 1944 it tried to weather the storm by limiting directors to three-month terms. There was a period in 1945 when there was enough interest to require volunteers to set up a schedule so that someone would be on hand at the clubroom every night to welcome visitors. But formal meetings suffered severe decline in attendance. One of them, in early 1945, found only Ackerman and Laney present. Several splinter groups helped to cause this situation. The Futurian Society of Los Angeles, noncompetitive with the LASFS in theory at least, organized on March 18, 1945, with Elmer Perdue, Kepner, Rogers, Morojo, Brown, Himmel, Joquel, and Saha as charter members. Its purpose was described as "discussions on any subjects of interest to the members irrespective of science fiction nature of the subject." It fell apart when some of its members moved to New York, only to find on their arrival that the similarly named group in New York had blown skyhigh. Late in 1943, the Knanves had organized as genuine rebels from the parent club. They rebelled after a dispute over a directorate election, and got the name from a typographical error by Yerke. This contained basically Laney, Kepner, Yerke, Bronson, Ed Chamberlain, Sam Russell, and Freehafer. Internal dissension broke it up.

The Outsiders (not to be confused with the later Outlanders) consisted of a dozen LASFS members who seceded in 1943. Mainly, they were Yerke, Bronson, Chamberlain, Freehafer, Russell, Laney, Pogo, Brown, Mike Fern, and Jules Lazar. Starting as a discussion group, it staged its first formal meeting in February, 1944. The Outsiders was intended as a partly social, partly sercon group. It plotted secretly a magnificent semi-pro future for fandom. But it was doomed from conception because too many members were individuals who were tired of fandom and had no other common ground with one another. Only four or five were left, three months later. It must not be thought that these cliques were stationary and that battle lines were definitely drawn. Freehafer and Russell managed to stay on good terms with almost everyone, for instance. Laney and Ackerman, leading the enemy camps, got along better much of the time than Ackerman did with Morojo, who was on his side but tiring of fandom. Ackerman also served as peacemaker at one crisis when Daugherty threatened to have Outsiders arrested whom he found in the clubroom. Russ Hodgkins, an old-timer, was another pacifying influence. Some of the revolting members rejoined in June, 1944.

Morojo

But the time of troubles took a new turn. Laney suddenly veered from Ackerman to homosexuality as a target. Survivors of the era still contradict one another about how many fairies were members and how ardently they pursued their sex lives in public. Laney at one extreme claimed that only half of the club's members were socially acceptable; others have asserted that only two members were homosexual and that only one of them made that fact plain. The arrival of the Slan Shack contingent in Los Angeles put new blood in a spillable condition. Burbee resigned as editor of *Shangri-L'Affaires*, now the official club organ, on November 13, 1947, because the club wanted to censor material about the homosexuality charges, causing further deterioration in the situation. But by then, "The club was left with few active fans," Rick Sneary recalls. "They didn't read fanzines. They didn't correspond. And they generally didn't know or care what was going

on in general fandom. The LASFS became mainly a science fiction club."
The last years of the decade are not as vivid in fandom's memories, but
they produced many instructive events. In 1948, for instance, a vice squad
put the LASFS under surveillance, suspecting it of illegal activities, then gave
up because, an officer of the law revealed, "they were just a bunch of harmless crackpots." *Shaggy* grew to the point that caused the club to invest $50
on a 36-page issue in 1949. The behavior of one drunken member caused the
club to be evicted from its clubroom in 1947. Daugherty rescued the club
by taking over the lease, subleasing to the LASFS one night weekly, and conducting a dancing class there on non-meeting nights. The ceiling in Tendril
Towers fell onto Himmel. He accepted the accident stoically, assuming that
it occurred because he worked for a Hearst newspaper. A rumor that Bradbury would attend a meeting brought out 33 individuals one Thursday night.
Ackerman had become so lukewarm to the LASFS that he missed meetings
for months on end in 1949. Instead he frequented the Bruin Science Fiction
Club, a college group at UCLA that claimed 90 members. A mysterious
organization, the Beverly Hills Fantasy Society, reportedly in existence for
many years without revealing its existence to fandom at large, supposedly
sent spies to LASFS meetings in 1947 and quickly decided that it preferred
to stay under cover as a result of their experiences.

The Outlander Society was created out of dissatisfaction rather than dissension. It was organized in October, 1948, for fans who lived in outlying
areas around Los Angeles. The original eight members were Len Moffatt,
Rick Sneary, Stan Woolston, John Van Couvering, Con Pederson, Bill Elias,
and Alan and Freddie Hershey. Ackerman enjoyed this company enough
to attend 24 of its 35 meetings during its first three years. These meetings
were usually all-day sessions without officers, dues, constitution, or bylaws.
Members maintained contact through an eternal chain letter between meetings. Guests included such important souls as Bradbury, Kris Neville, and
R. S. Richardson. Art Rapp defined it as fandom's "most articulate and
intellectual group." Part of that impression was provided by the nine issues
of its publication, *The Outlander*, from 1949 through 1952. The Outlanders
helped to start the propaganda for South Gate in '58 under the inspiration
of Sneary, and did not decline until Sneary began to lose part of his interest
in fandom.

An earlier effort to coalesce the territory outside Los Angeles took the
form of the Harbor Fantasy League. It organized in 1942, consisting of five
married couples from coastal cities like Wilmington and San Pedro. Pogo was
director and it started out by meeting every other week. Barbara Steedman
was the first secretary, Dan Lyons became treasurer, and Pogo and her husband, Russ Wood, edited the club's publication. The group attempted to
prevent infiltration by kids through restriction of membership to married

couples. But first it outraged Ackerman because a member suggested a visit to a psychiatrist for him, then the draft began to draw heavily on husbands, and the Harbor Fantasy League disbanded on August 1st of the year of its birth.

One of the few plays upon words in Los Angeles that was not played first by Ackerman seems to have been fanquet as a term for a formal eating session for fans. This seems to have been another of the many Daugherty creations. He planned, financed, and drew up the invitation list for what was planned as the first of a quarterly series of fanquets, then promoted the sale of 36 tickets at $2.50 each. The event was held at the Pacificon-hall-to-be, the Park View Manor at 2200 West Seventh Street, on February 10, 1944. The 16-page program booklet said that it culminated "several years of hopes for a science fiction banquet." As a sort of practice for the war-delayed Pacificon, it attracted three genuine celebrities, A. E. van Vogt, Ross Rocklynne, and Claude Degler. The second fanquet was staged at Daugherty's home and seems to have been nearly as successful as the first, despite confusion over the date when he miscounted the number of months in a quarter of the year. This one, on May 12th, was dedicated to the early days in science fiction, an early example of nostalgia's arrival in fandom. Old prozines and *Astounding* illustrations were auctioned off and given away as door prizes. The Pacificon's formal dinner was also called a fanquet. But the present series of fanquets as a consecutive tradition dates only back to 1949. In that year, the LASFS decided to honor Evans as the member who had earned the most money from science fiction during his first year in prodom; he had made five sales. It was staged on February 26th at the Unique Cafe. The van Vogts, Bradbury, Bryce Walton, and several other professionals were among the 39 on hand. Daugherty and Ackerman were the principal motivating forces.

The Westercon has been described as the creation of Evans and as an imitation of the Midwestcons. But there is something amiss with this reasoning, because the Westercons began a couple of years before the Midwestcons. The first annual West Coast Scienti-Fantasy Conference was staged at Park View Manor with Evans as chairman and the LASFS as sponsor on September 5, 1948. It suffered a severe case of professionals who failed to keep speaking engagements. E. Mayne Hull (Mrs. van Vogt) claimed bad health, L. Ron Hubbard claimed he had to be in New York City, Dr. Eric Temple Bell (John Taine) claimed that a close friend had died, and Bryce Walton didn't make any claims. However, Clare Winger Harris was there, admitting that her stories in *Amazing Stories* used to be pretty bad. Van Vogt spoke from his wife's viewpoint and suggested the merits of keeping prozines in an obscure part of the house. Bradbury told the group that writers should try to illustrate how terrible the future world will be when gadgetry rules in it.

John Scott Campbell, a particularly antique professional, discussed the possibilities of growing much larger or smaller. Dr. R. S. Richardson reviewed how Jupiter had turned from hot to cold and Venus had changed from a swamp to a dustbowl in astronomers' thinking in recent decades. Guy Gifford, who drew cartoons in *Planet Stories*, defined science fiction as fairy tales in disguise. On the fannish side, there was a drawing for the Big Pond Fund's benefit, in which Stan Woolston won the *Thrilling Wonder Stories* cover. Don Bratton described the potentialities of the Fantasy Foundation. Ackerman reviewed the current prozine situation. Daugherty served as auctioneer, but fans were apparently suffering from some type of collective financial crisis, for many offerings failed to get their minimum bids, and there were bargains like a $3.00 selling price for a mint copy of *House on the Borderland*. Los Angeles provided most of the 75 fans who attended.

Daugherty served as chairman of the second Westercon, again with LASFS sponsorship, on October 2, 1949, at the Knights of Pythias Hall. Joquel urged support for a rocket club to which his interests had flown. Daugherty was auctioneer. The event brought out many long-inactive fans, the Outlanders, and even Ashley, who was then rapidly taking on the qualities of a myth.

11. CONVENTIONS THROUGH THE DECADE

1. The Pacificon, 1946

The Pacificon intended in 1942 was postponed, soon after Pearl Harbor. Fans feared enemy action in the United States, it was growing increasingly difficult to travel, and there were threats of complete blackouts every night. The worldcon was rescheduled promptly after the end of the Second World War, and threatened immediately to involve fandom in fannish hostilities somewhat less dangerous but quite as prolonged as the late conflict. Late in November, 1945, Walter J. Daugherty mailed an announcement that Pacificon preparations were ready to resume. Fans who had paid a dollar in 1941 to join the Pacificon Society learned that 46¢ of their money had been spent. They were invited to send another 46¢ to permit the committee to get off to a fully solvent start, or better yet, to write off the remaining 54¢ and buy an entirely new membership. Fans also had a chance to vote between the July Fourth and Labor Day scheduling. The results of the balloting were never made public, but the July date was chosen.

Almost at the outset, Daugherty lost his temper completely over publicity matters. The LASFS had held planning sessions through the late summer and early fall of 1945. Daugherty had been named to act with full powers on all convention matters. He named a remarkable combination of fans to his advisory staff: his wife, Forry Ackerman, Andy Anderson, E. Everett Evans, and Francis T. Laney. He tried without success to change the name of the event to Post War Con. Without making it public, the planners chose tentatively the date for the Pacificon and A. E. van Vogt as the guest of honor. Daugherty was preparing to reveal these momentous decisions to fandom through the first issue of the *Pacificon News*, when Laney leaked them to Jack Speer for use in a newszine that Speer was then publishing, *Stefnews*. Daugherty exploded. Laney claimed that he had acted on the theory that the worldcon needed all the publicity it could get, and simultaneously alleged that he had intended to tell Speer to wait for a release date from Daugherty but forgot to do so. Daugherty sulked on fairly reasonable grounds, such as the fact that van Vogt had not been asked to be the guest of

Forrest J Ackerman (left), Mari Beth Wheeler, Francis T. Laney

honor when the announcement was made, and did little about the con for weeks. This interim was blamed in some fannish circles for causing the Pacificon to have a rather small attendance. But eventually, the event got plenty of promotion. The second convention news bulletin went to 775 fans, for instance, and the whole nation learned about the Pacificon when Tigrina wormed her way onto the *Queen for a Day* network radio program and talked for four minutes about it.

Extensive pre-con sessions were held before its formal July 4th start, at the LASFS clubroom. Rothman was officially the first out-of-towner to arrive. One fan whose identity has long been forgotten hitchhiked all the way from Massachusetts. Walt Liebscher stayed up all night before the opening day, to complete the mimeographing of a combozine. This lost fannish art consisted of special issues of leading fanzines published especially for the event and bound together for sale there. It featured a fine edition of *Shaggy* with a Burbee editorial and the results of Sneary's fantasy poll. The puritan element in Los Angeles excluded one contribution to the combozine on the grounds of obscenity. Its indignant editor later circulated it in FAPA where nobody noticed anything remarkable about it. In a pre-con caucus, there was a vain effort to stave off one of the most violent events to come, the impending collision between the NFFF and the new Fantasy Foundation, already causing trouble before the latter's official announcement.

There were more than 100 fans on hand when the convention opened on Independence Day. Although one or two fans flew from distant points, the final registration-book figures showed that only 120 fans attended, only 18 were non-Californians, and only 18 of the Californians lived an appreciable distance from Los Angeles. At the opening session, the customary introduction of notables was varied by Ackerman, who carried a microphone into the audience and told each one to stand and say something into it. This took an hour or longer. Van Vogt, wearing a blinding red and green necktie, then

Introductions by Ackerman

reminded some fans of their high school teachers with his hour-long talk, "To-morrow on the March." He predicted another war "because human beings have not yet learned to understand themselves. Notice that I did not say they haven't learned to understand others. It is themselves they don't understand." Much of this talk was devoted to hints about the merits of Korzybski-type semantics train-ing. These ranged from orthodox pep-talk remarks, like "If you want to succeed, you've got to give your time and thoughts and effort to it day and night," to more original suggestions to train the memory to retain everything important. If fans closed their eyes frequently and tried to remember the last things they saw in detail, "You will be amazed at the way that will sharpen your brain." Van Vogt claimed that self-improvement methods had taught him how to type, had given him a good speaking voice, and had permitted him to see without the use of glasses. Despite his memory claims, van Vogt failed to make the talk fully successful because he forgot some important transitional sections in his pre-pared manuscript.

Just as Mark Reinsberg had become ill at the start of the Chicon, so did illness strike down Ackerman on the opening day of the Pacificon. This Ackerman collapse had consequences of considerable import. The semi-secret Fantasy Foundation was to be sprung upon fandom at the Pacificon, and great hopes were held for its future with such a dramatic start. Acker-man's physical inability to do the politicking for the new group at the con-vention may have been one reason why the organization never attained the hoped-for scope. Ackerman had described the birth of the Fantasy Foun-dation and Laney had spoken about its publishing plans, when the illness intervened. Eyewitnesses mistook for a bad case of nerves what was really an attack of influenza in the gastric regions. Ackerman recovered from his collapse sufficiently to circulate around the hall for a while on that opening day, but the chills and fever grew so severe that Tigrina finally persuaded him to leave. He was unable to enjoy the rest of the con, but the fans gave him a Paul original that had been intended for auction-ing and filled a booklet with messages of good cheer. The fact that 80 memberships in the Fantasy Foun-dation were paid almost at once was the best medicine that Ackerman could have wanted.

Tigrina

Erle Korshak served as auctioneer. Prices in general ran high, but he accomplished his greatest feat when he sold for $2.50 an abstract by Ralph Rayburn Phillips after admitting that he didn't know which side was up. Also on the opening day, the convention heard a recording of "Satan's Phonograph," a Bloch episode from the *Stay Tuned for Terror* radio series. Bloch himself arrived late at the con, whereupon several carfuls of fans drove to Union Station to fetch him. He dined with them at a good restaurant and won

Erle Korshak, auctioneer

their hearts forever by picking up the bill. Bloch, who was making his debut to fans in general, explained that he had made two sales during the past week, his phonograph and his typewriter. It was the start of the happiest relationship with a filthy pro that fandom has ever known.

On July 5th, the open house announced for the morning hours at the fallen Ackerman's house was moved to the Bixel Street incarnation of Slan Shack. Phillips dominated the event with a discourse on humanity, religion, and abstract art. The convention itself resumed a half hour behind schedule. Daugherty, formally the chairman, got out from under by turning over the gavel to Russ Hodgkins, who endured a violent business session. This started mildly enough with a Speer resolution that urged fans to keep their hobby out of the eye of the general public as much as possible. It passed, without difficulty. Art Joquel next urged the appointment of a committee to work out a system for classifying fantasy fiction by theme under a decimal code, much as non-fiction is shelved in public libraries. Speer objected because he had already done most of the work on this very proposal, but the motion passed. The session warmed up a little during discussion of ways to make the fairest possible selections of future worldcon sites. Nothing was decided. Then all hell broke loose over the honorable old convention problem of what to do with the profits. Lou Goldstone offered a resolution that proposed their donation to the Fantasy Foundation. Daugherty immediately pointed out that he had already vetoed the con committee's decision to do this very thing. The National Committee for Atomic Information and the Emergency Committee of Atomic Scientists were next proposed as possible recipients of the funds. Goldstone offered an amendment that would give half of the profits to the foundation, the remainder to an atom group headed by Einstein. A hopeless parliamentary tangle ensued, and the motion failed amid complaints of fans that they didn't have any idea about the nature of the matter on which they were finally voting. Daugherty now created yet another sensation, by the disclosure that he knew the identity of the New York fan whose remark about Palmer's inability to edit a prozine had caused Ziff-Davis to cancel its plans to buy a $100 booster advertisement in the program book of the worldcon. The convention committee had meekly given the publishing firm a free ad. Perdue now proposed restricting the votes on convention sites to individuals whose homes were not in competing cities. Daugherty suggested as an alternate policy weighting votes so that individuals who came from the greatest distance would have the most say about next year's worldcon. The matter was tabled, despite fears that the event would soon settle into one portion of the nation, held captive by the predominance of attendees from that area.

The same evening, a caucus in Speer's room produced a compromise on the profit problem. The Fantasy Foundation directors agreed to let $150 go to the attempt to keep the atom under control. The remainder of the profits were to be divided equally between the Foundation and the NFFF.

Chief entertainer that evening was Theodore, a professional who had long been popular with Los Angeles fans. He almost struck because of noise outside the hall. But to many fans, he lived up to his reputation as a combination of Karloff, Dali, Nijinski, and Skelton. Charles Burbee made his only appearance of the con that evening. There was a weird session, over which Laney presided. Sam Russell spoke on weird fiction as a modern equivalent of the myths of past days and as a warning of doom that awaits men who fail to manipulate properly their newly acquired powers. Daugherty played his recording of Bradbury's "The Parasitic Hand" and Phil Schuman unveiled a dramatization of Lord Dunsany's "The Hurricane." It must be remembered that a recording in that pre-tape year was thoroughly impressive for its very existence, matters of quality aside. Yet another record, this time professional in origin, consisted of a *Suspense* dramatization of Lovecraft's "The Dunwich Horror." Another caucus of Foundation directors brought the revelation from Bob Tucker that Daugherty had agreed to follow the arrangements for disposition of the profits.

The third day produced still more problems. The hucksters' displays showed a premonition of what was about to happen, because someone had set up a small table dedicated to anti-NFFF propaganda. On it was a supply of mimeographed copies of the organization's constitution, overprinted with swastikas. The business session put a ten-minute limit on talks, to prevent the con from running into a fourth or fifth day. Goldstone's motion to split the profits between the NFFF and the Fantasy Foundation passed, 18-16. E. E. Evans then proceeded to extol the merits of the NFFF in a prepared speech, asked for suggestions on its future activities, and read a message from President Dunkelberger that told of the fake telegram from the Pacificon to Fargo alleging the dissolution of the NFFF. Rusty Hevelin identified the directors involved in the imagined conspiracy as himself, Laney, and myself, and revealed that the organization that was to supplant the NFFF was nothing more frightening than the Fantasy Foundation. This did not completely soothe the assemblage, because of resentment in Los Angeles fandom over Foundation planning: Evans and Gus Willmorth were peeved because they hadn't been invited to share the planning, and Daugherty had been squabbling with Laney over a number of matters, including this one. A long discussion preceded a successful motion by Evans urging Dunkelberger to let the directors run the organization for a while. Another motion cleared Laney and Hevelin of the conspiracy charges. My own character apparently remains suspect to this very moment. Bob Tucker presented a certificate of

merit signed by the board to Evans, "for loyalty to and advancement of the NFFF." The time for true confessions having arrived, Daugherty proceeded to identify Ray van Houten as the author of the prose that had angered Ziff-Davis, and the literary endeavor in question as a copy of an anti-Lemuria "publicity release." Opinion of the throng seemed to agree that van Houten had spoken truth but should have said it after the check for the adtisement was deposited.

Pre-con dinner at Clifton's Cafeteria— left to right: Max Sonstein, Lou Goldstone, Tigrina, Gus Willmorth, Forrest J Ackerman, and Ralph Rayburn Phillips

The masquerade ball that night was not much of a masquerade or ball, on the whole. Some fans dressed up in costume, a few others danced to the music of records, and the majority just sat there and enjoyed conversation. This upset Laney in the most extreme manner; he would apparently have been satisfied with nothing but the most violent variety of orgy. Daugherty, Elmer Perdue, and Rothman provided musical entertainment. Bob Hoffman, made up by a Hollywood expert, genuinely terrified a mundane girl who had been brought to the con for publicity purposes. She was Cay Forrester, then possessed of the distinction of being the All-American Girl of 1946, but assuming for the worldcon the added responsibility of serving as the Girl We'd Most Like to Be Stranded on the Moon With. Morojo, just over an operation, could not move around much, so she dressed as the Snake Mother, with a large headdress and nothing in particular from there down to the scales that began at her waist. Thus she had an excellent excuse for immobility, although it took three chairs pushed together to support her scaly lower areas. Dale Hart was an uncomfortable Gray Lensman, because Morojo had tailored his costume a trifle too snugly, and he could neither bend nor sit in it. Len Moffatt, as a fanzine story character, Vincent the Vampire, was carried rigid into the hall, then lay motionless so long that he alarmed less sophisticated fans. Art Joquel went around in red and black robes reciting the text of a black mass. Oliver King Smith, Earl Singleton's henchman in the fake suicide, drew upon his fannish past as the explanation of himself as the manifestation of thought energy: when fans learned that Singleton was alive, they had assumed that he had created an imaginary roommate to write the news of the alleged death to fandom. Tigrina dressed as Dracula's daughter, Evans as a birdman from Rhea, Himmel was the Stolen Dormouse, Phillips a Tibetan Buddhist, Charles Lucas a priest from *The Island of Captain Sparrow*, Pat Kenealy was Cthulhu, and Andy Anderson was the already legendary Helen Bradleigh. Prizes went to Joquel, Himmel, and Paul Carter, future cowboy, for the best characterizations; Morojo, Hoffman, and Chandler Davis as Quanna, for the most elaborate costumes; Hart, Tigrina, and Lucas, for displaying the most ingenuity of garb. A screening of *1,000,000 B.C.* followed.

The final day of the convention opened with a talk by a representative of the Federation of Pasadena Scientists, on civilian control of atomic energy. Despite the indecision about the need for money by atomic scientists, the audience gave him the loudest applause of any speaker during the con. At yet another business session, there was scarcely any difficulty encountered by Philadelphia when it asked for the right to stage the next worldcon. Rothman presented the city's bid. Tucker put in a bid for Fargo with a nomination speech. Mercifully, nobody sent a truthful telegram about it to Dunkelberger.

The fanquet concluded the con. Van Vogt spoke again, more briefly this time, with a claim that Ackerman had proved his point about the danger of exhausting endocrine reserves. Bloch cracked the first of a long and distinguished series of jokes at convention sessions. Leigh Brackett also spoke briefly. A survivor from Chicago, Richard Meyer, and the professional astronomer, R. S. Richardson, made their first appearances of the con. Ray Bradbury tried to run through some routines with Daugherty, but suffered memory lapses. Bob Olsen, an oldtime filthy pro, related anecdotes. When Daugherty announced that he was about to tell a joke, Perdue walked out. More than ninety fans and pros ate thin soup and halves of chicken, and mulled a lot of statistics that Don Day gave in a long talk, such as the fact that Ray Cummings had sold more science fiction stories than anyone else, 94. On Rothman's urging, hat-passing for atomic scientists produced $112, to which was later added $6, the outcome of a benefit poker session. (The Pacificon profits eventually provided $95.60 for the Fantasy Foundation and the National Fantasy Fan Federation. The check to the NFFF promptly bounced.)

The Pacificon received an odd mixture of praise and blame during the months that followed. Laney thought that $2.50 was an exorbitant price for a banquet, said that he had seen ten fairies among the group in one evening, and believed that the attendees in general gave evidence of social clumsiness. On the other hand, there was nothing at the Pacificon that upset lots of fans, like the Nycon exclusion act, and it did not destroy fandom in the host city as the Chicon had done. One potential fan, however, gafiated almost before he had started his career, because someone made a pass at him in an elevator. This was Sandy Kadet, who had become quickly liked, and seems to have been the only genuine example of a fan lost because of the homosexuality that Laney raged against in Los Angeles. Moffatt, a neofan during the first worldcons, and just back from looking at Nagasaki, might be an impartial critic: "There may have been background hassles and the beginnings or continuations of bitter feuds among some of the fans present. But on the surface, it was a happy, joyful con." It was also one of the last worldcons in which most persons present were inner circle fans and pros. It got next to no prozine publicity and Los Angeles newspapers ignored it, so the fringefans didn't know about it.

2. The Philcon, 1947

The PSFS announced near the start of 1947 its policy for the Philcon: "The delegates should have a good time. There should be plenty of opportunity for meeting fans, engaging in fangab, and conducting horsetrading among the collectors. There should be a fast-moving program which will stimulate the mind, and make the onlooker feel that science fiction fans are indeed unusual people who can do unusual things." Simultaneously with this cheerful announcement came evidence that that fascinating thorn in the side of worldcon committees, profits, had already begun to irritate Philadelphians. *The Philcon News* began early to drop obvious hints that the profits should help to pay the club's $25 monthly rent for the clubroom. It was the second straight convention that produced a fuss before it began. Milt Rothman had been the first to think seriously of a worldcon in Philadelphia, undergoing the inspiration while waiting in Paris for his demobilization after the war. The PSFS had acquired the same notion when he got home. After Rothman won the bid at the Pacificon, he was elected chairman of the Philcon, despite a busy life that contained dual status as teacher of physics and student of thermodynamics. He organized a convention society so informally that he did most of the preparatory work involved, later discovering that this had caused the program to be overweighted with scientific topics.

One day, Moskowitz and Sykora paid a visit to the PSFS with a proposal: a federation composed of that group, the ESFA, and the QSFL would help to put on the convention. The terror that was destined to engulf fans periodically for years to come, whenever New Yorkers seemed likely to have anything to do with a worldcon again, grasped some in Philadelphia. Rothman ruled that the Philcon Society, not the PSFS, was putting on the convention, and that the sponsoring group needed the help of neither one nor three local clubs. Moskowitz grew angry and refused to become New York representative for the Philcon. Sykora took this duty, then he got angry because Rothman didn't tell the PSFS to confirm his nomination. The situation did enough damage to the pride of the PSFS to force Rothman into a diplomatic stratagem. He pushed through the PSFS a resolution proclaiming that the club had created the Philcon Society to stage the convention. This quieted the tempers in Philadelphia, even though it was completely untrue. The New Yorkers consoled themselves by stirring up debate about how much of the profits should go to the PSFS. In the end, these matters unsettled things so badly that Rothman and Ben Waldo were forced to make a personal trip to New York to dislodge illustrations for auctioning from the offices of Mary Gnaedinger and John Campbell, and the little matter of deciding how much to charge for advertisements in the program booklet was forgotten. Advertisers were in the end told to pay what they felt like.

The Penn-Sheraton was chosen as site of the convention and warned to be ready for 200 to 300 fans. In the end, 175 registered, another 25 sneaked in, 102 attended the banquet, and 160 fans held Philcon Society memberships. There was no doubt about the identity of the first fan to arrive for this convention, because Degler was on hand as July began, in the belief that the event would be staged over Independence Day. He simply waited for the Labor Day weekend, using the name of John C. Chrisman. This also turned into the first real Worldcon, because Beak Taylor, Ned McKeown, and John L. Millard showed up from far-off, exotic Canada. There were other global undertones, because Ackerman had official status as head of the plan to bring a Britisher to some future worldcon. Plenty of celebrated pros were on hand: John W. Campbell as guest of honor, Willy Ley, George O. Smith, Hubert Rogers, Dr. E. E. Smith, Sam Merwin, Lester del Rey, Philip Klass, A. J. Donnell, L. Sprague de Camp, Alfred C. Prime, Lloyd Eshbach, Theodore Sturgeon, L. Jerome Stanton, Chan Davis, Dr. David Keller, and Alexander Phillips, among others. Ralph Milne Farley somehow withstood the strain of the Philcon immediately after attending the American Legion's national convention in New York City. The only things of note that happened before the opening was another of those fake telegrams, this one from California to the Los Angeles delegation, claiming that Walt Daugherty had impounded the contents of the LASFS clubroom so that he could use the

room exclusively for a dance studio; and an open house at the PSFS clubroom on the night of Friday, August 29th.

The convention opened Saturday afternoon with introductions by Rothman. New Yorkers were inexplicably scarce. Editors gave most of the talks
that afternoon. Merwin denied that he had strict taboos or requirements for
his magazines, he absolved himself of all responsibility for the blinding covers
of his magazines, and he said that the *Thrilling Wonder Stories* fanzine contest wasn't working out very well. Campbell confirmed
the report that he was attempting to break away from
atomic destruction as the theme of stories in *Astounding*, but complained that that was all that authors wrote
about for him. The duller part of Campbell's talk was
lifted from a book that he had written on atomic energy.
He predicted electrical use for the atom as its first peacetime function, said that an atomic power plant could be
in operation within ten years, and warned that scientists
were wishfully thinking when they hoped to get oodles
of energy by combinations of neutrons and protons.
Campbell got into a discussion when Farley used his in-

John W. Campbell

troduction to ask a resolution that would prohibit subversives from using
freedom of speech as a defense. Ackerman read a message from Ted Carnell
that explained how travel restrictions had prevented his crossing the ocean.
E. E. Smith read a short speech to a smallish group of fans and forbade
quotations from this manuscript in fanzines.

There was only one resolution presented during this session, but it was a
tough one. Speer lit out on Shaver, charging that his stories made fools of
science fiction readers and represented a threat to the mental health of many
persons. Speer asked the convention to oppose prozine material that might
prevent "impressionable youths from learning to think straight." He used
"lunatic fringe" in the talk, probably causing it to become a catch-phrase
that soon degenerated into a synonym for all those whom a fan disagreed
with. The Speer proposal drew both applause and objections. The latter
involved the probability that the worldcon attendees could hardly affect
the circulation or policies of the Ziff-Davis magazines and that a resolution
from them would provide Palmer with more grounds for claiming that he was
being persecuted by fandom. Phillips was authorized to write an alternate
resolution that would harass Ziff-Davis almost imperceptibly, by giving convention approval to a long list of prozines that would not include *Amazing
Stories* and *Fantastic Adventures*. The convention put off action until a later
session on this endorsement of magazines with "ethical and editorial policies
of honesty and repute." (In the end, the resolution ran into parliamentary
tangles, then had such a close vote that the whole matter was tabled for

action at the Torcon.) Someone suggested formation of a group that would subsidize the completion and publication of manuscripts left unfinished by A. Merritt at his recent death. There was discussion but no action.

The big item on the formal program that evening was a talk by Dr. Smith. He took to task virtually everyone—editors, authors, and fans—but defended the right of editors to set policy without consulting authors and fans. His talk emphasized the constancy of change in ways of writing science fiction stories. Rothman broke the news that Avon had dropped plans for two projected fantasy publications. There were numerous announcements from semi-pro firms about their plans. Hadley Publishing Co. promised *The Mightiest Machine* and a new edition of *The Skylark of Space*; Eshbach of Fantasy Press told about *The Black Flame* to come; Paul Spencer asked support for the NFFF publishing project, Keller's *The Sign of the Burning Hart*; Waldo plumped for Prime Press, particularly for its newly issued *Venus Equilateral*; Korshak boosted Shasta Publishers' checklist; Moskowitz told everyone to buy the Keller omnibus from Avalon; Ackerman spoke for Fantasy Publishing Company, Paul O'Connor for New Collectors Group, and someone else for the Carcosa House edition of *Edison's Conquest of Mars*. Blish smuggled in a plug for Vanguard Records. Aside from that, Tucker set some sort of worldcon record by completing in 105 seconds his talk on the topic "Et Cetera." The auction, by Korshak and Moskowitz, brought in more than $300. Nobody offered the $40 that was the reserve price on an Allen St. John cover, but Tom Hadley paid $31 for a Paul cover. Hadley, Dr. C. L. Barrett, and Jim Williams did most of the spending.

Perhaps the first of the big drunken worldcon parties followed in the Hadley suite where Fantasy Press and Prime Press provided much liquor. Fans gaped in disbelief at Campbell sitting on the floor, helping Hubert Rogers and Benson Dooling to sing a variety of bawdy ditties. The hotel staff did not interrupt, because there was a Sigma Alpha Rho convention in the hotel and the kids got blamed for all the noise that the fans made. This demonstrated Emerson's philosophy about compensation, as applied to fandom, because at the Pacificon the other convention in the meeting place had been that of Alcoholics Anonymous.

From time to time that Saturday night, the happy fans were vaguely aware of the existence of loud, intermittent noises. Several Philadelphians explained them away as a local phenomenon that occurred when sewer gas caused manhole lids to rise violently in a sort of municipal burping. However, the real facts were not at all like that. During a late drinking session in Hadley's room, Speer had suddenly remembered the existence of fireworks in the hip pocket of the Quintessence of FooFoo, his current auto. Ron Christensen, Al Lopez, and Chan Davis went along to help him retrieve this almost forgotten resource. Several roman candles later, policemen in a squad car gave the fans a warning about discharging fireworks within the city limits. The outraged fans retired to the Penn-Sheraton, pockets bulging with grenades. The ensuing excitement was blown into epic proportions through later accounts by Christensen, Tucker, Moskowitz, and others. Basically, Speer and Davis seem to have taken up strategic posts on upper fire escapes, after Lopez and Christensen chickened out. Firecrackers and skyrockets were alternated to provide variety, and the pair changed fire escapes frequently. When police returned, a strategic retreat ensued via back stairs and another outside staircase. They paid $5.00 apiece at the 21st District Station for disturbing the peace. The investment was at least partly justified because the pyrotechnics had helped Willy Ley to find his way to the hotel.

On the second day of the con, de Camp spoke on "Adventures in the Occult," covering the ground that his projected book, *Round About the Cauldron*, would deal with. He claimed that black masses are too long and tedious to sit through, and reported that he had had no success when he tested procedures outlined in Dunne's *Experiment With Time*. Davis conducted a discussion on the already unoriginal topic of whether science was catching up with science fiction. This led to a Campbell-Davis word battle over politics which the fascinated audience compared with the major engagements between space fleets in Doc Smith's space operas. It ended with a limerick battle. The group finally decided that science fiction was still considerably ahead of science. Korshak talked on books and their prices. He told the group that his test for the rarity of a volume was its ability to bring $100 from a customer. He listed as real rarities such items as Shiel's *The Rajah Sapphire*, the Weinbaum memorial volume, and John Collier's *Witch's Money*. Korshak also fascinated Lovecraft fans by the story of how W. Paul Cook had printed a 200-copy edition of HPL's *The Shunned House* in 1928 and left the sheets uncollated, and how R. H. Barlow finally bound up and sold a dozen copies for $2.00 apiece. Later that afternoon, Moskowitz took charge of the con and converted it into an ESFA meeting. During this, Dr. Keller spoke on "Editors I Have Known"; Joe Kennedy on fanzine publishing; and one Cullum, whose given name is apparently lost, on sequels to science fiction stories.

The evening was sacred to entertainment. Stanton was in charge of this program. Phil Klass, whose William Tenn penname was already celebrated, gave a monolog based on alleged mail from fans who thought he was one of the innumerable Kuttner pennames. Rothman compared Klass' explanation of the internal combustion of the carbon atom with Chaplin and the Folies-Bergère combined. George O. Smith gave a pantomime on how to split hairs, borrowing a specimen from the head of Mary Mair. Music emerged from Stanton and Ted Sturgeon, with an instrumental duo; Miss Mair, with a vocal setting of Sturgeon's "Thunder and Roses"; Davis, playing his own compositions on the piano; Kennedy, Fred Burgess, George Fox, and Algis Budrys, singing as a quartet a ditty about *Amazing* ("We shout to the skies the praises of Shaver; / We wish that he were a moldy cadaver"); and Rothman, playing the piano. Three parties followed. They were so large and so drunken that the dry element at the con took refuge in the meeting hall until the hotel staff locked them out at 2 a.m.

The final day began with a talk by George O. Smith, who told how science differs in practice from theory. He described utopia as "A place where all meters read alike" and complained that in this imperfect world, two signal generators can't be set on the same exact frequency and two identical radio components are different from one another. Willy Ley based his talk on part of a new book about space travel and the history of rocketry. He predicted a 230-mile upward trip by the navy's Neptune within a year, followed by an unmanned rocket that would commemorate its collision with the moon by setting off a flare. Dr. Thomas Gardner's talk dealt with spaceship drive mechanisms. He said that there are scientific reasons for not sending a rocket into space by exploding an atomic bomb under it. But he thought that an atomic pile smaller than current models might prove a practical drive. The banquet was served long after most stomachs needed it. Dr. Smith and Dr. Keller spoke briefly. Harry B. Moore sang a ribald tune. McKeown, Rothman, and Tucker put on various acts to while away the time. A few more remarks by Rothman closed the convention.

Since few foreigners had attended worldcons, the event became a worldcon the hard way, by moving out of the country the next year. At the Philcon's meeting to decide the next convention site, Speer was chairman. He urged allotment of four votes to each fan present from the Pacific Coast, in line with the Pacificon ideas about weighting votes from those living in far areas. This plan was voted down. Frank Stein nominated Milwaukee as the site for the next convention, but John Millard presented Toronto's case and Toronto won by an easy margin. The annual indecision on the proper holiday on which to schedule the con proved so agonizing that the group took the extreme measure of asking the NFFF to decide. It is not recorded that the NFFF ever did decide.

The Philcon was the closest thing yet to big business as a worldcon. Receipts were around $750. The committee paid $225 for the meeting hall and $145 to the printers. After other expenses were covered, profits amounted to $300. The PSFS inherited one-third of this sum. Another $75 was reserved for the NFFF and Fantasy Foundation, another $50 as a kitty for the next con, and the rest went to pay bus fares for impoverished fans and to buy magazines for a paralyzed reader discovered by Arthur Leo Zagat. The Big Pond Fund, confused since birth, ran into increased difficulties when its raffle winner turned out to be the completely vanished Abby Lu Ashley.

She was later discovered on the West Coast as a chiropractor. Milton Rothman thought it was the first commercial convention, in the sense that it brought together enough writers, agents, editors, and publishers to permit a big show of wares and to breed profits for various filthy pros. Del Rey, for instance, acquired a good agent as a result of a contact made at the con. Prime Press credited three big deals to the event. Paul Carter defined it as much better than the Pacificon, theorizing that this meant that pros make the difference between a mediocre and a good convention. Some of the pros also seemed impressed. Campbell had intended to stay only long enough to deliver his keynote address, but he liked the surroundings so much that he stayed three days. Keller was credited with being the only pro who kept his head sufficiently to stop talking at a sensible time, when given the podium.

3. The Torcon, 1948

The next two worldcons seem like an interlude in the sequence of things. Both were fairly small, they were planned and conducted with a minimum of friction, and they did not produce too much in the way of famous talks, celebrated fan antics, or startling revelations. The Torcon was distinctive as a worldcon held in a city where the fans were neither numerous nor particularly active, as the last worldcon staged over Independence Day, and as the first in a foreign nation. The Cinvention is unique for the fact that nobody guessed that it would be staged there until near the end of the previous year's worldcon.

Torcon sessions were held in the RAI Purdy Studios convention hall. The auditorium was decorated with original illustrations, fanzine displays, special editions of the *Sydney Futurian* and *Le Zombie*, and a panel containing future covers for *The Necromancer*. There was plenty of light, and the novelty of a sound system in good condition, although only Moskowitz and Keller possessed the ability to remember how to use the highly directional microphones. Most of the fans were housed in the Prince George Hotel, the Windsor Arms, and the King Edward. The Prince George was apparently an ultramodern, glass-doored establishment with pastel and chrome decorations in its giant lobby. Somewhat less impressive furnishings predominated elsewhere. Near the end of the convention, some fans became so discontented that they almost got up the nerve to throw a bathtub off the roof. Ron Christensen constructed a dummy which he hanged from the chandelier of his room, with a note attached: "I can't endure the Prince George Hotel any longer." In all fairness, it must be noted that the management soon tore apart and rebuilt the structure. The King Edward was better-liked, particularly for the phenomenal quality of its roast beef.

Another distinction possessed by the Torcon was that the convention committee chairman, Ned McKeown, managed to get the first session started on time on the afternoon of Saturday, July 3rd. After his welcoming address, Robert Bloch as guest of honor launched on an analysis of fandom and science fiction from Freudian principles. He argued that science serves as a father-substitute to readers of science fiction, as an infallible answerer for all problems. Bloch defended science fiction, however, for its glorification of the individual. Moreover, he con-

Ned and Mrs. McKeown

tended that fans are not as introverted as they seem to be, but give such an impression because they get few opportunities to act like extroverts. The speaker said that the neofan who praises a prozine story as great literature makes no greater mistake of evaluation than the professional critic who dismisses the best science fiction as trash. He called cons "a manifestation of the healthiest aspect of fandom. You have come here today not to save the world or to convert unbelievers or to grind the axe of self-aggrandisement— you have gathered here because of the pleasure you take in associating with others who share your liking for fantasy. I take a certain pride in writing fantasy, pride in the realization that what I write reaches an audience capable of such interest and reaction. It is not without significance that in a world so torn by discord today, such a group is still in existence, able to generate sufficient enthusiasm to make this convention a reality."

In the absence of most semi-pro publishers, messages were read from some of them, like James A. Williams for Prime Press and Abe Childs for the New Collectors Group. That evening, a movie on man's effort to conquer the atom possessed such monumental dullness that the projector was stopped at one point, to make sure that the fans still remaining in the hall had the patience to sit out the rest of it. George O. Smith restored good humor with a talk on interplanetary communication. He termed this possible already between Earth and Mars or Venus. Smith got into a complicated hassle with the audience over the degree of difficulty involved in conversations between planets because of the time lag, and finally almost fled to escape a group who continued to fire questions at him.

On Sunday afternoon, one of the great bidding duels in worldcon history occurred. Korshak got Alfred Prime and Harry Moore so fascinated by the Finlay cover for "The Devil's Spoon" that Moore finally paid $76 for it. The price for this cover, originally done for the June, 1948, *Famous Fantastic Mysteries*, was the highest yet paid for any single item at a fan auction. Original illustrations sold for prices ranging from $3 to $50, many of them bringing more than $10. The auction as a whole produced income in excess of $400, another worldcon record. Tucker delighted everyone in the evening by the humor of his "Little Kinsey Report" based on a survey of fandom. Sunday evening was supposed to provide reports from prozine editors, but the only member of the genus on hand was Wollheim, who dutifully described his *Avon Fantasy Reader*. Next came a roundtable discussion among Chan Davis, Milt Rothman, and Norm Stanley on the probable date for the arrival of interplanetary travel. The audience couldn't participate in the speculating very well, despite good intentions, because of audio difficulties.

It might be possible to write the whole history of worldcons as various aspects of a constant and desperate effort to keep New York City from winning next year's event. The Torcon's most famous happening sprang from this weltanschauung. The smoke-filled room in which mighty and secret deals are made has been mythical at many worldcons, but it became notorious because of the one that definitely functioned in Toronto. New York was known to be anxious to play host to the worldcon on the tenth anniversary of the Nycon. Various fans feared that the 1939 exclusion act had left scars that might resume bleeding at another Nycon, or that a similar mischance might occur. Moskowitz added to the anti-New York sentiment when he revealed that he didn't want the work involved in helping to promote a con. The smoke-filled room, actually several smoke-filled rooms, in Toronto, served to try to find a new home for the 1949 event. The fact that no other city wanted it badly made this a tough problem. Ackerman, Hevelin, and Evans feared that it was too soon to try to hold another worldcon in Los Angeles. Harry Moore proposed New Orleans as the host city, but this proposal was shouted down as fantastic. Fans from Milwaukee and Minneapolis were wooed as potential hosts, but turned down the propositions with shudders. Detroit fans had some interest in a worldcon, but this city was rejected as too close to Toronto. Finally, about thirty fans crammed into Korshak's room and spawned a mighty intellectual prodigy, in the form of remembering the existence of the city of Cincinnati. A telephone call to Charles Tanner provided Dr. C. L. Barrett with authority to enter the bid for the Ohio city. The few fans who went to bed that night slept with peaceful minds.

The business session itself, Monday afternoon, was almost an anticlimax. Moskowitz started it by summarizing the way worldcons had been fighting to prevent themselves from turning into sitting ducks for commercialization by interests looking for something to exploit. After all the worry, New York failed to enter a bid for the next worldcon. Barrett's motion for Cincinnati was hastily seconded by Evans for the West and by the Michigan delegation. As usual, a decision on whether to hold it on July 4th or Labor Day was tabled.

The big talk Monday was given by Dr. Keller: "Science—Master or Servant?" He devoted much of it to detailing the apparent increase in mastery over man possessed by science: "It is evident that he has become a slave to the machine. Every scientific discovery proved to be a two-edged sword. It could be used either to benefit or to destroy mankind." Dr. Keller warned that mankind would suffer destruction, if it did not subdue science and keep it in the status of a servant. Then he tied into this warning the audience before him, urging: "The writer should tell of inventions beneficial to man, dreams of the future in which society is happier, life more comfortable, old age more satisfactory. These scientific prophecies should benefit instead of harming our race. Science fiction literature is molding a new generation. The time has passed when the science fiction story can be considered simply a form of anesthetic pastime. If used properly, it can become a powerful means of bringing peace on Earth, good will toward men."

The convention formally recognized Sneary's crazy slogan of South Gate in '58, giving a letter from him on this fantastic theme a loud ovation. The final item on the formal program was a meal that had the labored trick name of buffanet. Bloch and George Smith served as masters of ceremonies. The former parodied the Tucker parody of Kinsey. Moskowitz recited "The Raven," then Stanley gave a talk on the semantics of such thing things as mill mills, drill drills, and birdseed seed. The Philadelphians presented a takeoff on the then celebrated radio soap opera, *Portia Faces Life*, in which Rothman was actor and musician, Smith served as announcer, and someone named Josie captivated everyone by her manner of wriggling. Dave and Pam MacInnes sang. George Smith read, with the help of sound effects by Tucker, the strange news stories that the Toronto press had provided as coverage of the con. (Sample headline: "Zap! Zap! Atomic Ray is Passé With Fiends." "Zap" had just been invented as a fannish tradition. One eyewitness traced back the word to a boring movie. Martin Alger allegedly asked Ben Singer if the reason for the boredom was the absence of anyone in the film who might draw a raygun and go "zap." The term instantly became associated with the water pistols with which almost all Torcon attendees were armed.)

Reaction to the Torcon was quite mixed. Those who liked to chatter and socialize without adulterants in the form of filthy pros were happy for the last time in worldcon history: not more than a half-dozen genuine pros were on hand. Some said that humor formed the predominant note of the whole event. Canada's different mores caused a few problems, like the ban that a house detective put on poker sessions in guests' rooms. One fan, Ben Singer, almost became a Canadian because he brought along a radio and sold it. He was allowed to return to his homeland only after paying $8.00 in import tax and giving the Canadian equivalent of the FBI enough information to make the purchaser a hunted man. Singer was involved in most of the more colorful legends emanating from the Torcon, such as the manner in which he almost took a rabbi along despite his militant atheism. The Kellers got into hot water twice. The author got miffed when some fans mistook his talk as intended to be humorous, and Sam McCoy so described it in a published conreport. Mrs. Keller angered some fans by her public references to the fact that Chad Oliver had had trouble getting his mother's consent to make the long trip from Texas. Tucker also stirred up the duller moments of the con by assuming from time to time the role of house detective and hotel manager. The con helped to create the legend of the Moskowitz vocal powers. Someone said that it was as easy to interrupt him as to derail the Super Chief with a hairpin. The younger element in fandom showed signs of coming to the fore. SAPS members took part of the transom from a door between their rooms, because it interfered with water pistols and firecrackers. George Young wore his beanie, except when Rapp borrowed it, creating another tradition. Despite the small attendance, room jam records were threatened. There were thirty persons in the Korshak room, in addition to the smoke, at a delicate point in negotiations on the next site. Smith's bathroom held twenty fans during an early morning limerick session.

The con may not have been responsible, but Toronto fandom was decimated soon after this event. Only Bill Grant remained active in that city well into the fifties.

4. The Cinvention, 1949

For a city that hadn't asked for the event, the Cincinnati fans put on a good if rather uneventful convention the next year. Don Ford, the chairman, did most of the advance work. The Cincinnati Fantasy Group cooperated with him, and derived an unusually fine profit for the trouble, $363.19. Part of the financial success derived from severe labors on the program booklet, for which 51 pages of advertising were sold. Public relations were perhaps the finest in worldcon history. The event got a sympathetic and generous press. There was a front-page story with three photographs on the opening day in the Cincinnati *Post*, an elaborate spread was featured in a special science fiction issue of the *Antiquarian Bookman*, a Sunday newspaper devoted a feature to the event a couple of weeks later, and Trans Radio Press, then serving news to most of the nation's broadcasting industry, got coverage from Dave Kyle and Tucker. A press service transmitted word of the events as far away as Australia. WLWT became the first television station to turn over a program to worldcon participants. Kyle moderated. Visible were such as Hannes Bok, Judith Merril, E. E. Smith, E. E. Evans, Jack Williamson, Fritz Leiber, Ted Carnell, Forry Ackerman, Lloyd Eshbach, Erle Korshak, Jim Williams, John Grossman, C. L. Barrett, Bob Tucker, and Lois Miles.

The first sensation of the Cinvention occurred before its formal opening. On September 2nd, the eve of the worldcon, Walter Coslet asked Palmer for his autograph. Palmer inquired: "As an ex-editor or as a fan?" This was the first word for most fans that the stormy petrel of the prozines had resigned from Ziff-Davis to become his own publisher. He apologized for failure to bring free copies of *Other Worlds* to the con, blaming his printer, and announced that he intended to print *Astounding*-type fiction in the new magazine. The convention itself lasted three days in the Hotel Metropole. Grossman and Gary Kroll had created a ten by thirty-foot backdrop for the convention hall. A $50 tip for the hotel staff permitted the fans to enjoy themselves without the interruptions of festivities that had plagued the Torcon.

The Torcon had also suffered from a lack of professionals. The Cinvention nearly went to the other extreme, and most of the pros gave talks at one time or another. If the previous worldcon's theme had been humor, this one impressed many fans as emphasizing the commercial growth of science fiction and the transition of many fans into pros. Jack Williamson, almost a legend as a professional writer, said that the element that makes science fiction exciting and worthwhile is "the intellectual interest in scientific possibilities, examined in the light of all their logical consequences." He decried efforts to prove that science fiction is better than more pretentious types of mundane fiction. "Considering the uses to which such discoveries as the atomic chain reaction are being put, you can't blame people who prefer to ignore such uncomfortable possibilities as long as they can," he added.

Vincent T. Hamlin, creator of Alley Oop, was the first comic strip genius to win a place on a worldcon podium. He identified himself as a reader of science fiction for 25 years, but said that he had not dared to put an interplanetary plot into his strip about cavemen until the White Sands Proving Ground had made the public moon-conscious. Dr. Smith claimed that business offices are to blame for poor covers on the prozines, and he warned that fans can do little about this art problem. Del Rey bemoaned the bad handling of love and sex in current science fiction stories. Lloyd A. Eshbach, a surprise choice as guest of honor, told about his 22 years of experience in science fiction, first as a writer, then as a semi-pro publisher, and he also put stress on the way fans were turning into pros. Leiber based a talk on science fiction and culture, but details of it seem to have vanished. Arthur J. Burks insisted that the average reader can do things to affect the policies of magazines. Palmer described plans for *Other Worlds*. He advanced them during the con by hiring an assistant editor he found there, Bea Mahaffey.

The group justified its worldcon designation in two ways. Ted Carnell was at hand, the first Britisher ever to make a trip to an American worldcon, thanks to the Big Pond Fund. The group was electrified when a telephone call came all the way from Australia. It was Sterling Macoby, who announced that he'd placed a news story on the event into the Sydney *Daily Mirror*. Dave MacInnes recorded most of the convention, on wire that seems irretrievably lost to fannish posterity.

Faanish aspects of the convention were not too significant. The biggest party occurred in the Shasta rooms. There was an NFFF meeting, where the group decided to publish an art portfolio and to make Boggs editor of a subscription fanzine that never came into existence. Judith Merril led a round table discussion in which Rothman, Leiber, Eshbach, Evans, and Ackerman participated. The Philadelphians put on a sequel to the previous year's space opera.

Back after a year's absence was the masquerade ball. Few fans took part. Lois Jean Miles wore a walkie-talkie on her head and not much else. If you don't recognize the name, it's because Kyle had hired her, a model, to symbolize Miss Science Fiction of 1949. Henry Chavot of New York attracted some attention for his yellow shorts, matching red jacket, and toy raygun. Rapp had a wild beard and giant pipe to symbolize a mad scientist. The auction brought quite high bids. An old *Thrilling Wonder Stories* cover for "Flight of the Star-Shell" was dignified with a price of $48. A cover for "Seven Footprints to Satan" sold for $31, and the first cover for *Other Worlds* won a top bid of $32. Today's Burroughs fans might quiver in the knowledge that $13 bought six volumes of Tarzan comic strips that Farley had painstakingly collected and bound. The auction showed a strong trend toward interest in original manuscripts. Two Lovecraft poems and HPL's autograph sold for $13, making the *Dawn of Flame* typescript a bargain at $12. A copy of *The Weapon Makers* in book form with corrections written in by van Vogt sold for $36. Farley's *Radio Planet* typescript supplemented by copies of correspondence about it between the author and *Argosy* sold for nine dollars.

Regular con-goers could be excused for the feeling that this was where they came in, when the business meeting settled down to another fight over the question of how to keep next year's con out of New York City. Things were more confused than at Toronto, because in Cincinnati the strategy was not worked out thoroughly before the site selection meeting, and because both Sykora and Stanton made bids for New York, creating an impression that there were competing groups active in New York. Ackerman entered a bid for Portland, Oregon. Harry Moore and Paul Juneau tried again for New Orleans. MacInnes offered Washington as the host city. What followed was reminiscent of certain political conventions. New York held a big lead on the first ballot. It got 48 votes, to 36 for Portland, 29 for Washington, and only 8 for New Orleans. But under the rules of the convention, a second ballot was needed, from which the two low cities were dropped. This ended in a 60-60 tie. There followed a considerable amount of politicking inside the hall and the roundup of some straying con-goers outdoors. In years to come, the doors of the meeting room were sometimes locked until balloting was ended, in commemoration of this occasion. The final ballot saw Portland gain the victory, 67-63. The only relaxation from the general tension and ill-feeling came when South Gate's mailed bid was acknowledged, covering as it did the far future year of 1958. Those who didn't vote against New York for fear of fusses apparently feared professional domination of another worldcon there.

The final checkup showed that the Cinvention had 175 registrants, about 15 stowaways, and income of $1,307, of which $980 came from auction profits. This was a big change in the decade since the first worldcon, because that Nycon had an income of $306 and still produced a $36 profit. With expenses at the Cinvention held down to $443, the chair-appointed finance committee had plenty of money to get rid of. It gave $150 to start off Portland, $50 to the NFFF, $150 for buying books and magazines for an unidentified British fan club for undisclosed reasons, the same amount for similarly vague purposes in Australia, and most of the rest to the Cincinnati Fantasy Group. The final report also showed that the banquet had attracted 116 persons.

An outsider's view of worldcons around this time might be of interest, before the worldcons became the monsters of the fifties. A New York pulp chain that was thinking of starting a prozine had sent an official to Cincinnati for reconnaissance purposes. Long afterward, his report found its way into print: "The people were middle class, bad dressers, not well-educated, no culture, little money. After you got to know them, they were likable, friendly and very sincere about the whole thing. That's fine, but I'd hate to live with them. They were all a believing sort, uncritical, anxious to please and be pleased; the led, not the leaders. These people lack affectation and there is just none of the phoniness you find at any Eastern literary tea party. They have a wonderful time."

An insider who had been to all the worldcons, Milton Rothman, also had opinions. He characterized the Pacificon as well-organized with a strong chairman but with too much of everything, making it impossible for any known human to withstand the strain of the four days' events. The Philcon had suffered from too much science and too little public address system. The Torcon left too much of the program to chance and things did not move rapidly enough. The Cinvention lacked timing and too many speakers failed to show up. In general, Rothman felt that fans were too anxious for publicity for their worldcons, as distinguished from good publicity; he feared commercialization, and he believed that worldcons must leave plenty of time for audience discussion, to prevent fans from busting gaskets in frustrated silence.

Meanwhile, as the forties ended, there was still no firm policy on a systematic way of choosing the next worldcon site, there was no decision on a way to split up profits without making everyone angry, and there was an occasional rumbling from the storm that was to break in the decade ahead, involving the sovereignty of the worldcons: whether they belonged to a host club or to a special con society or to fandom in general.

12. FANZINES: Oceans of Ink

1. Fan Polls

Polls and popularity votes were popular in fandom during the forties. It would be nice if their results could determine which fanzines were best-liked and most popular during that decade. But in fandom, polls were frequently taken mainly among individuals with special tastes in common. Most of them were conducted by someone who published a fanzine himself, and the results were distorted because his friends didn't dare leave him off the list or because he had disqualified himself from all consideration.

Despite these faults, the polls taken during the forties can provide some clues to the identity of the fanzines that got the most attention, and indirectly to the general atmosphere of fanzine fandom through these ten years. Art Widner was the busiest poll-taker at the start of the forties. In 1940, his poll revealed as the top five fanzines: *Spaceways*, *Sun Spots*, *Stardust*, *Le Zombie*, and *Snide*. The fickleness of interest among fans and the brief life of fanzines are shown by the fact that the Widner poll only two years later placed two newcomers among the top three: *Fantasite* and *VOM*. By 1944, Gerry de la Ree had become prominent as a pollster. He found that *Le Zombie*, *Acolyte*, and *VOM* were the favorites, but had a special category for newszines which *Fantasy Fiction Field* won. Two years later, de la Ree tried again and a new title was on top: *Vampire*.

As the decade neared its end, Don Wilson took a poll whose first five places went to *Gorgon*, *Dream Quest*, *Fantasy Advertiser*, *Fantasy Commentator*, and *Fandom Speaks*. But another group of voters almost simultaneously gave a different set of results when de la Ree got votes from Philcon attendees: *Variant*, *Fantasy Commentator*, *Shangri-L'Affaires*, *Fantasy Advertiser*, and *Vampire*. Unfortunately, nobody seems to have wrapped up the matter neatly by taking a poll on fanzine favorites in 1949.

2. Characteristics of Popular Fanzines

What conclusions come from such lists of titles of fanzines, some of which are frequently mentioned with nostalgia today and ardently sought by collectors, while others are completely forgotten by all but the most ancient fans? First, the fact that the fanzine field was almost as widely varied in the forties as it is today, with general-interest fanzines, faanish fanzines, and highly specialized fanzines equally capable of gaining the favor of fandom in general. Then, the inability of most fanzines to win popularity polls in ratio to the amount of money spent on their publication; only one of those fanzines lived luxuriously. Next, a striking difference from the most popular fanzines of the thirties: the favorites of the forties were mostly those that did not serve as organs for the perpetuation of feuds, and some of them strictly avoided material that could bring about the personal-insult type of controversy.

By the forties, it was obvious that most good fanzines had become one-man or two-man operations, another difference from the earlier custom of assembling big boards of editors. The majority of the most successful fanzines were those with a sharp personality of some type, either a reflection of the editor's own personality, like *Le Zombie*, or specializing in a particular type of material, like *Acolyte*. A few more traits possessed in common by most of the poll winners: They generally survived at least a year or two instead of flashing and burning out in two or three spectacular issues; most of them managed to appear at least four or five times a year; and the majority of them were reasonably plump, usually topping two dozen pages per issue. One final and shakier generalization might be that this decade placed a greater importance on conventional literacy as a factor in favor for fanzines than any other period in fandom's history. The kind of rough and ready writing and editing that inspired affection for a Max Keasler in the fifties was more likely to arouse indignation in the forties.

Some previous fan historians have credited my own publication, *Spaceways*, with helping to cause some of these tendencies in fanzine publishing. But I believe that *Spaceways* was an effect rather than a cause. I modeled it closely on fanzines that were already quite popular when it first appeared in 1938, particularly Madle's *Fantascience Digest*, which was moderately free from the inbred contents of other East Coast fanzines of the era, and *Scienti-Snaps*, Walter Earl Marconette's beautiful little publication that was so free from evidence of haste or fanaticism. Besides, some of the features of *Spaceways* that were prominent during its four years of existence were never imitated by most fanzines, such as its emphasis on material written by pros, a hangover from an earlier era in fanzines, and its large proportion of fiction. If *Spaceways* did affect fanzine fandom, it may have done so in a different way, simply by proving that a magazine that appears often enough for several years and contains something to interest many types of fans will find a great deal of favor.

3. The Content of Fanzines

The nature of material published in fanzines expanded somewhat during the forties. This happened because of outside influences, most likely, rather than through any deliberate intent to evolve. The conreport as a fannish art form began to solidify slowly during this decade, because suddenly there were many cons attracting lots of fans. To continue the old habit of writing objective, newspaper-type reports would have led to intolerable repetition. So the subjective conreport, in which the author plays a leading role, replaced the former listing of speeches, putting new emphasis on how the writer reacted to what he saw and heard, even describing in detail his adventures traveling to and from the con. Widner and Speer were among the most important pioneers in this addendum to fanzine material.

Simultaneously, fanzine pages were no longer as full of information about the prozines and gossip about the professional writers and editors. There were several pro-centered newszines appearing regularly, getting some of this material to fandom before the larger fanzines could publish it. Before the decade was half finished, the old situation of every fan reading every new magazine story and almost every new book with a science fiction theme vanished, in the flood of new books and magazines, so that an item about a professional work no longer carried meaning automatically for all readers of that fanzine. Then there were such problems as the prozines that filled an issue with eight or ten stories written by two or three authors; it was disheartening to try to track down a new author and prepare a biography on him, when he turned out to be a penname.

A related phenomenon was the smaller amount of effort that fanzine editors were making to imitate prozines. They were coming to realize that there is really no necessity to show the price on the cover of a fanzine that won't be bought at a newsstand, and that it isn't as important for a fanzine to issue a specified number of editions per year as it is for a professional magazine that sells advertising on the basis of commitments like these. Most fanzines stopped selling advertising space altogether, and the custom of trading free advertisements was almost forgotten as the fanzine review columns increased in popularity and provided the publicity for competitors.

The letter section, on the other hand, gained in importance from the subsidiary position that it had held in early fanzines in dutiful imitation of the prozines. Fans soon discovered how easy it was to use a letter section as a springboard from which to dive into topics only vaguely related to the material that the fanzine was publishing. It also became clear that Armageddon would not arrive if much space in a letter section was not concerned with science fiction matters at all. Soon, fandom discovered that, like the celebrated disembodied intelligences independent of a physical brain that had floated through much early science fiction, a letter section can exist indefinitely without any visible means of support. *VOM* was the most famous early example in general fandom of a letter section that stayed alive for years without any specific fanzine material on which to feed. The apa influence also may have helped to encourage general fanzines to put more emphasis on letter sections, because the apa equivalent of the letter section was the mailing comment, which might make up half or more of the total content of a bundle.

Tied in with the new freedom and scope for the letter section was the tendency for many fanzines to pay little or no attention to anything but fandom and fandom's non-science-fiction interests. Here again the apas led the way. Fandom-oriented fanzines of the thirties had mostly dealt with feuds or politics; during the forties, those that didn't emphasize fantastic fiction topics covered almost the entire range of interests in the outside world.

One fanzine trend crept up so unobtrusively that nobody has traced when it was first openly acknowledged as a practice. Giving away a fanzine for a letter of comment would have been complete heresy during the thirties. Some pioneer fanzine editors insisted on money for all copies, even if it meant exchanging dimes between editors who published at the same price with the same frequency. By the time *Spaceways* was alive, it had become customary to exchange fanzines with other publishers, even when one editor outpublished the other by a considerable amount of weight or merit. It was also accepted practice by then to send a free copy of an issue in which his material appeared to any contributor who was sophisticated enough not to offer to pay for that issue. *Le Vombiteur*, which Robert W. Lowndes began to publish at the end of 1938, seems to have been the first free fanzine outside the apas, other than an occasional special-purpose fanzine. Its first imitator, Bob Tucker's *Le Zombie*, lasted so much longer and became so much more popular that it deserves most of the credit for causing lots of fans to realize that the income from a few subscriptions hardly was worth the trouble of keeping track of how many issues were due each person and the futility of working hard on copies that drew only monetary response. But Tucker accepted money for *LeZ* as it grew older and larger. The LASFS began in 1941 to publicize the city's fandom by giving away *Shangri-L'Affaires*. Soon thereafter, Earl Singleton startled everyone by handing out copies of the first fat free fanzine, *Nepenthe*, and by 1944, Tucker could count 45 fanzine titles that were free without strings, or intended mainly for exchange and letter of comment purposes. The trend away from the subscription-centered fanzine must have helped to increase the quantity of the species. The number-conscious Tucker counted 81 titles issued during 1941, not including several dozen that were circulated in FAPA. By the end of the decade, the annual number of titles had grown to an estimated 200, if apa and other restricted-circulation magazines were counted.

4. The Format of Fanzines

Most important of all, perhaps, was the fact that the letterpress fanzine no longer dominated the field during the forties. A few fanzines probably wouldn't have seemed so superior to their hectographed and mimeographed brethren in the earliest years of fanzine fandom, if there hadn't been the unique figure of Conrad Ruppert, making his printing abilities available at rock bottom prices. Whether Ruppert was a cause or an effect, the die was cast by the forties: fanzines would be almost without exception reproduced by low cost, easily available machines, permitting almost any youngster to try his own hand at publication; moreover, these modest duplicating devices encouraged fanzines containing large quantities of words. If the printed publication had dominated fandom as it obsessed the mundane apas, the time required to set type by hand and the difficulty of finding someone with access to a linotype would have made enormously difficult the things that fandom accomplished: long essays, big bibliographic projects, endless chitter-chatter of a delightful nature.

But there were a few printed fanzines in the forties, and most of them were beauties of a short-lived breed. W. Lawrence Hamling managed to publish five professionally printed and lavishly illustrated issues of *Stardust*, relying heavily on the most famous pros as sources of material, claiming distribution approaching a thousand copies, and losing enough money to cause discouragement and suspension within a year. *Scienti-Snaps* evolved into a printed fanzine of similar aspect and ambition around the same time, and differed only in its greater speed of attaining oblivion, printing only one issue entitled *Bizarre*. Several of the newszines flirted on occasion with the printing press, and achieved slightly greater success before retreating to the

Stardust: Nov. 1940

more homely jelly or cylinder. Occasionally, something splendid came off the printing press into fandom. The second issue of *The Ghost*, published by W. Paul Cook in 1944, has claims to rank as the greatest single issue of any fanzine in history. An enormous printed fanzine entitled *Vortex* emerged in 1947 from San Francisco under the editing of Gordon M. Kull and George R. Cowie, almost indistinguishable in some ways from a prozine, but survived only two issues, each containing eighty-odd pages.

Curiously, one of the longest-lived of all fanzines is a printed one. In 1945 Bill Danner began to issue for VAPA a little fanzine entitled *A Dangerous Thing*, partly printed and partly mimeographed. He soon converted the format to all-printed, changed the title to *Stefantasy*, and moved over into FAPA for more than a decade. Now as an independent publication it still emerges several times a year.

The hectograph, which was in supreme favor in the primeval days of fanzine publishing, began to lose ground to the mimeograph in the late thirties, and suffered further disgrace as the forties moved ahead. The hectograph had the solitary virtue of low cost: one hecto ribbon and a few hecto pencils were the publishing equivalent of as many stencils and styluses as a week's salary would purchase. But the disadvantages of the hectograph are too numerous to be listed in a book of this size. Quickly the mimeograph became supreme even in circumstances where fewer than fifty copies of a fanzine were needed, like local clubzines and FAPA in its early years. Paste ink machines like the Gestetner did not make their major impact on fans until the fifties, and to that decade also belongs the greatest popularity of Ditto machines, occasionally confused by neofans with hectographs, because of their common custom of favoring purplish print.

5. Artwork in Fanzines

The rise of the mimeograph made it easy to publish large circulation fanzines and increased the probability that a fan could remain active for several years without going blind. But it had a bad effect on fanzines for the deterioration of the artwork that it created. Fan artists had been accustomed to use several colors and solid masses of hues when drawing for the hectograph. They had all sorts of trouble adapting their styles to the stark line work and anemic shading that are easiest to attain on the mimeograph. It was years before British fanzines proved how much fine detail and what firm, thick lines can be put onto a stencil with the naked hand, not to mention the additional subtleties that electronic stencil-cutting can produce. Perhaps in an instinctive effort to compensate for this situation, fanzines of the early forties contained a fair amount of artwork in a medium that has been abandoned completely by now, silk-screening. Organdy stretched across a wooden frame and paper masks, plus a squeegee to force ink through the paper and cloth were all that was needed for a crude sort of silk-screening. Jack Wiedenbeck drew and duplicated a magnificent series of multi-color covers for Battle Creek fanzines through a variant on this technique: an airbrush and cardboard masks. His magnum opus was the six-color back cover of the second issue of *Nova*, somehow accomplished with perfect register.

Ackerman was the pioneer in the use of lithography for fanzines. It was too expensive for most fans as a medium for producing entire issues, but the more pretentious fanzines were soon using this or some similar process to reproduce a particularly good cover drawing. About the time the decade began, 35-mm cameras were coming within the financial reach of many fans, resulting in occasional tipped-in photographic illustrations. *Fantasy Fiction Field* ran commercially produced prints regularly to give readers previews of what the covers of forthcoming prozine issues would look like.

It's hard to think of any method of reproduction that wasn't used at least once or twice in fandom during this era. Dale Tarr and Charles Tanner blueprinted part of the third issue of *Science Fiction World*, and made their own sensitized paper to boot. Elmer Perdue distributed a FAPA publication created with the aid of teletype tape. Another FAPA venture by Don B. Thompson looked like a positive blueprint but was actually a whiteprint dry process done with office machinery. Ackerman went to the United States Army's dogtag production facilities to graphotype an alleged publication. Limited-edition fanzines were those created with the aid of nothing more complex than carbon paper. Usually these were the first creative efforts of a fan, sometimes produced for the benefit of schoolmates before he knew of the existence of fandom. But one of the respectable pioneer Australian fanzines, *Ultra*, got its start that way. Eric Russell of Sydney distributed the few copies to a chosen few fans.

Several fans who wanted to mimeograph their publications made their own mimeos. Martin Alger kept track of expenses, and found that his investment came to $3.75 for the homemade machine on which he published a fanzine telling how to create similar do-it-yourself mimeographs. Dale Tarr was even more resourceful, getting results without putting a formal machine together through the simple process of plastering a stencil around a flannel-covered and ink-smeared gallon paint can, and rolling it over paper. Louis Russell Chauvenet, on the other hand, was the only prominent fan who achieved independence from the typewriter. *Detours*, his thin hectographed publication, was written in the distinctive Chauvenet penmanship, and was further distinguished by such elegancies as cellophane covers and pasted-on stars that showed why you were receiving it.

6. The Circulation of Fanzines

Fanzine circulation in those days was not too different from today's situation, except for a few special cases. The latter were publications that appealed to many borderline fans who were largely pro-centered in their interests and found too little to their taste in the majority of fan publications. *Fantasy Advertiser* reached a circulation of a thousand copies for some of its issues. *Fanews* claimed circulation of 500 copies for a while. However, appeal to the borderline group did not guarantee this type of success. That elaborate first issue of *Vortex* resulted in only 121 subscriptions. But the majority of fanzines must have appeared in editions ranging from 100 to 250 copies, rarely selling more than two-thirds of the total press run. *Le Zombie*, one of the most popular of all fanzines, had a normal press run of only 150 copies.

Most fanzines and fanzine editors, then as now, blossomed only briefly and could quickly be identified as annuals rather than perennials when the bloom began to wither. Sometimes a fanzine editor had an unusually vigorous but short career. Arthur Louis Joquel II of Los Angeles is a good example. Nobody had ever heard of him when he suddenly entered fandom in 1941 after 14 years of silently reading the prozines. In 14 months he produced 21 fanzines, then while working on a 116-page 22nd fanzine he startled all fandom by disappearing as abruptly as he'd appeared, after one unprecedented final gesture: he returned money due people on subscriptions and sent back manuscripts to their creators. My sense of duty is slightly stronger than my modesty, so I must relate that my own *Horizons* was the only fanzine that appeared regularly throughout the decade without changes in title or editor, or endless waits between issues. The *Fantasy Amateur* also lasted out the decade as a title, but had many editors because of its function as the official organ of FAPA. Many fine fanzine editors were active all through the decade with changes in name and nature of their publications. Joe Kennedy, for instance, began to issue hectographed little publications for his high school friends in 1941, then in 1945 captivated fandom with the light tone and entertaining contents of *Vampire*. Few fanzines gained such a reputation with so few issues: only nine. Kennedy produced fannuals in 1946 and 1947, ran a postal card newszine for ten months, and then concentrated on SAPS activities for the last part of the decade.

7. The LASFS Publications

Fanzines inspired by a local fan group came from many cities during the forties. The LASFS club publications had the most tumultuous biographies.

Originally there were two, *Shangri-La*
and *Shangri-L'Affaires*. They changed
policy, editorship, and appearance so
frequently that even the almost infallible R. D. Swisher was deluded into confusing the title of a fanzine column for
issues of a fanzine. *Shangri-L'Affaires*
made its first appearance in *VOM* for
March, 1941, in the form of a page
of news about fandom in Los Angeles
with that title. It became a roving feature in various other fanzines produced
in Los Angeles for the remainder of
that year, and broke free in December
when Charles D. Hornig used the title
for a one-page publication. *Shangri-La*
had been started in 1940 in an effort
to fill the vacuum that was left by the
passing of *Imagination!*—it was the re-

Shangri-La

sult of such a cooperative effort that nobody was listed as editor of the
first issue. By 1942, *Shangri-La* vanished, claiming that its name had been
changed to *Shangri-L'Affaires*. The club publication continued under the
latter title until after the big blowup in Los Angeles fandom. *Shangri-La*
serenely resumed title ascendancy late in 1948. It's hard to think of a Los
Angeles fan who didn't edit at least one issue of one title or the other. However, the editorship of Charles Burbee, which covered most editions from
1944 through 1947, saw the magazine's major triumphs. The geniality of
its general atmosphere and the relaxed suavity of Burbee's editorial writings
were something never quite duplicated in fanzine fandom. The most celebrated battle over control of a fanzine in that decade was touched off when
Burbee published two Laney articles about homosexuality in the LASFS,
as described in Chapter Ten. The climax came when the club voted to boycott a fanzine review column in *Amazing Stories* and Burbee announced in
an editorial that he was going to send *Shaggy* to the prozine anyway. Burbee
was kicked out of the editorship on November 13, 1947, and promptly sent
the rest of the club to the borders of a collective nervous breakdown by
spreading the false rumor that he intended to continue to publish an unauthorized club organ.

   Meanwhile, *Imagination!* really did have a successor with private rather
than club support, without creating a feud. Ackerman was so fond of the
letter section of *Imagination!* that when the fanzine died at the end of 1938,
he got the club's permission and Morojo's help to turn the letter section,

Voice of the Imagi-Nation, into a fanzine of the same title, as discussed in Chapter Six. Fifty issues emerged up to 1947.

8. A Melange of Miscellany

Two fanzines would probably have dominated the polls that weren't taken in the last year or two of the forties. One of them, *Peon*, survived so long that it really belongs to the fifties. Charles Lee Riddle started it in 1948 in a grandiose manner with a first issue that went to 300 fans and resulted in nearly a hundred letters and postal cards of comment. *Peon* was unique for all sorts of reasons, like the paper size that it preferred (slightly smaller than standard), its offer of a dollar for the best letter in each issue, and Riddle's ability to continue to publish it regularly year after year while making a living as a career man in the navy.

The Fanscient, the other big favorite, had been first published in September, 1947, by Donald B. Day for the Portland Science Fiction Society in a combination of lithography and mimeography. It lasted for 13 issues and three years, providing in its 464 pages an enormous amount of material about the most important professional writers of fantasy and their works, some good fiction, and articles with principally serious slants. Despite multicolor lithographing and as many as 64 pages to the issue, it paid for itself most of the way, and sold as many as 250 copies per issue. Fanzines have vanished for many reasons, but *The Fanscient* had a unique contributing cause for its demise: Day became interested in square dancing.

What about Arthur Rapp and *Spacewarp*? I feel that it belongs in spirit to the fandom of the fifties, even though the majority of its issues were dated in the previous decade, and it will be more convenient to discuss it when the time comes to consider the zeitgeist which it both foreshadowed and exemplified. Some other titans of fanzine fandom got their start as the forties were concluding but obviously these individuals like Max Keasler, William Rotsler, and Walter A. Willis reached their greatest heights in the later decade.

There was more specialization in the forties than generally remembered today. The Edgar Rice Burroughs fans have become numerous and loud in recent times. But Vernell Coriell was already publishing *The Burroughs Bulletin*, while he held membership in Terrel Jacob's Wild Animal Circus where he walked up a flight of stairs on his head and carried part of his precious collection around the country in a trailer.

There were fanzines published solely for conventions. *The Denventioneer* had eight titles bound together, a score of fanzines put out issues for the *Combozine* distributed at the Pacificon, and the *Philcon Memory Book* of 1947 offered some 130 pages representing about 15 fanzine titles.

That tradition somehow died out, but one that emerged in the last year of World War II has proved immortal. This was the one-shot fanzine, which in its purest form is stenciled by a group of fans on a single night and sometimes published as dawn is breaking. In theory at least, nobody has anything planned out before he sits down to the typewriter. Burbee first suggested the concept to Laney as "a Daugherty project, except that it will really happen." Elmer Perdue and George Ebey helped them to produce the first one, *Two Fingers*, in an unbroken eight-hour labor that started at 2 a.m. Tucker and Walt Liebscher soon responded with another one-shot, *Three Fingers*. The first one-shot inspired by a specific event and therefore possessed of some coherence of theme may have been *Ack on His Back*, which Laney and Burbee created when Ackerman was afflicted with a case of the measles.

There were specialized fanzines that failed to produce progeny for a while. Comics fandom is usually considered a phenomenon of the sixties. But Phil Bronson began his career as a fanzine publisher by producing *Scienti-Comics* in 1940. This was a devout imitation of the comic strips of the era with some fannish accompaniments. It even drew on a Robert W. Lowndes story from *Spaceways* as the source of one of its picture stories. In intent and appearance, this fanzine was just like the more primitive products of the current comics fandom.

Freakish items like that shouldn't monopolize attention, because fandom produced in those years an enormous amount of serious material of a bibliographic and chronicle nature. The lack of an index to indexes in fanzine form may have caused many labors of love to fall into limbo while a few remain celebrated because of their size or the widespread interest in their subject matter. The *Fancyclopedia* was the biggest and most famous of them, the biggest single publication that fandom had yet known when its 100-page first edition was issued in 1944. Jack Speer worked for four years on the writing of it, the NFFF provided financial assistance, and LASFS members did the actual production work. This first big compilation in dictionary form of fandom's traditions, slang, and big events was an enormous success, selling 103 copies before the bindings were in place on the loose pages. Bob Bloch called it "probably the most important step ever undertaken in the history of fandom," and said that it made fandom "permanent as a social phenomenon."

The other large fandom-oriented project completed in this decade was the *SF Check-List* that R. D. Swisher had begun in 1938. Other large scholarly projects were more concerned with professional publications. The *SF Check-list* and the indexes to the professional magazines are described in Chapter Three.

Fandom didn't forget its own. Once in a while, someone drew up an index to the contents of this or that famous fanzine of the past, like the one that Tucker issued in 1945 for *The Fantasy Fan*. Big directories of fans apparently began when Walt Daugherty published one with the help of other Los Angeles fans in 1942, listing some 600 names and addresses. J. Michael Rosenblum did the same thing for fans in the British Isles the following year. Occasionally a thoughtful soul did research on something recent enough to minimize the danger of errors and omissions, like the list of pioneer Australian fanzines published by *Cosmos* in 1940.

The most difficult index that fans could tackle, in many ways, was a bibliography of books with science fiction and fantasy contents. Searles made the first all-out attempt. He got much help from Unger, Evans, and Willy Ley, but no cooperation at all from a lot of major collectors, and enough competition from one direction to cause a feud. He began to release the listing piecemeal, including with each entry useful information on the nature of the book and directions on where to find reviews of some of the volumes. But the entire index was never published. It remained for a semi-pro source, Shasta, to publish in 1948 Everett F. Bleiler's *Checklist of Fantastic Literature*, with 5,000 titles, some of which were books of whimsy or way-out humor rather than genuine fantasy.

13. POSTWAR FANDOM ABROAD

1. British Fandom

When World War II ended, British fandom was among the many things that were decimated. Fans had been scattered by the conflict almost beyond the possibility of reassembly. The paper shortage had done in the native prozines. Little fanzine publishing remained, now that the incentive to keep peacetime traditions alive during the war had vanished. There was a little clubzine, *Cosmic Cuts*, produced by the Cosmos Club. The BFS issued its *Bulletin*. Rosenblum and Youd occasionally published for FAPA, and that was about it.

The Cosmos Club was one of the few British fan groups that managed to survive for a while the declaration of peace. It had been organized in 1943 by fans around Teddington, Middlesex, and didn't dissolve until late 1946. Frank Parker, Syd Bounds, Peter Hawken, John Aiken, and John Newman were its leading lights. Perhaps its main claim to distinction was the peculiarity that its members had found United States fandom before discovering a dispersed fandom in the British Isles.

The first important thing that fans in England did after the war was visit one another, now that travel had suddenly become untreasonable again. One weekend in August, 1945, produced a get-together of near-conference proportions on the part of Sam Youd, Benson Herbert, Joyce Fairbairn, Ron Lane, Michael Rosenblum, R. G. Medhurst, Walter Gillings, Roland Forster, Hal Chibbett, Maurice Hugi, Syd Bounds, and Canada's Norm Lamb. Doug Webster came out of the war-imposed isolation to tour major points of fan civilization in England.

A smidgin of fans were carrying on the British Fantasy Society as the war ended. Ron Holmes and Nigel Lindsay, who made up about half of the really active membership, soon combined its library and chain letter into a new group, called the British Fantasy League. This produced no violent reawakening of British fanac, for when 1948 ended, the group's membership contained only three important and active fans: Rosenblum, Ken Slater, and D. R. Smith. But another try at a national fan group was made in 1948, when Slater and various London fans founded the Science Fantasy Society, née Science Fantasy Fan Federation of the United Kingdom. Slater quickly got shipped to military duties in Germany, but Ken Bulmer and Vincent Clarke carried on the group. It acquired 150 members and stayed alive for three years, or longer if you count the extra span of life granted its official organ, *Science Fantasy News*.

London fandom was beginning to take on its postwar aspects around this same time. Thursday night meetings that became a famous fannish tradition began in 1947, first in the White Horse at Fetter Lane, later in the Globe at Hatton Garden. The London group was at this time without such organizational debris as officers, dues, and programs. And a little later, London reacquired another fannish focal point, a famous apartment to serve as the postwar equivalent of the old Flat. This was the Epicentre at 84 Drayton Park which Clarke and Bulmer shared in a manner that has become modern mythology. It was here that Bulmer invented the steam engine, from this point began the trips around London of the Fanvan, whose wheels kept falling off when traffic became heavy, and here was the chief non-tavern gathering point for London fans, except on the nights when the ceiling fell.

Many survivors of this era give Slater the credit for the eventual revival of British fandom. He had been a collector since prewar days. That first collection was dispersed when he gave the less valuable portions to the 1941 paper salvage drive and someone who was keeping the home fires burning gave away the rest. In September, 1947, Slater first published a fanzine called *Operation Fantast* that was to prove more important than the national fan clubs. It was, incredibly, the first general circulation fanzine that any individual had published in the British Isles for nearly a year. In ten quarto pages, it proclaimed its intent: "To encourage and promote greater interest and enthusiasm in stf., to complete files of magazines with missing issues." The British Fantasy League published at about the same time a handbook that may have shown Slater how *OF* could later attain fuller effectiveness. He issued a second *OF* the following January, which told of a plot to revive the BFS, then Slater was ordered to Germany. With the help of the girl he left behind him, Joyce Teagle, he produced from the Continent a third *OF* in March, and distributed with it as a rider another fanzine, Norm Ashfield's *Alembic*. The dam broke and the flood that later resulted from the ensuing trickle of new British fanzines didn't ebb until the mid-sixties. Walter H. Gillings began to publish fannish items in his *Fantasy Review*, Holmes listed books that could be borrowed from the BFL, and by the summer of 1948 came the first real British con since the 1944 Eastercon at Teddington. We'll reserve for the second volume of this history the rest of the account of how *Operation Fantast* burgeoned during the fifties.

This Whitcon, organized by John Newman, was held on Whitsunday with little advance preparation and a surprising total of 50 participants. London fans who had begun to meet at Fred Gram's home sponsored it at the White Horse on May 15th, although the con-hungry fans began to assemble the previous day. Most of the audience came from somewhere in the London area, although others made it from Ilford, Sheffield, and Yarmouthshire, and auction materials arrived from the United States. The earlier visitors were guided by natives on Saturday afternoon to bookshops at Charing Cross Road. There was a general assembly for tea at a Lyons Corner House, then a subway trip to the White Horse for the main meeting, where A. Bertram Chandler was the guest of honor. As chairman, Gillings called the meeting to order, told how hard it was to publish prozines in Great Britain, and said that *Fantasy* had folded because of the paper shortage. Carnell also had doleful news: the collapse of Pendulum Publications, an event that was preventing the publication of the fourth issue of *New Worlds*. But he revealed plans to form a new publishing group with financial support from fans.

A ghost from fandom's past, Arthur C. Clarke, spoke about science fiction and astronautics. He illustrated the change in things by reminding his audience that once the British Interplanetary Society had contained mostly fans in its membership. Now, he estimated, only twenty per cent of the members were fans. Ted Tubb was the main auctioneer, selling easily everything except Ziff-Davis publications. This auction produced about $70, and nearly $50 of that sum went to the Big Pond Fund, about which we'll hear more in a moment. Slater couldn't attend, because of duties in Germany, but he sent two pounds with instructions to employ it in toasts to his health. Dave Newman also spoke. Daphne Bradley occupied another key role at the con: she was the only unattached female.

The Whitcon was successful enough to encourage Slater to publish in August his plea for a new national fan organization. His pamphlet, *The Time Has Come*, aroused enough response to bring about a small conference in London on September 26th, then an open meeting of London fandom on October 9th.

2. Irish Fandom

But what actually emerged around the year's end was a small fanzine rather than an imposing national organization, it came out of Ireland rather than London, and it symbolized the start of an entirely new atmosphere, literacy, and cast of characters in the British Isles' fandom. Irish fandom had been born, and the most important early event in the parturition can be pinpointed to August 26, 1947. That was the date of the historic moment when Walter Alexander Willis discovered why it was so hard to find American science fiction magazines in Belfast: James White was also hunting them. It was the first meeting of two fans in that city, in one sense, although Willis had met a girl named Madeleine Bryan some time before without realizing that she was a fan, then married her after he observed the manner in which she dashed into a newsagent's shop to purchase a copy of *Astounding*.

These spanking new Irish fans got in touch with the British Fantasy Library at the start of 1948. Willis rescued an abandoned small press from a drug store's back room, and with the help of White, began to set type. When the font ran out of i's halfway down the first page, White produced his first woodcut. Months later, they had *Slant*, the first Irish fanzine, ready to mail. It didn't get mailed until near the end of the year, because the publishers couldn't find enough names and addresses of people who might like it. The full importance of Irish fandom, through its demonstration of how entertaining intelligent people can be in person and in print, will become clear in the account of the fifties.

3. The Big Pond Fund

Meanwhile, a less happy event had been the mysterious and total failure of the Big Pond Fund. Many American fans had been in England while in the service during the war, building personal friendships, but British fans had been unable to appear in the United States. Ackerman conceived the plan to import a Britisher through contributions from all fandom, and named the project the Big Pond Fund. He chose one of his oldest fannish friends, Ted Carnell, as the object of the project, and fixed the 1947 Philcon as the occasion for the visit. The event was formally announced in late 1946, with Rothman as its chairman. Fans were more prosperous than ever before, thanks to the wartime boom. Carnell had been a major force in British fandom until service duties forced him to slow down, and he had no enemies in the United States. There was no reason why the project should fail, but it did. Ackerman donated five dollars to start it off and began selling for a dollar apiece tickets to a raffle of much valuable fantasy material as an extra inducement to obtain contributions. But by the following August, only $75 was on hand, a sum that Ackerman defined as an insult instead of an invitation to Carnell.

Perhaps a combination of circumstances could be blamed. Many fans in 1947 were too new in the field to know about Carnell's fanac, for he had published no fanzine since 1943 and had turned into a filthy pro in 1946, when he began to edit *New Worlds*. Dissension over the Fantasy Foundation may have entered the situation, because Ackerman had announced that the FF would get the money if the Big Pond Fund didn't reach the necessary amount. In the end, Ackerman announced that he would hold the money for some future importation of a British fan, and Carnell consoled the contributors with a letter of thanks in which he explained how difficult his trip would have been in any event on the $140 that was then the maximum that Britishers could take to other nations. As things turned out, Carnell eventually made the trip with this and other money, to the Cinvention.

In the same thank-you letter, Carnell wrote a remarkably prophetic passage, as if he foresaw the Trans-Atlantic Fan Fund (TAFF) that was to come: "The fund is a great idea in the sense that such a project can be inaugurated upon a two-year basis as soon as world conditions improve. There is no reason why a delegate should not visit each other's country on alternate years, or bi-yearly, to attend conventions and cement still further the friendships that have been formed over many years' standing."

British fandom continued to recover slowly during 1949. It failed to produce a monster con, but London was the scene of a one-day gathering at the Raglan that brought out most of the active notables and caused Vincent Clarke to coin a nickname that became famous later: LonCon. Fanzines were still rare enough to cause a stir when a new issue of something went out. By now, Willis was certain that the Science Fantasy Society was "an unmixed disaster for British fandom," causing among many other bad things the frittering away of the precious fanac time of Vincent Clarke who was publishing the official organ when he could have been doing more creative things. After Clarke and Bulmer got tired of trying to keep the organization alive, Slater made one final effort to salvage it, when he appointed Egerton Sykes as secretary. That didn't work, either, and the group vanished in time for *Operation Fantast* to become an important force.

4. Fans Turn Pro

The cast of principal characters in British fandom was sharply different after the war, partly because so many of the best wartime fans were now selling instead of giving away their writings. Christopher Samuel Youd, for instance, had built up an imposing reputation as one of the most capable handlers of prose, poetry, and intellectual ferment in the British fanzine world, just before and during the war. He had begun to publish in 1939 *The Fantast*, perhaps the most literate of all the British fan publications. He once described his fanzine as "an outlet for the literary activities of

Christopher S. Youd

those unfitted, for one reason or another, for the wider world of letters. Some, we hope, will graduate from our small beginnings." Originally a vigorous pacifist, Youd changed his mind before the war was very old, and won ten pounds for writing the second best war story in the February, 1940, issue of *Lilliput*, a mundane British publication. His entrance into the service cast *The Fantast* into the editorial hands of Doug Webster, and stopped Youd's publishing. Demobilized in late 1946, Youd began editing a professional venture, *New Frontiers*, that survived only two issues. But then he received a grant of £250 from the Atlantic Awards in Literature, in return for his promise to spend a year in creative writing. Almost immediately, he sold a science fiction story to Gillings, and quite soon achieved a success as John Christopher. He demonstrated little interest in fandom after that, although he asked to stay on the mailing list for Rosenblum's fanzines as late as 1955.

Dave McIlwain was less celebrated as a fanzine publisher, although the five issues of his *Gargoyle* at the start of the forties demonstrated a lively personality. After the war he became a prolific novelist, using the name of Charles Eric Maine. John Frederick Burke, who published *The Satellite* regularly for two years around the end of the thirties, was another who was lost to fandom through success as a filthy pro. "Such a positive drive toward writing that it is not possible for him to fail" were the words with which Youd predicted his success. William F. Temple, somewhat older than these other British fans, also turned his typewriter to professional purposes a bit sooner. He was published in two of the first four issues of *Tales of Wonder*, and used to nourish the hope that selling to the prozines would help him to achieve his own particular utopia, that of lying in bed as long as he liked every day in the year.

But it was Arthur C. Clarke who attained the most formidable reputation as a writer of science fiction, out of all those early British fans. His nickname of Ego seems to have come when he divided up the work of sharing a flat with Temple by doing the talking while Bill did the housework. The pair had begun this arrangement partly to rescue Clarke from the dangers of a boardinghouse room so small that he was reputed to have been wedged helplessly between the walls for three days after putting on a double-breasted suit. As early as 1939 or thereabouts, Clarke was forgetting national boundaries in an effort to write the Great American Novel. He didn't quite succeed but the story metamorphosed eventually into *Against the Fall of Night*. His first story to see print was "Loophole," in the April, 1946, *Astounding*, although he had previously sold a story to Gillings while still on duty as a flight lieutenant in the RAF. Clarke not only proceeded to create a series of superb novels and short stories, but was one of the few people to illustrate the Gernsback desideratum of fans leading science in its advance. He became chairman of the British Interplanetary Society, lectured all over the world on space travel, and starred on television programs.

5. Australian Fandom

Australia's fans were badly scattered individuals, mainly unknown to one another, during the years when United States fans were corresponding and inventing such things as fanzines and fanac. Marshall L. MacLennan was probably the best known in later years of these primeval fans from Down Under. He read the August, 1928, issue of *Amazing Stories*, immediately began collecting, and had virtually completed his set of the prozines when in 1934 a thief swiped everything. Undauntedly, MacLennan fought fate systematically. He drew up a schedule providing biweekly visits to 120 back issue shops. Within a year he had reconstructed his prozine collection, amassed 200 books, and obtained many fanzines.

The first signs of organized fandom in Australia appeared in 1935, when a Sydney chapter of the Science Fiction League was organized with W. J. J. Osland as director and William Hewitt as secretary. With the help of Thomas M. Mallett, they acquired two things: the 27th charter in the SFL, and a recruit, Charles La Coste, who was the only member of this group with fannish survival value. Someone owned a printing press but the coming of fanzines to Australia was postponed when he used it only to produce advertising leaflets that proclaimed the glories of science fiction and urged readers of it to join the SFL chapter. This group survived about a year, with a half-dozen members meeting biweekly at the homes of one another, and making little or no contact with fans on other continents.

If you interpret "fanzine" loosely, the first of them in Australia appeared in Sydney in 1937. This was a 12-page publication called *Space Hounds* that survived ten issues. It was not duplicated in the normal sense but manifested itself only in the form of one handwritten copy per issue, produced by a group of students at Landwich Intermediate High School who met regularly because of their common interest in science fiction. Bert Castellari, Ron Lane, Ron Brennan, Kevin O'Keefe, and Bill Veney called themselves the Meteorite Club. This club was visible only slightly longer than the visible evidence of its namesake.

But in 1938 Veney contacted another teenager, named Eric F. Russell, who was to cause worldwide confusion throughout fandom because the name already belonged to a British pro who occasionally acted fannish. The two formed the Junior Australian Science Fiction Correspondence Club, recruiting in the process a younger brother, Edward H. Russell, as well as Castellari and Lane.

About the same time, John Devern organized in South Australia an Adelaide chapter of the SFL. He published the first duplicated fanzine in Australia, a 16-page hectographed *Science Fiction Review*, in February, 1939. This immediately became immensely rare, because its press run was only about 18 copies, and only two copies were ever accounted for, by falling into the hands of Veney and Eric Russell. Devern soon vanished as completely as the other 16 copies of this pioneer fanzine. But his brief example inspired the Sydney fans to produce the first mimeographed fanzine on that continent, *Australian Fan News*, whose sole issue was dated May, 1939.

Already, Sydney fans had discovered another fannish pastime that they seemed to enjoy as much as fanzine publishing. This consisted of feuding. Vol Molesworth formed a rival club, the Junior Science Correspondence Club, and in 1939 claimed 14 members, twice the population of the earlier group. Fans with brief careers like Ruduk Volsoni and Ken Jeffreys published two issues of a fanzine and got recruits for the newer group by advertising in a comics magazine. The JSCC lasted only a few months.

All this sounds quite boyish, but it should be remembered that active Australian fans were even younger than their counterparts in England and the United States. In 1939, for example, Edward Russell had not yet attained the dignity of his teens, Levy was 14, and Veney and Castellari were 15. Perhaps this lack of maturity prevented the first prominent filthy pro in Australia from taking an interest in fandom. He was Alan Connell, who began selling to the prozines around 1940, and had the cover story, "Dream's End," in Gernsback's *Wonder Stories* of December, 1935.

Moreover, Australian fans were cranking a mimeograph without much exposure to fan publications from other lands. Some copies of *Spaceways* seem to have lit the fuse on a fanzine explosion when they relieved this particular type of Australian famine. Eric Russell began at the end of 1939 to publish his *Ultra*, first as a carbon-copied booklet but mimeographed with its third issue, and growing to as large as a 50-page issue before it vanished at the end of 1941. Veney and Castellari created in January, 1940, *Futurian Observer*, a newszine devoted to Australian events that achieved the impressive record of 57 issues in the following two years. Molesworth had begun at the end of 1939 to publish *Luna*; then by the middle of 1940, a half-dozen fans cooperated on a major fanzine project, *Zeus*. By 1941, there were eight active fanzine titles on the continent.

The next important organization was the Futurian Society of Sydney, organized on November 5th, 1939, at Veney's home. Wollheim persuaded them to choose the name of his New York group, after discovering to his horror that they were almost ready to call themselves the Sydney Science Fiction League. This group became the finest that Australia had known, with membership reaching a round dozen at times, 18 meetings in the first ten months, and such activities as formal discussions, psi experiments, and round-robin story creations. Another activity was dissensions. One of many squabbles arose over the proposal by David R. Evans that independent fanzine publishing should be scrapped in favor of one all-out cooperative clubzine. The group was still cohesive enough to try to form a Futurian Association of Australia, intended to organize the boondocks, in July, 1940. Veney was president and Eric Russell was secretary when the group tried to recruit such distant new fans as Melbourne's Warwick Hockley, Brisbane's J. Keith Moxon, and Hobart's Don Tuck. By September, Evans had succeeded Veney as president, and personalities were clashing so violently that the club dissolved at its September 22nd meeting.

Meanwhile, Australia was suffering from a difficulty unique in the history of known fandoms: almost total inability to find prozines, either native or imported. The government banned the importation of the American prozines in June, 1940, two years after *Weird Tales* had been stopped from going Down Under. There were no local editions of American magazines or independent native prozines, as in Canada or England. Then the production of fanzines became almost impossibly difficult, because it required a permit from a frightening Division of Import Procurement to buy enough paper to put out an amateur magazine, and most applications were rejected.

Australia did come close to having a fan-inspired prozine during the early part of the war. Evans had a conference with the publisher of a monthly humor magazine, *Quiz*, in 1941, and won permission to accumulate manuscripts for a possible prozine. But nothing came of this. Fans were forced to subsist on the limited diet provided by British reprint editions of *Astounding* and *Unknown* that survived submarines, and an occasional native book. The first of these seems to have been a sixpenny booklet issued in January, 1942, in Sydney: *The Living Dead*, whose 80 pages were written by one J. W. Heming. Nevertheless, the global trend for fans to become pros penetrated even this island fastness: Molesworth somehow sold seven novelettes.

Several individuals almost became martyrs to fandom. Donald H. Tuck had a copy of *VOM* seized, probably because of an unusually picturesque VOMaiden on the front cover. Another fan underwent grilling by an intelligence officer who had become aroused by mysterious abbreviations in a letter to Tucker.

Official actions couldn't still the social impulses in fannish souls. La Coste had the delicate job of presiding over the first Sydney fan conference. This was staged at Veney's home on December 6, 1940, when ten fans gathered. The event was intended to settle fannish conflicts and to clarify the condition of the Futurian Society of Sydney. The group decided, futilely, that fanzine editors shouldn't make detrimental statements about the FSS without approval by a censor, while holding membership in the club. The reorganized FSS had stricter controls on the admission of new members, came back to life officially on January 28, 1941, and survived for another two years before another suspension. There were unofficial meetings of the officially suspended group even after that, until after peace had returned. Two other cons occurred in these early years. A second Sydney Conference on April 6, 1941, drew about 15 fans, who alternated throwing buns at one another with arguing. The most spectacular achievement was to change the name of the Futurian Association of Australia to the Australian Futurian Association. The third con on January 4, 1942, brought out only eight fans, no particular hostility, and a decision to keep the Futurian Association in the status of a non-active organization.

Fandom showed few signs of life in the final years of the war and the early stages of the peace. About 30 fans' whereabouts were known on the continent when the Futurian Society of Sydney reawoke and staged its 78th meeting on August 9, 1947, the first since the end of shooting. Eric Russell was elected director and Molesworth became secretary-treasurer. Within a month it had picked up new members who became well-known, like Hockley and Ralph Smith. But some older fans were drifting away. Castellari, once a power, sold part of his collection and gave the remainder to the club library at the end of that year. By the following year, the homes of the Molesworths and Graham Stone in Coogee were the official club headquarters. About this time, Stone and Sterling Macoby made a surprising discovery: a group of serious-minded fans who, unknown to the rest of fandom, had been meeting weekly for years at the Quality Inn as an offshoot of the Book Collectors Society of Australia. The hidden fans boasted a university lecturer, S. L. Larnach, among their membership, but they were mislaid soon after their discovery. The FSS repeated on a somewhat larger scale its previous history by growing to a roster of a score of members and reaching a semi-deceased condition by 1950 through disinterest and squabbles.

In Melbourne, fandom had suspended totally during the war. Then Bob McCubbin returned from service in Japan in 1948, spotted Race Mathews staring at a copy of *Amazing* in a bookstore, and the two strangers began to chat over this rare phenomenon. They formed the Melbourne Science Fiction Group, which enlisted such members as MacLennan, Gordon Kirby, Dick Jenssen, and Lee Harding. A particularly valuable recruit was Mervyn Binns, because he worked in the same McGill's shop that had inspired the whole thing. He saw to it that science fiction was always on sale there. The group lived many years, possibly because it resisted firmly all efforts to organize rigidly and retained an informal structure that contained neither officers, dues, nor clubrooms.

In the same remarkable manner as in America, the arrival of the fifties brought sharp changes in Australia's fanac. Nick Solntseff of New South Wales put out in 1950, for instance, the first big Australian fanzine in many years, *Omara*. In that same year, Jack Murtagh of New Zealand reawoke impulses of life in many cataleptic fans by his extensive visiting tour of Australian fans. He baited their interest with entrancing stories about his near-complete prozine collection, made possible by New Zealand's policy of permitting its residents to subscribe to American publications. The Australian Science Fiction Society also accompanied the coming of a new decade, filling a vacuum that the Futurians seemed likely to leave.

6. Canadian Fandom

The Torcon of 1948 is obvious evidence that Canada's fandom thrived after the war. In the immediate postwar years, a new generation of Canadians produced many more fans than in the old days, but the new generation did not participate in American and British fandom as much as their elders had done. Bob Gibson, Ted White, and Norm Lamb all returned to civilian life during 1946, and Les Croutch continued to publish, trade, correspond, and write as furiously as ever. But most of the other names in Canada were new. Charles R. Johnston, Robert Loosemore, C. J. Bowie, Cecil de Bretigny, Dave Stitt, and Norman L. Barrett were heralded as particularly promising members of the new Canadian fandom, but the fame of most was confined to their native land. A Montreal Science Fiction Society was organized on November 15, 1946, by students of McGill University. Jack Bowie-Reed, Basil Rattray, and Moe Diner, the organizers, found two dozen members in little more than a year, thanks to publicity in Montreal newspapers and school publications.

Toronto had acquired its Derelicts by 1948. However, the fans who made that name famous were not yet in evidence: Beak Taylor and Ned McKeown were the main powers at this time. Hamilton possessed in the same year an active group called the Lakehead Science Fiction Society, headed by J. Clare Richards. Ottawa had also acquired a fan club, whose president was Lew Holland, with Ron Anger as secretary, and Bowie-Reed as liaison officer. The last-named is an enigmatic figure in fandom: almost unknown outside Canada and forgotten by now, he seems to have achieved remarkable success in unearthing fans and forming clubs by applying the political organizing techniques that were involved in his vocation. One observer gave him credit for formation of five clubs; and partly due to his work, fan groups existed in such obscure places as Picton and Deseronto.

Before gafiating, Fred Hurter had formed during the war a Canadian Amateur Fantasy Press, designed to unite and promote fanzines. The next try at a national fan group came in 1948, when Toronto, Hamilton, and Montreal fans organized the Canadian Science Fiction Association. Bowie-Reed was its national organizer and the Lakehead SFS of Hamilton was chosen to guide its destinies during the first year, with James Templar as president and Paul Rebey as secretary-treasurer. It published a newsletter, did not achieve the indexes that it planned to publish, and Richards took over the presidency when Templar quit before the year had ended. The organization thrived sufficiently to try to sponsor a World Science Fiction League. But after a couple of more years, it retrogressed to a mere paper existence.

Canada had at least ten fan clubs in various centers toward the end of the decade. They were generally characterized by lots of discussion of science fiction and scientific possibilities. There was little of the faanish fandom that is supposed to be the beginning of the end of fan groups, but the groups didn't last long, anyway. Collecting was popular, with good collections of magazines and books frequently discovered in the possession of someone previously unknown to fandom.

If Canadian fanzines were few, some of them were remarkably long-lived. Croutch had begun to publish in the late thirties a carbon-copied listing of his stock for trading. He expanded it gradually in the forties, began to run it off on a mimeograph, changed the title to *Light*, and kept it alive longer than any but a half-dozen or so other fanzines in history. Fred Hurter produced *Censored* for the first time in 1941—its title derived from the fact that his original title turned out to have been used before—published it a year or two, suspended it, and revived it; it lived into the new decade. Beak Taylor began to publish *Canadian Fandom* during the war and it didn't disappear completely until the late fifties, despite a series of changes of editorship.

7. Other Foreign Fandoms

Fandom was very slow to appear in nations whose native languages are not English. It's quite likely that there is more than coincidence between this fact and the late appearance of magazines devoted to science fiction in many European nations. But there is always the possibility of a double effect of the language barrier: if it prevented many nations from importing large quantities of American prozines, it may also have prevented us from learning about early manifestations of fandom in those nations.

Of course, there were a few instances in which fanac was conducted in a faraway nation by Americans who were residing there for extended periods of time. Thus, Ron Maddox became the first African fan, when this American youngster accompanied his parents to that continent in 1948, and collaborated with friends back in the United States to edit fanzines in Nairobi and Ethiopia. Japan was host for years to two fans who had achieved their major fame in mundane apas. Helen Wesson moved to Tokyo at the end of 1946, to join her serviceman husband. She had recently become interested in fandom through acquisition of several issues of *The Acolyte*. She contacted Laney, and immediately became celebrated as the only known woman who had kept him up most of the night just talking. While in Japan, she published a fanzine, *The Unspeakable Thing*, and reported on native fantasy materials. Her co-editor was Burton Crane, a remarkable fringefan who was in charge of the Tokyo office of the *New York Times*. He was a big wheel in mundane apas, too, and had the unexpected side distinction of enormous popularity in Japan as a recording artist specializing in popular tunes.

German fandom hardly existed as such in this decade, despite the popularity of science fiction in book form in Germany. Herbert Häussler could not find any other fans in Germany to correspond with, although he'd been in contact with Ackerman from 1935 onward. Even the rocket enthusiasts had little opportunity to split off into a science fiction fandom, because the German equivalent of the BIS, the Verein für Raumschiffahrt, was dissolved after Hitler came into power. Willy Ley was the only other German science fiction enthusiast who bobbed up in American fanzines before the fifties; his name could be found in *Cosmology* long before he gained his American fame as a science popularizer and rocketry expert.

Georges Gallet, a combination of fan and pro, was the only French representative of fandom during the forties. If there is a link between prozines and fanzines, it snapped in France, because that nation got a native-language prozine quite early: *Anticipations*, which published in Belgium a total of 14 issues in 1945 and 1946, mostly translated from American and British prozines. France was also in the fannish news occasionally by reason of encounters there among American fans just before and after V-E Day.

Mexico had a prozine that translated prozine and fanzine stories from English during the late forties, and there may have been a few isolated fans somewhere in Latin America, because Sykora published an "international edition" of *Fantasy Times* in early 1949, "slanted towards fans in Latin America" and containing one news item translated into Spanish. Equally mysterious is the exact extent of fanac in South Africa toward the end of the decade. One sheep farmer at Colesburg named P. Haupt and a Johannesburg resident named B. Burman were mentioned in fanzines in the United States as suffering from the import ban just imposed from the United States to South Africa.

The most publicized foreign fandom during the forties has never yet been discovered. This is the fandom which has been rumored time and again to exist in Russia as an outcome of the equally unsubstantiated reports of prozines in that land. In 1944, for instance, *Fantasy Fiction Field* told of a Russian prozine that had been appearing ever since 1907. A clerk at a New York City store specializing in Russian literature once told Wollheim that it had stocked both prozines and science fiction books before the war. The popularity of science fiction in Russia became definitely evident after the war, and *Literaturnaya Gazyeta* was even inspired to publish in 1949 a denunciation of the American brand of science fiction.

However, nobody ever produced a name and address of a genuine Russian fan or an actual copy of a Russian prozine. It seems probable that the magazine rumors resulted from popular science publications that ran illustrations of predicted new inventions and an occasional science fiction story, like the Russian magazines that fooled the South Gate con-goers in 1958. Russian restrictions on the use of duplicating machines seem to eliminate any possibility of fanzines.

INDEX